American Freethought

AMERICAN FREETHOUGHT

The History of a Social Movement, 1794–1948

by David C. Hoffman

Johns Hopkins University Press
Baltimore

© 2025 Johns Hopkins University Press
All rights reserved. Published 2025
Printed in the United States of America on acid-free paper
2 4 6 8 9 7 5 3 1

Johns Hopkins University Press
2715 North Charles Street
Baltimore, Maryland 21218
www.press.jhu.edu

Library of Congress Cataloging-in-Publication Data

Names: Hoffman, David C, 1968– author.
Title: American freethought : the history of a social movement, 1794–1948 / David C. Hoffman.
Description: Baltimore, Maryland : Johns Hopkins University Press, 2025. | Includes index.
Identifiers: LCCN 2024035511 | ISBN 9781421451800 (hardcover ; acid-free paper) | ISBN 9781421451817 (ebook)
Subjects: LCSH: Free thought—United States—History.
Classification: LCC BL2757 .H74 2025 | DDC 211/.4097309034—dc23/eng/20250103
LC record available at https://lccn.loc.gov/2024035511

A catalog record for this book is available from the British Library.

Special discounts are available for bulk purchases of this book. For more information, please contact Special Sales at specialsales@jh.edu.

EU GPSR Authorized Representative
LOGOS EUROPE, 9 rue Nicolas Poussin, 17000, La Rochelle, France
E-mail: Contact@logoseurope.eu

*For my Dad, Ray David Hoffman, PhD,
in his ninetieth year, a gentle man of science*

CONTENTS

Acknowledgments ix

INTRODUCTION
Freethought as a Social Movement 1

1
Prelude to American Freethought
The Age of Reason and the French Revolution 15

2
The First Wave of American Freethought
Deists of the Early Republic 47

3
The Second Wave of American Freethought
Revival and Transformation 88

4
The Third Wave of American Freethought
The Golden Age 130

5
The Fourth Wave of American Freethought
The Journey to Disestablishment 188

CONCLUSION
Freethought Today and Tomorrow 213

Notes 221
Index 277

ACKNOWLEDGMENTS

There are more people and institutions that I should acknowledge and thank than I have space to do so here, so I will tender my short list and offer apologies for the numerous omissions and generalizations.

First, thank you to my immediate family, who have put up with many years of distracted behavior ("Dad, you promised to make me mac and cheese as soon as you finished a paragraph! That was two hours ago . . ."). Thanks to my colleagues at the Marxe School of Public and International Affairs and Baruch College, who have provided me with so much freedom to pursue my chosen projects and so many opportunities for intellectual growth. The project has benefited over the years from grant support from the PSC CUNY Research Award Program, the Mellon Foundation, and generous course release provided by the Marxe School. Thanks to all the many people who have commented on and encouraged this project, including Sharon Hoffman, Laura Davulis and the rest of the team at Hopkins Press, the anonymous reviewers of this manuscript, my wonderfully astute copy editor Michael Baker, members of the Science Circle at the Unitarian Universalist Church at Washington Crossing (UUCWC), and colleagues at the CUNY Graduate Center, who saw the very earliest stages of this project during a Mellon-sponsored humanities seminar many years ago. Thanks to all the good people at the UUCWC who have given me a place to stand and feel accepted for who I am as I have explored the history of religious outcasts in America. The words of a frequently sung Unitarian Universalist hymn have a special appeal to freethinkers like me: "Come, come, whoever you are: wanderer, worshiper, lover of leaving! Ours is no caravan of despair. Come, yet again, come!"

American Freethought

INTRODUCTION

Freethought as a Social Movement

There has been a tendency among the proponents of secularism to believe that the freedom of speech, the freedom of the press, and the freedom of religion written into state and national constitutions in the founding era would by themselves naturally lead to a decline in the political power and public influence of religions that make supernatural claims based on the authority of revelation. As Thomas Jefferson wrote in an 1822 letter to Benjamin Waterhouse, he believed a rational, nonsupernaturalist religion, which he identified as Unitarianism, would quickly triumph in the new nation: "I rejoice that in this blessed country of free inquiry and belief, which has surrendered its creed and conscience to neither kings nor priests, the genuine doctrine of one only God is reviving, and I trust that there is not a young man now living in the United States who will not die an Unitarian."[1] Thomas Paine too thought that it was probable that the American and French political revolutions would be "followed by a revolution in the system of religion," the triumph of deism over Christianity in Europe and America.[2] Two hundred years later it seems odd to think about a single "system of religion" in a country that has become as richly pluralistic in religion as America. Relations between church and state have been transformed in important ways, but the change has been incremental.

The United States has, in a legal and political sense, become a more secular nation in the two hundred years since Jefferson made his prediction, but the progress has not been easy. A Christian nationalist understanding of America came to prominence in the early nineteenth century that is exemplified in the writings of Supreme Court justice Joseph Story, who ironically *was* a Unitarian, albeit a rather conservative one. This philosophy provided a justification for the continued establishment of Christianity in state and local laws well into the twentieth century. Story was well known as a legal scholar, serving as Dane Professor of Law at Harvard College for many of his years on the bench. His 1833 *Commentaries on the Constitution of the United States* is an important text in the history of constitutional law. The section that comments on the Establishment Clause of the First Amendment remains a favorite citation of jurists seeking to uphold Christian privilege: "Probably at the time of the adoption of the constitution, and of the amendment to it, now under consideration, the general, if not the universal, sentiment in America was that Christianity ought to receive encouragement from the state, so far as was not incompatible with the private rights of conscience, and the freedom of religious worship. An attempt to level all religions and to make it a matter of state policy to hold all in utter indifference would have created universal disapprobation, if not universal indignation."[3] Story goes on to write, "The real object of the amendment was not to countenance, much less to advance, Mahometanism, or Judaism, or infidelity, by prostrating Christianity, but to exclude all rivalry among Christian sects, and to prevent any national ecclesiastical establishment which should give to an hierarchy the exclusive patronage of the national government."[4]

It was Story's vision of church-state relations to which freethinkers, whom Story referred to as "infidels," opposed themselves, and it was in large part due to their efforts that it was transformed. The "acids of modernity," to borrow Walter Lippmann's phrase,[5] did not magically dissolve the faith of Americans in the supernatural or in scriptural revelation, nor did they quickly eat through the legal bulwarks of Christian privilege that Story helped to erect. Instead, the project of disestablishment was advanced by the persistent campaigning of many generations of freethinkers and secularists. This book tells the story of how the efforts of these freethinkers changed the religious landscape of the United States.

Before beginning the story of American freethought, I should say a few words about the meaning of the terms "freethought" and "freethinker." As I use the term, a freethinker is someone who dissents from a religious tradition for what appear to them to be rational reasons. A freethinker is *not* necessarily an atheist or an agnostic. Over the years, theistic deists, spiritualists, and Unitarians have all made substantial contributions to the freethought movement. Atheists were rare in the freethought movement until the twentieth century, and the words "agnostic" and "secular" did not even come into common usage until the second half of the nineteenth century. American freethinkers have called themselves many things over the years: deists, theophilanthropists, infidels, free inquirers, secularists, liberals, and humanists, to name a few. The label "freethinker" became popular in the 1870s and remained so throughout the period sometimes called "the golden age of freethought," which ran up until the turn of the century. During that time organizations like the New York Freethinkers' Association sprang up, the *New York Times* ran many stories about the activities of freethinkers, and freethought historians wrote books like *Four Hundred Years of Freethought* (Samuel Porter Putnam, 1894) and *Fifty Years of Freethought* (George E. MacDonald, 1929). But although in the last quarter of the nineteenth century "freethought" became a predominant term for Americans who dissented from Christian orthodoxy—and a few who dissented from Jewish orthodoxy—the term had been borrowed from an earlier era. "Freethinker" had been adopted by English deists as a self-description already in the early eighteenth century.

Anthony Collins, an English jurist and friend of philosopher John Locke, published what was perhaps the first freethought manifesto in 1713: *A Discourse of Free-thinking: Occasion'd by the Rise and Growth of a Sect Call'd Free-thinkers*. In this work he defined freethinking as "the use of the understanding in endeavoring to find out the meaning of any proposition whatsoever, in considering the nature of the evidence for or against it, and in judging of it according to the seeming force or weakness of the evidence."[6] Collins argued that such a use of reason, common in the fields of science and law, should also be applicable in religion, and particularly in forming judgments about the truth of the claims and assertions of the Bible. The English deist Peter Annet used "freethinking" in a similar way in his 1739 publication, *Judging for Ourselves, or Freethinking the Great Duty of Religion*. He titled a periodical that he wrote and published in the early 1760s *The Free Enquirer*. So "freethought" was a long-established term for rational religious dissent by the time it started to be widely used in America. I have chosen to use the terms "freethought" and "freethinkers" to describe the movement and its members throughout its history, even at those times when members rarely used the term, as a matter of convenience and conformity to scholarly usage. I also happen to think it is one of the more attractive and strategically keen labels that the movement has given itself.

In addition to clarifying how I use the word "freethought," I should also say a few introductory words about the time frame that I have selected for this book. Why is the book specifically about American freethought from 1794 to 1948? Although beginnings and endings in history are often somewhat arbitrary, I have chosen to focus on the period between the publication of Thomas Paine's deistic manifesto *The Age of Reason* in 1794, an event that arguably launched American freethought as a social movement, and the 1948 *McCollum v. Board of Education* Supreme Court decision that ended religious instruction in public schools. The McCollum decision was among the first of a series of mid-twentieth-century Supreme Court decisions that realized many of American freethought's long-standing goals. These goals also included ending religious tests for state offices, ending the threat of blasphemy prosecutions for questioning the existence of God or the authority of Christian scripture, and ending prayer and Bible reading in public schools. It seemed fitting to begin the story of American freethought with the publication of its most foundational text and conclude it with a Supreme Court decision that finally began to realize the goals it had been pursuing for generations. But because American freethought did not arise from a vacuum, and because it did not cease to exist after 1948, I will also include some discussion of events that took place before *Age of Reason* and after *McCollum v. Board of Education*.

The title of this book asserts that freethought is a social movement, and this claim also merits a preliminary discussion. Freethought was and is a social movement in exactly the sense defined by Charles J. Stewart, Craig Allen Smith, and Robert E. Denton in their foundational work on the subject, *Persuasion and Social Movements*. Stewart and his colleagues define a social movement as "an organized, uninstitutionalized and large collectivity that emerges to promote or resist change in social norms and values, operating primarily through persuasion encountering opposition in its moral struggle."[7] The freethought movement is and was composed of a plethora of associated organizations. Historically these organizations have included the Deistical Society of New York, the Society of Moral Philanthropists, the Free Press Association, the Society of Free Enquirers, the United States Moral and Philosophical Society for the General Diffusion of Useful Knowledge, the Infidel Society for the Promotion of Mental Liberty, the Infidel Association of the United States, the New York Freethinkers' Association, the National Liberal League/National Secular Union, the National Defense Association, the Free Speech League, the Society of Freethinkers, and Freethinkers of America. Contemporary freethought organizations include the American Humanist Association, Americans United for the Separation of Church and State, the Center for Freethought Equality, the Freedom from Religion Foundation, the Secular Coalition for America, the Center for Inquiry, and the Freethought Society. The freethought movement is thus qualified as both organized and large. The movement has had significant success in institutionalizing the changes it has sought but finds continued reason for existence in promoting new projects and in defending the advances of disestablishment. Like its better-known sister movements, feminism and abolition, the freethought movement has had no tools other than those of persuasion available to it in its moral struggle to promote the separation of church and state and create a society where all varieties of honest religious belief and honest nonbelief find acceptance. Freethought is a classic American social movement.

Importantly for my history of the freethought movement, I view the ability to form publicly visible organizations to be another essential characteristic of social movements, in addition to those characteristics discussed by Stewart, Smith, and Denton. A movement that, because of official repression or persecution, must operate clandestinely and cannot declare its existence or goals publicly does not fit the usual pattern of a *social* movement, even though it is a movement of sorts. The contrast between a clandestine activity and a social movement is apparent if one contemplates the difference between the trade and use of marijuana in places where it is illegal (clandestine activity) and the movement to legalize marijuana (social movement). Prudence dictates that people who are gathering to use an illicit drug do not advertise the fact. But people who organize to campaign for the legalization of an illegal drug, without admitting the use of that drug, can do so publicly with much less fear of official sanction. Crucially for this book, prior to about 1794 in America, freethought was mainly a clandestine activity in which a good number of people engaged, but few advertised. A bold few admitted they were deists but stopped far short of organizing visible campaigns to promote deism. It was mainly after the publication of *Age of Reason* that openly deistic organizations began to grow in America. This is why I locate the beginning of freethought as a social movement in 1794.

My history of the American freethought movement is informed by social movement theory. Although the term "social movement" entered the lexicon of social science as early as 1850,[8] it was in the 1970s and 1980s that the academic study of social movements became firmly established as scholars and researchers were inspired by the movements for civil rights, feminism, gay rights, and the environment they saw occurring all around them. In that period, European and American scholars took differing and independent approaches to the study of social movements. In Europe, New Social Movement

Theory described social movements of the '60s and '70s as products of postindustrial society and tried to understand how their members forged collective identities.[9] In America, at first Collective Behavior Theory emphasized the role that strains and breakdowns play in the formation of social movements, and later Resource Mobilization Theory and Political Process Theory gave more attention to the importance of material and political opportunities in movement formation and growth.[10] Recent social movement theorists and scholars have mostly overcome the earlier isolation of European and American schools of thought and have tended to draw creatively on the whole tradition of social movement research as they explore new areas of inquiry.

With the exception of introducing a distinction between clandestine and social movements, I will not attempt to advance social movement theory in this book but will draw language and concepts from it when they prove useful for describing the American freethought movement. Among the concepts employed in social movement theory that I think are illuminating with regard to American freethought are *collective identity*, *movement framing*, *repertoires of action*, and *movement waves*.

Alberto Melucci's work emphasizes how a period of *collective identity* formation always must precede collective action in the life cycle of social movements.[11] The freethought movement had a particularly long and dynamic phase of collective identity formation as deists, agnostics, pantheists, atheists, and others struggled to find ways to see themselves as sharing a core identity.

Movement framing research inquires into the language that a movement uses to describe itself and its goals. David Snow and Robert Benford write that movement framing means to "assign meaning to and interpret relevant events and conditions in ways that are intended to mobilize potential adherents and constituents, to garner bystander support, and to demobilize antagonists."[12] As the list of organizational names a few paragraphs back attests, freethinkers struggled over the years to find the optimal self-description, but the identity-framing challenges they faced were mitigated by a good ability to frame issues of common concern. I argue that three frames have dominated American freethought over the course of its existence: (1) an antiscriptural frame that positions the Bible as being superstitiously revered by Christians as the Word of God, (2) a "scientific hope" frame that positions science as a pursuit that can do a better job of improving human life than Christianity, and (3) a separationist frame that points to legal privileges afforded to Christianity as a continuing source of injustice and a barrier to progress.

Movement repertoires, as conceptualized by Charles Tilly, are a movement's toolkit of protest strategies and tactics.[13] Many movements have tactics like petition drives, marches, conventions, declarations, and speaking tours in their repertoires. Sometimes a movement can advance when an effective new tactic is added to its repertoire, such as when the Black Lives Matter movement achieved a new level of recognition when Colin Kaepernick inspired other NFL players to take the knee during the national anthem. A key development in the history of the freethought movement, I will argue, occurred when freethinkers' repertoire expanded in the early twentieth century to include legal challenges to laws and practices they saw as unconstitutional violations of their right to disbelieve. The addition of a legal strategy to the freethought repertoire helped the movement realize many long-standing goals.

Finally, *movement waves* refer to waves of movement activity. Social movements often develop through successive periods of expansion, maintenance, and latency. The beginning of a wave is frequently marked by an expansion or revival during which the movement transforms to accommodate new participants. In the process, participants come to realize that they are part of a collective enterprise and to identify with the movement. After a period of expansion, it is common that the structures that the movement has built persist without much new growth during a period of maintenance. As maintenance passes into inactivity, the movement can enter a phase of latency. During periods of latency, many movement participants retain their identification with the movement even though they are no longer engaged in collective action on behalf of the movement. They maintain their connections with other movement participants and circulate information about issues of common concern. This makes it possible for collective action to be mobilized quickly when the time is right for the next wave of activity.[14] By way of illustration, one can imagine a peace protester who had become convinced that US military intervention was wrong during the Vietnam era. Even after the war, they continued to think of themselves as a peace activist and maintained connections with other peace activists, so that, during the Iraq War, protests could be organized quickly as the movement became active again.

Determining where one wave has ended and another has begun is admittedly still far from an exact science. But I believe there is a reasonable case to be made that the freethought movement experienced four waves of activity in the period I will write about in this book. One began in the mid-1790s in a surge of republican enthusiasm sparked by the French Revolution and Thomas Paine's *Age of Reason* and ended in 1810 after Paine's death. A second began in the mid-1820s with Benjamin Offen's establishment of Paine birthday celebrations and ended with the onset of the Civil War. The third wave of activity began in the mid-1870s. It swept up more followers than either previous wave and was marked by efforts to pass legislation to strengthen separation of church and state. A fourth wave began with a resurgence of the movement in the 1920s and is marked by a shift from a legislative strategy to a legal one to advance the movement's goals.

My account of the American freethought movement differs, I hope usefully, from other accounts both in taking a long view of the movement, from the late eighteenth to the middle of the twentieth centuries, and in trying to understand the strategies that have led to its successes. A majority of academic literature on the freethought movement concentrates on limited periods and aspects of the movement's history. Examples of period-specific studies include Sidney Warren's *American Freethought, 1860–1914*,[15] Albert Post's *Popular Freethought in America, 1825–1850*;[16] Amanda Porterfield's *Conceived in Doubt: Religion and Politics in the New American Nation*,[17] which covers a period from the 1790s through the War of 1812; and Eric R. Schlereth's *An Age of Infidels: The Politics of Religious Controversy in the Early United States*,[18] covering a period from the mid-1790s through the 1830s. These studies delve deeply into the rich tapestry of the public discourse on religious belief and disbelief in the periods they focus on but can't tell more than a single chapter of the story of American freethought.

Leigh Eric Schmidt's *The Church of Saint Thomas Paine: A Religious History of American Secularism* is a study focused on how American secularists developed, consciously or unconsciously, practices analogous to those of religion in the nineteenth century.[19] While Schmidt's innovative book does take a longer view of freethought than the other studies I have thus far mentioned, it is focused exclusively on the quasi-religious practices of secularists and is not an attempt to understand freethought as a social movement. Another title by Schmidt, *Village Atheists: How America's Unbelievers Made Their Way in a Godly Nation*, is mainly a study of four individual nineteenth-century freethinkers.[20] *Free-thought on the American Frontier*, edited by Fred Whitehead and Verle Muhrer, is a unique anthology of freethought voices with an obvious and narrow focus.[21] A book that covers about a century of freethought history, but which also has a very specific focus, is Christopher Cameron's *Black Freethinkers: A History of African American Secularism*.[22] This enlightening volume focuses on African American freethinkers from the Civil War through the 1970s. I know of only two books about American freethought that span a period from the eighteenth through the twentieth centuries: Harvey J. Kaye's *Thomas Paine and the Promise of America* and Susan Jacoby's *Freethinkers: A History of American Secularism*.[23] Kaye's book is a brilliant exploration of Thomas Paine's influence on American thought and politics. But as important a figure as Paine was to later generations of freethinkers, a point that I will also stress, a study of Paine's influence is not quite the same thing as a study of the freethought movement itself. Jacoby's *Freethinkers* is most certainly a study of the freethought movement that begins with Paine and ends up in the twenty-first century, but my account differs from hers in paying greater attention to American freethought's organizational and thematic development and the strategies that led to its successes as a social movement.

Just as an awareness of freethought as a social movement is largely absent in the literature specifically about freethought, the freethought movement is absent in the literature on social movements. Many of the most prominent books about social movements are full of case studies. For instance, Charles Tilly's *Social Movements, 1768–2008*, which has been revised and updated many times since it first appeared, lists numerous nineteenth-century social movements in the United States, including abolition, socialism, prison reform, and anti-immigration. But freethought is strangely absent.[24] Many other volumes, like Suzanne Staggenborg's *Social Movements*, focus exclusively on twentieth- and twenty-first-century social movements and also neglect freethought. I hope that my study of freethought as a social movement will enrich the social movement literature with its discussion of the movement's unique collective identity and framing challenges.

This book seeks to provide a comprehensive history of the American freethought movement through the mid-twentieth century. A comprehensive understanding of the history of the freethought movement is important because it reveals the fragility of American secularism. The history of repeated difficulties the movement encountered in trying to achieve its goals demonstrates how contingent and fragile the current state of secularism in the United States is. The religiously inspired campaigns against reproductive rights and gender-affirming care that have borne fruit in recent years are the latest manifestations of a deep and consistent current in American politics that freethinkers always struggled against. In the mid-twentieth century freethinkers met with substantial success in their quest for secularization.

But perhaps even twentieth-century achievements in the areas of school prayer, religious tests for office, and blasphemy laws may not be permanent.

One place where the fragility of American secularism is very apparent is in the contemporary critique of the separationist principle upheld by the Supreme Court beginning in the late 1940s. The foremost purveyor of this critique is constitutional law scholar Philip Hamburger. Hamburger's 2002 book, *Separation of Church and State*, remains a difficult-to-remove thorn in the side of secularism more than twenty years after its publication. The book argues, in a historically savvy way, that during the twentieth century the Supreme Court extended the principle of separationism much further than there is any constitutional basis for doing. Hamburger argues against the relevance of Jefferson's remarks about a "high wall of separation between church and state" in his 1802 letter to the Danbury Baptists to the interpretation of the constitution. He argues that the founding generation sought to prevent a complete union of church and state but did not mean that church and state should be strictly separated. Hamburger holds that contemporary ideas about the separation of church and state originated in nineteenth-century nativism, which sought to employ separationist rhetoric to mask a Protestant attempt to prevent Catholics from exercising power through public institutions in the same way that Protestants had. He charges that the twentieth-century Supreme Court justices who promoted church-state separation, Justice Hugo Black chief among them, were also motivated by anti-Catholicism and even the influence of the Ku Klux Klan. He concludes that "because of its history—both its lack of constitutional authority and its development in response to prejudice—the idea of separation should, at best, be viewed with suspicion."[25] Hamburger's book initially received much praise for the depth of his historical analysis and plucky challenge to what had become a settled principle of American jurisprudence.[26]

Defenders of separationism took their time in replying, but now Hamburger's antiseparationist history had been definitively answered by Steven K. Green in a series of books including, *The Second Disestablishment* (2010); *Inventing a Christian America* (2015); *The Third Disestablishment* (2019); and *Separating Church and State* (2022). It is beyond the scope of this book to pay as much attention to the twists and turns of the history of church-state separation as Green has. But because the history of church-state separation as told by Hamburger runs parallel to the history of the freethought movement, and because Hamburger has misrepresented the history of the freethought movement in places, I think it would be appropriate for me to intersperse remarks about his version of the history of church-state separation within my history of the American freethought movement. The history of church-state separation is salient to the present moment as the most conservative Supreme Court in a generation struggles with church-state separation issues in cases like *Kennedy v. Bremerton School District* (2022), where the court sided with a football coach who had been fired for praying in public in the middle of the football field after games. The conservative Supreme Court in combination with the prominence of Hamburger's clever but misleading interpretation of history represents a strong threat to secularism in America.

In addition to revealing the fragility of American secularism, taking a big-picture view of American freethought has given me several insights into the movement. One is that, although it is tempting to think that a movement which championed secularization must itself be profoundly secular, the first wave of American freethought is best understood as a movement of religious dissenters, and religious elements of the movement persist to this day. This is partly because many freethought leaders began their careers as Christian preachers. Such figures include Elihu Palmer, Abner Kneeland, William J. Potter, Francis Ellingwood Abbot, Charles B. Reynolds, George Chainey, and Moncure Conway. These leaders often described their outlook in religious terms, proclaiming that they were proponents of deism, or a "religion of humanity." Their project was not to do away with religion but rather to make religion rational and nonsupernaturalist. This was an enterprise proposed by Thomas Paine himself in *The Age of Reason*, a work that called for the replacement of the "false theology" of Christianity with the "true theology" of scientific deism. Especially in the antebellum period, freethinkers often held meetings on Sunday mornings just as other religious denominations did. Some groups, such as that led by Elihu Palmer in New York, can easily be considered independent congregations of deists. It was an organization called the Free Religious Association, which aimed to promote "pure and genuine religion in the world," that led the post–Civil War revival of American freethought.

Another group of religiously inclined freethought leaders in the later part of the nineteenth century were spiritualists who had been led to dissent from religious orthodoxy by their belief that the spirits of the dead remain in the world to help guide the living. To them, spiritualism was a religion, and they considered their religion to be a rational one, founded on the evidence of thousands of séances. Among their number were Robert Owen and his son

Robert Dale Owen, Andrew Jackson Davis, Victoria Woodhull and her sister Tennessee Claflin, Ida Craddock, and Amy Post and her husband, Isaac. As lecture tours and conventions displaced Sunday gatherings as foci of freethought activity after the Civil War, freethought lost some of its religious character, but even today liberal religious traditions such as Unitarian Universalism, Quakerism, and Humanistic Judaism remain deeply entwined with freethought. The idea that American freethought began as a religious dissent movement is strongly supported by Leigh Eric Schmidt's documentation of the religious elements of American secularism in *The Church of Saint Thomas Paine*. This book takes the argument a step further by claiming that in the first wave of freethought religiosity was not just one element among many, it was a core characteristic, and it remains an important element of the movement even today.

In addition to revealing the persistent element of religiosity within freethought, taking a big-picture view of freethought also enables us to see the most important ways that the movement has changed over its lifetime, and to try to make sense of those changes. I will explore four important shifts in the movement throughout the book. The first is the move, already alluded to, away from a religious mode of organization to a more fully secular one. The second is the shift away from the dependence on the leadership of freethinking immigrants who had fled persecution in Europe that characterized the movement's antebellum period to the dominance of native-born American leaders after the Civil War. The third is the shift away from the thematic prominence of opposition to the divine authority of scripture and other Christian doctrines that characterized early American freethought to the thematic prominence of calls for the separation of church and state that became the focus of movement activity after the Civil War, a key development that fueled the golden age of freethought beginning in the 1870s. Finally, after the movement began to focus on church-state separation, there was a shift from nineteenth-century attempts to legislate greater separation to twentieth-century attempts to win it through legal action. These changes in the character of American freethought have not been apparent to historians who have focused only a single period of American freethought. But they become visible in the context of a comprehensive history of the movement. And they are important not just as historical observations but also because they hold lessons for contemporary freethinkers.

As much as I think it is important to achieve a comprehensive understanding of the freethought movement, I think it is also important to tell the stories of individual freethinkers in some detail to better understand how they came to identify with the movement, the choices they faced about framing, and how they contributed to the movement's repertoire of strategies and tactics. The story of the movement is, at least in part, an interweaving of the stories of the people who participated in the movement. Consequently, in many places my writing is somewhat biographical in character. I hope, by raising new questions about their place in the history of freethought as a social movement, my account offers new insight into familiar figures like Thomas Paine and Robert Ingersoll. It also introduces a few lesser-known characters to the story of freethought, figures such as Elihu Palmer, the blind preacher who helped to found one of the first openly deistical societies in the country; Ernestine Rose, the atheistic daughter of a Polish rabbi who called on freethinkers to honor the "rights of man" by granting women more rights; Francis Ellingwood Abbot, who formulated the influential "Nine Demands of Liberalism"; Ida Craddock, a fervent spiritualist who was persecuted for writing a sex manual; Joseph Lewis, an early twentieth-century freethinker responsible for pioneering the movement's successful legal offensive; and Queen Silver, a precocious child who started giving public lectures in defense of atheism before she was ten.

Outline of the Book

Before there was an American freethought movement, there was *The Age of Reason*. Thomas Paine's deistic manifesto attacked the authority of Christian scripture and championed a scientific deism that he hoped would displace Christianity. In speaking out against orthodox Christianity, Paine said things that many had considered unsayable, making it possible for private doubts to be uttered publicly and creating conditions where freethinkers could openly organize themselves. Freethinkers admired Paine and were influenced by his framing of key issues for more than a century to come. Chapter 1 tells the story of how Paine came to write *Age of Reason* in the midst of the French Revolution, discusses key aspects of how and why Paine framed political and religious issues as he did, and shows the persistence of these frames in the freethought movement. It also shows some of the ways that the French Revolution itself was an important prelude to the American freethought movement. Chapter 2 deals with the first wave of freethought activity in the United States. It follows one of the first organized groups of deists in America led by Elihu Palmer as they laid the foundations of a movement that later freethinkers would build on. The chapter inquires into the conditions that led this early incarnation of freethought to arise in the final years of the eighteenth century. Chapter 3 deals with a second wave of deistic activity in the United States. It describes how, by organizing celebrations of Paine's birthday, an English émigré named Benjamin Offen revived Palmer's deistic movement more than a decade after it foundered. It also relates how the revived movement was transformed through the involvement of Frances Wright and Ernestine Rose. These women helped open freethought to more of the religiously dispossessed and built bridges with the feminist, workers' rights, and abolitionist movements. Chapter 4 discusses a wave of freethought activity that surged in the mid-1870s and was characterized by a new focus on the separation of church and state. Chapter 5 covers freethought's resurgence in the 1920s and details the rise of the legal strategy that brought great advances in the mid-twentieth century. The conclusion brings the story of the American freethought movement up to the present and draws lessons from the movement's history for the freethinkers of today.

CHAPTER ONE

Prelude to American Freethought

The Age of Reason and the French Revolution

I believe in one God, and no more; and I hope for happiness beyond this life.

I believe the equality of man, and I believe that religious duties consist in doing justice, loving mercy, and endeavouring to make our fellow-creatures happy.

But, lest it should be supposed that I believe many other things in addition to these, I shall, in the progress of this work, declare the things I do not believe, and my reasons for not believing them.

—Thomas Paine (1794), *The Age of Reason*

When I took up this treatise, I considered it as one of those vicious and absurd publications, filled with ignorant declamation and ridiculous representation of simple fact, the reading of which, with attention, would be an undue waste of time; but afterwards, finding it often the subject of conversation in all ranks of society; and knowing the author to be generally plausible in his language, and very artful in turning the clearest truths to ridicule, I determined to read it, with an honest design of impartially examining its real merits.

I confess, that I was much mortified to find, the whole force of this vain man's genius and art, pointed at the youth of America, and her unlearned citizens (for I have no doubt, but that it was originally intended for them) in hopes of raising a skeptical temper and disposition in their minds, well knowing that this was the best inlet to infidelity, and the most effectual way of serving its cause, thereby sapping the foundation of our holy religion in their minds.

—Elias Boudinot (1801),
writing in reaction to Thomas Paine's *The Age of Reason*

The Age of Reason: Swan Song or Phoenix?

The above passage from Elias Boudinot's *The Age of Revelation; or, The Age of Reason Shewn to be an Age of Infidelity* (1801) testifies to the impact of Thomas Paine's deistic manifesto, *The Age of Reason*.[1] It simultaneously articulates a stunned horror at its success. Boudinot was a devout Presbyterian who had served as president of the Continental Congress during the Revolution. Afterwards, he was appointed by Washington to be director of the

Mint of the United States. He was also the first president of the American Bible Society. Although he knew little of the real circumstances that had given birth to Paine's treatise on religion,[2] he was not mistaken about the growing popularity of deism in the United States inspired by Paine's book in the mid-1790s. Deism is a system of beliefs that affirms the existence of God but denies the intervention of God in the universe by supernatural means. Although deism had been mostly dormant in the English-speaking world for half a century, Boudinot had good reason to fear that Paine's deistic revival had the potential to offer a serious challenge to the religious sensibility of American Protestants, who looked to scriptural revelation for the surest truth. Although the opening of Paine's "profession of faith" from *Age of Reason*, quoted above,[3] seems mild and inoffensive, the book rapidly develops a forceful attack on all religions that depend on the authority of a divinely inspired text, especially Christianity.

The popularity of deism rose dramatically in the mid-1790s in the north Atlantic world. *The Age of Reason*, published in two parts in 1794 and 1795, brought deism to a mass audience in France, the United States, and Britain. It also provoked great controversy. Paine penned the work in Revolutionary France, where leaders of the Revolution actively promoted deism through the "Cult of Reason" and the "Cult of the Supreme Being." Paine himself supported the Theophilanthropic Society, which came into being toward the end of 1796 for the purpose of putting deistic beliefs into practice in France.[4] In the United States in 1795 and 1796, deism and *The Age of Reason* were in vogue among the students at Yale, Harvard, Dartmouth, and other colleges,[5] and a small network of deistic societies and papers sprang up in mid-Atlantic cities, led by followers of Paine such as Elihu Palmer and John Fellows.[6] *Age of Reason* went through seventeen American editions by 1796. In Britain, *Age of Reason* sold well even as a bookseller, Mr. Thomas Williams, was prosecuted for selling it.[7] *The Age of Reason* was by far the most widely read deistic work ever produced, but its popularity would precipitate a strong negative reaction against deism, and against Paine personally.

Some historians view *The Age of Reason* as the swan song of Enlightenment deism in America, a final energetic performance of religious rationalism before the evangelical movement known as the Second Great Awakening changed everything. "Evangelical heart-religion, nurtured in numberless revivals... penetrated the very citadels of Enlightenment," writes historian John Turner. "Devastation fell on reasonable religion. So successful proved the assault that by the 1830s the last crippled Deists had been driven into that outer darkness where dwelt only disreputable radicals."[8] The story of *Age of Reason* has not been well served by the way academics traditionally partition historical periods. Because it appeared at the very end of what is usually thought of as the Enlightenment, the continuing importance of *Age of Reason* in the nineteenth century, and the continuity between deism and the freethought movement, was not fully appreciated by twentieth-century historians of the American Enlightenment like Gustav Adolf Koch and Herbert Morais. *The Age of Reason* appeared at the limit of their historical jurisdiction, and they never looked beyond that arbitrary event horizon to see what became of it.

More recent historians of the Enlightenment such as Henry May and Jonathan Israel have done more than their predecessors to acknowledge Paine's continuing influence in nineteenth-century America but still miss the continuity between Paineite deism and later forms of American freethought. Israel's career-summing magnum opus, *The Enlightenment That Failed*, acknowledges the revival of Paineite deism in the 1830s but frames it as a phenomenon limited mainly to radical immigrants fleeing the European revolutions of 1848.[9] An important thesis of *The Enlightenment That Failed* is that what Israel calls the "Radical Enlightenment," defined as the strand of Enlightenment thinking that opposed religious authority, ended in disillusionment with the revolutions that swept Europe in 1848 and 1849, and so he too misses the fact that American freethought, a movement that continued to perpetuate the legacy of *Age of Reason*, only gained strength in this period and had its most vibrant days still ahead of it. From the perspective of American freethought, it is perhaps more fitting to think of the "Radical Enlightenment" not as an enlightenment that failed but as an enlightenment that faltered—one that, after stumbling in 1810 and being revived in 1825, was carried forward into the twentieth century by figures like Robert Ingersoll, Clarence Darrow, and Joseph Lewis.

There is reason to think that the *Age of Reason* was less like a swan's dying song and more like a phoenix consumed in the flames of controversy, from the ashes of which arose a fledgling freethought movement in America. After going into eclipse for fifteen years, a time during which Paine was prominent only in the posthumous attacks of opponents, his works began to be republished. Old friends and new admirers began to meet at yearly celebrations of his birthday. Inspired by Paine's writings, particularly *The Age of Reason*, new societies devoted to propagating freethought formed, such as the Society of Free Enquirers and the Society of Moral Philanthropists. As the movement continued to grow through the nineteenth and into the twentieth century, American freethinkers continued to be inspired by Paine and *The Age of Reason*.

Because of *Age of Reason*'s role in the genesis of the American freethought movement, and its strong and continuing influence on it, it makes sense to begin a study of the American freethought movement with a chapter about *The Age of Reason*. I'll tell the story of how Paine came to write *The Age of Reason* and note some key aspects of how he framed religious issues that would have lasting resonance. In the process, I will discuss the campaign of dechristianization that took place while Paine was writing *Age of Reason*, and the rise of the Cult of Reason and the Cult of the Supreme Being. These events, in themselves, are also important preludes to American freethought. I will begin by narrating the events of Paine's life that led up to his writing of *The Age of Reason*. This story is an unlikely tale of a poor Quaker staymaker's son, a man with only a grammar school education, who became the best-known political writer of his era.

The Adventures of a Staymaker's Son

Thomas Paine was born in a rented, thatch-roofed cottage with a garden in the town of Thetford, England, about ninety miles north of London, on January 29, 1737.[10] He was the child of an unusual marriage between Frances Cocke, a middle-class Anglican woman who was the daughter of an attorney, and Joseph Pain, a Quaker tradesman eleven years her junior. The marriage was unusual not only because of differences in class but also because Quakers were generally not permitted by their community to marry outside their faith. Joseph Pain was somehow able to defy this norm without being completely rejected by his fellow Quakers.[11]

As the child of an interfaith marriage, Paine had a rare perspective on the religious tension of his time. The Church of England, or Anglican Church, which Paine's mother was born into, was the established church. Its priests were supported by mandatory tithes and its official head was the king. It was governed by a hierarchy of bishops led by the archbishop of Canterbury. Those who practiced other varieties of Protestantism, such as Quakerism, were known as dissenters. They received no support or encouragement from the government and, together with Catholics and Jews, were barred from holding public office. In earlier times, they had been officially forbidden to meet for worship at all. Paine grew up with one foot in the world of the Anglican establishment—a world of priestly vestments, stained glass, sacraments, hierarchy, and ceremony—and one foot in the world of disenfranchised Quaker dissenters, who gathered in a starkly simple meetinghouse, had no formal hierarchy, and believed that each person had a God-given inner light that should be trusted above all else.

Paine's father's trade was the making of "stays," a word that referred both to the whale bone ribs that gave stiffness to ladies' corsets, and to the corsets themselves. He earned a meager living working in a shop in their rented cottage. Because his father was a tradesman with the status of a freeman, Paine was entitled to attend the local grammar school free of charge. He did so from the age of seven until the age of thirteen, but that was all the formal education he ever received.[12] After he graduated, he apprenticed with his father, spending long days in the tedious work of fitting and sewing whale bone ribs into cloth girdles while often dreaming of adventures in far-off places.

In 1756, at the age of nineteen, Paine ran off to London, intending to join the crew of a privateer called the *Terrible* as she set off to capture French prizes at the start of the Seven Years' War. Privateers were ships given official leave by a "letter of marque" to wage war on enemy commerce for profit. Had Paine not been dissuaded at the last minute from boarding the *Terrible* by his father, who dropped everything to pursue his son, he would likely have died with most of the rest of her crew.[13] But from that point on, Paine would make his own way in the world. His desire for adventure at sea not yet sated, in 1757 he joined the crew of the privateer *King of Prussia*. The voyage was successful, and Paine returned to London flush with his share of the ship's takings. He used it to attend public lectures by James Ferguson and Benjamin Martin, two popularizers of Newtonian science. These lectures covered a range of topics in natural philosophy, but Paine was especially impressed by the lectures on astronomy. The six months that Paine spent pursuing the only kind of higher education available to him were important for the future course of his life. In *The Age of Reason* Paine later claimed that it was in Martin and Ferguson's lectures that he first encountered deistic ideas. Martin and Ferguson were not deists, but they did justify the study of science with the idea that the study of God's creation brings the human mind closer to the Creator. This element of natural theology was an essential part of Paine's deism. Just as importantly, it was through the connections Paine developed through Martin and Ferguson to men of science that he met Benjamin Franklin, who was instrumental in bringing him to America and making possible the astounding career that followed.

After the death of his first wife in childbirth, Paine took up a career as an excise tax collector, eventually settling in the busy commercial city of Lewes in the south of England in 1768. There he blossomed as he became involved in local politics. He began to write poetry to amuse himself and his friends. He got so much confidence as a writer and political actor that he composed a petition on behalf of all his fellow excise officers, arguing that better pay and working conditions would reduce the corruption that the profession suffered from. He delivered the petition personally to the Board of Excise in London in early 1774. But 1774 turned out to be a bad year for Paine. Not only did he fail to secure improved pay and working conditions, but he was permanently dismissed from the excise service for having left his posting without permission. About that same time, the tobacco shop that Paine had been running for his second wife's family failed and he was forced to sell all his possessions to cover debts. Paine's second marriage ended along with his career as an excise officer and shopkeeper.[14]

Paine traveled back to London, where he turned to Benjamin Franklin for guidance. Franklin was impressed by Paine's ingenuity and love of scientific learning. He advised the thirty-seven-year-old to travel to America to make a fresh start in life, providing him with the letters of introduction he would need to get established in Philadelphia.[15]

In America, after getting a start as the editor of the *Pennsylvania Magazine*, Paine achieved fame as the author of *Common Sense*, a pamphlet that was critical in making a conflict with Britain over taxation into a war for political independence. It portrayed the colonial struggle for independence as having profound consequences for the future of the whole human race: "'Tis not the concern of a day, a year, or an age; posterity are virtually involved in the contest, and will be more or less affected even to the end of time, by the proceedings now."[16] Printed, reprinted, excerpted, and read publicly throughout the colonies, it reached as much as a fifth of the total population.[17]

After independence was declared, Paine volunteered for the army, serving as an aide first to General Daniel Roberdeau and then to General Nathanael Green. He was with the army when the British took Brooklyn and George Washington was forced to retreat in the dead of night to Manhattan. He was likely watching across the Hudson River from New Jersey as the British took Fort Lee, the last American stronghold on Manhattan. After the fall of Fort Lee, Paine made a dismal retreat across New Jersey with the army to the relative safety of Pennsylvania.[18] To help keep up morale, Paine composed what would become the first of a series of essays called *The American*

Crisis. "These are the times that try men's souls," he wrote.[19] Legend has it that his first *Crisis* essay was read to Washington's troops before they recrossed the Delaware and made the successful surprise attack on Trenton, on Christmas night of 1776.[20]

As the war dragged on, Paine continued his *Crisis* series and accepted an appointment as secretary to the Committee of Foreign Correspondence of the Continental Congress, a body charged with securing foreign support for the Revolution. After a divisive controversy over the conduct of an arms procurement agent in France named Silas Dean prompted Paine's resignation in January 1779, he accepted a commission to use his pen to promote the levying of taxes to support American troops. After the war, Pennsylvania awarded Paine $500, New York a 277-acre farm in New Rochelle, and the US Congress gave him a $3,000 grant, all to honor his service as a Revolutionary propagandist.[21]

Paine's new wealth allowed him to pursue the career of a gentleman inventor, following in the footsteps of his mentor Franklin. Around 1785 he had an idea for a new kind of bridge that would be made of iron and that could span wide rivers without support columns. With the help of a British cabinetmaker named John Hall, he built a series of prototypes, the longest of which was thirteen feet. In an effort to win a contract to build a full-scale bridge over the Schuylkill River in Philadelphia, Paine displayed this model first in Franklin's home and then in the Pennsylvania State House. After the Pennsylvania Assembly decided the bridge project would be too expensive for the present, Paine took Franklin's suggestion to travel to Europe to try to get a commission there. Paine's bridge plans got a favorable review from the French Royal Academy in 1787, and in 1788 the British ironworking firm of Walker Brothers undertook the casting of a hundred-foot prototype at their foundry in Rotherham. This was completed in May 1788 and set up in an open field next to an inn in the hamlet of Lisson Green, near London, where at first it drew crowds of curiosity seekers. It remained an attraction until 1791.[22]

Paine watched the French Revolution unfold as he was pursuing the later phases of his bridge project. He had been so absorbed with his bridge-building aspirations that he had published very little from 1787 until *Rights of Man* in 1791, but he did keep up with events, crossing the English Channel frequently to see friends in France. He was kept informed of events there through correspondence and visits with Thomas Jefferson, who served as US minister to France between 1785 and 1789, and who Paine had got to know during the American Revolution. He was also on good terms with the

Marquis de Lafayette, a French noble who had served as an officer under Washington during the American Revolution, playing a key role in the American victory at Yorktown, which forced the British to begin peace talks.

By 1790 the new French National Assembly had adopted a statement of governing principles called *The Declaration of the Rights of Man and Citizen*, which was largely the work of Lafayette.[23] It continued to attempt to construct a stable constitutional monarchy with the reluctant compliance of King Louis XVI. Back in England, a conservative Whig named Edmund Burke published an influential criticism of the French Revolution called *Reflections on the Revolution in France*. Burke, who had once been on friendly terms with Paine, thought it was folly to found a government on a declaration of rights. "Government is not made in virtue of natural rights, which may and do exist in total independence of it," Burke declared.[24] Burke thought that, if the ancient political establishments of Europe fell to radicals who replaced them with theoretical declarations of rights, so too would fall civilization. Many British reformers who supported the French Revolution wrote replies to Burke. The very first was by the pioneering feminist Mary Wollstonecraft. Her *Vindication of the Rights of Men* was published before the end of 1790.[25] Its title presaged her 1792 *Vindication of the Rights of Woman*.

With a pamphlet war breaking out around him, Paine, with his history as a successful pamphleteer, felt he might again be able to influence the course of important events through his writing. While still supervising the bridge installation at Lisson Green, he completed his own refutation of Burke just before the end of January 1791. It was published March 16 with the full title *Rights of Man: Being an Answer to Mr. Burke's Attack on the French Revolution*. It was a point-by-point refutation of Burke employing an irreverent wit that could be appreciated even by those who had not read Burke's *Reflections*. This was fortunate, because more people read Paine's reply to Burke than Burke's original statement. Burke's *Reflections* sold approximately 17,500 copies and would have been the most widely read political essay in Britain if Paine's *Rights of Man* had not exceeded 100,000 in sales.[26]

The phenomenal success of *Rights of Man* in 1791 gave Paine a unique opportunity to reach a mass audience with a vision of a new political order. He did just that in February 1792 with *Rights of Man, Part the Second: Combining Principle and Practice*. Where the first part of *Rights* had closely followed Burke's text in order to discredit it, the second part presented a bold political agenda rooted in Paine's political philosophy with a structure somewhat parallel to that of *Common Sense*. Just as Paine had closed *Common Sense* with a chapter that addressed the ways and means of achieving an independent America, he closed the second part of *Rights of Man* with a chapter titled "Ways and Means." This final chapter of *Rights of Man* argues that if the expense associated with war and the royal court were eliminated, even with a momentous reformation of the tax system to make it more progressive, there would be sufficient revenue to provide financial assistance to the poor and the elderly and to pay for the schooling of children whose parents cannot afford it, with enough left over to make small one-time payments to newlyweds, upon the birth of every child, and to defray funeral expenses. To achieve these benefits, all Britain would need to do would be to sign a mutual defense pact with France and Holland in which all powers agree to reduce their navies by 90%, and then to reduce all the expenses associated with British government to £500,000 per year, a sum that would support modest salaries for legislators and civil servants, but little else. Although Paine was clever enough not to make a direct call for the end of the British Court, the finances of his plan made no provision for its continuance. Paine was proposing to defund the monarchy and the military.

Although Paine had done nothing like calling for armed rebellion in *Rights of Man*, his blueprint for a British republic looked like a ticking revolution bomb to King George III and Prime Minister William Pitt. On May 21, 1792, the king issued a proclamation against "seditious publications" that ordered magistrates to discover the identity of the authors and printers of any seditious publications and transmit this information to "our principal secretaries of state."[27] Paine was indicted for sedition the very next day. Thus began a campaign to defame and prosecute Paine.

Paine must have presented the defenders of the establishment with a ticklish problem. His writings certainly did have the power to inspire those who would be happy to witness the birth of a British republic and who were emboldened by the French Revolution to work for such a change. But Paine's popularity was such that there was a high risk that violence, and perhaps revolution, would break out if they moved against him before he had been discredited. So, the trial was postponed until December as a campaign to discredit, defame, and humiliate Paine got into full gear. Many hostile replies to *Rights of Man* were published and endorsed by government officials and clergy, as well as reactionary societies like the Association for Preserving Liberty and Property Against Republicans and Levelers. Among the surviving artifacts of anti-Paine propaganda from 1792 is a broadside claiming to be "Intercepted Correspondence from Satan to Citizen Paine."

At the top is a fantastical Cerberus-type creature with a horned Satanic head between Paine-like heads, one of which is depicted shouting "Rights of Man" and the other shouting "Sedition." An inscription on the pedestal where the creature sits reads, "Pain, Sin, and the Devil: Tres Juncti in Uno."[28] Perhaps more personally insulting to Paine was a false letter, which was widely circulated, that purported to be from his mother to his second wife, in which his mother writes about what a terrible person her son is.[29] Although Paine had a large following of loyal supporters, feeling began to run high against him thanks to these efforts, to the point that there were anti-Paine rallies where effigies of him were hung and burned.[30] According to one account, it was Paine's friend the poet William Blake who warned him that his life was in serious danger, and on September 13, 1792, Paine took a packet from Dover to Calais, departing England for the last time in his life, where he would soon be convicted of sedition *in absentia*.

Paine had a good reason for going to France in addition to the increasingly dire threat to his life in England. In France, the new constitutional monarchy established in 1791 had failed on August 10 after an angry republican mob had stormed the royal Tuileries Palace in Paris and surrounded the Legislative Assembly, where the king and his family had taken refuge. To appease the mob, the assembly was forced to suspend the king from his constitutional duties, imprison the royal family, and declare that a National Convention would be elected to replace the Legislative Assembly and create a new and truly republican constitution for France. The outgoing Legislative Assembly voted to make Paine a citizen eligible for election as an expression of gratitude for his defense of the Revolution. Paine shared this honor with a number of other patron saints of republican revolutions, including Joseph Priestley and George Washington. Such was Paine's fame as a defender of the Revolution that he was elected to represent the department of Calais in the National Convention, whose members were to create a new and fully republican French constitution.

Paine took his seat in the convention the week after his arrival in Calais. A few days later he delivered a speech that expressed his gratitude for being elected. The speech made it clear that he saw the French Revolution as continuing the principles of the American Revolution. "The principles on which that Revolution began, have extended themselves to Europe; and an overruling Providence is regenerating the Old World by the principles of the New."[31] Just as he had believed the American Revolution was of vital importance, not just for the future of America, but for the future of humanity, he now believed the French Revolution to be the next step in the same process of world liberation: "It is no longer the paltry cause of kings, or of this or of that individual, that calls France and her armies into action. It is the great cause of ALL. It is the establishment of a new era, that shall blot despotism from the earth, and fix, on the lasting principles of peace and citizenship, the great Republic of Man."[32] This speech, like all the speeches that Paine presented to the convention, was written in English and translated into French. Paine did not have sufficient command of the French language to write or speak proficiently. It is likely that Paine's lack of fluency in French prevented him at first from understanding the danger of the political maelstrom he had entered. Neither Jefferson nor Lafayette was there to guide him any longer. Jefferson had returned to the United States to take up his duties as secretary of state and Lafayette had been captured and imprisoned by the Austrians the previous summer, after resigning his commission as general after the fall of the constitutional monarchy that he supported.

Politically, Paine allied himself with the moderate Girondin faction in the convention. Girondins represented provincial and bourgeois France. They took their name from the province of Gironde, because the twelve deputies from that region formed the core of the loosely knit group. A leading member was Jacques Pierre Brissot, who, like Paine, was both an abolitionist and a member of the American Philosophical Society. Brissot had been associated with Paine at least since 1789, when the two were among the founders of a short-lived paper called *Le Républicain*.[33] Another key figure among the Girondins was Madame Roland, a brilliant woman whose frequent salons promoted cohesion and exchange among Girondin politicians and their allies. The Girondins were among the most vocal advocates of spreading the Revolution across Europe through a war of liberation, a goal that Paine shared even if he was not so bellicose in his rhetoric.

In the convention, the Girondins increasingly found themselves opposed by another faction called the Montagnards. The Montagnards were strongly associated with the Jacobin political club. Founded in 1789, the Jacobin Club was originally a place for open political debate that got its name from the deserted Dominican monastery where it met, which was called the Jacobin Monastery because it was located on the Rue Saint-Jacques. The organization split over the question of whether the king should be removed in June of 1791, when he and his family attempted to flee Paris and travel clandestinely to Montmédy, a citadel near the border of Austrian territory protected by a general and 10,000 troops still loyal to the king. After the royals were apprehended about thirty miles short of their goal and returned to Paris, the king was relieved of his duties. Rumors spread that he was seeking to ally himself with Austria and Prussia against the Revolution. The conservative members of the Jacobin Club who supported the king without qualification left to form the Feuillant Club. Members like Georges Danton and Camille Desmoulins, who wanted a republic without a king, formed their own Cordeliers Club. The then-more-moderate Maximilien Robespierre stayed in the Jacobin Club and gained increased control over it, for the time taking the position that there should still be a constitutional monarchy but that Louis XVI should no longer be the king. As Robespierre moved toward the political left, moderate members of the Jacobin Club like Brissot were expelled, and the club eventually became an echo chamber for Robespierre's increasingly despotic policies.

When Robespierre and the Jacobins did come around to the republican side, they did so with a vengeance. They courted the poor of Paris, known as the *sans-culottes*, or "men without britches," because they wore trousers rather than the knee-length britches with stockings that were fashionable among men of rank in the eighteenth century. The Jacobins nurtured ties to the *sans-culottes* using a paper called *L'Ami du peuple* (*Friend of the People*), published by Jean-Paul Marat, and gained control of the Paris city government, known as the Paris Commune. Using these tools, they were instrumental in organizing the storming of the Tuileries Palace and the end of the constitutional monarchy. The Jacobins, Cordeliers, and other far-left deputies in the convention together were referred to as Montagnards, or "mountain men," by their opponents because they sat in the highest seats in the Convention Hall. They also chose to sit on the left side of the president, a practice that gave rise to modern "left" and "right" political terminology. The Montagnards were at first a minority in the convention but had ties to the Jacobins, who could mobilize the *sans-culottes* to violent action at key moments.

The early days of the convention were a time of optimism. An invasion of France meant to restore the monarchy launched in spring of 1792 by a coalition of Austrian and Prussian forces was stopped short of Paris at the Battle of Valmy on the very day the convention first met, September 20, 1792. A string of French military victories followed as the *sans-culottes* volunteered by the tens of thousands to serve at the front. Revolutionary armies pushed into enemy territory, capturing Brussels and Frankfurt.[34]

But the hopefulness of the convention's early days soon gave way to partisan conflict and then increasing peril for Paine and his Girondin allies. Girondins and Montagnards mostly took different sides on the question of whether the king's life should be spared after he had been tried and found guilty of treason by the convention, with Montagnards calling for execution and Girondins calling for imprisonment or exile. Paine, although an ardent supporter of the Revolution, had always maintained a strong respect for Louis XVI rooted in his crucial support for the American Revolution and his apparent openness to reform. During the debate, Paine rose and delivered a plea that the life of Louis should be spared for humanitarian reasons. "As France has been the first of European nations to abolish royalty, let her also be the first to abolish the punishment of death, and to find out a milder and more effective substitute."[35] His speech helped to get 288 votes to save the king's life, but it did not carry the day.[36] Instead, it drew negative attention from the Montagnards, some of whom blamed his Quaker heritage for his leniency toward the king.[37] A few days later, on January 21, 1793, Louis's last protestation of innocence was drowned by a drum roll as the blade of the guillotine fell.[38]

Partisan tensions further escalated in the convention in early 1793, when revolts broke out in a number of French provinces. An uprising in the province of Vendee was the largest of many. At about the same time, the French advance in the Austrian Netherlands stalled, and a key general named Charles-François du Périer Dumouriez, who had ties to the Girondins, defected to the enemy. These and other circumstances conspired to bring the Girondins under suspicion: they were the faction most associated with provincial France and were suspected of supporting the provincial insurrections. Marat and another writer-publisher named Jacques Hébert began calling the Girondins traitors and advocating their expulsion from the convention in their newspapers. In response, Girondins led an unsuccessful attempt to impeach Marat, who was a member of the convention, and engineered the arrest of Hébert. The Paris Commune, controlled by the Jacobins, retaliated by replacing the leader of the Paris National Guard with a man loyal to their side, François Hanriot, and organizing an armed demonstration of the *sans-culottes*. Then, on June 2, 1793, the National Guard and the *sans-culottes* completely surrounded the convention. A delegation from the commune demanded the expulsion and arrest of twenty-nine deputies identified as Girondins, Brissot among them. When the members of the convention tried to leave, they were stopped by the ready guns of the National Guard. Most deputies were shocked and abstained from voting, but the Montagnards delivered the legally required votes to expel the Girondins.[39]

The expulsion of the Girondins foreshadowed the approach of a period known as the Terror. The Terror was an effort by the Montagnards of the National Convention, Robespierre chief among them, to break the spirit of anyone sympathetic to the revolts in the provinces. They also aimed to eliminate ultraradicals like Hébert and other *"enragés,"* whose influence over the *sans-culottes* was dangerous and no longer useful now that the Girondins were out of the way. The Terror created a parajudicial system meant to be used as a weapon of war. The Law of Suspects, passed by the convention on September 17, 1793, was the legal cornerstone of the Terror, making it a capital crime to give any sign of being a "partisan of tyranny," or an "enemy of liberty," or to be an aristocrat who had not "constantly demonstrated" commitment to the Revolution.[40] People suspected of being guilty of these or other vague counterrevolutionary offenses were identified by or reported to Surveillance Committees and brought to trial before one of the Revolutionary Tribunals, which comprised a separate court system that used increasingly streamlined sentencing procedures to process ever more cases. Although only 177 people were executed in Paris by the end of 1793,[41] including the surviving Girondins and former queen, Marie Antoinette, as many as thirty people a day were executed in Paris alone in the following year. In all, more than 16,000 people were tried and executed throughout France during the ten months of the Terror.[42] And if the mass executions practiced because of the civil wars are included, the number of victims rises to more than 35,000 by some estimates. But the executions were just the tip of the iceberg; 300,000 to 500,000 suspected persons were sent to prison, far too many for even expedited trials, so most just sat in captivity until the fall of Robespierre.[43] The victims were not only rebels and aristocrats, but many who were deeply invested in the new republic, including the radical journalist Hébert and his followers, and also Danton and Desmoulins, leaders of the Cordeliers Club and the movement to remove the king after his flight. It seemed that anyone could become an enemy of the Revolution.

Paine's situation grew steadily more dire over the course of 1793. The expulsion of the Girondins, the enactment of the Law of Suspects, the trial and execution of the Girondins: in each of these events Paine heard the footsteps of his doom approaching. By his own account, given at the beginning of *"Part the Second"* of *The Age of Reason*, it was the realization that his life was likely nearing its end that prompted Paine to finally publish his true thoughts on religion. But the story of how Paine came to write *The Age of Reason* is more complicated than that of a closet deist coming out with his beliefs in public on what he believed would be the eve of his death, as dramatic as that story is in itself. Deism, after all, was not a worldview that anyone was born into. So, it is reasonable to wonder how Paine became a deist in the first place, how his deism was similar or dissimilar to the deism of his contemporaries and predecessors, and why he framed his deism as he did in *Age of Reason*. I hope to answer these questions at least partially in the next section.

Inventing *The Age of Reason*

John Adams's recollections of an evening spent with Paine in 1776 suggest that Paine had begun to contemplate writing a book that expressed his views on religion quite early in his career as a political writer. In his 1802 autobiography, Adams tells of an encounter with Paine that took place several months after the January 1776 publication of *Common Sense*. Adams believed that the plan for a unicameral legislature Paine proposed in *Common Sense* was misguided. He published his own *Thoughts on Government* in April to argue for a bicameral system that he considered more prudent. After reading *Thoughts on Government*, Paine paid a call to Adams to discuss their differences. After an exchange of views with Paine about the relative merits of unicameral and bicameral legislatures, Adams went on to discuss another misgiving he had about *Common Sense*, in which Paine cited 1 Samuel 8 in the Old Testament to argue that God disapproves of monarchy.[44] Although a sincere Christian, Adams belonged to a Unitarian-leaning congregation that questioned the doctrine of the Trinity and was no biblical literalist.[45] He found Paine's application of 1 Samuel 8 to be naïve. He told Paine,

> that his reasoning from the Old Testament was ridiculous and I could hardly think him sincere. At this he laughed and said he had taken his ideas in that part from Milton; and then expressed a contempt of the Old Testament, and indeed of the Bible at large, which surprised me. He saw that I did not relish this, and soon checked himself with these words: "However, I have some thoughts of publishing my thoughts on religion, but I believe it will be best to postpone it to the latter part of life." This conversation passed in good humor, without any harshness on either side; but I perceived in him a conceit of himself and a daring impudence, which have been developed more and more to this day.[46]

If we believe that Adams correctly remembered this conversation with Paine twenty-six years after the fact, then it would appear that Paine was a fully formed closet deist less than two years after he had arrived in America, just waiting for the right moment to tell the world what he actually thought about religion. This seems possible, but not an absolute certainty. It is at least equally possible that Adams's distaste for *The Age of Reason* colored his memory. But the whole incident raises not only the question of when Paine started to think about writing *The Age of Reason* but also the question of when he became a deist.

Paine gives some hints about the origins of his deism in *Age of Reason* itself. He recalls how revolted he was as a child of "seven or eight" by a sermon he had heard read by a relative; it was called *Redemption by the Death of the Son of God*. Even as a young child, Paine had found the idea that an omnipotent and benevolent God would be able to forgive humanity's sins only through the gruesome death of his own son to be absurd. Surely if an omnipotent God wanted to forgive sins, he could just do it without engineering the crucifixion of an innocent man. Paine believed that "God was too good to do such an action, and also too almighty to be under any necessity of doing it." The story behind Christian redemption theology made "God Almighty act like a passionate man, that killed his son when he could not revenge himself in any other way."[47] While it is not likely that the young Paine had much opportunity to act on or even speak about such doubts, according to his account he carried them from a very young age. The full implications of rejecting Christian redemption theology might have taken many years to dawn on him, but sooner or later he was bound to ask, "If the story of God's sacrifice of his own son cannot be true, what does that mean about the trustworthiness of the Bible from which that story is taken?"

If Christian redemption theology was uninspiring to Paine, as a young man he stumbled across a kind of theology that he did find inspiring: natural theology. Natural theology in the eighteenth century was understood to be any theology that relied on human reason and the observation of nature to understand God and his divine will. It was distinguished from the theology of revealed religion, which relied on scriptural revelation to understand God. Revealed religion was a necessary complement to natural theology for many Christians. But deists believed that natural theology alone was all that was necessary to understand God and lead a good life.[48] In the scientific literature of Paine's time, scientifically minded Christians commonly used natural theology to justify the scientific study of God's creation.

Paine became inspired by natural theology through attending the popular science lectures of James Ferguson and Benjamin Martin in London. In *Age of Reason,* Paine mentions attending Martin and Ferguson's lectures in the winter of 1757–1758, during the period when he was in London living off the prize money from his privateering cruise on the *King of Prussia.* By the time Paine saw them, Martin and Ferguson were accomplished showmen who kept audiences enthralled with demonstrations and scientific instruments, which they made conveniently available for purchase. One of the most crowd-pleasing devices was the orrery, which was a mechanical model of the solar system.[49]

Martin and Ferguson were also among the many men of science in Paine's time who seasoned their public science with natural theology. In the first winter Paine saw him lecture, Ferguson's book, *Astronomy Explained upon Sir Isaac Newton's Principles,* first published in 1756, went into its second edition. The introduction of this work reads, "Of all the sciences cultivated by mankind, Astronomy is acknowledged to be, and undoubtedly is, the most sublime, the most interesting, and the most useful ... our very faculties are enlarged with the grandeur of the ideas it conveys ... and our understandings clearly convinced, and affected with the conviction, of the existence, wisdom, power, goodness, and superintendency of the SUPREME BEING! So that without hyperbole, 'An undevout Astronomer is mad.'"[50]

Paine was almost certain to have heard similar natural theology–based justifications for scientific inquiry in Ferguson's lectures. Martin's lectures ranged even more broadly than Ferguson's through topics in physics and chemistry. And they also were seasoned with natural theology. As stated in the advertisement for his course,[51] much of the lecture material was contained in *A Plain and Familiar Introduction to the Newtonian Philosophy* (1751).[52] The penultimate page of the preface to this work refers readers to Martin's *Panegyrick on the Newtonian Philosophy* (1749), which contains this forceful natural theology defense of science: "The Business of this Science is to enable us, in a proper manner, to consider the HEAVENS, that is, the infinite Space, the interminable Void, the *To-pan,* or *Universe* of all created worlds, the Sun and the Stars which God has ordained ... it astonishes the Mind with a certain and indubitable Proof of Prospect of an Infinity of Worlds, and creates an Idea every way worthy of, and adequate to the Notions we ought to entertain of an infinitely wise, perfect, and powerful Being."[53] Paine is likely to have heard some version of this natural theology justification of science echoed in Martin's lectures.

In *Age of Reason,* Paine recalled the profound influence that Martin and Ferguson's lectures had on him:

> As soon as I was able, I purchased a pair of globes, and attended the philosophical lectures of Martin and Ferguson, and became afterwards acquainted with Dr. Bevis, of the Society called the Royal Society....[54]
>
> ... After I had made myself master of the use of the globes and of the orrery, and conceived an idea of the infinity of space, and of the eternal divisibility of matter, and obtained, at least, a general knowledge of what is called natural philosophy, I began to compare, or, as I have said before, to confront, the internal evidence those things afford with the Christian system of faith.[55]

Although Martin and Ferguson fed Paine's love of science and inspired his taste for natural theology, natural theology in itself was not deism. Most proponents of natural theology were Christians, as were Martin and Ferguson themselves, and some even deployed natural theology to attack deism in a tradition of Christian apologetics called physico-theology.[56] But, at least by the time he wrote *Age of Reason*, Paine had liberated natural theology from Christianity and made it a cornerstone of his deism.

The path that led Paine from Martin and Ferguson's lectures to *The Age of Reason* was a long and winding one that sometimes veered away from deism. After his *King of Prussia* prize money had been spent, Paine moved to the Dover area and went back to working as a staymaker. Under the influence of an employer named Benjamin Grace, he practiced Methodism for a period between 1758 and 1759, even reading John Wesley's sermons to the congregation when no preacher was available.[57] This argues that Paine did not become a fully realized deist as an immediate effect of Martin's and Ferguson's lectures. But Paine's faith in Christianity seems to have weakened after the death of his first wife in childbirth in 1759. A 1767 letter to Paine from Jacob Duchè, a Swedenborgian minister who struggled to reconcile reason with Christianity, implies that Paine had voiced doubts about the divinity of Jesus. In it, Duchè tells Paine of how the writings of the religious mystic William Law had helped him overcome his doubts about the divinity of Jesus. Duchè implies that Law's writings might also strengthen Paine's Christian faith.[58] But if Paine read Law, it did not have the effect that Duchè hoped. Paine's deism is likely to have grown quietly stronger in America through exchanges with his deistic mentor Benjamin Franklin and his deistic friend Thomas Jefferson, but there is little indication of it in his published writings, which employed biblical references and offered no direct challenge to Christianity.[59] Prior to *Age of Reason*, Paine—like Franklin, Jefferson, and most other American deists—kept his deism mostly to himself.

The Age of Reason was composed in several distinct phases, each arising from a different set of circumstances. Like *Rights of Man*, it was a work that appeared in two parts. *The Age of Reason, Being an Investigation of True and Fabulous Theology* was published in early 1794. *The Age of Reason, Part the Second* was published about a year later. But, as scholars have discovered relatively recently, a large portion of the first part of *Age of Reason* was published during the first half of 1793 in French under the title *Le Siècle de la Raison, ou Le Sens Commun Des Droits De L'Homme* (literally "the century of reason, or, the common sense of the rights of man"). Only two imperfect copies of this curious work are known to exist, one at the American Philosophical Society in Philadelphia and the other at the Bibliothèque nationale de France in Paris, but they provide clear evidence that all but four of the seventeen chapters of the first part of *Age of Reason* appear in French in the first half of 1793.[60]

Le Siècle de la Raison is a curious work for several reasons. It does not list Paine as the author, but rather François-Xavier Lanthenas, a deputy of the National Convention who translated *The Age of Reason* and many of Paine's convention speeches and pamphlets into French. Further, it contains not only Paine's unattributed work but also a separate essay by a "citizen Néez" described as a *tableau frappant*, or "striking portrait," of "despotism and fanaticism, ancient and modern." It is mainly a defense of a policy called the Civic Constitution of the Clergy, a policy that Paine likely opposed.

The Civic Constitution of the Clergy was a policy adopted in 1790 after the Revolutionary government had nationalized church property to fund itself. It made all Catholic clergy in France employees of the state and prescribed that they swear an oath of loyalty. But only about half the clergy complied, and only 7 out of 160 bishops took the oath. The pope issued a Bull condemning the Civic Constitution of the Clergy on May 4, 1791, but that only increased the determination of the government to compel clerical compliance with it. After the new constitutional monarchy came to power, a great deal of clerical representation in the legislature was lost, and new rules were proposed to penalize the "non-juring" clergy who refused to swear their allegiance. These rules were blocked by the king's veto but took effect after he was deposed on August 10, 1792. This was the state of things when Paine arrived in September. As non-juring clergy were suspected of supporting the provincial counterrevolutionary rebellions that broke out in 1793, the anticlerical sentiment that had already been on the rise hit a fever pitch.[61]

There is good reason to think that Paine would not have been happy with the arrangements under the Civic Constitution of the Clergy. In *Rights of*

Man, he had clearly stated that he disapproved of established, or "law religions," as he called them, and the Civic Constitution of the Clergy made Catholicism more of an established religion in France than it had ever been by putting it under the direct control of the Revolutionary government. If the religious regime established by the Civic Constitution of the Clergy had continued to this day, the Gallican Church would be a doctrinally Catholic equivalent of the Anglican Church, the established religion of England. Paine believed that the establishment of any religion inevitably led to abuses of power by the state, which could justify any state action that had the approval of the clergy in its pay. It also allowed the church to squash all rational critique of its doctrines by calling on state power to repress religious dissent. In *Rights of Man* Paine took the American model of prohibition on religious establishment at the federal level and in some states to be ideal, and the only way to prevent organized religion from becoming oppressive: "Persecution is not an original feature in *any* religion; but it is always the strongly marked feature of all law religions, or religions established by law. Take away the law establishment, and every religion re-assumes its original benignity. In America, a catholic priest is a good citizen, a good character, and a good neighbor; an episcopalian minister is of the same description: and this proceeds independently of the men, from there being no law establishment in America."[62] When Paine arrived in France in September 1792, he would have found the Revolutionary government's takeover of the Catholic Church to be in stark contradiction to this ideal of religious freedom he had discussed in *Rights of Man*.

Although we can probably never know for sure what prompted Paine to approve the publication of a large portion of *The Age of Reason* in French without his name being attached to it (or even if he did approve this publication!), I would guess that *Le Siècle de la Raison* is the result of Paine adapting a manuscript that expressed his view on religion, which he had been working on for some time, to address the debate about the Civic Constitution of the Clergy as it stood in the first half of 1793. *Le Siècle de la Raison* makes no direct reference to the situation in France, but it does begin with the words "Every national church or religion has established itself by pretending some special mission from God."[63] The relevance of these words to the Civic Constitution of the Clergy is underscored by citizen Néez's staunch defense of that institution included in the same volume. Néez brushes aside the papal condemnation of the Civic Constitution of the Clergy and argues that France will be more Christian now that the tables have been turned on the church:

"Will we be less Christian, my descendants, I ask you; my faith, yours, will it be less vibrant and less firm, just because the visible leader of the church will no longer be able to increase his temporal treasure with our money, because the French clergy will be our pensioner, instead of our rich oppressor . . . ?"[64] I believe that Paine saw his book on religion as being relevant to the debate about the Civic Constitution of the Clergy but was not ready yet, in early 1793, to publish the work under his own name, reasonably fearing the negative repercussions it might have in the English-speaking world. So, he attempted to influence the debate through a French version of his book without his name on it. The result was *Le Siècle de la Raison*.

Paine begins *Age of Reason, Part the Second* with an account of the circumstances under which he wrote the first part that at first appears difficult to reconcile with the publication of *Le Siècle de la Raison* in early 1793. But the difficulty is only apparent. "I had originally reserved it to a later period in life," Paine wrote of his planned book on religion, "intending it to be the last work I should undertake." As the Terror swept France in 1793, Paine wrote that he "saw many of my most intimate friends destroyed; others daily carried to prison; and I had reason to believe . . . that the same danger was approaching myself." Paine clearly frames the Terror as the reason that he sought to finish and publish *Age of Reason* sooner than he might have wished, but even as he does so, he hints at the existence of an earlier version of the work. After the passage of a law excluding foreigners like himself from the convention, in late December 1793, he realized that he likely only would have "a few days of liberty" remaining. So, he writes, "I sat down and brought the work to a close as speedily as possible; and I had not finished it more than six hours, *in the state it has since appeared* [emphasis added] before a guard came there, about three in the morning, with an order signed by the two Committees of Public Safety and Surety General, for putting me in arrestation as a foreigner, and conveying me to the prison of the Luxembourg." The clause "in the state it has since appeared" allows for the existence of an earlier version of the work, which surely must have been *Le Siècle de la Raison*. So, Paine's impending doom was more the reason he "brought the work to a close" and put it into the hands of his friend Joel Barlow to publish rather than the reason he started writing it, which he had undertaken months or even years earlier.

Paine was not wrong about the threat to his freedom and his life. He spent nine long months as a prisoner in the Luxembourg, a palace that had been converted to hold victims of the Terror. "During the whole of my imprisonment, prior to the fall of Robespierre," Paine later wrote, "there was no time when I could think my life worth twenty-four hours, and my mind was made up to meet its fate."[65] Paine very nearly died without the aid of a guillotine. In prison, he contracted a life-threatening illness that kept him in a delirium for much of June and July 1794 and left him with little memory of that period. Paine remained in prison for many months after the fall of Robespierre in July 1794, languishing in bureaucratic limbo as one of some 300,000 people detained as suspects under the Terror. The American minister to France at the time, Gouverneur Morris, was no fan of Paine. He justified his refusal to make any effort to aid Paine in a letter to Thomas Jefferson dated January 21, 1794:

> Lest I should forget it, I must mention that Thomas Paine is in prison, where he amuses himself with publishing a pamphlet against Jesus Christ. . . . I incline to think that if he is quiet in prison, he may have the good luck to be forgotten. . . . I believe he thinks that I ought to claim him as an American citizen; but considering his birth, his naturalization in this country, and the place he filled, I doubt much the right, and I am sure that the claim would be, for the present at least, inexpedient and ineffectual.[66]

Even though he did not have "the good luck to be forgotten," Paine did survive. No one was more surprised about this than Paine himself. At first, Paine thought it had been his ill health that had prevented him from being brought before a tribunal for sentencing. But later he learned from a cellmate that one day not long before the fall of Robespierre the door of his cell had indeed been marked with the faithful symbol that indicated the inhabitants should be taken out and tried that night. The door, however, had been wide open the day it was marked, so that when it was shut at night the mark was on the inside of the door and could not be seen by those who came to collect the doomed prisoners. So, Paine and his companions were left undisturbed. Paine was finally released in November of 1794 due in large part to the efforts of a new American minister to France, James Monroe, who had recently replaced Gouverneur Morris.

The two most significant changes made to *Le Siècle de la Raison* before Paine passed it off to Joel Barlow for publication on the night of his arrest were the addition of a new first chapter and the replacement of the title. Both these changes can be viewed as responses to a massive change in the Revolution's attitude toward religion that occurred between the publication of *Le Siècle de la Raison* and *The Age of Reason*, a period in which the country experienced a wave of "dechristianization" that saw many Catholic churches appropriated by citizen groups for deistic worship. The convention had made dechristianization possible in November 1793 when it empowered local governments to renounce Catholicism and take over churches for other forms of worship.[67] Because dechristianization was carried out by local governments, its character was different from place to place. In Paris, where anticlerical sentiment ran high, dechristianization was voluntary and radical. Priests were pressured by citizens to give up their positions and salaries and surrender their churches to a new "Cult of Reason." It is estimated by Michel Vovelle, a prominent scholar of dechristianization, that between 18,000 and 20,000 clergy out of about 115,000 renounced their vocation. Another 20,000–25,000 left France, and between 3,000 and 5,000 were executed.[68] Notre-Dame Cathedral was one of many churches that were converted into Temples of Reason and Philosophy. Citizens of Paris held a Feast of Reason there on November 10. They selected a young woman to represent the Goddess of Reason. After dressing her in a classical tunic and Phrygian cap, they carried her through the streets on a sedan chair accompanied by a train of flower girls and followed by a great crowd. Then they enthroned her on the altar of Notre-Dame, where the crowd danced and sang hymns to Reason and Liberty.[69]

Voluntary dechristianization was most common around Paris and in north-central France.[70] But not all dechristianization was voluntary. In provinces that had rebelled against the Revolution, the Cult of Reason was forced on populations to check the counterrevolutionary force of the Catholic Church. Certain members of the convention were selected to be *envoyés en mission* and sent into rebellious provinces armed with virtually unlimited powers to crush resistance. Joseph Fouché carried out a particularly notorious campaign of dechristianization in Nièvre.[71] But Feasts of Reason were most often voluntary expressions of a patriotic form of deism. Citizens gathered at dechristianized churches on the rest days of the new Revolutionary calendar to worship the Supreme Being just as Catholics had previously used the spaces on Sundays for worship. These rites were celebrated with newly composed poems and hymns, such as those contained in Marie-Joseph de Chénier's *Office des décades, ou Discours, hymnes et prières en usage dans les temples de la raison* (1794).[72] Although some might have embraced the Cult of Reason only to stay on the right side of the Revolution, the outpouring of deistic liturgical material that accompanied dechristianization testifies to the sincere devotion of many followers. Liturgical worship, which had been in the hands of Catholic priests for centuries, was now in the hands of the people.

While there is every reason to suppose that Paine approved of dechristianization as a development that weakened the privileged status of the Catholic Church, he feared that what was fundamentally a deistic movement would be hijacked by people he considered to be atheists, just as the Revolution had been hijacked by the Jacobins. Many Revolutionary leaders shared the Creator God deism of Voltaire, Rousseau, and Paine himself, which held that an omnipotent and benevolent God had created the universe and then retreated into the background to watch providence unfold. But others followed the more strident materialism of Jean Meslier, Claude-Adrien Helvétius, Denis Diderot, and Baron d'Holbach. D'Holbach's 1770 *Système de la nature*, which argued that a self-caused cosmos is all that exists and defended atheism, was especially influential.[73] Although many of the materialist revolutionaries might have called themselves pantheists who, like Baruch Spinoza and John Toland, believed either that nature *is* God or that God is imminent in nature, Paine saw all such thinkers as atheistic. He argued against materialism in an 1801 speech he gave to the Theophilanthropic Society, one of the organizations that had sprung up during dechristianization to promote deistic forms of worship. While Creator God deists, like many Christians, held that a prime mover God was necessary to explain what had set the universe into motion, the materialists argued that the potential for motion is inherent in matter, and so no prime mover is necessary. Paine attacked this argument directly in his 1801 speech. "Motion is not a property of matter," Paine told his fellow Theophilanthropists. "Were motion a property of matter, that undiscovered and undiscoverable thing called perpetual motion would establish itself. It is because motion is not a property of matter, that perpetual motion is an impossibility in the hand of every being but that of the Creator of motion. When the pretenders to Atheism can produce perpetual motion, and not till then, they may expect to be credited."[74]

After he returned to the United States in 1802, Paine wrote to Samuel Adams that one reason he had for writing *The Age of Reason* was to counter the atheistic tendencies of the Revolution that began to emerge more strongly than ever during dechristianization. "The people of France were running headlong into Atheism," he told Adams, ". . . and I had the work translated and published in their own language to stop them in that career."[75] The content of *The Age of Reason* does not support the idea that the sole purpose of the book was to counter atheism, as is sometimes claimed on Paine's behalf.[76] More than half the work is given to Paine's efforts to discredit the doctrine that the Bible is the word of God and cannot reasonably be interpreted as an argument against atheism. But Paine was concerned about the progress atheism was making, perhaps because his understanding of human rights was at root a theistic one. It supposed "the right of man" to have been granted to humans by the Creator at the dawn of time. If there was no Creator God, there could be no human rights on this theory. Although Robespierre himself was a Creator God deist, Paine may have attributed the excesses of the Terror in part to a lack of belief in a Creator God. If the cosmos was eternal or self-caused and if no Creator God had existed to bestow rights upon humanity, then human rights were mere human conventions and could be altered or abolished at the whim of the state, as happened during the Terror.

Paine's changes to *Le Siècle de la Raison* should be understood not only in the context of the Terror but also in the context of dechristianization. While much of the work was still taken up with criticism of Christian doctrine, both the new title and the new first chapter put the emphasis more on what Paine believed rather than what he did not believe. The old title, *Le Siècle de la Raison, ou Le Sens Commun Des Droits De L'Homme*, had promised a century of reason and human rights. But the new title, *The Age of Reason, Being an Investigation of True and Fabulous Theology*, assured readers that there is a "true theology" that is older and stronger than the "fabulous" myth of Christian redemption theology. *Le Siècle de la Raison* had led off with an attack on national religions, but the very first page of *Age of Reason* proclaimed Paine's belief in God. Both these changes can be readily understood as responses not so much to the success of dechristianization but to the rising element of materialism within dechristianization that Paine found troubling.

Paine began work on *Age of Reason, Part the Second* about ten months after being released from prison at a time when he was living with Monroe and his family and had been reinstated to the National Convention with backpay for the time he had spent incarcerated. Paine seems to have been driven to add a sequel to *Age of Reason* by the replies of early critics who relied on the authority of scripture to back their arguments. "I observe," he writes, "that all my opponents resort, more or less, to what they call Scripture Evidence and Bible authority, to help them out. They are so little masters of the subject," he continues, "as to confound a dispute about authenticity with a dispute about doctrines; I will, however, put them right, that if they should be disposed to write any more, they may know how to begin."[77] Paine had not been able to find an English-language Bible anywhere in Paris when he had started writing the first part of the work. The references to the Bible in the first part of *Age of Reason* were all from memory, as Paine attests at the beginning of *Part the Second*.[78] Now he was able to use the Monroes' Bible to hone his criticisms of the authority of scripture. So, he set out to review the whole of the Old and New Testaments chapter by chapter, laying bare all the unbelievable claims, unworthy conduct, and outright contradictions of the Bible in order to show that it cannot be a divine revelation. Paine's critics, of course, did not abandon their belief that the Bible is the word of God because of Paine's arguments, but the strident antiscripturalism of *Part the Second* had a lasting impact on American freethought.

Viewed as a whole, Paine's deism had both a moderate component and a radical component. Paine's Creator God deism was theologically moderate in comparison to the religious views of French intellectuals such as Jean Meslier, Claude-Adrien Helvétius, Denis Diderot, and Baron d'Holbach. Although most of *Age of Reason* cannot be read as an argument against atheism, it is likely that Paine did hope that the parts of the work that argued for the existence of a Creator God on the basis of natural theology would steal wind from the sails of his more materialistic rivals for the hearts and minds of the French people. If Paine's Creator God deism was theologically moderate, the *Age of Reason* was radical in its attempt to prove that there was nothing at all sacred about any portion of Christian scripture. Many earlier deists—such as Edward Herbert, John Toland, Matthew Tindal, Anthony Collins, Thomas Woolston, and Thomas Morgan—held that scripture could not be read literally, but most stopped short of saying that the Bible was not in some way sacred. For them, reason demanded that the miracles and supernatural occurrences described in scripture be understood symbolically or as allegories, but it did not compel them to reject the sacredness of the Bible. The Irish pantheist John Toland, for instance, considered his views to be consistent with "the Mosaic Formation of the World."[79] And Thomas Woolston wrote in 1727: "That the literal History of many of the Miracles of Jesus, as recorded by the Evangelists, does imply Absurdities, Improbabilities, and Incredibilities, consequently they, either in whole or in part, were never wrought, as they are commonly believed now-a-days, but are only related as prophetical and parabolical Narratives of what would be mysteriously and more wonderfully done by him."[80] Woolston read the Bible nonliterally, looking for hidden messages about God's will and God's plan. Paine, on the other hand, read the Bible with extreme literalness in order to discredit it. He made the thesis of *Part the Second* "that the Bible is not entitled to credit, as being the word of God."[81] Only Peter Annet among the previous English deists had taken such a strident antiscriptural view. The radical antiscripturalism of *Age of Reason* set the tone for the early stages of the American freethought movement, but it was just one of at least three themes from the book that influenced the movement. I will conclude this chapter with an exploration of these themes, and the way they were used as "frames" in the freethought movement.

The Age of Reason and Movement Framing

The conditions under which *The Age of Reason* was created in France were vastly different from those under which it was received in America, nonetheless it frames issues of religion and politics in ways that would be enduringly important for American freethought and it pioneers a style of strategic biblical criticism that many American freethinkers would follow. The three frames from *Age of Reason* that were important in American freethought were the separationist frame, the antiscriptural frame, and the scientific hope frame.

"The Adulterous Connection Between Church and State": The Separationist Frame

Paine portrays established national religions as the root of sundry evils in the opening pages of *Age of Reason*. The frame these passages employ can be labeled the separationist frame. Although, as I have argued, Paine probably introduced separationist rhetoric into *Age of Reason* to oppose the nationalization of the Catholic Church imposed by the Civic Constitution of the Clergy, his separationist rhetoric had an appeal far beyond this immediate circumstance. Prominent examples of Paine's separationist framing include the following:

> All national institutions of churches, whether Jewish, Christian, or Turkish, appear to me no other than human inventions set up to terrify and enslave mankind, and monopolize power and profit.... [82]
>
> ... The adulterous connection of church and state, wherever it had taken place, whether Jewish, Christian, or Turkish, had so effectually prohibited, by pains and penalties, every discussion upon established creed, and upon first principles of religion, that until the system of government should be changed, those subjects could not be brought fairly and openly before the

world; but that whenever this should be done, a revolution in the system of religion would follow.[83]

The separationist frame Paine employed in *Age of Reason* would become a staple of the freethought movement, although Paine's writings were certainly not the only place that freethinking Americans would have encountered separationist ideas. Although it was not as prominent in the earlier decades of the movement, separation of church and state was literally at the top of the agenda as freethought became politically active in the 1870s. The very first plank of the platform adopted by the National Liberal League in 1877 read, "TOTAL SEPARATION OF CHURCH AND STATE to be guaranteed by amendment of the United States Constitution: including the equitable taxation of church property, secularization of the public schools, abrogation of Sabbatarian laws, abolition of chaplaincies, prohibition of public appropriations for religious purposes, and all other measures necessary to the same general end."[84] Separation of church and state remains the central political goal of contemporary organizations like Americans United for the Separation of Church and State, the Freedom from Religion Foundation, and the Secular Coalition for America.

The separationist frame allows for the formulation of a very specific political agenda but has the advantage of not requiring any very specific system of beliefs. Deists, agnostics, and atheists can all embrace it, as can many traditional Christians. Indeed, historically some of the greatest advocates of separationism in American history have been Bible-believing Baptists like Isaac Backus and John Leland, who worked to end the establishment of the Congregational Church in New Hampshire, Connecticut, and Massachusetts.

"A History of Wickedness": The Antiscriptural Frame

A second frame employed by Paine in *Age of Reason* that was important for later American freethinkers is the antiscriptural frame, which emphasized that the Bible is not divinely inspired. It is both more uniquely characteristic of freethought and more prevalent in *Age of Reason* than the separationist frame, and it gave rise to a staple of the early repertoire of freethought: sermonizing against the Bible. The illegitimate scriptural authority frame is related to the separationist frame in that, as Paine put it, "Every national church or religion has established itself by pretending some special mission from God, communicated to certain individuals."[85] Thus the best way to attack established religion is to attack the illegitimate scriptural authority it is grounded in. Large portions of *Age of Reason* are devoted to doing just that. It is the task of the great majority of *Age of Reason, Part the Second*, where Paine states that his purpose is to "shew... that the Bible is not entitled to credit as being the word of God."[86]

Paine argues that the supposed divine authority of the Bible is illegitimate in multiple ways. He argues against the authenticity and authority of the Bible from what he calls "moral evidence," demonstrating that the Old Testament is full of "obscene stories... voluptuous debaucheries... cruel and torturous executions," and "unrelenting vindictiveness." It is a "history of wickedness that has served to corrupt and brutalize mankind."[87] Paine provides abundant examples of what he sees as the "wickedness" that fills the Bible. To cite just one example, Paine calls attention to a passage from the book of Numbers in which—after the Israelites had conquered the Midianites, killed all their warriors and royals summarily, and looted all there was to be looted in their lands—Moses tells them to kill all the men and boys among them, and the women too except for the virgins. The virgins they were told to "keep alive for yourselves."[88] This is just one instance of the executions and debaucheries in the Old Testament catalogued by Paine.

With regard to the New Testament, he argues that the stories of Gospel writers are not to be believed because they are inconsistent with each other: "if the writers of these four books had gone into a court of justice to prove an alibi... and had they given their evidence in the same contradictory manner as it is here given, they would have been in danger of having their ears cropt for perjury, and would have justly deserved it."[89] Extending the legal approach to the legitimacy of the Bible, he argues it is based on "hearsay evidence and second hand authority."[90] He also cites a lack of both "external evidence" and "internal evidence" to support the truth of scripture. For instance, he asks why Roman and Jewish historians did not independently report an event as spectacular as Jesus's ascension, which he reckons was an event as novel and spectacular as the assent of a balloon in his own time.[91] Such external evidence for the truth of the Bible is missing. Further, the vengeful and pecuniary nature of the biblical God's justice is not consistent with the behavior of a good and benevolent God and is therefore internal evidence that the Bible is not the word of God.[92] A good portion of the first part of *Age of Reason*, and the vast majority of *Part the Second*, is taken up with these and other arguments for the illegitimacy of the authority of scripture and the illegitimacy of any authority founded in scripture.[93]

Many figures in the freethought movement employed the antiscriptural frame in ways that strongly echo, and sometimes invoke, Paine. As we shall see in chapter 2, Elihu Palmer's lectures to the Deistical Society of New York in the late 1790s and early 1800s often employed elements of Paine-like Biblical criticism, as did Benjamin Offen's lectures to the Society of Moral Philanthropists in the 1820s and 1830s. To cite just one example of these antibiblical lectures, we can look to Offen's *A Legacy to the Friends of Free Discussion*, which collects many of the lectures he delivered to the Moral Philanthropists at their Sunday meetings at Tammany Hall in New York. Offen strikes a very Paine-like chord in his "General Introduction" when he states, "Sincere believers in Divine revelation are not aware what monsters the Bible makes of them but for which they would be humane compared to what they are under its influence." For an example of the inhumanity that the Bible inspires people to, Offen points to the case of Thomas Paine: "For all his faithful devotedness to the independence of America, how is his name and memory spoken of at the present time? From the pulpit every kind of falsehood and detraction is poured forth concerning him."[94] Offen's memorial to Paine leaves little doubt that his antibiblical lectures were inspired by him. As we shall see, the practice of antibiblical sermonizing was a core activity of the freethought movement in its early days.

"The Creation We Behold": The Scientific Hope Frame

A third frame from *Age of Reason* that was important for later freethinkers is the scientific hope frame. There is more to *Age of Reason* than denouncements of the "adulterous connection between church and state" and the Bible's "history of wickedness." Paine also emphasizes the positive message that God's power and benevolence are made manifest in creation and that the scientific study of God's creation is an act of worship that has many positive benefits for humankind. God's creation is the true scripture, not the Bible, so it is to the universe that humans must direct their reverence: "the Creation we behold is the real and ever existing word of God," Paine says. "It proclaimeth his power, it demonstrates his wisdom, it manifests his goodness and beneficence . . . the moral duty of man consists in imitating the moral goodness and beneficence of God manifested in the creation towards all his creatures."[95] In other passages, Paine says more about how the reverent study of creation has benefited humans: "The Almighty lecturer, by displaying the principles of science in the structure of the universe, has invited man to study and to imitation. It is as if he had said to the inhabitants of this globe that we call ours, 'I have made an earth for man to dwell upon, and I have rendered the starry heavens visible, to teach him science and the arts.'"[96]

The scientific hope frame is the part of Paine's deism that he traces back to the London lectures of James Ferguson and Benjamin Martin that he used his prize money from *King of Prussia* to attend as a young man. Somehow, in the many years between 1757, when he heard the lectures, and 1793, when he wrote *Age of Reason*, Martin and Ferguson's devout Christian natural theology was transformed in Paine's mind, perhaps in part through the influence of his deistic mentor Benjamin Franklin and other American deists, into the positive core of his deism.[97] A. Owen Aldridge has pointed out the existence of a strain of American deism that, just like Paine, takes nature itself to be the only true revelation.[98] Examples of this tradition include an anonymous pamphlet titled *Sermon on Natural Religion by a Natural Man*, published circa 1771, and *Reason, the Only Oracle of Man*, by the American Revolutionary militia leader Ethan Allen, written soon after the Revolution but not published until 1784. *Reason, the Only Oracle of Man*, which Allen might have co-written with fellow deist Thomas Young, proclaimed, "As far as we understand nature, we are become acquainted with the character of God, for the knowledge of nature is the revelation of God." It is full of language about "the globe with its productions, the planets in their motions, and the starry heavens in their magnitudes."[99]

The scientific hope frame was at least as prevalent in later American freethought as the separationist and illegitimate scriptural authority frames. To cite one example, a broadside advertisement for the early freethought newspaper *Temple of Reason*, published between 1800 and 1803 in New York City, announces the prominent place that astronomy will have in the publication as it nods to Paine: "The Creation is the Bible of God, as Mr. Payne very elegantly and justly observes, and Astronomy may be considered as its title page, printed in the most luminous and brilliant characters: everyone who looks up, may read and discover the author."[100] For another example, consider that a major focus of the activity of Frances Wright in the late 1820s was to establish "Halls of Science" in cities across America where citizens could go on Sunday mornings to be educated on useful scientific topics rather than attending traditional religious services. "Turn your churches into halls of science," Wright told her followers.[101] The same impulse to promote science led Wright and other freethinkers to campaign for more widespread secular education. The scientific hope frame was also a favorite theme of Robert Ingersoll toward the end of the nineteenth century. "Nothing but education—scientific education—can benefit mankind," Ingersoll proclaimed in one lecture.[102]

Over the course of the movement's history, the scientific hope frame has been more inclusive of different belief systems than Paine's usage of it at first allowed for. Paine's idea was that a benevolent Creator God had structured the universe for the benefit of humankind and that the pursuit of science would reveal many beneficial things that God had put there for us to discover. Thus, as originally formulated, the scientific hope frame was open to deists and perhaps some pantheists, less to agnostics, and not at all to atheists. For Paine, science was a grand hunt for the Easter eggs that God had hidden throughout creation. But Paine's was not the only interpretation of the scientific hope frame. It proved possible for an agnostic or an atheist to accept the general idea that humans must look to science to find hope of improving their lives without embracing fully the idea that "creation is the Bible of God." Thus, scientific hope was as important to the agnostic Ingersoll as it was to the deistic Paine.

Because they were inclusive toward a range of belief systems, the combination of the separationist frame, the antiscriptural frame, and the scientific hope frame gave direction and coherence to the freethought movement despite the diversity of theological views held by even the earliest groups of freethinkers. Although *Age of Reason* was not the only place where freethinkers could encounter separationist arguments and optimism that science could improve the standard of living, *Age of Reason* brought separationism and scientific hope together with Paine's style of biblical criticism in a way that made it a foundational text of the freethought movement. In chapter 2, I'll tell the story of the beginnings of American freethought as a social movement in the years immediately following the publication of *Age of Reason*, a story in which Paine himself, beyond the influence of his book, played a role.

CHAPTER TWO

The First Wave of American Freethought

Deists of the Early Republic

> It has been the peculiarly honorable lot of Thomas Paine, the firm advocate of truth, the undaunted champion of reason, and the resolute and unconquerable enemy of tyranny, bigotry and prejudice, to open the door to free and impartial enquiry. He has boldly entered the field himself, and taught the world, that no true system of principles, however sacred they may be held in the public opinion, and however strongly protected and enforced by the terrors of man's vengeance here, and eternal punishment hereafter, is too awful to be canvassed by reason, or too sublime to be comprehended by common sense.
>
> Anonymous New York Pamphleteer (1794),
> *The Examiners Examined*

This chapter is the story of the first wave of freethought in the United States. It will explore the conditions, events, and personalities that contributed to the rise of organized deism in America in the last years of the eighteenth century. Prior to the 1790s, deism in the United States, as in most of Europe, was a clandestine activity that flourished in carefully cultivated underground networks. During the Revolution and its aftermath, privately deistic and liberal Christian members of the political elite were able to make great advances on behalf of religious freedom by securing provisions in state constitutions and the passage of the First Amendment. These religious freedom protections created the opportunity for deists to organize openly. But few did until Paine's *Age of Reason* gave deism a new prominence and inspired many to believe that deism should supersede Christianity. When the catalyst of *The Age of Reason* was added to the American stew of republicanism, clashing Protestant faiths, covert deism, and a wide-open future, the underground intellectual movement that was deism was transformed into a true social movement. As the anonymous New York pamphleteer quoted in the epilogue says, *Age of Reason* opened "the door to free and impartial enquiry."[1] In the wake of *Age of Reason*, groups of religious rationalists began to coalesce and engage in activism to challenge Christianity's attempts to control the future of the new nation. Both because it called for a "revolution in the system of religion" and because Paine wrote it, *Age of Reason* associated deism with the Democratic-Republican political faction that was forming around Thomas Jefferson, charging deism with the political energy that would put Jefferson in the White House in 1800 but also making "infidelity" a prime target for Federalist political attacks. In this charged atmosphere, a trained-minister-turned-deist named Elihu Palmer became a "movement entrepreneur" by using his ministerial skills to create the Deistical Society of New York with the help of a bookseller named John Fellows. After his return to the United States in 1802, Paine's association with the Deistical Society contributed to both the group's prestige and its notoriety. Attacks on *Age of Reason* and the Deistical Society helped foster a common sense of identity among the many varieties of "infidels" in the fledgling movement. Even though the movement foundered after the deaths of Palmer and Paine, it laid the groundwork for a deistic revival in the 1820s.

Before I begin to recount the story of freethought as a social movement in the United States, a story that properly begins with the publication and popularity of *Age of Reason* in 1794, I will say a few words about the conditions that made it possible and encouraged its growth. Those conditions included the existence of a tradition of English language deism in which some of the Revolution's leaders participated, and the adoption of constitutional protections of religious freedom that occurred during the Revolution and in its aftermath.

Deism before *The Age of Reason*

Neither the popularity of *Age of Reason* nor the rise of organized deism in America would have been possible if there had not already been a well-established tradition of English-language deism. Deism arose in reaction to the wars of religion that ravaged Europe in the sixteenth and seventeenth centuries as well as to European encounters with non-Christian peoples during the Age of Discovery. The core tenet of deism is the belief in a benevolent and omnipotent God. Deists typically believed that God would not reveal himself through scripture alone, since scripture was available only to a small portion of humanity. They believed that a "natural religion" or "natural theology" can be discovered by any human through the use of reason, and that this natural religion is sufficient for salvation. If God is truly good and just, argued Charles Blount (1654–1693) in *The Oracles of Reason* (1693), he must have made the rules to be followed to achieve "future happiness" available to all people. But because of barriers of geography, time, and language, the revelations of scripture are not universally available, so natural religion must in itself be sufficient if God is truly benevolent. "No rule of revealed religion was, or ever could be made known to all men," Blount writes. "Therefore, no revealed religion is necessary to future happiness."[2]

What could be called the golden age of English deism occurred in the period of political liberalization that followed the Glorious Revolution of 1688 that put William and Mary on the throne. The Toleration Act of 1689 decriminalized religious dissent, although without giving dissenters full civil rights.[3] This, together with the demise of the Licensing Act in 1695, which had previously given the government strict control over all printing presses, created an environment where religious ideas could be discussed with greater liberty than before. A brief period of nearly complete freedom to express religious views ended after the 1696 publication of John Toland's *Christianity Not Mysterious, or, A Treatise Showing that there is Nothing in the Gospel Contrary to Reason, nor above it, and that no Christian Doctrine Can Be Called a Mystery*.[4] The fervor caused by this book prompted the passage of the Blasphemy Act of 1697,[5] which made it criminal to deny the Trinity or the authority of the Bible. Consequently, by the beginning of the eighteenth century, dissenters could openly assemble and practice Christianity as they saw fit, provided they were willing to forego the state support provided to conforming members of the Established Church and provided they did not flagrantly violate the Blasphemy Act. This act was especially burdensome on deists, who frequently denied the literal truth of scripture, and Unitarians, who denied the Trinity. In this environment of bounded freedom, a contest grew up between deistic daredevils willing to risk loss of position and criminal penalties for publishing heretical views, and the ready army of orthodox churchmen seeking to advance their careers by writing replies, which as frequently served to perpetuate the viewpoint of those they attacked as they did to stifle them. Those attacked as having deistical views sometimes were professed deists, but often were not. Even among professed deists, there was much theological diversity.

Deists were not the only rational religious dissenters on the British scene in the seventeenth and eighteenth centuries. There were also pantheists, who followed Baruch Spinoza's idea that nature itself was God. There were neo-Epicureans, who found inspiration in the materialistic ideas of the ancient Greek philosopher Epicurus popularized by the rediscovery of Lucretius's didactic poem *De Rerum Natura* in the fifteenth century. But in the English-speaking world the most organized group of rational religious dissenters were the Unitarians. After being expelled from the Polish-Lithuanian Commonwealth in 1658, a group known as the Polish Brethren that followed the theology of Faustus Socinus took up residence in Holland. It was there they began to be called Unitarians because they rejected the doctrine of the Trinity, believing that Jesus was an inspired human being but not an aspect of God.[6] Unitarian theology in the tradition of Faustus Socinus was introduced in Britain by John Biddle, a headmaster at Gloucester, during the period of the Civil War and the parliamentary ascendancy that followed it. In a period of relatively high toleration for all varieties of dissent, Biddle's anti-Trinitarian views were considered so radical that he was tried and imprisoned on several occasions, leading to an early death in 1662.[7] But Unitarian ideas continued to spread as Polish Brethren who had settled in Amsterdam published theological tracts and one of Biddle's followers, an Anglican clergyman named Stephen Nye, published *A Brief History of the Unitarians, Called also Socinians* in 1687.[8] The first avowedly Unitarian congregation in England was founded by Theophilus Lindsey, an Anglican cleric turned dissenter, at Essex Street in London in 1774, with the aid and support of Joseph Priestley, who in addition to being a dissenting theologian was the scientist who discovered oxygen.[9] Although Priestley's friend Lindsey was the driving force behind the new Chapel at Essex Street, and the regular minister there, it was Priestley who became the theological voice of institutionalized Unitarianism in Britain.[10] Having made a career as an educator at dissenting academies and a minister to dissenting congregations, Priestley began expounding a non-supernatural Christianity in a series of publications that began to appear in the period of the chapel's founding. His *History of the Corruptions of Christianity* (1782)[11] and *An History of the Early Opinions Concerning Jesus Christ Compiled from Original Writers Proving that the Christian Religion Was at First Unitarian* (1786)[12] both made the scripture-based cases that primitive Christianity viewed Jesus as human and not divine. Not only did Priestley embrace the Unitarian position on the full humanity of Jesus, but he was also a thoroughgoing materialist who tried to work out a theology completely consistent with the laws of the natural world in *Disquisitions Relating to Matter and Spirit* (1777).[13] Unitarians differed from deists mainly in their approach to scripture. While both groups believed in a Creator God and rejected the doctrine of the Trinity, most Unitarians at that time clung to a strong belief in the authority of scripture, while deists thought that scripture was at best inspired allegory and at worst a garbled collection of untrustworthy histories and folktales.

Deism, Unitarianism, pantheism, and neo-Epicureanism were part of a broader Radical Enlightenment whose activity prior to the American Revolution has been described by historian Jonathan Israel as involving "furtive copying and discussion of forbidden subversive texts primarily in Latin and French, and clandestine networking."[14] Deists and other Enlightenment religious rationalists often needed to disseminate their ideas clandestinely out of a justifiable fear of persecution. Israel details how the *cercle spinoziste* in seventeenth-century Holland published its most challenging works anonymously, even giving Eleutheropolis as a pseudonym for Amsterdam as the place of publication.[15] If English deists were more prone to take public credit for their challenging views than their Dutch counterparts, they were also more likely to be prosecuted for them.

The necessity for deists and other rational religious dissenters to keep out of the public view is made clear by the long list of people who suffered official or popular reprisal for promoting their unorthodox beliefs in the English-speaking world. George van Parris was burned at the stake in London in 1551 for denying that Jesus was the son of God.[16] John Biddle was imprisoned six times for his Unitarian beliefs in the seventeenth century and died in prison in 1662.[17] John Toland was condemned for his deistic book *Christianity Not Mysterious* in 1697 and needed to flee his native Ireland to avoid being burned along with his book.[18] William Whiston lost his position as Lucanian Professor of Mathematics, previously held by Isaac Newton, and was expelled from Cambridge University for denying the existence of hell in 1710.[19] Thomas Woolston was sent to prison on a blasphemy conviction in 1729 for denying the literal truth of the Bible and remained in prison until his death.[20] Peter Annet was sentenced to the pillory and hard labor for the same offense, dying in prison in 1769.[21] And Unitarian scientist Joseph Priestley had his house and chapel burned by a royalist mob in 1791 for a combination of political and religious reasons.[22] If these persecutions touched only a few of the most prominent religious rationalists in the English-speaking world, they reminded the rest about the risks of expressing their views openly to the public. The necessity of covert activity was a circumstance that kept deism from becoming a full-fledged social movement. Deists could not safely belong to publicly visible organizations that promoted deism. Unitarians ran almost as much risk, as the 1791 attacks on Priestley in Birmingham demonstrate. For much of the eighteenth century, in most European states, being an active deist meant privately reading dangerous books and sometimes discussing them within a network of trusted others who had been carefully recruited to the cause. If "clandestine" is too strong a word for the level of secrecy practiced by American deists like Jefferson and Franklin, even these powerful men found it necessary to be "private" and "discreet" about their religious beliefs.

Seventeenth- and eighteenth-century deism is best thought of as a religious dissent movement allied with the Radical Enlightenment. The history of British dissenting religious traditions goes back to the Uniformity Act of 1662, which made the use of the Book of Common Prayer compulsory in religious services conducted in the Anglican Church. More than 2,000 clergy chose to give up their tithe-supported positions, because they felt they could not in good conscience endorse the content of the Book of Common Prayer.[23] These nonconforming clergy and their followers became known as dissenters. Many continued to preach to congregations that now needed to meet at private residences rather than openly in chapels, and that risked prosecution if they were discovered. Dissenting groups included the Quakers, Unitarians, and Baptists, who are familiar because they have survived to this day, and many others less familiar because they have not survived, such as Ranters, Seekers, and Familists. Because they denied both the literal truth of scripture *and* the divinity of Christ, deists were considered to be uncommonly dangerous dissenters. Even after the Toleration Act of 1688 decriminalized most forms of religious dissent, deists continued to be convicted of blasphemy for publishing their religious beliefs. It remained too dangerous for independent deistic congregations to form. But deists were religious dissenters nonetheless. Because participation in deism was more a literary than a liturgical activity, deists, while more isolated from each other than other dissenters, were perhaps also more widely diffused than dissenters whose activities centered on in-person religious services. The necessary secrecy and the high intellectual standards that needed to be met for a person to become a trusted participant in the Radical Enlightenment underground prevented deism from becoming either very visible or very large. Deism did, however, have widespread influence as an underground intellectual movement, if not a social movement, and that influence most definitely extended to some of the key figures in the founding of the American republic, people like Benjamin Franklin, Thomas Jefferson, and Thomas Paine. These men and other religious rationalists channeled the energies of the American Revolution into a major realignment of church and state.

The Revolutionary Disestablishments

The deistic tradition was an important part of the intellectual background of the American political elite during the Revolutionary era, but the advances for the cause of religious freedom that were made during and soon after the Revolution were not the result of the activism of a mass movement of religious rationalists. These advances were triumphs for deism as an underground intellectual movement, not freethought as a social movement. The wave of state constitutional reforms that disestablished state churches during the Revolution and the subsequent adoption of federal First Amendment protections of religious freedom, called the "first disestablishment" by legal scholar Steven K. Green and others, occurred *before* the first wave of American freethought as a social movement.

To understand the process of disestablishment in the United States, it would be useful to first briefly consider the case of the fully established seventeenth-century Church of England, which was the model for religious establishments in many American colonies. Prior to the Toleration Act of 1688, the Church of England was near the high point of establishment. Clerical salaries and the upkeep of church properties were funded by mandatory tithes, as they had been for centuries. The 1662 Uniformity Act ensured orthodoxy within the Church of England by enforcing the use of the Book of Common Prayer at Anglican services. It also forced the ejection of dissenting clergy.[24] The Corporation Act (1661)[25] and Test Acts (1663 and 1673) barred anyone not receiving the sacrament of communion at an Anglican church from holding a public office.[26] The Conventicle Act (1664) forbade unauthorized worship meetings in public and in private.[27] English common law standards on the offense of blasphemy made possible the criminal prosecution of those who expressed heterodox beliefs. In sum, the church was state supported. Civil penalties were imposed for not belonging to and attending an Anglican church, and criminal penalties could be imposed on those who gathered at alternative worship services or expressed heterodox beliefs. The Toleration Act of 1688 removed the criminal penalties on alternative worship but left much of the other architecture of establishment intact.[28] To deny the divinity of Christian scripture or the divinity of Jesus Christ remained criminal acts under the blasphemy laws.

On the eve of the American Revolution, most colonies had church establishments that mimicked aspects of the Anglican establishment in England. The Anglican Church itself was the established church in all the southern colonies. Taxes or tithes were collected to support the clergy. Congregationalist churches, founded by Puritan migrants but increasingly heterodox, were supported by a similar system in all of the New England colonies except for Rhode Island, which was a haven for those with dissenting religious views. In New York Anglicanism was established only in the metropolitan region and dissenting Protestant sects were broadly tolerated. Maryland had an Anglican establishment that officially tolerated Catholics. There was no religious establishment in the form of state support in Pennsylvania, as this was antithetical to the principles of its Quaker founders. Pennsylvania exercised control over both Delaware and a large part of New Jersey (called West Jersey) for extended periods of time, leaving these states too with a tradition of disestablishment. In addition to supporting particular churches, most states, including even Pennsylvania, required religious tests for public officials, usually involving professing belief in some set of Christian doctrines.[29] William Penn's Pennsylvania Charter of Privileges, for instance, required that anyone who served in public office must "profess to believe in Jesus Christ, the Savior of the World."[30] By 1774, freedom of worship for Christians was generally permitted in the colonies with the exception that Catholics were prohibited from practicing their faith in Massachusetts and a few other colonies, and dissenting sects like the Baptists were sometimes persecuted at the local level.[31] In earlier times Massachusetts Bay notably had expelled Anne Hutchinson and her followers in 1638 for their heterodox beliefs and had gone so far as to hang four Quakers between 1659 and 1661 for repeatedly returning to the colony to protest its restrictive laws on religion.[32]

The first wave of religious disestablishment commenced with the Revolution and was largely the result of a wave of wartime republicanism. It is far from surprising that the war with England brought about the disestablishment of the Church of England in the states where it was established.[33] Later attempts to revive a more pluralist establishment in southern states, such as Patrick Henry's 1784 "A Bill Establishing a Provision for Teachers of the Christian Religion," were defeated, although not without difficulty.[34] The Constitution of 1787 and the First Amendment were landmarks of disestablishment at the federal level. But until 1947 the provisions of these documents, including the Constitution's Article VI prohibition of religious tests for national office and the First Amendment's Establishment and Free Exercise Clauses, applied only to the federal government, not to state governments. This allowed compulsory public support for churches to survive in Congregationalist New England.

The role that religion played in the founding of the United States has been the topic of vigorous debate in popular history in recent years. Christian nationalist popular history writers such as David Barton, Michael Medved, and Rick Saccone have sought to minimize the role of Enlightenment thought and deism in the American founding.[35] Such claims have been answered in great detail by Steven Waldman, Steven K. Green, Sam Haselby and, from a Christian perspective, John Fea, and I will not attempt to replicate their efforts in this book.[36] But it might be useful here to characterize the role of religion in the American founding. Contrary to Christian nationalist writers, I contend that the United States did *not* have an unambiguously Christian founding. In support of this claim, one can point to the strong deism of some important figures in the founding movement including Franklin, Jefferson, Paine, and Ethan Allen.[37] There is also the fact that the Constitution constitutes the country in the name of "the people," not in the name of God or any people particularly chosen by God. The Constitution makes no reference to God whatsoever. Further, Article VI, Clause 3 of the Constitution states that "no religious Test shall ever be required as a Qualification to any Office or public Trust under the United States." In addition, the First Amendment forbids Congress to make laws "respecting an establishment of religion," and the Treaty of Tripoli, signed by President Adams in 1796, states that "the Government of the United States of America is not, in any sense, founded on the Christian religion."[38] One can point to James Madison's *Memorial and Remonstrance against Religious Assessments*, written in response to Patrick Henry's 1784 effort to impose a tax in the state of Virginia to support "Teachers of the Christian religion," for a good summary of arguments for church-state separation in circulation during the founding period. Jefferson's Virginia Statute for Religious Freedom, in addition to his letter to the Danbury Baptist Association,[39] from which the now-common metaphor of a wall separating church and state was drawn, provide further evidence that Jefferson too was a strong proponent of church-state separation. In a passage from his 1821 autobiography, Jefferson gives what is probably his most robust statement concerning what he envisioned the scope of Establishment Clause protections to be. In this passage, Jefferson recalls a failed attempt to amend a key clause of his Virginia Bill for Religious Freedom prior to its passage in 1786. The amendment would have changed the meaning of his bill in a way he did not at all want. In his recollections he discloses the fullness of the religious disestablishment that he and, as he saw it, most other Virginia legislators envisioned. "Where the preamble declares that coercion is 'a departure from the plan of the holy author of our religion,' an amendment was proposed, by inserting the word 'Jesus Christ,' so that it should read, 'a departure from the plan of Jesus Christ, the holy author of our religion;' the insertion was rejected by a great majority, in proof that they meant to comprehend, within the mantle of its protection, the Jew and the Gentile, the Christian and Mahometan, the Hindoo and Infidel of every denomination."[40] Jefferson believed that the solid rejection of the "Jesus Christ" amendment proved that the Religious Freedom Statute's "protection of opinion was meant to be universal."[41] Jefferson's letter to the Danbury Baptists confirms that he hoped the protection afforded by the federal Establishment Clause would be just as universal as those of the Virginia Statute for Religious Freedom. At minimum the evidence supports the statement that important figures within the founding movement argued that government should not be associated with religion, Christian or otherwise, and that, for a variety of reasons, which included fears of the federal government favoring one Christian sect over another, their views prevailed in the drafting of the federal Constitution.

All this said, it is also hard to make the case that the United States had an unambiguously secular founding. All the leading figures in the Revolutionary movement—including deists like Franklin, Jefferson, and Paine—believed in a God who created the universe, if not in the divinity of Jesus or that the Bible is the revealed word of God. Those who made arguments for religious freedom and church-state separation often made them in explicitly theistic terms. Madison's "Memorial and Remonstrance" argues that the state must stay out of religion because "the duty which we owe to our Creator and the manner of discharging it, can only be directed by reason and conviction, not by force or violence" and contends that any establishment of religion "is adverse to the diffusion of the light of Christianity."[42] "Almighty God has created the mind free," begins Jefferson's Statute for Religious Freedom, "all attempts to influence it by temporal punishments or burdens, or by civil incapacities, tend to beget habits of hypocrisy and meanness."[43] In addition to the fact that some of the strongest arguments for church-state separation had a theistic foundation, Congress continued many of the religious practices it had adopted in the colonial era.[44] Despite the injunction of the First Amendment against establishing any religion, Congress appointed official chaplains who opened sessions with prayer, as they still do. Madison, in his "Detached Memoranda," objected that he believed this went against the Constitution,[45] but he was evidently in the minority in thinking this. Washington and Adams regularly proclaimed national days of prayer, and, though Jefferson refrained from this practice, even Madison was prevailed upon by Congress to proclaim a day of prayer during the War of 1812.[46] With regard to the personal religious beliefs of those in the founding movement, for every strongly deistic Franklin, Jefferson, Paine, and Allen you can find, you can also find a strong Christian like John Jay, Samuel Adams, Patrick Henry, or Elias Boudinot.[47]

In sum, the federal government created by the founding movement was neither unambiguously Christian nor unambiguously secular. It was, however, bold and unprecedented in its ambiguous secularism. The proper place of religion in government and in national life was one of many contested issues in the founding period, and it has continued to be contested ever since.

One of the places where different views on the place of religion in American civic life can be seen in the period is in the congressional deliberations of the religion clauses of the First Amendment that took place in 1789. On August 15, 1789, the House took up consideration of the addition of the phrase "no religion shall be established by law, nor shall the equal rights of conscience be infringed" to the First Amendment. Representative Peter Silvester of New York immediately raised the concern that the addition might "have a tendency to abolish religion altogether." But Daniel Carroll of Maryland countered that because the "rights of conscience are ... of peculiar delicacy" they "will little bear the gentlest touch of the governmental hand." Madison weighed in on behalf of the clause, of which he was the principal author, saying that it meant "that Congress should not establish a religion, and enforce legal observation of it by law, nor compel men to worship God in any manner contrary to their conscience."[48] Already in this debate there is a tension between those who wished to prevent Congress from in any way compelling worship and those who feared that the clause itself might "abolish religion." Perhaps to address both these fears, the final wording of the First Amendment has two clauses pertaining to religion. The Establishment Clause states that "Congress shall make no law respecting an establishment of religion." The Free Exercise Clause adds "... or prohibiting the free exercise thereof."

The final language of the Establishment Clause had the effect of preventing federal interference with the New England state religious establishments. "Congress shall make no law respecting an establishment of religion" does as much to prevent Congress from prohibiting state religious establishments as it does to prevent the founding of a federal religious establishment.

This arrangement was likely politically necessary to secure passage, but not everyone was happy with it. Surprisingly, opposition to the continuing establishment of Congregationalism in New Hampshire, Connecticut, and Massachusetts came mainly from Baptists, led by such people as Isaac Backus and John Leland. The Baptist reading of the New Testament led them not only to believe in the spiritual necessity of adult baptism but also to oppose state-sponsored religion. One of the strongest Baptist calls for disestablishment was John Leland's 1791 pamphlet titled *The Rights of Conscience Inalienable, and, Therefore, Religious Opinions Not Cognizable by Law; Or, The High Flying Churchman, Stripped Of His Legal Robe, Appears a Yaho[o]*. Among the many arguments against established religions set forth in the work are the following:

1. That individuals, not governments, are accountable to God for their actions. "If government can answer for individuals at the day of judgment, let men be controlled by it in religious matters; otherwise, let men be free."[49]
2. When religion is established, inevitably, "Uninspired, fallible men make their own opinions tests of orthodoxy...."[50]
3. That religious establishments keep the best people from holding public office through religious tests: "Good men cannot believe what they cannot believe, and they will not subscribe to what they disbelieve and take an oath to maintain what they conclude is error; and, as the best of men differ in judgment, there may be some of them in any state: their talents and virtue entitle them to fill the most important posts, yet, because they differ from the established creed of the state, they cannot—will not fill those posts; whereas villains make no scruple to take any oath."[51]
4. That religious establishment diminishes reverence for the Bible: "Establishments metamorphose the church into a creature, and religion into a principle, of state, which has a natural tendency to make men conclude that *Bible religion* is nothing but a *trick of state*; hence it is that the greatest part of the well informed in literature are overrun with deism and infidelity."[52]

This last point strongly foreshadows Paine's arguments in *The Age of Reason*, reaching a similar conclusion about established religion from a very different starting point. Leland felt that using the Bible as an instrument of state power had already diminished, and would continue to diminish, reverence for the Bible as a sacred text. Paine, behaving exactly as Leland predicted, tried to discredit the idea that the Bible was a sacred text expressly to prevent it being used to prop up established religion.

Despite sharp differences on the status of the Bible as a sacred text, Baptists had reached the same conclusion about established religion as freethinkers like Jefferson and Paine, namely, that it was not a good thing. This was the reason that the Danbury Baptist Association, representing twenty-three Baptist churches in Connecticut and three in New York, sought and received President Jefferson's support in 1801 as they launched a petition to end the Congregationalist establishment in Connecticut. Jefferson's famous letter to the Danbury Baptists is his reply to their request for support that asserts the Establishment and Free Exercise Clauses of the Constitution were intended to build "a wall of separation between church and state." Despite this unlikely alliance between freethinkers and disestablishmentarian evangelicals, disestablishment did not come until 1817 in New Hampshire and 1818 in Connecticut. Citizens of Massachusetts did not end public support for the Congregational system until 1833, and it happened then in part because orthodox Congregationalists were dismayed that some churches had become openly Unitarian but were still receiving public funds.[53] The debate about the Congregational establishments in New England was part of the background of the first wave of the freethought movement. Elihu Palmer and other early leaders of the movement naturally came in on the side of disestablishment, but, in this period, they were far less influential than the Baptists whom fate had ironically sided them with.

The religious disestablishments of the Revolutionary era ended direct state aid to churches but left many other aspects of religious establishment in place at the state and local levels. It was an unprecedented but only partial victory for separationists. Elements of a continuing establishment of Christianity included religious tests for public office, the continuing criminalization of blasphemy, restrictions on activity on Sundays called Sunday laws, or "blue laws," and school-based religious activities like prayer and Bible reading. These elements of ongoing Christian establishment were challenged, but not eliminated, during the nineteenth century.

The Age of Reason on the American Scene

Despite the great uproar that it would later provoke, conditions in America were actually quite favorable to the reception of *The Age of Reason* in the mid-1790s when it first appeared. In December of 1791 the ratification of the Bill of Rights was an apparent victory for the spirit of republicanism, echoing and Americanizing the principles of the *Declaration of the Rights of Man and Citizen* enacted in France two years earlier. As the foremost defender of the ideas of the French Revolution in its early days, Paine was generally well thought of in America. *Rights of Man* had been warmly received and much reprinted, probably eventually reaching as many Americans as had *Common Sense*.[54] Before news of the Terror fully registered in America, many Americans felt they shared a common republican ideology with Revolutionary France, and no book better articulated that ideology than *Rights of Man*. In 1793, Philadelphians formed at least two Democratic-Republican clubs to promote republicanism. (The anti-Federalist or anti-administration party in this period can be called Jeffersonian, Democratic-Republican, or simply Republican.) By the end of 1794 at least twenty-four more such clubs had come into being in cities both north and south, and most paid homage to Paine, *Common Sense*, and *The Rights of Man* in the toasts that punctuated their meetings.[55]

In this period when Paine, the French Revolution, and *The Rights of Man* were all popular, it is no wonder that publishers jumped at the chance to print *Age of Reason*. In England, publishers risked imprisonment for printing the work, but no such danger existed in America. The inherent interest of the book's subject matter combined with the fame of the author fed public appetite for *Age of Reason*. Publishers produced tens of thousands of copies through eighteen editions and sold them at low prices, much to the chagrin of critics like Elias Boudinot, who was scandalized that copies of it were being sold for a half penny each, "whereby children, servants, and the lowest people, had been tempted to purchase."[56] A Presbyterian minister from Virginia named Moses Hoge, a man deeply concerned about the "infidelity" that Paine's book was inspiring, told a friend in 1799 that he had credible information that 100,000 copies of *Age of Reason* had been sold in America just in the previous year.[57] Paine himself sent 12,000 printed copies of his book to America to be sold at a low price.[58]

The Age of Reason reached a broad spectrum of Americans, from stable boys to college students. Lyman Beecher, who would become a minister and father of Harriet Beecher Stowe, recalls in his autobiography that *Age of Reason* was in vogue during his sophomore year at Yale, from 1794 to 1795: "That was the day of the infidelity of the Tom Paine school. Boys that dressed flax in the barn, as I used to, read Tom Paine and believed him. I read and fought him all the way. Never had any propensity to infidelity. But most of the class before me were infidels and called each other Voltaire, Rousseau,

D'Alembert, etc., etc."[59] Such was Paine's influence at Harvard, it is reported, that Richard Watson's *Apology for the Bible* was distributed to counter it. Most students at Dartmouth were said to have abandoned Christianity, at least temporarily.[60] Paine's version of deism became fashionable in America not only because it was accessible to readers with only a basic education but also because it was politically aligned with a swelling tide of republican political sentiment.

One historian who paints a particularly vivid picture of the heyday of "infidelity" in the mid-1790s and how much it owed to *Age of Reason* is John H. Spencer, who wrote a history of Baptists in Kentucky. Spencer attributes much of the "infidelity" of the period to the sympathy of early Kentucky settlers to the aims of the French Revolution. France was an "infidel nation" that was "anxious to free men from the thralldom of religion," a project for which "Kentucky presented a most promising field" as both ministers and Bibles were in short supply on the frontier. "Of all the infidel books circulated in the country about this time," writes Spencer, "the *Age of Reason* was the most widely influential and mischievous." He goes on,

> The *Age of Reason* was just the book for the backwoods of America and was just from the source to make it most popular. It was written in the darling French Republic and by the honored patriot Paine. It was printed in cheap pamphlet form and circulated in the Mississippi Valley in immense numbers. It could be seen in the cabin of the farmer, on the bench of the tailor, in the shops of the smith and the carpenter, on the table of the lawyer, and at the desk of the physician. It was not put by the side of the Bible, but it was used instead of the Bible. Bibles and all other religious books were extremely scarce in the west at that period.
>
> ... At this period infidel principles prevailed to an alarming extent in the eastern states. They were fashionable in the gay and literary circles of society, they were prevalent in Yale College and other similar institutions, and a very general impression existed that Christianity was supported by human authority and not by argument. But infidelity prevailed in a cruder form and to a much greater extent in the west.[61]

Part of *Age of Reason*'s appeal was that it integrated deism into republican ideology at a time when many Americans felt themselves to be participating in an international republican movement, but the book's politics also proved to be a liability. As tensions between Federalists and Democratic-Republicans increased during the Adams administration, the republican affinity for religious "infidelity" became a target for Federalist attacks. Paine in particular was an easy target because a ready supply of prefabricated lies and half-truths about him had been amassed during the British campaign to defame him following the publication of *Rights of Man*, and these could be easily recycled by the American Federalist press.

The Age of Reason would not have been as avidly taken up in America as it was if there were not already a reserve of latent deism waiting in the country. Few had tried to evangelize for deism as *Age of Reason* did, but many leaders of the Revolutionary movement in America had given signs of their private endorsement of a deistical outlook. The examples are well known. Benjamin Franklin admits to having become a deist at the age of fifteen in his autobiography.[62] Thomas Jefferson created a version of the New Testament for his personal use with all the supernatural parts removed. He also wrote in his *Notes on the State of Virginia* that "it does me no injury for my neighbor to say there are twenty gods or no God," a strong statement against any interference with a freedom of belief and disbelief.[63] George Washington, although he famously proclaimed the value of religion in his 1796 Farewell Address, only once mentioned Jesus Christ in a public comment, and that in a context that did not imply his own belief in Christ's divinity. Washington went out of his way to refer to God as "Providence," "The Governor of the Universe," the "All Wise Creator," and the "Great Spirit" in his speeches, a pattern that is consistent with private deism or at least a strong respect for the deists in his audience.[64]

Occasionally, deism would be asserted more forcefully. Boston Revolutionary leader Thomas Young defended his deistic principles in print in a 1772 letter to the *Massachusetts Spy* after he had been attacked by a political rival named Aaron Davis, Jr., because of his deism.[65] And after the Revolution, New England militia leader Ethan Allen wrote America's first deistical book, *Reason, The Only Oracle of Man*, possibly in collaboration with Young. Allen could not persuade anyone to publish the book until 1784. After it was published, the publisher, Mr. Haswell, got cold feet and destroyed the books before they could be sold.[66] The incident speaks to both the presence of deistic beliefs in America before *Age of Reason*, and a pervasive fear of discussing them too openly. *Reason, The Only Oracle of Man* is one of the few precedents for Paine's contention that God intended to reveal himself through creation, not through scripture. If that idea was widespread among American deists, then *Age of Reason* was a bold amplification of a notion that many already harbored.

Another circumstance that increased the impact of *Age of Reason* in America was the fact that only a small minority of Americans at the time had any meaningful association with a church. Using the best available data, Rodney Stark and Roger Finke estimate that in 1776 only about 10% of the total population of America (and 12% of the white population) were active church members.[67] If we believe the commentary of Yale president Timothy Dwight, religious participation declined even below this level as a result of the Revolutionary War and the republican enthusiasm it sparked and so was at a very low ebb in the mid-1790s.[68] Thus, many Americans who encountered *Age of Reason* were religiously unaffiliated. They would likely have read the book with an open mind and would not have encountered any counterarguments unless they sought them out. Paine's deism rushed in to fill the void in organized religious life and in some places became so fashionable that people joined deistical organizations as much for social as for religious reasons. This was the case with William Vaughan, a young tailor in Winchester, Kentucky, who eventually became a well-known Baptist minister. As Baptist historian John Spencer tells the story,

> This was the period of infidelity in Kentucky. Tom Paine's *Age of Reason* was extensively circulated and was very popular. Deism was the fashionable religion of the day. Most of the professional men and such others as desired to make the impression that they were wise, or learned, avowed themselves infidels.
> Mr. Vaughan was fond of reading and had a great thirst for knowledge. He procured the writings of Paine and Volney, and, after reading them, professed infidelity and joined an infidel club in Winchester. He ceased going to religious meeting and became recklessly profane. Like many other towns, at that period, Winchester had no place of worship. Even Louisville had no house of worship at that time. Mr. Vaughan joined the infidel club merely for the pleasure and the social and intellectual advantages he expected to derive from it.[69]

As the foregoing passage implies, various sorts of infidel clubs sprang up across the country in this period, but it is difficult to know exactly what Spencer means by "infidel club." Both a deistical society and a masonic lodge would likely have counted as infidel clubs for him. There is, however, good evidence for at least three deistical societies that originated in the 1790s, one in Philadelphia, one in New York City, and one in Newburgh, New York, but there were likely many more.

Thanks to *Age of Reason*, in the 1790s deism was transformed from a mostly clandestine form of religious dissent into an open social movement.

Age of Reason made it fashionable for college students, frontier tailors, and many people in between to openly question the truth of revealed religion. Some of the reasons for this transformation involve what has been called "political opportunity" in the literature on social movements.[70] Through Paine's writings and reputation, deism was able to attach itself to the larger international republican political agenda. Although only a minority of Democratic-Republicans were professed deists, American deism drew energy from republicanism, making deism into a movement that was as much about changing the authority structure of society as it was about changing personal beliefs. But the favorable political circumstances of the mid-1790s alone would probably not have led to the creation of deistical organizations if it were not for the efforts of "social movement entrepreneurs" who devoted themselves to creating such organizations.[71] One such movement entrepreneur was Elihu Palmer, who used the skills he had acquired studying to be a minister to create a deistical organization based in New York that would leave a lasting legacy for American freethought.

Elihu Palmer, John Fellows, and the Birth of the Deistical Society of New York

Elihu Palmer was the leading light of the Deistical Society of New York and was instrumental in establishing the freethought movement in America, creating a network of supporters who propagated Paine's legacy throughout the nineteenth century. He was well known in his own day, but many of the details of his life were lost to history until Kirsten Fischer's valuable biography of him, *American Freethinker*, brought them back to light. Palmer was born in 1764 and grew up on a farm in a very rural region of eastern Connecticut, near the hamlet of Scotland.[72] He was drawn to the life of a minister from a young age, but he eventually needed to leave organized Christianity because of the unorthodoxy of his religious ideas. Palmer's theological outlook was similar to, but not identical with, the theology of *The Age of Reason*. Palmer had already associated himself with deism before he read *Age of Reason*, but Paine's work created a broader audience for Palmer and influenced his rhetorical style.

Palmer moved from the moderate Calvinism of his parents' congregation in Connecticut to his own brand of deism slowly over the course of his life rather than through some singular conversion experience. Palmer received a scholarship to study divinity at Dartmouth in the mid-1780s, graduating in 1787.[73] At Dartmouth, he belonged to an extracurricular debating society called the United Fraternity, the more liberal of the college's two fraternal societies.[74] In the course of extracurricular discussion and debate, activities which were regularly sponsored by the fraternal societies, he would certainly have encountered the doctrine of Universalism, which held that all souls could achieve salvation rather than just those that were predestined to, as Calvinism would have it, and also the Unitarian outlook, which questioned the doctrine of the Trinity, and often the divinity of Jesus. Both Universalist and Unitarian outlooks were held by various liberal ministers in New England's Congregational churches. Congregational churches were so called because local congregations had the final word on who they would employ as minister, and the theology of ministers chosen by different congregations could vary quite a bit, from Calvinist through Universalist to Unitarian. Although the Dartmouth curriculum included only one course in theology for seniors,[75] it would have been important for fledgling ministers to become familiar with, and to debate, the various theological ideas that were being entertained by different congregations across the region. Palmer might also have encountered the works of earlier English deists at Dartmouth, such as John Toland, whom he later expressed admiration for. Probably already by the end of his college education, Palmer's personal theology was moving beyond the mysterious and supernatural aspects of Christianity, but not beyond what might be quietly accepted by some liberal New England congregations.

After graduating, Palmer served the usual term as an apprentice minister, before accepting a full-time position with a probationary period. His apprenticeships went well. The first was with the Unitarian-leaning John Foster in Brighton, Massachusetts, and the second with the Universalist-leaning Thomas Allen in Pittsfield, Massachusetts. Unfortunately, the position he then moved into was with a more traditionally Calvinist Presbyterian congregation in Newtown, New York, in what is now Queens. In his preaching, he avoided "the peculiar and mysterious doctrines of the Christian religion, confining himself to moral precepts."[76] It was discovered, while visiting a local doctor, that his views were "far from orthodox" when he professed not to believe in the doctrine of original sin, and it was subsequently decided that Palmer would not be a good fit for the traditionally minded congregation.[77] So his employment ended at the conclusion of his six-month probationary period.

Always resilient, Palmer started over in Augusta, Georgia, in 1789, where he undertook a period of legal apprenticeship and made a living as a chaplain and professor of rhetoric and oratory at Richmond Academy, a college preparatory school.[78] Still following his passion for preaching, Palmer managed to become a part-time minister at St. Paul's Episcopal Church,[79] where his engaging style of sermonizing won over parishioners in spite of any reservations they may have harbored about his unorthodoxy. The next couple years were happy and relatively prosperous. Palmer met his future wife on a trip back to his hometown. Over the summer of 1790 he courted and married, and then returned to Georgia in September with his wife, whose name has not been preserved. Mrs. Palmer, it seems, did not adapt well to the southern climate and culture, and by 1791 the Palmer family, which would grow to three and then four, settled in Philadelphia, where Elihu hoped to find larger audiences for his sermons.[80]

Disappointment and tragedy lay in store for the Palmers in Philadelphia. Elihu first found a pulpit as a guest minister with a congregation of Universalists, but soon the more conservative members of this newly minted denomination, anxious to minimize doctrinal differences from other sects, requested that Palmer no longer preach to them. His Universalism was welcome, but his Unitarianism went too far.[81] As there was not yet any organized congregation of Unitarians in Philadelphia, Palmer was happy to accept the invitation of the Deist Society of Philadelphia to deliver a series of talks in 1792. The fact that there was a Deist Society in Philadelphia before the publication of *The Age of Reason*, as well as the acceptance of Palmer in Massachusetts and Georgia, shows that, even before Paine's bombshell, deism in America was not confined to a few eccentric founders. Unfortunately for Palmer, orthodox critics of deism also preceded Paine on the American stage. It was advertised that Palmer would "deliver a Discourse at the Long-Room in Church-Alley against the divinity of Jesus Christ" in March of 1792.[82] The discourse was to be delivered at 10 a.m. on Sunday, at a hall that was a short walk from the largest church in the city, the Episcopalian Christ Church. These circumstances combined to raise the ire of the local Episcopalian bishop, William White, who pressured the landlord of the venue to break the rental agreement with Palmer and the Deistic Society. A war of newspaper polemics between Palmer, White, and other clergy followed in which Palmer made a brave show, but when the smoke cleared, Palmer was without a pulpit in Philadelphia.[83] Palmer retreated with his family to Wilkes-Barre, Pennsylvania, for a year before returning to Philadelphia, where tragedy struck. The Palmers were living on Front Street without the means to relocate yet again when the yellow fever epidemic of 1793 invaded the city on mosquito wings. Both Palmer and his wife contracted the horrible disease, which causes severe internal bleeding, eventual liver failure, and jaundice before death. Benjamin Rush, Paine's friend during the time he was writing *Common Sense*, was the physician who attended Palmer, but Palmer refused his proposed treatment of letting blood. The disease took a terrible toll. Palmer's wife died of it, and Palmer was left blind.[84] Without the help of friendly neighbors, the blinded preacher could never have managed to care for his two small children as he recovered from his illness.

Between 1793 and 1796, Palmer rebuilt his life as best he could, spending time both with family in Connecticut, where his two young sons had gone to be raised in their grandfather's household, and in Augusta, where he still had close friends.[85] The loss of his eyesight did not keep Palmer from either encountering new literature or composing new works; in fact, his most prolific days as a writer still lay ahead of him. Friends must have read him the first part of *The Age of Reason* soon after it appeared, correctly guessing that it would appeal to him.

Sometime in 1796, passing through New York as he traveled between Connecticut and Georgia, Palmer made a friendship with a deistical bookseller and publisher named John Fellows that would alter the course of his life. Fellows was born in 1759 in Sheffield, Massachusetts. During the Revolution, he served under his uncle Colonel John Fellows, with whom he is sometimes confused, in the Continental army, and then attended Yale College, earning his bachelor's degree in 1783.[86] He went into business as a publisher and bookseller around 1793, selling titles that catered to those with a taste for republicanism and deism. He was granted the American copyright for the first part of *Age of Reason* in 1794 on Paine's behalf, a fact of which he informed Paine by letter.[87] He underwrote publication not only of *Age of Reason* but also Gilbert Wakefield's reply to it, and an anonymous defense entitled *The Examiners Examined; Being a Defense of "The Age of Reason."* Other books that he had a hand in publishing include Paine's *Decline and Fall of the English System of Finance*, an English edition of Voltaire's *Philosophical Dictionary*, and several works by Paine's friend Joel Barlow, including *A Letter Addressed to the People of Piedmont, On the Advantages of the French Revolution, and the Necessity of Adopting Its Principles in Italy*.[88] Fellows also sold a pamphlet he had composed himself, *On the Character and Doctrines of Jesus Christ*, in which he, like Paine, argued that Jesus was an exceptional moral teacher, but not a divinity.[89]

Soon after Palmer and Fellows met, they hatched a plan to create a deistical society that would meet regularly every Sunday. It is not known exactly how Palmer and Fellows got to know each other. Palmer may have been directed to Fellows's bookstore as a place where he could get the latest deistical publications, or perhaps they were introduced by a mutual friend. But as they became acquainted Fellows learned of the blind orator's desire to return to his vocation in a context where he could freely express his views. Fellows was sympathetic with Palmer's aims and impressed with his abilities, so he proposed that Palmer begin a series of lectures in New York and helped him get an assembly room where he spoke on Sunday mornings.[90] The two worked together to establish the Deistical Society of New York to help support him.[91] Palmer authored a statement of the society's principles that aligned its deistic theology with a hoped-for triumph of international republicanism. In the preamble, he wrote: "At a time when the political despotism of the earth is disappearing, and man is about to reclaim and enjoy the liberties of which for ages he has been deprived it would be unpardonable to neglect the important concerns of intellectual and moral nature."[92] He then listed eleven principles to which all members of the society should subscribe:

1. That the universe proclaims the existence of one supreme Deity worthy the adoration of intelligent beings.
2. That man is possessed of moral and intellectual faculties sufficient for the improvement of his nature and the acquisition of happiness.
3. That the religion of nature is the only universal religion; that it grows out of the moral relations of intelligent beings, and that it stands connected with the progressive improvement and common welfare of the human race.
4. That it is essential to the true interest of man that he love truth and practice virtue.
5. That vice is everywhere ruinous and destructive to the happiness of the individual and of society.
6. That a benevolent disposition and beneficent actions are fundamental duties of rational beings.
7. That a religion mingled with persecution and malice cannot be of divine origin.
8. That education and science are essential to the happiness of man.
9. That civil and religious liberty is equally essential to his true interests.
10. That there can be no human authority to which man ought to be amenable for his religious opinions.

11. That science and truth, virtue, and happiness, are the great objects to which the activity and energy of the human faculties ought to be directed.[93]

The Deistical Society drew much of its membership from the local Democratic-Republican Club, of which both Fellows and Palmer were members, and also from the Tammany Society, which also backed Jefferson in the election of 1800 and was only beginning to become the political machine it would be in the future. Members of the Deistical Society included Philip Freneau, a poet and former publisher of the republican newspaper the *National Gazette*, and David Denniston, who began publishing the *American Citizen* in 1800 at the request of his relative George Clinton, onetime governor of New York and Jefferson's political ally.[94] The association of the Deistical Society and these anti-Federalist political clubs established the association of freethought and liberal politics that would still be thriving one hundred years later in the close relationship between *The Truth Seeker* journal and the National Liberal League. Certainly not all republicans were deists or freethinkers, but the association was strong enough to fuel federalist claims that being a republican was synonymous with being a deist.[95]

Palmer must have been very pleased with the reception his speeches got in New York. Before the end of 1796, he had taken up residence at Powell's boardinghouse, which was an easy walk to Fellows's bookstore at 60 Wall Street.[96] In addition to lecturing regularly in New York, he made frequent excursions to speak to freethinking groups in Philadelphia, Baltimore, and Newburgh, New York.[97] With the help of Fellows, Palmer had achieved a small but steady income from speaking and a position at the head of a supportive community of freethinkers. The Sunday morning meetings of the Deistical Society started out as being a kind of mirror image of Sunday Christian worship. In many ways the Deistical Society operated like a small Christian congregation under the leadership of a chosen minister. Fellows's connections to New York freethinkers and republicans drew in members, and Palmer's oratorical and ministerial skills kept them interested and built community feeling.

In this encouraging environment, Palmer started work on a book that would express his own version of deism: *Principles of Nature, Or, A Development of the Moral Causes of Happiness and Misery Among the Human Species* (1801). Palmer arranged for a copy to be delivered to Paine in France, and he was no doubt gratified, and perhaps relieved, to get Paine's favorable response. "I see you have thought deeply on the subject," Paine wrote, "and expressed your thoughts in a strong and clear style."

Although Palmer's theology differed from Paine's in some respects, *Principles of Nature* carried forward the most important themes of *Age of Reason*, in which Paine had contrasted the "true theology" of scientific deism with the "fabulous theology" of revealed religion. *Principles of Nature* makes the same contrast, and perhaps even more sharply. The opening chapter praises the long process through which human reason has acquired an understanding of the earth, the heavens, and the workings of the mind. "The sources of hope and consolation to the human race are to be sought for in the energy of intellectual powers," Palmer writes. "The strength of the human understanding is incalculable; its keenness of discernment would ultimately penetrate into every part of nature were it permitted to operate with uncontrolled and unqualified freedom."[98] For Palmer, as for Paine, the progress of a scientific understanding of the universe is the greatest hope for future human happiness. But "human understanding" has unfortunately not been able to operate with "unqualified freedom." It has long been opposed by the forces of "supernatural theology," which, in Palmer's understanding of history, is responsible for plunging Europe into twelve centuries of darkness. He blames the union of church and state for the Dark Ages, when science was almost forgotten:

> The whole earth has been made the wretched abode of ignorance and misery— and to priests and tyrants these dreadful effects are to be attributed.... The political tyranny of the earth coalesced with ... [a] phalanx of religious despots, and the love of science and of virtue was nearly banished from the world. Twelve centuries of moral and political darkness in which Europe was involved had nearly completed the destruction of human dignity, and everything valuable or ornamental in the character of man. During this long and doleful night of ignorance, slavery and superstition, Christianity reigned triumphant—its doctrines and divinity were not called in question.[99]

All three of the frames used by Paine in *Age of Reason*—separationism, antiscripturalism, and scientific hope—are present in some form in the opening chapter of *Principles of Nature*, as well as throughout the book, but there are many differences from Paine too. Where Paine focused single-mindedly on disproving the divine authority of scripture in *Part the Second* of *Age of Reason*, Palmer launches a more general attack across a range of Christian beliefs. Many chapters single out one or more themes in Christian theology to dispute such as the Trinity, the authority of the Bible, original sin, biblical stories of creation and the flood, miracles, prophecies, martyrs, the devil, death, and damnation. Palmer also had a different conception of God than Paine. Where the idea of a Creator God was essential to Paine's outlook, Palmer argued that nature was eternal, a position that would seem to exclude the idea of a Creator.[100] However, Palmer does speak of God as Creator in other passages.[101] Palmer followed d'Holbach, whom Paine opposed, in believing that all matter is to some degree animate.[102] In one place Palmer speaks of God as the intelligence of the universe: "NATURE is considered as possessing a central power. A brain or cogitative faculty whose operations on a higher scale are supposed to be analogous to the brain or thinking faculty of man. And this perhaps would be the most philosophic method by which to arrive at the idea of supreme intelligence or the governing power of the universe."[103] Although Palmer declared himself a deist, his beliefs at times seem far closer to pantheism than Paine's. Underneath the basic agreement between Paine and Palmer that religion should not be dictated by the state, that scripture has no divine authority, and that science is the best hope for human improvement and happiness, there were also many points of disagreement that Paine chose to overlook in his approval of Palmer and his book.

Because of his blindness, Palmer would probably not have been able to write his book without the help of Mary Powell, the wife of the proprietor of the boardinghouse where he lived. Palmer's oratorical skills were such that he could compose and deliver electrifying speeches with little aid from anyone else despite his lost eyesight. But to commit words to paper he needed someone to take dictation. It was almost entirely Mary who read to him the books and journals he was curious about and who took dictation for his own compositions. Fellows says she was "a woman of good sense, and fine moral feelings" and she was devoted to "promoting the cause of truth."[104] A decent amount of time after Mary's husband, Benjamin, passed away, she accepted Palmer's proposal of marriage, and the two wed in 1803.[105]

In December 1803, Palmer, with Mary's aid, began publishing an eight-page weekly journal called *Prospect, Or, View of the Moral World* in addition to giving weekly lectures, now on Sunday evenings.[106] Palmer's paper continued a strong strain of scientific deism together with criticism of Bible stories and Christian doctrine. The little community of deists and freethinkers had previously been served by the *Temple of Reason*, a weekly that commenced on November 8, 1800, during the most contentious election in the history of the country up to that time. The title recalled French deism in the period of dechristianization when many cathedrals were converted into Temples of Reason or of the Supreme Being. It was published by Dennis Driscol, a refugee from the losing side of the Irish Rebellion of 1798, which unsuccessfully attempted to establish an Irish republic based on American and French models.[107] The paper naturally endorsed Jefferson for president.[108] The *Temple of Reason* was explicitly devoted to the defense of Paineite deism. A broadside announcing the publication opens, "This paper is chiefly intended to combat the enemies of Deism." After outlining the various subjects that would be addressed, from the existence of God, the "polytheism" of the Trinity, and the deistic views of Jesus, Driscol wrote, "The foregoing subjects shall be supported from the best Deistical authors, both living and dead; and if no others had been quoted, the *Age of Reason*, by Mr. Payne, would be sufficient."[109] The journal was published off and on until the beginning of 1803, when financial issues caused by nonpaying subscribers forced its closure. But it was less than a year until Palmer gave the Deistical Society a new journal, promising "free, open, and bold" discussions of theology.[110]

The brief run of *Prospect*, from December 1803 to March 1805, was a prosperous time for the Deistical Society. As it drew together a theologically diverse group of deists and pantheists, agreement on the three great themes of *Age of Reason*—separation of church and state, the rejection of the divine authority of the Bible, and science as the best hope for human happiness—proved to be stronger than the points they were divided on. Both the prestige and the notoriety of the society increased as Thomas Paine, now returned from France, became involved with its activities and began contributing to *Prospect*.

Thomas Paine and the Deistical Society of New York

After a fifteen-year absence from America, Paine arrived in Baltimore on October 30, 1802. Politics had shifted since the days of the American popularity of *Rights of Man* in the early 1790s. As the political contest between Federalists and Democratic-Republicans had heated up in the second half of the decade, the Federalist press had turned Paine into a symbol of the union of "infidelity" and radical republicanism of the sort that had failed dramatically in France. Paine's arrival in Baltimore was an early nineteenth-century media event. "You can have no idea of the agitation which my arrival occasioned," Paine wrote to his friend and biographer Thomas "Clio" Rickman. "From New Hampshire to Georgia (an extent of 1,500 miles), every newspaper was filled with applause or abuse."[111] By this point in his life, Paine was no stranger to either fame or to controversy, and he sounds happy to have so much attention paid to him, even if he might have wished that he was not being called rude names in half the papers in the country. Paine had fled the growing despotism of Napoléon in France only to land in the middle of a fierce political struggle in America at a time when politically neutral newspapers were all but nonexistent. Although Jefferson had won the hard-fought election of 1800, Federalist papers like the *Gazette of the United States, Daily Advertiser* and the *New-York Evening Post* were doing whatever they could to see that he would be a one-term president, as the papers in Jefferson's camp had succeeded in making John Adams.

Federalists must have viewed Paine's arrival in the United States as a present of sorts. What better way could have been invented to defame Jefferson than to trumpet his association with that radically republican "infidel" Thomas Paine? Thanks to the Pitt administration's campaign to defame him after the publication of the *Rights of Man*, and the scores of indignant replies to the infamous *Age of Reason*, anybody who wished to attack Paine had plenty of prefabricated lies, half-truths, and malign epithets to choose from. Nasty articles about him began to appear in the Federalist press even before he arrived in America. The January 10, 1803, edition of the Federalist *New-York Evening Post* printed a song about Paine's return to America that told of Satanic assistance on his Atlantic crossing: "The furies swell'd his sails / The Devil and Lapland witches join'd / To give him favoring gales." Paine is depicted riding in a crow's nest atop a mast pole "with a jug of liquid fire." The song goes on to tell of Paine's reception by "King Thomas," that is, Thomas Jefferson, and of Paine drinking himself to death while writing after filling "four sheets with *I* and *me*."[112] Paine quipped about the Federalist abuse: "But I hope they will not leave off. I shall lose half my greatness when they cease to lie."[113] Rather than defending him, Republican papers like the *Philadelphia Aurora* downplayed the potentially damaging connection between Paine and Jefferson. Despite all the controversy surrounding Paine, to Jefferson's great credit he received his old friend at the White House often during Paine's stay of nearly three months in what was then called Federal City (Washington, DC).[114]

Paine's biographies are full of accounts of confrontations and incivilities inflicted on him during his final years by those who felt justified because he had written against their religious or political views. I will only cite a couple of examples here. In March 1803, Paine and his freethinking friend Joseph Kirkbride decided to travel up to New York City from Bordentown, New

Jersey, where Kirkbride lived. They traveled to Trenton and there tried to get an express stagecoach to New York, but when Kirkbride gave Paine's name to reserve a seat, two different coach owners refused to take him as a passenger; one cited Paine's deism as the reason, and another expressed a wish that his coach not be struck by lightning, which presumably might be hefted at Paine by an angry God. A mob assembled to intimidate the horse and driver that eventually did agree to take them.[115] Paine was frequently discriminated against and insulted in similar ways. One very well-documented incident rises above the others because it concerns an official action against him. On election day in 1806 Paine tried to vote in New Rochelle, New York, where he was then living. Elisha Ward, an election supervisor who hailed from an old Tory family, refused to accept his ballot on the grounds that Paine was not an American citizen, giving the following justification: "You are not an American; our minister at Paris, Gouverneur Morris, would not reclaim you when you were imprisoned in the Luxembourg prison at Paris, and General Washington refused to do it."[116] Paine was outraged, and he filed a lawsuit against the election officials. In the course of pursuing this lawsuit, he wrote to George Clinton, then the US vice president, James Madison, and Joel Barlow to ask for testimony and evidence. Fantastically, it seems that Paine lost his case.[117]

Paine became involved with the Deistical Society in 1804, after he had taken up residence at the farm that had been given him in New Rochelle and New York could be reached by coach in only a few hours. In France, Paine had been involved with the Society of Theophilanthropists, a non-Christian deistic group of "Adorers of God and Friends of Man," which began holding public worship services in 1797.[118] Paine would have recognized the Deistical Society as being very similar. Indeed, Palmer and Fellows had considered calling their group the Theophilanthropist Society, no doubt having heard of the French group, but ultimately decided the "Deistical Society" was a name of greater clarity.[119] Paine was also drawn to the society through connections to its leading members. Paine had been impressed by Palmer's *Principles of Nature*, and he corresponded with Fellows in 1797 concerning his American edition of *Age of Reason*.[120] Paine sometimes boarded in the same house as Fellows when staying in New York.[121] The first of at least twelve pieces that Paine wrote for Palmer's *Prospect* appeared in February 1804,[122] and by July Paine had gotten to know Fellows well enough to ask him to travel up to his farm and help him get his financial affairs in order.[123] In spring of 1805, Paine stayed with William Carver, a member of the

Deistical Society he had first met long ago in Lewes. Carver lived on Cedar Street, where Elihu and Mary Palmer also lived, and it is reported that Paine frequently visited them.[124] It would be surprising if Paine did not often attend Palmer's Sunday lectures when he was in town and mix with all the members of the freethinking community.

There was a considerable range of theological positions within the New York–centered network of deists. Paine's God had created the universe and then became a benevolent observer of the world he had set in motion, perhaps indirectly influencing events through the mysterious force of providence. Palmer's God, however, was a vital force that existed throughout the universe and guided its operations in accordance with the laws of nature. "There is no such thing as dead matter," wrote Palmer in *Principles of Nature*, "all is alive, all is active and energetic."[125] He elsewhere writes that humanity "should be taught to revere the power, which animates and enlivens the great system of nature."[126] Like the Baron d'Holbach, whom he quotes as "Mirabaud" (a pseudonym used by d'Holbach), Palmer believed that motion was inherent in matter, and therefore a prime mover was unnecessary.[127] God was a part of the cosmos, not something outside of it. Paine had spoken against d'Holbach's idea of active matter in an 1801 address to the Theophilantropist Society while still in France. To Paine, at that time, this line of thought ran too close to atheism, a term that d'Holbach acknowledged might be used to describe his system.[128]

Another point on which Paine and Palmer had differences of opinion was the possibility of an afterlife. On this subject Paine wrote, "I trouble not myself about the manner of future existence. I content myself with believing, even to positive conviction, that the power that gave me existence is able to continue it, in any form and manner he pleases, either with or without this body."[129] Palmer, on the other hand, wrote that death is "the disorganization of intelligent beings,"[130] "the counterpart of our original construction." "Change or mutability is essentially connected with the uniform harmony and preservation of the great fabric of the universe, and no one can expect to be excepted from the operation of this general law."[131] Palmer thought that a person's vital force rejoins the vital substance of the cosmos after death, just as the body eventually decomposes and is dispersed into nature. Despite these theological differences, Paine and Palmer did not challenge each other's divergent views in print, although they might have discussed them in private. Their common antipathy toward revealed religion was more important to them than whether matter was self-moving, whether God was a benevolent observer of the universe or a vital force within it, or whether a personal consciousness survived death.

The heterodoxy of the Deistical Society was further increased by others associated with the group. Palmer admired the eccentric English traveler John "Walking" Stewart, who was a vegetarian and engaged in meditative practices he learned on his travels in India and Thailand.[132] Stewart, who associated with the Deistical Society during its most vibrant years, believed in the "unity of all beings," which he called "homo-ousia,"[133] and was critical of Paine for continuing to support the French Revolution after the Terror.[134] But Paine and Stewart could agree to disagree even about the French Revolution for the sake of the shared central project of demolishing the religious and civil authority of scripture.

Dissent from the goal of undermining scriptural authority seems to have been the one thing that would mean exclusion from the otherwise heterodox Deistical Society and its associated publications. When Swedenborgian minister John Hargrove, who considered himself a deist of sorts, wrote a friendly letter to Driscol arguing that the Bible must be read in a "spiritual" rather than a "literal" sense, he hoped it would be printed in the *Temple of Reason*. "The *literal* sense, in many passages, proclaim[s] war and death against the principles of true science and reason," he wrote. "But when the genuine or *spiritual* sense is explained . . . every passage appears fraught with heavenly wisdom."[135] Driscol shot back a blistering response to Hargrove without printing his submission, saying "the *Temple of Reason* is not established for every furious fanatic and wild visionary to *rant* and *cant* away in it."[136] After another attempt to start a dialogue and another harsh rejection, Hargrove published his letters and Driscol's responses himself.[137]

Besides an uncompromising rejection of the authority of scripture, even at the cost of alienating freethinking Christians who did not insist on biblical literalism, another topic on which the opinions of nearly all these freethinkers agreed was the promise of science. Palmer proclaimed in the opening issue of *Prospect* that he hoped the journal would be "useful to the public in the great cause of science and virtue."[138] In the second issue Palmer printed an aphorism that stated: "SCIENCE is the sun of the moral world; when its rays shall have penetrated the darkness of every understanding, a new era will be commenced in history, and man will become the friend of sensitive existence."[139] "A Subscriber" reaffirms the commitment of the Deistical Society to science in general in the twelfth issue of *Prospect*: "'Tis owing to science that men are enabled to throw off the shackles of prejudice, divest themselves of the trammels of superstition, and erect the religion of nature on the firm basis of truth."[140]

It is not surprising that an organization promoting thought that ran so counter to religious orthodoxy attracted negative attention from the Federalist press, especially after Paine became personally associated with it. However, one of the most paranoid misrepresentations of the Deistical Society was published by a member of a Republican faction. Within the Democratic-Republican fold, followers of Vice President Aaron Burr, who would kill Alexander Hamilton in a duel in 1804, vied for power with followers of New York governor George Clinton, both in New York and on the national level. A Burr supporter named John Wood published a pamphlet called *A Full Exposition of the Clintonian Faction, and the Society of the Columbian Illuminati* in 1802. This work tried to blacken Clinton and his followers by associating them with a secret "Theistical Society" led by Elihu Palmer. Of this Society, Wood wrote, "Like felonious robbers, they associated with, feigned, and courted the habitudes of industry and religion during the day, that they might with more security in their nightly cabals, mangle the divine Revelation into a banquet of pleasure, and season the works of the Fathers, with the seeds of Epicurean philosophy. All their intercourse, all their actions and dealings were infectious. They were the hidden instruments of vice and torment; like poisonous plants, corrupted themselves and corrupting all about them."[141] The "secret" "Theistical Society" was in fact the not-at-all-secret Deistical Society, and some Clintonians, like David Denniston, were indeed members. The term "illuminati" linked Wood's accusations to a large body of European anti-Enlightenment conspiracy literature that blamed the French and other revolutions on secret societies of "illuminati" and Freemasons.[142] The term "Columbian," means that this was supposed to be a New World branch of this clandestine international network of illuminati. Federalist newspapers loved Wood's propaganda bomb and reprinted many passages; however, in an era when hyperbolic political rhetoric was common, the ultimate effect on the Clintonian faction and on the Deistical Society was negligible.[143]

Throughout the years of his association with the Deistical Society, Paine had increasingly serious issues with his health. Palmer visited Paine on his farm late in the summer of 1805 and wrote to his friend Robert Hunter of his concern about Paine's declining health, predicting that this "firm cog in the wheel of human life" was nearing his end.[144] But, tragically, it was Palmer who was to pass away first in the spring of 1806, at just forty-one years of age. About six months after he had written of his concern for Paine's health, he fell ill on a lecture trip to Philadelphia, and in just a few days died of pleurisy, an inflammation of the lining of the lungs.[145] His unexpected death must have been a devastating blow to his wife and friends and to the Deistical Society, which had been held together by Palmer's weekly lectures, especially after Palmer had suspended publication of *Prospect* in March of 1805 due to the perennial problem of nonpaying subscribers and a lack of funding.[146]

Paine outlived Palmer by about three years. Palmer's death and the suspension of the activities of the Deistical Society must have caused Paine great sadness, but the members of the society continued to socialize with him and helped to care for him as his health declined through his final years. Paine spent more and more time in New York City as he wearied of the hostility he experienced in New Rochelle. Not only had he been denied his right to vote there, but a court had sided with a long-time tenant farmer who refused to pay him any rent for the many years he had lived and worked on the farm.[147] Then the new tenant farmer, Christopher Derrick, tried to shoot him on Christmas Eve in 1804. That evening, Paine was in his cottage talking to the son of Andrew Dean, a friendly neighbor who farmed the north part of Paine's land.[148] Derrick took a shot at Paine through a window from the outside with a borrowed gun, but he succeeded in shooting only the side of the cottage. Derrick was apprehended, but apparently acquitted.[149] The underlying problem with Paine's situation was that the farm that had been given to him was confiscated from a British loyalist during the Revolution, and such political attachments were pretty typical of the region, which became a Federalist stronghold in the 1790s. Paine came to feel much more welcome in New York City.

In 1806, while staying with William Carver, a friend from the Deistical Society, Paine suffered a stroke, which he called "a fit of apoplexy," that left him bedridden, either because of the effect of the stroke or because the stroke had caused him to fall down a flight of stairs. Paine called the experience an "experiment in dying."[150] He hired Mary Palmer, who had fallen on hard times since the death of her husband, to care for him and for a time she also lived in Carver's house. On medical advice, Paine moved out of Carver's house as the weather grew cold because his room there had no fireplace. With the help of John Fellows, he found lodging with John Wesley Jarvis, a twenty-six-year-old painter who had done an excellent portrait of him the previous year.[151] The jaunty young painter wrote to a friend that Paine was "one of the most pleasant companions I have met with for an old man."[152] Soon Paine recovered enough that he could walk and went on to take other lodgings over the next two years. He visited his farm for the last time in his life in 1807, when he failed to obtain justice on the matter of his right to vote.

Paine reached out to his friend Marguerite de Bonneville as he felt death approaching in 1809. In his last years in France, Paine had taken up residence with his young friend Nicolas de Bonneville and his family, consisting of his wife Marguerite and two sons, Benjamin and Thomas. The youngest was named in honor of him. Paine had been happy living with them, playing the role of an adopted grandfather, until Nicolas, a writer and publisher, had run afoul of Napoléon and been forced to go into hiding. With France becoming unsafe, Paine had arranged for Marguerite and her boys to come to America and helped Marguerite get established as a French teacher. Now, she was the closest thing he had to family. At Paine's request, according to her reminiscences, Marguerite rented a house in Greenwich Village during the last weeks of his life, so that she could sit with him every day. As death came closer his body began to swell. Paine received many visitors in his final days.[153] Some, like the painter Jarvis, came just to comfort him, others, like the Quaker Willit Hicks, to make a final attempt to "save his soul." No one succeeded in getting him to renounce what he had formerly written on the topic of religion.[154] He died the morning of June 8, 1809.

The often-repeated story of Paine's sparsely attended funeral in New Rochelle is somewhat misleading because most of his friends lived in New York and had paid their final respects before his body was taken back up to his farm, where it had been arranged for him to be buried. Jarvis made a plaster cast of his face for the purpose of sculpting a bust, and his body was laid in a good mahogany coffin. Marguerite laid a rose on his chest before the casket was closed and put on a carriage. She gives the following touching account of the burial:

> This interment was a scene to affect and to wound any sensible heart. Contemplating who it was, what man it was, that we were committing to an obscure grave on an open and disregarded bit of land, I could not help feeling most acutely. Before the earth was thrown down upon the coffin, I, placing myself at the east end of the grave, said to my son Benjamin, "stand you there, at the other end, as a witness for grateful America." Looking round me, and beholding the small group of spectators, I exclaimed, as the earth was tumbled into the grave, "Oh Mr. Paine! My son stands here as testimony of the gratitude of America, and I, for France." This was the funeral ceremony of this great politician and philosopher.[155]

Paine left the bulk of his estate to the de Bonneville family, who eventually sold all but the gravesite, mostly to help pay for the education of Benjamin and Thomas, as Paine had intended. Some of the land was to be sold immediately so that smaller sums could be paid to other friends, including Mary Palmer and Clio Rickman.[156] When Napoléon fell in 1814, Nicolas was finally able to come out of hiding and join his family in America. Nicolas and Marguerite returned to France in 1819, but at least Benjamin remained in the United States, where he had a successful military career, retiring as a brigadier general in the US Army.[157]

Although the deaths of Palmer and Paine brought an end to the period of deistic activism that had begun in the republican enthusiasm of the mid-1790s, they had planted the seeds of a more enduring movement. The spirit of Palmer's *Prospect* would be briefly revived by John Fellows in 1810 in the form of *The Theophilanthropist; Containing Critical, Moral, Theological, and Literary Essays, in Monthly Numbers*.[158] Although this publication was short-lived, it would be succeeded by more successful ones beginning in the 1820s such as *The Correspondent*, *The Free Enquirer*, *The Beacon*, and, eventually, *The Truth Seeker*, published by new generations of freethinkers who would toast Elihu Palmer at annual celebrations of Thomas Paine's birthday.[159]

The End of an Era, but Not the End of a Movement

The history of the freethought movement is marked by waves of activity and latency, especially in its early development. This chapter has been about the movement's first wave, from the mid-1790s to the death of Paine. Deistic freethought was transformed from an underground form of religious dissent into an open social movement in 1794, when American readers took up *The Age of Reason* in a moment of transatlantic republican enthusiasm. The initial success of this movement was quite substantial, but its progress was checked by strong opposition and the disappointing fate of republicanism in France. The association of deism with political republicanism gave Federalists the opportunity to denounce the "infidelity" of their opponents, particularly Paine, but these attacks gave freethinkers of many varieties a common antagonist and strengthened their unity.

In this first flowering of the freethought movement, American freethinkers, following Paine, mostly thought of themselves as deists. Their deism was a form of religious dissent that carried forward Paine's antiscripturalism and his hope that science would improve life, and to a lesser degree his separationism. Their main activities included going to deistic lectures, often offered on Sunday morning as an alternative to Christian religious services. They also read and produced deistic literature. The Deistical Society can easily be seen as an independent congregation of deists that met on Sunday mornings to listen to discourses that they believed would improve both themselves and the world, just like Christians. The community financially supported the deistic preacher who led them, just as Christian congregations supported Christian preachers.

Implications for the Current Interpretation of the Establishment Clause

In his *Separation of Church and State*, antiseparationist, constitutional law scholar Philip Hamburger has some insightful but also some misleading things to say about the period covered in this chapter. Throughout his book, Hamburger is fittingly focused on the specific phrase "separation of church and state," likely because Jefferson's use of the phrase in his letter to the Danbury Baptists was a key citation in Supreme Court justice Hugo Black's 1947 *Everson v. Board of Education* decision, which justified the separationist principles that would rewrite the rules for church-state relations in the mid-twentieth century. "Neither a state nor the Federal Government can, openly or secretly, participate in the affairs of any religious organizations or groups, and vice versa," wrote Black. "In the words of Jefferson, the clause against establishment of religion by law was intended to erect 'a wall of separation between church and State.'"[160] Thus did Black justify his decision with evidence concerning what Jefferson understood the words of the Constitution to mean, and he offered similar evidence concerning Madison, the main author of the Establishment Clause. Surely, even a strict constructionist would approve! But not Hamburger. After examining the circumstances surrounding Jefferson's epistle to the Baptists, Hamburger concludes, "The constitutional authority for the separation of church and state is without historical foundation."[161]

How does Hamburger reach the conclusion that "separation of church and state" is "without historical foundation" as a constitutional principle? The story, according to Hamburger, goes something like this. The idea of church-state separation first entered American political discourse in the 1740s as something that ministers in established churches *accused* religious dissenters of seeking.[162] To them it was obvious that social order and good government depended upon religion and that to separate government from religion would bring chaos and decline. Because "separation of church and state" had been made to sound poisonous by establishment ministers, that specific phrase was seldom used in the debates about state constitution reform that took place during and after the Revolution, or in the debates about the Constitution and Bill of Rights.[163] But after Federalist preachers started using their pulpits to support Adams's campaign against Jefferson in the election of 1800, Jefferson's Democratic-Republican allies began to hold up separation of church and state as an *American ideal* that the ministers were violating. In Hamburger's words, it was an attempt to separate the "federalist clergy from republican politics."[164] Jefferson won the election by the skin of his teeth and with the help of the Baptists and other religious dissenters who were working to end religious establishments. Jefferson's letter responding to a petition of the Danbury Baptists that called for the disestablishment of Congregationalism in Connecticut was not only a gesture of gratitude and continued allegiance to these political allies, it was also an opportunity for Jefferson to promote his views on church-state separation. But according to Hamburger, the Baptists did not share these views and because of this they did not publish or even acknowledge Jefferson's reply to them. The apparent silence of the Baptists on the topic of Jefferson's letter is the main support for Hamburger's claim that "the constitutional authority for the separation of church and state is without historical foundation."

There are moments of great insight in Hamburger's story about the early history of the phrase "separation of church and state" in American political discourse, but there are also some serious difficulties with it. Hamburger's dogged tracing of the usage of the phrase throughout the eighteenth century is to be admired, and his treatment of the phrase's specific political meaning circa 1800 is insightful. But his conclusion that "separation of church and state" is "without historical foundation" has several problems.

The first problem with Hamburger's conclusion concerns constitutional interpretation. On strict constructionist principles, which I do not endorse but do abide by here for the sake of argument, we should look solely to the words of the Constitution and the intentions of those involved in crafting and ratifying them to find legitimate meaning. Like much constitutional language, the words "Congress shall make no law respecting an establishment of religion" had a range of meanings for the people who crafted and voted to approve them. Hamburger is probably right that one of those meanings was that the government should not favor one religious group over another but is not barred from all involvement with religion. This can be called the "nondenominationalist" interpretation because it holds that the government cannot favor one denomination over another. The nondenominationalist interpretation became the prevailing constitutional norm in the United States for most of the nineteenth century in no small measure because of Justice Joseph Story's endorsement of it in his influential 1833 *Commentaries on the Constitution of the United States*, where he held that the First Amendment was intended primarily "to exclude all rivalry among Christian sects."[165] But the nondenominationalist interpretation of the Establishment Clause was not the only interpretation available. Hamburger himself points out that Madison held that religion is "not within the purview of Civil Authority" during the 1784 debate about using state money to support "teachers of the Christian religion."[166] And in the 1789 debate about the Establishment Clause, Representative Carroll of Maryland warned against "the gentlest touch of the governmental hand" in religious matters. Representative Livermore of New Hampshire proposed that "Congress shall make no law touching religion."[167] Although they did not use the phrase "separation of church and state," Madison, Carroll, and Livermore were all strong separationists. Years later in his "Detached Memoranda," Madison wrote that "the establishment of the chaplainship to Cong[res]s is a palpable violation of equal rights, as well as Constitutional principles."[168]

Clearly Madison, the principal author of the Establishment Clause, maintained consistently throughout his career that any government involvement in religion is a violation of it, and in this he agrees with Jefferson's "separation of church and state" language. Black's *Everson* decision highlights the Jefferson/Madison separationist interpretation of the Establishment Clause in a way that is as historically legitimate as Hamburger's highlighting of the nondenominationalist interpretation. It seems to me that, even on strict constructionist principles, when different groups originally supported a constitutional provision without agreeing on the meaning of that provision, it is part of the legitimate scope of current constitutional interpretation to choose between, or somehow balance, the different meanings that were assigned to it by its original architects and ratifiers. Justice Black perhaps should have done more to acknowledge the competing nondenominationalist interpretation of the Establishment Clause in his decision, but Hamburger is *not right* to say that the separationist interpretation of the Establishment Clause is "without historical foundation." The separationist interpretation of the Establishment Clause is not delegitimized by the existence of the nondenominationalist interpretation any more than the nondenominationalist interpretation is delegitimized by the existence of the separationist interpretation.

They are both original meanings of the clause. Even within the limits of strict constructionism, both interpretations, even though they are in conflict, are historically legitimate.

Beyond ignoring the views of the author of the Establishment Clause in his discussions of the Establishment Clause, Hamburger does not acknowledge the extent to which early nineteenth-century Baptists were really separationists. As we have already seen, in his 1791 pamphlet *The Rights of Conscience Inalienable*, John Leland argues not only against government support for favored denominations but against religious tests for public office, which he believes would bar many good people from public service but allow oath-breakers to rise unimpeded. He also argues against any form of governmental endorsement or promotion of the Bible, which he believed would diminish reverence for the Bible. Hamburger reviews the writings of Leland and many other Baptists of the period and concludes that "what Baptists sought not only differed from separation of church and state but conflicted with it."[169] While it is true Leland does not use Jefferson's specific language, he opposed not only state financial support for any religious group but also religious tests for public office and governmental promotion of the Bible. The only point on which Leland might have disagreed with Jefferson's vision of separation is in the matter of official days of prayer and thanksgiving. Does that one point of disagreement mean that "separation of church and state" is "without historical foundation"? That, to me, does not seem warranted.

Another problem with Hamburger's story is the way it makes the Danbury Baptists representative of the will of the entire American people. Even if we grant that the Baptists were not separationists in the Madison/Jefferson sense (and I *do not* grant this), why would their nonsupport of Jeffersonian separationism delegitimize the separationist interpretation of the Establishment Clause? Would deistic nonsupport of the nondenominationalist interpretation of the Establishment Clause delegitimize that interpretation? Hamburger does not answer this question directly but seems to imply that the separationism of Jefferson and Madison was a private interpretation that lacks historical legitimacy because it lacked support from any religious group. Hamburger suggests that if even the Baptists, whom he takes to be the most separationist group of religious dissenters in the country, did not endorse Jeffersonian separationism, then few Americans other than Jefferson, Madison, and a handful of eccentric associates like Paine believed in it. If separationism lacked support of any religious group, Hamburger insinuates, why should a view that was, in effect, Jefferson and Madison's personal interpretation of the Establishment Clause, be credited as historically legitimate? One obvious answer to this question is that Madison was the main author and a key proponent of the clause. Therefore, by virtue of his authorship, his interpretation of it is historically legitimate. But even if one is willing to go so far as to ignore the views of the principal author of a constitutional provision if those views lacked broader support, it is not right to say that the separationist interpretation of the Establishment Clause was not supported by any religious group. Even if the Baptists are left out of the picture, the separationist interpretation had the emphatic support of a group of religious dissenters whose existence and views are completely ignored by Hamburger, a group to which Jefferson himself belonged. That group is the deists, who were no less religious dissenters than the Baptists. The words "deist" or "deism" only appear in two places in Hamburger's entire book, once to acknowledge that Paine was a deist, and once in a quotation where Baptist leader John Leland wonders if Jefferson is a deist.[170]

It is obvious that Hamburger never grappled with the presence or significance of deism in the early republic. But as I have argued, deists were an important, if not a very large or visible, group of religious dissenters. Because of their non-Christian perspective, deists would have been among the first to foresee the difficulties that would be involved with nondenominational government involvement in religion. Even seemingly innocuous government proclamations of days of prayer and thanksgiving tend to support the sectarian doctrine that God intervenes in human affairs, a doctrine that most deists rejected because of its supernaturalism. If even the proclamation of a day of prayer that welcomes all varieties of prayer equally is necessarily sectarian because it endorses the sectarian doctrine of an interventionist God, is it really possible for the government to be involved with religion without being sectarian? Deists thought not. Thus, even if one endorses the dubious principle that the views of an author of a constitutional provision cannot be relied on in the interpretation of that provision if they lack broader support, as Hamburger does, and even if one misleadingly downplays Baptist separationism, as Hamburger does, it is not right to say that separationism lacked the support of any religious group. It had the support of deists.

Finally, it is problematic that Hamburger rests his argument that the Danbury Baptists rejected Jeffersonian separationism mainly on the fact that we have no record of any response they made to Jefferson's letter. The main evidence Hamburger offers that the Baptists rejected separationism is a silence, the lack of a Baptist response to Jefferson's letter. An obvious objection to Hamburger's argument from silence is that the Baptists may have written a response which has been lost to history. Hamburger tries to reduce the force of this objection by pointing out that Jefferson's letter is not mentioned anywhere in the minutes of the Danbury Baptist Association, which are preserved.[171] He makes this seem like an intentional snub. But what Hamburger does not take fully into account is a colorful, well-known, and well-supported story that is rather inconvenient for his narrative because it handily explains the silence of the Baptists. When Jefferson signed his letter to the Danbury Baptists on New Year's Day of 1802, John Leland himself, a moral leader of disestablishmentarian Baptists, was present in Federal City, as Washington, DC, was then called. Leland had traveled to Federal City to present the president with a 1,235-pound wheel of cheese as a gift of thanks for his support of their cause.[172] Apparently, Jefferson timed the signing of his final draft of the letter to correspond with Leland's visit. He probably wanted to maximize the public relations value of a visit from a friendly Baptist minister to a president whose private deism made him vulnerable to accusations of atheism. Although Hamburger dutifully describes the cheese episode, he does not seem to realize the implications of the event for his narrative.[173] Because their gratitude toward Jefferson had already been expressed in person by Leland and accentuated by his gift of cheese, it would have been quite natural for the Danbury Baptists to have made no further reply to Jefferson. After you give a president a 1,200-pound wheel of cheese that has been carried by your chosen representative in a wagon from Connecticut to Washington, DC, what more can you say? For this reason, the silence of the Baptists is probably not as meaningful as Hamburger makes it out to be. To put it another way, if he wants us to believe that the Danbury Baptists snubbed Jefferson because they disagreed with the separationism he extolled in his letter to them, Hamburger needs to explain the big cheese.

Up Next: The Second Wave

When Paine wrote *Age of Reason*, he hoped that deism would quickly displace Christianity everywhere that religious establishments were no longer supported by state coercion. But by the time of Paine's death, it had become clear to all that the "revolution in the system of religion" would not come overnight, if it was ever going to come at all. With the passing of its leaders, Paine and Palmer, the movement went into a phase of latency that would last until the mid-1820s. In this quiet period of about fifteen years, people did not forget that they had been deists in the 1790s. Some did recant their former deism, such as William Vaughan of Kentucky, who went from being a deistic tailor to a Baptist minister. However, many others, like John Fellows in New York, quietly maintained their deism by following the tradition of clandestine dissent that had long been practiced by agents of the Radical Enlightenment. These true believers made possible the freethought revival of the 1820s that began the movement's second wave, which is the topic of chapter 3.

CHAPTER THREE

The Second Wave of American Freethought
Revival and Transformation

At an 1860 celebration of Thomas Paine's birthday in Cincinnati, Moncure Daniel Conway, who would write what is still one of the most complete and useful biographies of Paine, said: "Thomas Paine's life up to 1809, when he died, is interesting; but Thomas Paine's life from that time to 1860 is more than interesting—it is thrilling!"[1] This comment came toward the end of a second wave of American freethought activity that had begun in the mid-1820s with the introduction of the practice of celebrating Paine's birthday. What transpired between those 1820s celebrations in New York and Conway's Cincinnati Paine birthday speech in 1860 was certainly thrilling for those who were caught up in it. The freethought movement expanded from a timid handful of former members of the Deistical Society into a national network of thousands knit together by freethought periodicals like *The Free Enquirer* and *The Boston Investigator* and traveling lecturers like Frances Wright and Ernestine Rose. It was invigorated by cross-pollination with followers of the British utopian socialist Robert Owen and organized its first national conventions. It now framed itself not as a deistical movement, but as a movement of "free enquirers" or "infidels." Freethought built bridges to other movements: feminism, labor, and abolition. The movement's progress could well be described as "thrilling."

This chapter will tell the story of the second wave of American freethought: how it began and how it expanded and transformed as it embraced a wider variety of theologies and causes. I'll begin with some notes on the period of dormancy between 1810 and 1825 before discussing Benjamin Offen's revival of the movement, the arrival of Owenite freethinkers on American soil, and the rise of national freethought organizations, publications, and conventions.

The Dormant Years: The Second Great Awakening, the American Bible Society, James Cheetham's *Life of Thomas Paine*, and the War of 1812

The dominant trends in American religion in the period from 1810 to 1825 were not conducive to the flourishing of freethought. It was the heart of a period of religious revivalism known as the Second Great Awakening, which saw Christian church membership soar. Beginning around 1800, across many denominations, perhaps spurred to action by the fad for "infidelity" in the 1790s that had been sparked by the French Revolution and *The Age of Reason*, church leaders began a sustained effort to grow church membership and build new churches. Such efforts were especially successful in largely unchurched frontier states like Kentucky, where just a few years earlier *Age of Reason* had such a profound influence. The campaign to win converts featured new techniques of evangelization such as the "camp meeting." Presbyterian minister James McGready pioneered the camp meeting in 1800 as a way of evangelizing large numbers of people in areas with few churches. The events would last for several days and featured entertainment and socialization in addition to multiple preachers speaking simultaneously in different parts of the camp, delivering highly emotional messages about attaining salvation through personal faith in Jesus. McGready's first camp meeting was in Red River, Kentucky. When he repeated the meeting in Cane Ridge, Kentucky, the next year, he drew more than 10,000 worshipers. Although McGready's fellow Presbyterians were reluctant to adopt his methods, Methodist and Baptist preachers soon began to organize their own camp meetings. The membership of these denominations soared as the camp meetings were held throughout frontier territories and the countryside in the first decades of the nineteenth century.[2]

Back east, in 1816, a group of well-placed churchmen and civic leaders came together to form the American Bible Society, devoted to making inexpensive or free Bibles available all over the nation. Among its members were John Jay, who had served both as chief justice of the US Supreme Court and governor of New York, and Francis Scott Key, author of "The Star-Spangled Banner." Its first president was Elias Boudinot, who had been scandalized by how cheaply copies of *Age of Reason* had been sold. It seems likely that he and other founders of the society hoped to head off future outbursts of infidelity by making sure that the Bible was as widely available and inexpensive as any book that set out to attack it. An 1849 history of the society framed the distribution of Bibles as a patriotic act. Citing evidence that the Continental Congress had undertaken the importation and printing of Bibles during the Revolution, the author asks, "Who, in view of this fact, will call in question the assertion that *this is a Bible nation?*"[3] The society quickly set up a national network of auxiliary societies to which it sold Bibles at cost. It soon undertook the distribution of Bibles to the army and navy, to sailors, in prisons, to Native Americans, and in many foreign nations. The American Bible Society was not the only organization formed to aggressively disseminate Christian literature in the period. At least seven "tract societies" were formed for the purpose of publishing and disseminating Christian literature by 1814, including the New York Religious Tract Society (1813) and the Evangelical Tract Society of Boston (1811), many of which later merged with the American Tract Society. The national networks of religious publishing societies, working in concert with local churches and ministers, flooded the country with quantities of conservative Christian literature that collectively far exceeded the circulation *Age of Reason* had achieved.[4]

In this period of fervent evangelization, Paine continued to be attacked posthumously. In October 1809, only about four months after his death, a defamatory biography was published by James Cheetham, a former editor of a Clintonian paper called the *American Citizen*. Paine had a bad falling out with Cheetham in 1807 after the editor had rewritten one of Paine's contributions to *American Citizen* and printed it without Paine's permission. The conflict became politicized after Paine wrote Cheetham a furious letter calling the editor out for putting words in his mouth. Cheetham responded by attacking Paine in *American Citizen*. Paine, in turn, retaliated with an article in the *Public Advertiser* titled "Cheethem [sic] and His Tory Paper" that called Cheetham "a disgrace to Republicans."[5] Nursing a grudge, Cheetham compiled a biography of Paine filled with many of the misrepresentations, half-truths, and falsehoods promulgated by Paine's detractors, even drawing on an angry letter that Paine's friend William Carver had written during a quarrel that he later regretted. Cheetham concluded the preface to his biography by saying, "I have written the life of Mr. Paine, not his panegyric."[6] That is an understatement, but much of the rest of the book is not at all understated.

After the biography was published, Marguerite de Bonneville sued Cheetham for libel because of his false claim that she was Paine's mistress. She won the lawsuit, even though the judge otherwise commended the book for "tending to suppress Paine's writings."[7] Although it had been proven in court that Cheetham's biography contained at least one important falsehood, the book continued to be printed unaltered. Cheetham's view of Paine, strongly echoing and amplifying the royalist and Federalist narrative about him, became the dominant view in America and Britain, overshadowing Clio Rickman's defense of his friend. But Cheetham himself did not survive long after the publication of the biography. He ran afoul of the rising Tammany Hall political machine when he berated it as a Jacobin political club in *American Citizen*. He seems to have died after a mob of Tammany supporters attacked his house in September 1810, somewhat proving his point about the organization's Jacobin tendencies.[8]

With the continuing attacks on Paine and the public prominence of fervent Christian religiosity, it is not surprising that most freethinkers laid low in the years after Paine's death, reverting to the clandestine forms of religious dissent that had been characteristic of deism prior to the 1790s. But even as they did so, politics shifted in a way that would make it easier for freethinkers to eventually reemerge. The War of 1812 against Britain, during which the British burned the Capitol and the White House, brought an effective end to the pro-British Federalist party. Faced with the real prospect of a British reconquest, former Federalists like John Quincy Adams temporarily joined the Democratic-Republicans. Consequently, the divisive partisanship that had led to the politicization of "infidelity" abated.

Benjamin Offen's Freethought Revival

On January 29, 1825, a group of freethinkers including former members of the Deistical Society came together to celebrate Thomas Paine's birthday in New York. This was arguably the moment when American freethought was revived, and a new wave of activity began. The celebration of Paine's birthday became a central ritual of the movement continuing into the twentieth century. Such "Paine Festivals" generally consisted of a dinner, followed by speeches and toasts to liberal causes, and then dancing. Until 1839, women were excluded from the dinner and toasting portion of the celebration, and only invited for the dancing. The Paine birthday celebrations began a process that would transform freethought from a movement of religious dissenters who emulated many of the practices of Protestant Christianity, including Sunday morning meetings centered on sermonic oratory, into one that employed increasingly secular methods of organization and activism.

Paine birthday celebrations began in Britain and then spread to America. In Britain, the celebrations were dangerous for the participants because of the Seditious Meetings Act passed in 1795 and strengthened in 1817 and 1819. These laws imposed penalties on gatherings of more than fifty persons that "deliberated about any grievance established in church or state."[9] Paine's books were all outlawed by laws prohibiting the printing of seditious or blasphemous material, and these provisions were invoked to sentence Daniel Isaac Eaton to pillory and prison for publishing an addendum to *Age of Reason*.[10] Despite these perils, Paine's supporters had begun to gather to celebrate his legacy by 1818, when, on January 21, in the London satiric reform paper the *Black Dwarf*, a notice was printed that a committee was being formed to organize a birthday dinner in honor of Paine.[11] By 1823, more than five hundred people attended an event in London, and the practice spread to many other towns, including Bath, Edinburgh, Birmingham, Manchester, and Newgate.[12] Historians of British reform agree about the importance of these celebrations in forming networks of reformers and freethinkers in early nineteenth-century Britain.[13]

The practice of celebrating Paine's birthday was brought from Britain to America by a Sussex-born shoemaker and reform activist named Benjamin Offen, who came to New York in 1824 hoping to escape the politically oppressive environment at home. In New York, he was surprised to find that Paine was ill-spoken of by all but a small group of freethinkers. Finding the surviving members of the Deistical Society, such as John Fellows and William Carver, had much in common with him, he organized the first American Paine birthday celebration in 1825 to bring them back together and reenergize enthusiasm about Paine's political and religious ideas.[14]

In just a few years, the coalition of political and religious reformers that gathered yearly to celebrate Paine's birthday had created a network of organizations that was broader based and more vibrant than those that had surrounded the Deistical Society in its heyday. In the late 1820s Offen started a series of lectures at Tammany Hall, the meeting place of the Tammany Society of New York, that revived the spirit of Elihu Palmer's lectures. As Palmer's lectures were sponsored by the Deistical Society, Offen's were sponsored by the Society of Moral Philanthropists, a freethought organization with a more inconspicuous name than its predecessor.[15] Offen's lectures covered many of the same themes as Palmer's had, laying heavy emphasis on the Bible's lack of divine authority. Offen later published a collection of the lectures as a book, the main thesis of which was that "the Bible . . . is not divine revelation."[16] The community also soon got a newspaper. George Houston's *Correspondent* started publishing in 1827, promising to "fearlessly advocate the paramount importance of the laws of *Nature*, and the dignity of *Reason*."[17] The first issue included a letter titled "Authenticity of the Scriptures," which argued that Christian scripture is not authentic, and the first number of a series called "Deism Defended."[18]

Houston worked with Offen to found the Free Press Association, an organization that defended freedom of the press and that was the official sponsor of many Paine birthday celebrations beginning in 1828.[19] Offen makes explicit the need for a Free Press Association in the second paragraph of the introduction of his collected lectures, where he writes: "In most Christian countries (America excepted) this work would be answered by either fine, or imprisonment, or probably both. But fortunately for the cause of truth and free discussion, theological power here is so happily balanced, that persecution for religious opinions is impracticable."[20] It might be added that the persecution of religious opinion was more impractical in New York at the time than it was in other parts of the country where freethinkers faced the real threat of blasphemy charges.

By 1831, Paine birthdays began to be celebrated at Tammany Hall, which allowed its space to be used by other organizations of which it approved. The move to this space indicates that the celebration of Paine's birthday had the blessing of New York's most powerful political organization. The celebrations grew in size and extravagance. By 1833, it was reported that "150 gentlemen" and "upward of 500 persons of both sexes attended the ball" at Tammany Hall.[21] *The Correspondent* and other freethought periodicals record the growing popularity of Paine birthday celebrations first in New York and then across the country throughout the late 1820s and 1830s.[22]

New Harmony: Owenite Freethought Arrives in America

At the same time that freethought was being reestablished in New York, a new group of freethinkers had arrived from Britain and was establishing itself in New Harmony, Indiana. They were followers of the utopian socialist Robert Owen and were attempting to create a utopian community based on his principles. Owen was born in Wales in 1771, the son of a tradesman who made saddles and shoes for horses. He trained as a draper but worked his way up to become a manager in a Manchester textile mill. In 1799 he and some business partners bought a textile mill in the Scottish town of New Lanark from David Dale, the father of the woman Owen married later that year. Owen settled in at New Lanark to manage the mill and the company town, which housed some 1,800 people, including 500 children from the poorhouses who labored in the mill.[23] By this time, Owen had already fixed upon the principle that would guide his actions as a manager and that formed the basis of his philosophy, namely, that people are not responsible for their own behavior but rather that behavior is conditioned by the environment: "The character of man is, without a single exception, formed for him."[24] The key to improving human behavior and promoting human happiness, therefore, is to improve education and the conditions under which people live. People should be corrected when they do wrong, but not blamed. Conditions must be engineered to cause people to do right. He believed that if this is done, there are no limits to what humans can attain. Owen put this principle into practice as best he could at New Lanark by improving sanitation, controlling the sale of alcohol, and providing free education to the workers and their families. He also gradually improved wages. He eventually built a new school for the town, which he called the Institution for the Formation of Character, run at the mill's expense.[25]

One of his greatest successes was his reform of the company store. While in many mill towns the company stores were set up to make a further profit off the workers by forcing them to buy inferior goods at high prices, Owen acquired quality goods at wholesale prices for the store and passed the savings on to the workers. He was perhaps most loved by the workers for continuing to pay their wages during a period of four months when the mill ceased production due to a US cotton embargo during the War of 1812.[26] Owen was able to make these improvements to working conditions while keeping the mill profitable. However, some of his original partners were upset that higher profits had not been realized because of Owen's investments in the community. In 1816 he found it necessary to seek out a new set of partners, which included the philosopher Jeremy Bentham, to buy out his original partners.[27] Around that time, he became active as an advocate for industrial reform, attempting to persuade his fellow factory owners to limit the working day to twelve hours, including meal breaks, and not to employ children under ten years of age, reforms that were already in place at New Lanark but almost nowhere else.[28] By contemporary standards the working conditions at New Lanark were, of course, harsh, but they were the most progressive of Owen's era.

As he began to campaign for laws to improve working conditions, Owen got the idea that his success at New Lanark could be replicated elsewhere. In 1817, in a report to the county of Lanark, he proposed the creation of communal agricultural villages as a way of providing employment for the poor and bringing prosperity to the countryside. They would be farming towns that functioned like factories. Ideally, each village would have 800 to 1,200 people who would cultivate up to 1,200 acres of land. The villagers would all live together in connected buildings forming an open square. There would be communal arrangements for both eating and education. Owen expected the economy of scale would allow such villages to return a healthy profit. He also expected that some of the villages he envisioned would be owned collectively by the inhabitants, but he left open the possibility that they might also be partly or fully owned by investors or public charities.[29]

It was also in 1817 that Owen began to publicly proclaim how much he blamed religion for the social ills of his day. In a speech given at the City of London Tavern on August 21, and printed in the papers the next day, he said, "My friends, I tell you that hitherto you have been prevented from even knowing what happiness really is, solely in consequence of the errors—gross errors—that have been combined with the fundamental notions of every religion that has hitherto been taught to men. . . . By the errors of these systems he has been made a weak imbecile animal, a furious bigot and fanatic, or a miserable hypocrite."[30] Owen's position might not have been as radical as it is sometimes portrayed, for only a year before he had proposed the reform, not the elimination, of the "national church," and his plans for utopian agricultural villages allowed for there to be churches.[31]

In 1825 Owen tried to realize his vision of a utopian farming community in the American state of Indiana. He was lucky to be able to acquire a ready-built town that suited his purposes exactly. It so happened that a community of celibate communitarian German pietists had built a town called Harmony in southwestern Indiana beside the Wabash River. They were led by a devout man named George Rapp and his adopted son, Fredrick. Rapp and his followers had first come to America in 1804, building the first town of Harmony in western Pennsylvania. That first Harmony was sold to Mennonites at a handsome profit in 1814, and the group had moved west and built a second Harmony. Although the town was well built and prosperous, in 1825 Rapp decided the group should move back to Pennsylvania, where they would build yet another new town that they would call Economy. He sold the second Harmony in Indiana to Owen and a business partner, a respected geologist named William McClure, again at a handsome profit. Happy to acquire a turnkey utopia so easily, Owen renamed the town New Harmony and hoped it would be an American New Lanark. Owen's children William and Robert Dale both played a role in the leadership of New Harmony, and his daughter

Jane was also a resident.[32] But while the hearty German peasants who followed Rapp built prosperous communities from the ground up and thrived wherever they went, the middle-class British and French social experimenters of New Harmony and the diverse collection of Americans who joined them struggled with the challenges of community organization.

By the time he founded New Harmony, Owen had adopted protosocialist ideas about equal distribution of wealth and communal ownership of property.[33] He experimented with these ideas in New Harmony, which was governed by a series of constitutions over the years of its existence guided by these principles. The first constitution, intended to be temporary, established a "Preliminary Society." All members of the community were expected to work for the common good and in return they would receive roughly equal housing, education for their children, and a line of credit with which they could buy goods at the community store. The town was governed by a committee appointed by Owen.[34] The second constitution placed legislative power in the hands of an assembly consisting of all adult members of the community, who also elected the chief officers of an executive council. It included a list of duties and rights of the citizens, including "community of property" but did not greatly clarify the practical duties of citizens with regard to work.[35]

Very soon, New Harmony began to be divided by disputes both ideological and practical. Some of the Americans who joined were deeply religious, and while there was a small chapel at which ministers or priests of any denomination could preach,[36] Owen himself was a deist who considered all religions to be essentially superstitions.[37] So, some of the religious members broke away with Owen's blessing to form an independent collective on the property that Owen owned. Then a group of English farmers who couldn't stomach the sloppy agricultural methods most of their neighbors employed also seceded to form their own community. Another dispute was between Owen and his partner William McClure concerning how the school should be run, and this led McClure to break away to form yet another independent collective. A perennial problem was that the community never produced as much as it consumed, so Owen himself ended up footing the bill for the citizens' lines of credit; moreover, except in extreme cases, there was no practical way to ensure that citizens did a roughly equal amount of work to justify their equal lines of credit, and some took advantage of the system, exacerbating the unfavorable balance of production and consumption. Disharmony often reigned in New Harmony. It was also a financial failure. The community devolved into a collection of independent collectives living on Owen's land. Owen finally placed the whole under the authority of a board of trustees and charged each collective with paying a reasonable rent for the real estate it was occupying. Some of the collectives persisted a considerable time under this arrangement, but most soon dissolved or relocated.[38]

Despite the ultimate failure of New Harmony's experiment in communitarianism, there were many innovative and successful aspects of the town that had lasting influence. The town featured a civic center called New Harmony Hall that was a center of community life and hosted the first known secular public address by a woman in the United States, delivered by Frances Wright on July 4, 1828.[39] It had a nationally influential newspaper printed at a trade school called the School of Industry. The School of Industry and newspaper survived for years after the dissolution of New Harmony. Owen and his followers did not lose faith in the idea of collective ownership, and many more attempts were made to make it work in practice. While achieving an enduring collectively owned and self-governing community always proved elusive, collectively owned business enterprises and housing proved to have staying power. Today cooperative farms and food stores, cooperative housing, and credit unions owe something to Owen's ideas.[40]

One of the ways that New Harmony was important to the broader community of American freethinkers was through its newspaper. Although New Harmony was small and isolated, its paper had a national circulation. The paper, which was at first called the *New Harmony Gazette*, was distributed in many cities across the country, including Louisville, Cincinnati, Pittsburgh, New York, Boston, Philadelphia, Baltimore, and New Orleans.[41] The first issue is dated October 1, 1825, and contains an address by Robert Owen to the people of New Harmony, the first New Harmony Constitution, and a plan by Frances Wright to end slavery in the United States by settling slaves in communities like New Harmony where they would learn useful skills and earn enough to buy their freedom. The paper was founded by Robert Owen, run initially by an experienced editor named William Pelham, later by Owen's son William, and then by Robert Dale Owen and Frances Wright. After the dissolution of New Harmony, under the co-editorship of Wright and Robert Dale Owen, the paper changed its name to *The Free Enquirer* and it relocated to New York in 1829. By this time, it had distribution in at least fourteen of the twenty-four states that were in the Union.[42] Its national circulation is estimated to have been about one thousand paying subscribers.[43]

The freethought content of the *New Harmony Gazette* often takes a backseat to social reform and community business, but it has some moments of prominence. One of them is a transcript of an address that Owen delivered to the community on the Fourth of July 1826, which he called a "declaration of mental independence." In it, after appropriately commemorating the fiftieth anniversary of American independence, he declared mental independence from "a trinity of the most monstrous evils. . . . I refer to private, or individual property—absurd and irrational systems of religion—and marriage, founded on individual property combined with some of these irrational systems of religion." "All religions have proven themselves to be superstitions," he continued, that enslave the believer "through the fear of nonentities created solely by his own disordered imagination."[44] This address was indeed revolutionary for Owen, who had not used such strong rhetoric against religion before.[45] The remarks about marriage are among the earliest articulations in America of the free love position. Owen held that marriage was a contract between human beings, not a divine institution, and that such a contract should be able to be easily dissolved when it no longer served the interests of both parties: "It is a law of nature that our affections are not at the control of our will . . . it should be as reputable, and equally authorized by law, to dissolve marriage . . . when the union promises to produce more misery than happiness."[46] The issue of the *New Harmony Gazette* in which Owen's declaration of mental independence appeared also declared independence from the Christian calendar. Rather than simply giving the standard date as all previous issues did, it was dated "Fifty First Year of American Independence" and "First Year of Mental Independence" and "July 12, 1826, of the Christian Era." This style of dating, in imitation of the calendar of the French Revolution, is clearly intended to decenter the Christian calendar. Although references to mental independence disappeared in later years, the paper continued its post-Christian dating practices for as long as it was published. After the paper became *The Free Enquirer*, freethought became more dominant in it. The paper developed a more robust social reform agenda than Palmer's *Prospect* or Houston's *Correspondent*, printing items favorable to the separation of church and state, women's rights, and marriage liberalization. Its separationist pieces opposed legislative chaplains, judicial oaths, mandatory Sabbath observances, and blasphemy laws.[47]

Owenite freethinkers and their publications had a profound effect on the direction of the American freethought movement, reframing the movement in ways that aligned it with labor, abolition, and feminism. This shift is already apparent in Owen's Declaration of Mental Independence, where religion is just one of the trinity of evils that oppress humankind. While Paineite freethinkers like Benjamin Offen and George Houston were content to speak out against the divine authority of scripture and clear the way for scientific progress, Owenites went a step further and tried to reform the inequalities of property and sexual relations that scripture had been used to justify. In the 1820s and 1830s few freethinkers did this more actively than Frances Wright, who combined a vision of a republic united by a devotion to science rather than religion with a strong urge to correct injustices that had been perpetuated against workers, women, and the enslaved.

Frances Wright: Utopian Abolitionist and Apostle of Science

Frances Wright was one of the most luminous of the British activists who immigrated to the United States in the early nineteenth century. She is honored today as a pioneering feminist and abolitionist who was the first woman to go on a public speaking tour in America, but she also should be remembered for carrying forward Paine's vision for science by promoting secular scientific education for both women and men. One of the more overlooked projects of her career was to establish "halls of science" in population centers across the country. These were to be public institutions that were meant, in a new way, to realize *Age of Reason*'s dream of replacing the "false theology" of revealed religion with science. But, in addition to pursuing this project that was so much in keeping with *Age of Reason* and the Paineite freethought tradition, she forged new connections between freethought, feminism, and abolitionism, rebranded the movement as centering on "free enquiry" rather than "deism," and chose not to embrace the fervent antiscripturalism of freethinkers such as Paine, Palmer, and Offen.

Wright was born in Dundee, Scotland, in 1795. Reform ran in her blood, although she never knew her parents. Her father, James Wright, Jr., was from a wealthy merchant family with deep roots in the region, and her mother, Camilla Campbell Wright, was related to the Campbells of Argyll and to English nobles.[48] James had been afforded an excellent education by the family fortune and grew into a reform-minded numismatist who argued that coins should bear emblems of commerce and industry rather than "silly morsels of heraldry."[49] He admired Thomas Paine and the ideals of the French Revolution and promoted a cheap publication of *The Rights of Man* in 1794. Consequently, according to Frances's autobiography, he "became an object of government espionage."[50] Wright had a younger sister, Camilla, and a younger brother, Richard. In 1798, when Wright was two and a half, her mother and father both died within three months of each other, and she was sent to England to grow up in the household of her maternal grandfather, Major General Duncan Campbell, as the ward of her mother's maiden sister, also named Frances. In this wealthy Tory household, by her own account, she was "surrounded at all times by rare and extensive libraries" and was tutored in any subject she wished to learn. Writing of her childhood in the third person, Wright recalls that she "applied herself by turns to various branches of science and to the study of ancient and modern letters and the arts."[51] Her brother was raised by her father's uncle, who was a professor at the University of Glasgow, and enlisted in the service of the East India Company as a cadet at the age of fifteen. Sadly, he was killed in an encounter with a French vessel before ever reaching India.[52]

Wright and her sister acquired sizable personal fortunes in 1803 when Major William Campbell, their mother's brother, was killed in action in India, leaving each of his nieces a quarter of his estate and his surviving sister, who was Frances Wright's guardian, the remaining half. Camilla, Wright's sister, had been brought up by foster parents in Dundee. But she joined Wright in England in 1806 after she and her guardian aunt had moved to a twenty-room "cottage" in the coastal village of Dawlish.[53] The two sisters quickly formed a tight bond. Camilla would accompany Frances on most of her future adventures for as long as she lived. Although cheered by the reunion with her sister, Wright longed to escape the stuffy confines of her gilded cage. At a young age she had happened across a reference to the American Revolution, but nowhere in the libraries of classical works that surrounded her or among the social connections that she was permitted was she able to satisfy her curiosity about how the American experiment in republican government was turning out, or for that matter find any sympathetic account of the French Revolution.

When she was eighteen, Wright was allowed to visit her father's uncle in Glasgow, the "liberal, amicable, talented, and extensively known" Professor James Mylne, who had been "the most confidential friend" of her father.[54] It was from him that she learned of her father's true political views, which agreed remarkably with those that she was developing. Through him she gained access to the Glasgow University library, where she was shown to a "remote and little-frequented compartment" filled with "volumes and pamphlets from floor to ceiling . . . all that had ever appeared in print respecting the American colonies."[55] Intellectually famished for information about the country that had long been the subject of her intense curiosity, she devoted herself to reading it all. She had far more freedom living with her great-uncle in Glasgow than she had formerly living with her aunt in England. She stayed for three years, touring the Highlands and the Lowlands when she wasn't studying, writing plays, and composing a piece of literary fiction that purported to be the translation of a Greek manuscript discovered in Herculaneum. She later published it under the title *A Few Days in Athens* (1822). The work demonstrated her affinity with the Greek philosopher Epicurus, who is a central figure. Epicurus was said to be the first ancient Greek philosopher to accept women as students, and a female student portrayed in *A Few Days* seems to be modeled on Wright herself. *A Few Days in Athens* may signal Wright's attraction to the neo-Epicurean school of thought that had been allied with the Radical Enlightenment since the rediscovery of Lucretius's Epicurean poem *De Rerum Natura* in the sixteenth century.[56] Despite these intellectual adventures, Wright longed to see the wider world, especially America. In 1818, she made secret plans to voyage to America with her sister Camilla. She made the financial arrangements for the trip herself and told no one save one female confidant as well as Professor Mylne, and she told the professor only when she was just about to depart, after it was too late to stop her.[57]

Wright's trip to America brought her more eventual success than anyone could have foreseen. She and her sister toured the country for two years. During this time, she finished writing a play called *Altorf: A Tragedy*, about the Swiss struggle for independence from Austria, and saw it produced in New York in 1819 and Philadelphia in 1820.[58] This brought her some fame, but her book, *Views on Society and Manners in America*, would do more to change her life. It was a collection of twenty-eight letters written to an anonymous friend in England, perhaps the confidant with whom she had shared her travel plans. The letters were filled with Wright's astute observations about the politics, sociology, and the landscape of America. Published in 1821, the book was predictably panned by Tory reviewers, but so impressed English utilitarian philosopher and reformer Jeremy Bentham that he recommended it to friends and invited Wright many times to dinner at his London home, known as the Hermitage. Bentham introduced Wright to his circle of reformist friends, which included Robert Owen and James Mill. James Mill was, along with Bentham, a leading light of the utilitarian movement in British philosophy and an advocate of political reform. His son, John Stuart Mill, would follow in his footsteps, but he was only fifteen in 1821. Wright, for a time, became for the unmarried and childless Bentham the protégée that these other reformers had in their sons. Bentham's utilitarianism became Wright's personal ethic. She also was impressed by Robert Owen's plans for utopian communities.[59]

Wright's association with Bentham and his circle, and the usefulness of her book to Europeans curious for a sympathetic account of the American experiment, helped gain her a following on the continent that included some very prominent admirers. In 1821, she accepted an invitation from the Marquis de Lafayette to visit him in France. Lafayette had languished in an Austrian prison from 1792—when he had abandoned his position in the Revolutionary army after the storming of the Tuileries Palace and the deposition of the king—until 1797, when Napoléon negotiated his release after defeating the forces of the First Coalition. He was able to return to France after Napoléon became consul, but he remained a staunch constitutional republican in politics, and he did not lend his support to either Napoléon or to the Bourbon monarchy when it was restored in 1815. A relationship between Wright and the "venerable soldier of liberty" developed into one that Wright described as "a friendship of no ordinary character," saying that she "possessed his most intimate private, and political confidence."[60] Soon Wright and her sister became frequent guests at the Chateau La Grange, the country estate the general had inherited from his wife, who had passed away in 1807. In 1824, Lafayette declined Wright's suggestion of marriage but did so in a way that did not alienate her.[61]

In 1824, President Monroe and Congress invited Lafayette to visit the United States. Wright and her sister followed him as he toured the country in 1824 and 1825, although they did not stay strictly in his train. They stayed on in America when he returned to France. As Wright toured the southern states, and especially after a visit with Jefferson at Monticello, where Lafayette spoke strongly against slavery, she became deeply concerned with the slavery issue.[62] As Wright visited New Harmony and the new Rappite community of Economy in Pennsylvania, she began to form a plan she thought would end slavery in the United States.[63]

By the time Lafayette returned to France in September 1825, Wright's plan to end slavery had matured. The United States had banned the importation of enslaved people from other nations in 1808, but they could still be bought and sold within the country. Influenced by her discussions with southern plantation owners, Wright believed that the inexperience of enslaved Africans in directing their own affairs was as serious an obstacle to the abolition of slavery as was the dependence of the economy on enslaved labor. Enslaved people needed a period of "moral, intellectual, and industrial apprenticeship" before they would be ready for full enfranchisement.[64] She thought such an apprenticeship could be provided in a utopian community like New Harmony.

Inspired by New Harmony and Economy, Wright planned a utopian community where enslaved people could get an education that would prepare them for freedom. She called it Nashoba, which is the Chickasaw word for "wolf," because it was on the Wolf River in western Tennessee, about fifteen miles east of Memphis. She hoped that slavery could be ended by paying plantation owners for their enslaved workers, who would then be resettled in communities like Nashoba, where they would learn to read and write, to farm independently, and to work in useful trades. Nashoba was meant to generate profits that would be used to buy out more of the enslaved, who would be placed in similar communities that would generate more profits to buy out still more enslaved people until all enslaved people had been bought out, educated, and emancipated. Although Wright got moral support from Thomas Jefferson,[65] and land acquisition advice from Andrew Jackson,[66] she needed to fund the expense of buying enslaved families and land for the community from her own fortune. She appointed ten trustees, who included herself and Camilla, Lafayette, Robert and Robert Dale Owen, and other veterans of New Harmony.[67] The trustees created a scheme where the enslaved inhabitants, who were never more than twenty in number, would buy their freedom in five years, during which time they would have been educated.

Wright labored to make the community prosper, but there were many difficulties to overcome. Land was cleared and a walled compound was built of logs, but, due to a lack of funding, the promised school was never completed, and the workers of the community remained enslaved as the trustees thought was best. The site of Nashoba was swampy. Wright, her sister, and other members of the community were often seriously ill, very likely with malaria. After a serious bout of illness in 1827, Wright left Nashoba under the charge of her sister and two of the trustees, James Richardson and Richeson Whitby, and sailed for Europe accompanied by Robert Dale Owen, who had become friends with her during her visits to New Harmony. The object of the trip was to recover her health and enlist more support for her enterprise. In her absence, as reported in the abolitionist newspaper the *Genius of Universal Emancipation*, Richardson began punishing men and women with the lash, and Camilla Wright, who did not share her sister's commanding personality, did not stop him.[68] This was only one of the scandals that thwarted future attempts at fundraising. On her voyage home, Wright composed a defense of the ideals that she believed should guide Nashoba, *Explanatory Notes, Respecting the Nature and Objects of the Institution of Nashoba, and of the Principles Upon Which It Is Founded*. In it, she doubled down on her principles, arguing that, once educated, formerly enslaved people of African descent would be able to participate socially and politically on equal terms in the United States.[69] But by the time she got back to Nashoba, it was in disarray. Richardson had left, and her sister had married Whitby, the other trustee she had left in charge. Soon Camilla became pregnant and left for the more healthful environs of a small house in Memphis.[70]

Wright brought the project to an end in early 1830, when she chartered a ship and sailed with the enslaved residents of Nashoba from New Orleans to Haiti, a republic that had outlawed slavery. In Haiti, Wright finally emancipated the Nashobans, and they were generously resettled by President Jean-Pierre Boyer.[71] When all was said and done, although the Nashobans had not received much that might be considered a useful "apprenticeship," Wright had bought the freedom of some twenty enslaved human beings and found a way that they could start new lives with good prospects. But Wright had planned to start a franchisable utopian community that would gradually bring about the end of slavery while preparing enslaved people for freedom, and this plan lay in tatters, a victim of malaria, of socially ingrained cruelty toward Blacks even among professed abolitionists, and of a widespread disinclination to invest in the dream.

As the Nashoba community was entering its final years, Wright began a career as a public lecturer, a career that was unprecedented for any woman in America. It was launched with a Fourth of July address at New Harmony Hall in 1828, where two years before Robert Owen had declared "mental independence." This speech has been described as the first address given by a woman to a mixed-gender crowd at a public ceremony in America.[72] In front of a New Harmony crowd that was naturally sympathetic to her person and her principles, Wright delivered a subtle and original Fourth of July address that distinguished between vainglorious "patriotism," a term with which she did not have much sympathy, and true love of country. Rather than joining the parade of mere patriotism, "It is for Americans . . . to nourish a nobler sentiment . . . to know why they love their country, and to *feel* they love it, not because it is their country, but because it is a palladium of human liberty, the favor'd scene of human improvement."[73] In Wright's lexicon, Paine's "rights of man" had become "human liberty," a term that gracefully included Black and brown people and women. More subtly, Wright hoped that the United States would become a "palladium" of human liberty. Palladium is a silvery-white metallic element that had only been discovered in 1803 and was named after the asteroid Pallas, whose name refers to the Athenian goddess Pallas Athena.

When she spoke on public occasions Wright often assumed an appearance that was reminiscent of a Greek goddess like Athena, and also of the women who had portrayed the goddess Reason at Feasts of Reason during the French Revolution. Wright's friend, the English travel writer and novelist Frances Milton Trollope, could be scathingly critical of anyone, friend or foe, who did not live up to her standards of taste. She had only radiant things to say about Wright's persona as a public speaker: "It is impossible to imagine anything more striking than her appearance. Her tall and majestic figure, the deep and almost solemn expression of her eyes, the simple contour of her finely formed head, unadorned excepting by its own natural ringlets; her garment of plain white muslin, which hung around her in folds that recalled the drapery of a Grecian statue, all contributed to produce an effect unlike anything I had ever seen before, or ever expect to see again."[74]

As successful as her New Harmony speech was, Wright was preaching to the choir there. She was more interested in social change than mere applause, so she started touring. She gave a series of three lectures in August in the courthouse of Cincinnati.[75] She would go on to speak in Philadelphia, New York, Boston, Baltimore, St. Louis, and Boston among other cities and towns.[76] Wright gave speeches in many contexts and for many occasions. She delivered orations for the Fourth of July and for Paine's birthday.[77] She also at least once joined Offen in addressing the Society of Moral Philanthropists at Tammany Hall on Sundays.[78] But the mainstay of her lecture tour was a series of three speeches delivered on successive nights. The first was an extended definition of knowledge, as opposed to belief rooted in faith or hope; the second concerned the necessity of free inquiry for the attainment of knowledge; the third discussed the good that could arise from knowledge and ended with a call for the creation of a "hall of science ... where the citizens of all ages may assemble for the acquisition of useful knowledge, and for the cultivation of that social feeling and brotherly fellowship without which no real republic can have an existence."[79] The speech goes on to describe an institution that sounds very much like a free public university, a lecture space that would be integrated with museums and libraries, and a school of industry like the one in New Harmony. All this could be accomplished if citizens would spend just a small portion of the $20 million that she estimated Americans spent yearly on building churches and maintaining clergy. "Turn your churches into halls of science," she enjoined her hearers, subtly alluding to the dechristianization of the French Revolution.[80] Wright's lectures were always well attended by previous converts to the freethought movement, newly minted doubters, and many who were simply curious to see a woman speak in public. In many cases they spurred the formation of Fanny Wright Societies that raised funds to build halls of science.[81] Soon Wright would create her own hall of science in New York City.

As Wright's fame increased, she and Robert Dale Owen maintained the comradeship that had developed between them during their days of utopian experimentation and travels in Europe, and they undertook a number of new joint enterprises.[82] One was to keep the *New Harmony Gazette* going. In October of 1828 co-editors Wright and Owen, together with Robert L. Jennings, revived the journal as the *New Harmony and Nashoba Gazette, or, The Free Enquirer*, a weekly journal published on Wednesdays.[83] It was printed at the School of Industry in New Harmony. They continued the *Gazette* at New Harmony until the end of February 1829. With the March 4, 1829, issue, the paper shortened its title to *The Free Enquirer* and announced its place of publication to be New York City.[84] In this issue appear a printed version of one and a half lectures from the series that Wright had given at the Park Theater beginning at the end of the previous January, and later issues would carry the rest. This began the period of Wright's most intense engagement with the New York scene, a period that brought her into contact with those who were carrying on in the tradition of the Deistical Society.

Soon after relocating to New York, Wright followed her own advice to turn churches into halls of science. Sometime in March, she bought the defunct Ebenezer Baptist Church on Bloom Street and began the renovations that would transform it.[85] On Sunday, April 12, the new Hall of Science had an open house where visitors could sign up to attend Sunday classes on "mathematics, astronomy, natural history, reading, writing, composing, and public speaking."[86] The classes were open to all women and men, a quietly revolutionary arrangement. The announcement was brilliantly timed to coincide with the publication of the final lecture in Wright's series in *The Free Enquirer*, where she called upon listeners to "take for your teachers experimental philosophers, not spiritual dreamers. Turn your churches into halls of science, and devote your leisure day to the study of your own bodies, the analysis of your own minds, and the examination of the fair material world that extends around you!"[87]

The Hall of Science had its grand opening on Sunday, April 26, with Wright giving the dedication speech. As in other speeches, in this one Wright portrays religion as divisive and the scientific pursuit of knowledge as a project that could bring social and political unity. The idea, promoted by Paine, that creation is the only kind of truth that is universally available to all humankind is foundational to Wright's view of science. The Hall of Science was as much an attempt to realize a vision of science as the "theology that is true" as the Deistical Society had been, but Wright tried to avoid the confrontational antiscripturalism of Paine, Palmer, and Offen in carrying out this project. Where Paine had written that purveyors of revealed religion are "not bold enough to be honest, nor honest enough to be bold," Wright wrote that followers of science should be "honest enough to reveal what they know, and bold enough to be silent (for, alas! In these days of error even silence may be a crime;) bold enough, I say, to be silent where they are ignorant."[88] Later she elaborated,

> I would apply this exhortation equally to the sceptic as to the believer, and to the believer as to the sceptic. Are we believers? Let us believe as we may, but let us believe peacefully, in the depths of the heart, that our belief offend not that of our neighbor. Do we see with the eye of faith? Let us see what we may and dream what we will, but let us dream at home. In our own closets be our worship, whether of god or gods, saints, angels, prophets, or blessed virgins; but here—here in the hall of union, sacred to peace and to knowledge, let us study that book which all can read, and reading, none dispute—the field of nature, and the tablet of the human mind.

Paine had been an enemy of national churches and a champion of freedom of belief, but in his worldview, and in his experience, religious belief was never a completely private matter. Citizens could, and should, hold each other publicly accountable for their beliefs. Paine confronted the religiously orthodox for ignoring the God-given voice of reason, and they confronted him for his "infidelity." In contrast, Wright said, "Let us . . . dream what we will, but let us dream at home." While Benjamin Offen was still exposing the contradictions of scripture in his lectures at Tammany Hall, Wright's Hall of Science would give people the option of learning about a range of useful subjects on Sundays while others worshiped, but it would not host religious discussions of any kind. Wright had abandoned the project of rationalizing religion that had been so central to Paine, and she simply sought to create a public space for science that was free from religion, an approach that is still common in our own time. It is unclear whether Wright sought to create a similar ethos in the Society of Free Enquirers, a freethought organization she established around this same time. It appears that some chapters did host religious discussions. A speech delivered to the Boston chapter of the Society of Free Enquirers proclaimed that the society was opposed to doctrines and not religions.[89]

Wright discussed her views on the separation of church and state in an October 1829 speech given at the Hall of Science on the topic of the Sunday mails controversy. As early as 1809 Christian activists began protesting the fact that some rural post offices remained open on Sunday to allow country folk to drop off and collect mail when they came to town for church. Some Christians saw this as a violation of the commandment to "keep holy the Sabbath." During a resurgence of the controversy in 1829 Wright implied that she did not think religion could long survive in America without government support and cautioned against attempts by desperate clergy to end the separation of church and state:

> In Europe the pride of the priesthood runs high, for it is backed by the power of Kings.... In England, secure in a church fast welded to the state, they can set at naught the doubts of the heretic or the lukewarm zeal of their own followers—fattening equally on the tithe of Jew as of the Christian, of Sceptic as of full Believer.... The priest of America, on the other hand, stands in the power of his craft alone to protect an alter robbed of its main supports—a King, nobility, and standing army; without the power of setting bayonets in motion, of instigating massacres, or even of enclosing within prison walls the friends of peace and common sense ... the alter must replace the constitution in these [United] states, or the alter must fall; the two are in direct opposition. And well does the Priest know, and fully does he understand the discrepancy. Deeply in the depth of his heart has he sworn to effect a counter revolution by wedding church and state, in this land, blessed by liberty, or, in his failure, to pull after him the whole fabric of superstition.

As it turned out, the prospects of religion in America were not nearly as bleak as Wright imagined, nor were clergy quite so desperate.[90]

Around the time she was establishing the Hall of Science, co-editing *The Free Enquirer*, and establishing the Society of Free Enquirers, Wright and Robert Dale Owen also became involved in the short-lived but influential

Workingmen's Party. The party's first leader was a mechanic named Thomas Skidmore. His reputation as a political leader was built on his radical 1829 pamphlet, *The Rights of Man to Property! Being a Proposition to Make It Equal Among the Adults of the Present Generation, and to Provide for Its Equal Transmission to Every Individual of Each Succeeding Generation on Arriving at the Age of Maturity*. It is a mark of Paine's continuing influence that Skidmore evokes him in the title and praises him in the text, before setting out a proposal more radical than anything Paine ever contemplated: a total and equal redistribution of all real estate and the abolition of inherited wealth. Skidmore reasons that all humans must have been granted an equal portion of the world at the creation, and that any inequalities that have arisen since must be due to injustice. He criticizes Paine for allowing there to have the rich and poor people already in existence when the first governments came to be. If those first governments allowed some to claim more of the common inheritance of all humanity than others, they could not have been just governments. "How is it then that a writer so sagacious as Paine . . . should have committed such a blunder, as that of attempting to erect an equal government, upon a foundation where inequality had already found an existence, and that without attempting to extirpate it?"[91]

Skidmore's demand for the redistribution of property was the most radical plank of the platform of the party of workingmen that formed around him. Other demands included the passage of a mechanic's lien law, which would allow workers to legally claim property they have worked to improve if the owners did not pay them what had been contractually agreed to, the abolishment of debtors' prison, and legal guarantees of a ten-hour working day. The new party commenced its organizing meeting on April 23, 1829, and by October they had hammered out their platform, which now included a demand for universal free education that had been the addition of Robert Dale Owen, who had become secretary of the organization. Owen was promoting a version of an idea that Wright had been championing in her lectures, that free and universal education would quickly lift up the lower classes and create a more equal society. It was widely recognized that Owen's main contributions were inspired by Wright, who could not herself fully participate in party politics because of her sex. The new party succeeded in winning one seat in the State Assembly in November of 1829 in competition against Tammany Hall and the National Republican Party. The Owens-Wright position on education soon became the rallying cry of the moderate majority of the Workingmen, and Skidmore's property redistribution plank was abandoned.

Skidmore left the party to form his own Agrarian Party. By 1830 the now-divided Workingmen's Party lost prominence as Tammany Hall regained its strength in city politics and the Democratic Party (which had evolved directly from the Democratic-Republican Party) swept state-level elections. The Workingmen's Party soon disappeared as a political entity but could claim some real successes. This is because Tammany and the state Democratic Party had won partly through adopting elements of the Workingmen's platform and rapidly implementing the reforms: a mechanics' lien law passed the state legislature in 1830, debtors' prison was abolished in 1831, and appropriations for education were increased.[92]

Skidmore's use of Paine's legacy to back his property redistribution scheme shows how Paine's name was sometimes appropriated by actors on the far left, but a better idea of how the people who gathered to celebrate Paine's birthday were exercising their stewardship of his legacy can be learned by looking at the records of who they toasted at those birthdays. The February 9, 1833, issue of *The Free Enquirer* carried extensive coverage of the January 29 Paine birthday celebration at Tammany Hall. Among the toasts were one by J. P. Clark concerning churches and chapels: "May they be converted into Temples of the Sciences, and the Philosopher be cherished instead of the Priest."[93] This is nearly a quotation from one of Wright's speeches, save that the hall has become a temple. Soon after "A Free Enquirer," probably a member of the organization Wright had started, offered a toast to "the cause": "That cause for which Paine braved the power of a vindictive clergy, for which Carlile and Taylor have suffered years of imprisonment, for which Cooper has been wantonly persecuted, and to which a Wright, an Owen, and many other distinguished characters have devoted the prime of their lives. It must and shall prosper."[94] Wright was acknowledged as a leader of "the cause" that the Paine birthday celebrants all believed they served, and the issues she brought to it—female education and property rights, the abolition of slavery, and fair treatment of workers—influenced the future direction of the movement.

Abner Kneeland: Blasphemy Law Martyr

The freethought movement found inspiration in the boldness of Paine's *Age of Reason* but also took a lesson from what it had cost him, viewing Paine as someone who had willingly sacrificed his good name and the tranquility of his declining years to further the cause of freethought. Everyone who became prominent as a freethinker to some degree suffered the same disparagements that Paine had. A few freethinkers endured worse than Paine in that they were prosecuted for their beliefs and given prison sentences, further strengthening the tradition of sacrificing for the cause of freethought and motivating freethinkers with anger at the injustice of their treatment. Because they looked at sex as a biological function and marriage as a human institution, some freethinkers ran afoul of obscenity laws, which deemed any discussion of sex "obscene," even if it was medical advice about sex and contraception for married people. Dr. Charles Knowlton was a medical doctor whose *The Fruits of Philosophy, or, the Private Companion of Young Married People* gave medical advice on contraception and sex.[95] Its publication landed him in a Massachusetts jail for three months in 1832. Knowlton fought back by helping to found the United States Moral and Philosophical Society for the General Diffusion of Useful Knowledge in 1836, whose purpose included defending the right to diffuse useful medical knowledge about sex and reproduction. But although Knowlton's case was well known, it was those freethinkers who faced prosecution for blasphemy that were most clearly emblematic of the persecution of freethought. The most well-known "blasphemy law martyr" of the first half of the nineteenth century was Abner Kneeland.

As someone who followed his conscience through a lifetime of theological transformations, Abner Kneeland was a freethinker in the fullest and best sense. The son of a carpenter, he was born in Massachusetts in 1774. As a young man he worked in the family trade, as well as being a schoolteacher and spelling book compiler. He joined a Baptist congregation in Vermont in 1801 and began preaching to it in 1802. In 1803, he met Hosea Ballou, a Universalist preacher with a streak of Unitarianism who believed freethought offered a healthy challenge to Christianity and was not nearly as wrong as Calvinism.[96] Kneeland adopted a similar Unitarian Universalist theology and won a good name in the New England Universalist General Convention, eventually establishing himself at a Boston-area church in 1811. However, his doubts about even the broadly liberal theology of his fellow Universalists caused him to renounce the ministry and start a dry goods business with his wife. Ballou persuaded the popular minister to return to his fold.[97] Between 1816 and 1829, Kneeland preached to congregations at Whitestown, New York, Philadelphia, and New York City, but his theology continued to evolve toward materialistic pantheism, especially after he became friendly with Robert Owen and Frances Wright in New York City.[98] He invited Wright to speak to his congregation before once again resigning from the ministry in 1829 and joining Wright's Society of Free Enquirers.[99]

The Society of Free Enquirers granted Kneeland a small salary to lecture regularly to its Boston chapter in 1831, and he rapidly became a star of the freethought movement. In 1831 he started the highly successful freethought paper, the *Boston Investigator*, sharing the editorship with Frances Wright from 1837 to 1838. New York freethinkers sometimes mocked Kneeland's teetotaling, alcohol-less celebrations of Paine's birthday, but they admired his success in building a freethinking community. His lectures in New England and New York drew hundreds of people, and his paper achieved a circulation of more than 2,000, twice that of *The Free Enquirer*.[100]

Kneeland might have pursued his chosen career of freethought lecturing and publishing unmolested if he had been able to stay in New York City or if he was sent to one of the frontier territories, but Massachusetts had traditionally been committed to keeping any heterodoxy within the broad boundaries of Congregationalism. It is perhaps not a coincidence that Kneeland ran into trouble in 1833, the year that Massachusetts ended state funding for Congregational churches and anxiety about the future of orthodox Protestantism in the state ran high. Late in the year several articles Kneeland published in the *Investigator*, and one that he both wrote and published, drew censure from the authorities. The articles he had merely published, "On the Soul," "On Faith," and "On Prejudice," were eventually dropped from the case because it could not be proven he had knowledge of their contents. The focus of the prosecution came to be on the article Kneeland himself had written, which was an explanation of his theological differences with Universalism:

> I still hold to universal philanthropy, universal benevolence, and universal charity. In these respects, I am still a Universalist. Neither do I believe in punishment after death, so in this also I agree with the Universalists. But as it respects all other of their religious notions in relation to another world, or a supposed other state of conscious existence, I do not believe in any of them; so that in this respect I am no more a universalist than I am an orthodox Christian. As for instance,
> 1. Universalists believe in a god which I do not; but believe that their god, with all his moral attributes, (aside from nature itself,) is nothing more than a chimera of their own imagination.

2. Universalists believe in Christ which I do not; but believe that the whole story concerning him is as much a fable and a fiction, as that of the god Prometheus, the tragedy of whose death is said to have been acted on the stage in the theatre at Athens, 500 years before the Christian era.
3. Universalists believe in miracles which I do not; but believe that every pretension to them can either be accounted for on natural principles or else is to be attributed to mere trick and imposture.
4. Universalists believe in the resurrection of the dead, in immortality and eternal life, which I do not; but believe that all life is mortal, that death is an eternal extinction of life to the individual who possesses it, and that no individual life is, ever was, or ever will be eternal.[101]

It was charged that in writing and printing this statement, Kneeland had violated a Massachusetts antiblasphemy statute dating from 1782, which imposed a penalty of up to two years in prison plus a $300 fine on any person who "shall willfully blaspheme the holy name of God by denying, cursing, or contumeliously reproaching God, his creation, government, or final judging of the world."[102] Kneeland contended that he had not blasphemed because he had not denied the existence of God. He believed that God is nature, and he had not denied the existence of nature. Instead, he had professed his disbelief in the particular idea of God held by Universalists. He further contended that even if he had violated it, the Massachusetts statute on blasphemy was in violation of the Massachusetts constitution of 1780, which stated that "no subject shall be hurt, molested, or restrained, in his person, liberty, or estate, for worshipping God in the manner and season most agreeable to the dictates of his own conscience, or for his religious profession or sentiments, provided he doth not disturb the public peace or obstruct others in their religious worship."[103] Kneeland also asserted that the blasphemy law was unconstitutional because it violated the freedom of the press guaranteed by the Massachusetts constitution.

Kneeland went through four trials defending his right to write and publish his true thoughts on religion. After a conviction and a hung jury on the appeal in 1834, he lost his second appeal in 1735.[104] The most dramatic summation of the case against him was delivered by the prosecutor, Mr. Parker, in the second trial, who linked him to Frances Wright and warned the jury of the dire consequences of giving an inch to her "system" by failing to convict Kneeland of blasphemy:

And now, gentlemen, I leave you to do your duty. I hope I have done mine. If open, gross, palpable and indecent blasphemy, and all the consequences of the Fanny Wright system—atheism, community of property, unlimited lasciviousness, adultery, and the thousand evils of infidelity, receive no check, the reproach will not fall on me. . . . Look then with care, gentlemen, to your great responsibility in this trial, to your duty and to your verdict. Take care that this day you offend not God, nor injure man, that you violate not the law, and the constitution; that your children rise not up in judgment against you, and that you avoid the maledictions of the world.[105]

But if feeling against Kneeland ran high, so did support. Unitarian minister William Ellery Channing, abolitionist William Lloyd Garrison, transcendentalists Theodore Parker and Ralph Waldo Emerson were among the 170 prominent supporters who signed a petition calling on the governor to pardon Kneeland.[106]

The Massachusetts Supreme Court made the final ruling against Kneeland in 1838. Kneeland represented himself in this proceeding. Writing for the majority, Chief Justice Lemuel Shaw defended the constitutionality of the Massachusetts blasphemy law at length, citing antecedent colonial blasphemy laws and blasphemy law then in force in New Hampshire, Vermont, Maine, and New York. He pointed out that a New York blasphemy law had been upheld as constitutional by the New York Supreme Court in *The People v. Ruggles* (1811) despite that state's robust constitutional protections of religious liberty. He used an original intent argument without any textual backing to uphold the constitutionality of the blasphemy statute in Massachusetts, saying, "It is impossible to believe that the authors of this article [protecting religious liberty] intended to prohibit the legislature from reenacting a [blasphemy] law, which had been in force from the first settlement of the country, a law thought essential to preserve the sanction of oaths, prescribed and required in every clause almost of the constitution, and which had hitherto been deemed essential to the peace and safety of society."[107] The ruling held that general constitutional guarantees of religious freedom don't protect blasphemy because blasphemy is a threat to the "peace and safety of society." Kneeland's appeal was denied, but the court apparently had some respect for Kneeland's argument, as he was sentenced to only sixty days in jail, far less than the maximum of two years.

Although Kneeland lost his case, he won a tremendous amount of sympathy for himself and for the freethought cause through the continuing coverage of the legal battle in the *Boston Investigator*, whose circulation was driven to new heights by the controversy. The *Iowa News* bemoaned that Kneeland, known as the editor of the *Investigator* even on the Iowa frontier, would spend the anniversary of the Battle of Bunker Hill in jail: "What a spectacle was there for a freeman to witness! A grey-headed man of three score years, against whom naught but the charge of blasphemy has been made, torn from his family, and like a felon, locked in a prison, while the *supposed* freemen are rejoicing midst the deaf'ning peals of the wide-mouth'd cannons' roar in honor of the triumph of the American flag."[108] The case also succeeded in getting the strong dissenting opinion of Justice Marcus Morton against the constitutionality of the blasphemy statute into the legal record. When Kneeland was released from jail on August 17, 1838, a crowd of some three hundred freethinkers were there to celebrate and called on him for a speech. But the experience had soured him on Boston, and the next year he and his family and close followers traveled west and established a community called Salubria on land they had purchased in the southeastern part of the Iowa Territory. He lived there until he died in 1844. His *Boston Investigator* continued to thrive in his absence, publishing until 1901, when it was absorbed by *The Truth Seeker*.[109]

Commemorating Paine: William Cobbett and Gilbert Vale

In addition to rallying around persecuted contemporaries, freethinkers in the first half of the nineteenth century continued to be knit together by the commemoration of the author of *The Age of Reason*. Commemoration took the form not only of the annual Paine birthday celebrations but also attempts to build a monument in honor of him. The first attempt made to honor Paine with a memorial was undertaken by an adversary-turned-admirer named William Cobbett in 1819, and it turned out to be spectacularly ill fated. However, a successful campaign to build a memorial for Paine came to fruition in 1839. Its organizer was Gilbert Vale, editor of a freethought periodical called *The Beacon*. He also commemorated Paine by writing a sympathetic biography that tried to counter the distortions and errors of his earlier defamatory biographers.

William Cobbett, who made the first ill-fated attempt to build a monument for Paine, was born in Surrey, England, in 1762 (or 1763). Cobbett embarked on a career in the military as a young man but found it prudent to flee England for France in 1792 after he published a pamphlet protesting the poor pay and living conditions endured by common soldiers.[110] He spent some happy months in the French countryside and was on his way to Paris in August 1792 when he heard of the storming of the Tuileries, the massacre of the Swiss Guards, and the deposition of the king. These events turned him against the "accursed Revolution" for many years to come.[111] He immediately resolved to leave for America, where he was drawn to the Federalist side in politics largely because of the anti-British tone of the Democratic-Republicans and because of their continuing support of the French Revolution. When the scientist and Unitarian minister Joseph Priestley arrived in America after his home had been burned by a royalist mob in Birmingham, Cobbett ridiculed him in a 1794 pamphlet.[112] Gaining a following among Federalists, Cobbett opened a bookstore in Philadelphia and began publishing a Federalist-leaning paper, *The Censor*, which was succeeded by *Porcupine's Gazette*, so called because Cobbett's needle-sharp wit had earned him the nom de plume Peter Porcupine.[113] Like many others, he published attacks on Paine's *Age of Reason*.[114] Cobbett's fortunes took a bad turn after he wrote against Benjamin Rush, the Philadelphia physician, for his conduct during a 1797 outbreak of yellow fever, charging that his practice of bleeding patients had cured no one and in fact cost many lives. Although Rush was following an established medical practice, this was very possibly true. It was at least true that bleeding had cured no one. Nonetheless, Rush sued Cobbett for libel and won a judgment of about $8,000.[115] Rather than pay the settlement, which he considered unjust, Cobbett returned to England, where his previous transgression had been forgotten, and resumed his publishing career. His new journal, *Cobbett's Weekly Political Register*, often gave voice to his hopes for British political reform, and this led to trouble. He served two years in prison after criticizing the flogging of soldiers and in 1817 he fled back to America rather than face another trial for libel.[116]

Over the years Cobbett became more sympathetic to Paine's ideas. He was particularly struck by how well Paine's *Decline and Fall of the English System of Finance* had foretold the problems caused by bank-issued paper notes that had come to plague both the United States and Britain.[117] In 1819, he felt that enough time had passed that he could safely return to England once again. He determined to take with him the earthly remains of Thomas Paine, because he thought the revolutionary deserved a more honorable resting place than the neglected grave in New Rochelle. Before setting sail, he traveled to New Rochelle, dug up Paine's coffin, and had it loaded onto the ship that would take him from New York to Liverpool. He wrote of the exploit in his *Political Register* in 1820: "Our expedition set out from New York in the middle of the night; got to the place (22 miles off) at peep of day; took up the coffin entire; brought it off to New York; and, just as we found it, it goes to England. Let this be considered the act of the reformers of England, Scotland, and Ireland."[118]

Unfortunately, Cobbett was not able to secure the necessary financial support to build the memorial for Paine he had dreamed of, and the bones were still in his possession when he died in 1835, having become a Member of Parliament working for reform. An account of what happened next can be found in a little 1847 pamphlet by a Paine admirer named James Watson, who was later interviewed by Paine biographer Moncure Daniel Conway. According to Watson, the bones passed briefly into the possession of Cobbett's son James. But James was unable to pay his father's debts, so a court appointed George West to take charge of the estate, which included a farm, in a receivership arrangement. A judge ruled, however, that Paine's bones were not part of the estate, and so they remained in the custody of West until 1839, when he passed them on to Benjamin Tilly, who had been Cobbett's secretary and who intended to realize Cobbett's dream of a grand memorial tomb for Paine.[119] But Tilly also died without accomplishing this goal. Around 1890, Paine's biographer Conway investigated what then became of the bones and found that most likely they had been sold to a rag and bone collector by the Ginn family, with whom Tilly had been boarding in 1860 when he died. Mrs. Ginn is said to have claimed she did not know the bones were human, but Conway was skeptical of this. There is a legend that the bones were made into buttons and sold one by one. Conway also discovered reports that Paine's skull and right hand had been in the possession of Reverend Robert Ainslie, but no trace of them was later found.[120] Conway did track down what he believed to be Paine's mummified brainstem and this, along with some of his hair, was eventually reburied at New Rochelle.[121]

Despite the loss of Paine's body, Gilbert Vale, editor of the freethought journal *The Beacon*, was successful in erecting a monument to him at New Rochelle in 1839. Born in London in 1788, Vale, like many other reform-minded Brits, gave up on much progress being made in his own country and immigrated to New York in 1827.[122] He soon was accepted into the social circle that included Benjamin Offen, George Houston, William Carver, John Fellows, and other former members of the Deistical Society. He made a living by teaching navigation, as well as through lecturing and publishing.[123] In January 1831 he began a series of Sunday lectures on perspective drawing at Wright's Hall of Science.[124] With connections both to Wright's Owenist

Hall of Science and Offen's Paineite Society of Moral Philanthropists, Vale must have been a valuable intermediary between the two traditions of freethought.

In 1836 a national freethought society was created called the United States Moral and Philosophical Society for the General Diffusion of Useful Knowledge, holding a convention in Saratoga Springs.[125] It was founded by Dr. Charles Knowlton, who had been imprisoned in Massachusetts for having published a book that contained medical advice on sex and contraception. The organization started publishing its own journal in New York, called *The Beacon*. Vale was selected to be the editor of what would be for a time the flagship journal of American freethought. By 1837 Vale had taken Offen's Sunday morning lecture slot at Tammany Hall, usually speaking on scientific topics, and Offen shifted his sessions of scriptural criticism to the evening.[126] Possibly because of his connections to the national United States Moral and Philosophical Society and to the Tammany Society network, Vale succeeded in raising the funding for a Paine Memorial where Cobbett and Tilly had failed. The memorial in New Rochelle was completed in 1839. By that time, little remained of Paine's original grave. After Cobbett had cracked it open, souvenir hunters had chiseled away most of what was left. The sculptor and architect John Frazee undertook the work of building a monument at the site of the grave for free, and $1,300 was raised to pay for the marble and other materials required. The monument was a simple rectangular column that bore Paine's likeness as well as the words "Thomas Paine, Author of *Common Sense*." It was surrounded by a substantial wall with an iron gate to guard the front.[127]

Paine's supporters got the first sympathetic biography of him since 1819 with the publication of Vale's *Life of Thomas Paine* in 1853.[128] Vale might have published the book in reaction to recent sensationalistic accounts of Paine's life . . . and his afterlife! In 1847, Thomas Paine had received a sympathetic treatment in George Lippard's popular *Washington and His Generals: Or, Legends of the Revolution*, a novelistic history of the American Revolution. But despite Lippard's admiration for Paine, his book called Paine's rejection of Christianity a mistake. "Here was the terrible mistake of Thomas Paine," he wrote. "He mistook the cloud which marred the sun for the sun itself; he mistook the abuses of men; the frauds of hypocrites; the lies of fabulists which have been done and uttered in the name of Christianity; for Christianity itself."[129] Lippard's Paine was the Paine of *Common Sense* and *Rights of Man*, not the Paine of *Age of Reason*. Even more sensationalistic than Lippard's novelized history was Reverend Charles Hammond's account of how Paine's disembodied spirit possessed him and took him on a pilgrimage to the "seventh circle of the spirit world" in his book *Light from the Spirit World: The Pilgrimage of Thomas Paine and Others to the Seventh Circle in the Spirit World* (1852).[130] Hammond was a medium and a Universalist minister who taught at Monson Academy in Massachusetts and who had been caught up in the wave of spiritualism that swept the country in the early 1850s.[131] His treatment of Paine is also sympathetic, but in his tale the spirit of William Penn convinces Paine that he was wrong to reject Christianity, enabling Paine to ascend to higher spiritual planes. The success of these two books demonstrated that the public was ready to take a fresh look at Paine, and Vale likely wanted to add to the record a sympathetic biography that did not represent *Age of Reason* as a grave error or rely on the channeling of spirits for its information.

When Vale started gathering material for his biography of Paine, there were still living witnesses to Paine's final years in America, so Vale had the personal testimony of Carver and Fellows, as well as access to witnesses who could debunk false claims about Paine's deathbed recantation of his religious views. One of several important historical contributions made by Vale's biography was to debunk the widely circulated myth of Paine's habitual drunkenness. Paine was saddled with the label in England after the publication of *Rights of Man*, and it was revived and blown out of all reasonable proportion when he returned to America. Because even today many Paine biographies repeat accounts of his drinking that originated with his religiously and politically motivated detractors, I think it might be worth quoting the discussion of the topic that Vale was able to compile from eyewitnesses who were sympathetic to Paine:

> Mr. Jarvis, the celebrated painter, with whom Mr. Paine lived, informs us distinctly that Mr. Paine was neither dirty in his habits nor drunken: nay, he good humoredly added that *he* always drank a great deal more than ever Paine did. Mr. John Fellows lived in the same house with Mr. Paine, above a twelvemonth, and was his intimate friend for many years after his return to this country, and never saw him but once even elevated with liquor, and then he had been to a dinner party. We know more than twenty persons who were more or less acquainted with Mr. Paine, and not one of whom ever saw him in liquor. His habit appears to have been to take one glass of rum and water with sugar in it after dinner, and another after supper. His limit at one period when at Rochelle was one quart of rum a week for himself and friends.[132]

To drink two or three cups of rum punch with meals per day was moderate by the standard of Paine's time. I don't doubt that Paine occasionally drank too much, but I am also quite sure that detractors like those who forged letters supposedly from his mother to defame him and accused him of conspiring with the devil would not hesitate to grossly exaggerate his drinking. It should be kept in mind that Paine far outlived the average life expectancy of his time.

Ernestine Rose and the Rights of Woman

Ernestine Rose was a woman whose sustained efforts helped to establish the women's rights movement in America and the passage of the Married Women's Property Act in New York State. She was also a freethinker who attended and spoke at Paine birthday celebrations from her first years in America until the Civil War, established the practice of welcoming both men and women to all portions of the Paine celebrations, and frequently pointed out that it is fitting to honor Paine by working to promote the rights of women and the freedom of oppressed and enslaved peoples.

She was born Ernestine Polowsky in 1810, the daughter of a rabbi, in the Dutchy of Warsaw. Her religious views were molded by childhood debates about scripture with her father. Her first biographer, Jenny d'Héricourt, who based her account on an 1856 interview, wrote, "The God of Madame Rose is the *Univers-vivant*. She is convinced that the Bible, the Koran, the Vedic texts, and all other books reputed to be divinely inspired are the source of slavery, despotism, intolerance, injustice, and error; that humanity cannot really advance in the path of the true and the good until it is able to rid itself of this sacred baggage which the past continues to place on its shoulders."[133] The term *"Univers-vivant,"* literally the "living universe," suggests that like Spinoza, d'Holbach, and Palmer, and unlike Paine, she thought the universe is self-caused and the only thing that might be called a supreme being. At times she described herself as an atheist.[134]

At the age of sixteen, Ernestine Polowsky rejected an arranged marriage and left her father's home, giving up an inheritance her recently deceased mother had left her. She traveled throughout Europe for a decade, funded by the sales of perfumes and colognes she made herself and room-deodorizing perfumed paper that was her own invention. In England, she met Robert Owen, who likely recognized in her something of the spirit of Frances Wright. He invited her to speak at gatherings of his followers despite the fact that she was just learning English. Her views on the evils of religion and private property already agreed pretty well with those of the Owenites, and she was warmly received. Soon she married a member of the group: William Rose, a jeweler and silversmith who was not of Jewish ancestry. In early 1836 the Roses set out for America together in the company of a group of Owenites who intended to found another community like New Harmony. The group arrived in New York City in May and then headed west. But the Roses, while still holding to their Owenist ideas, decided to make their home in the city rather than following the group to the frontier. They settled in the Lower East Side and opened a shop where Ernestine sold her perfume and William repaired jewelry and silver objects. Rose and her husband soon found their way to the Sunday lectures at Tammany Hall, just a few blocks from their home, sponsored by the Society of Moral Philanthropists at which Offen and Vale were regular speakers. They found they had common cause with the views on religion expressed there, and thus the Roses were drawn into freethinking Paineite circles. In time they would become central figures, especially the outspoken Ernestine.[135]

Ernestine Rose first made an impression on the members of the Society of Moral Philanthropists by starting a debate with Benjamin Offen on the subject of private property. At first unbidden, and then by invitation, Rose spoke out against Offen's espousal of Paine's classically liberal views on property, taking a strongly Owenite stance against private property and arguing for what she called a "community of property." The discussion was open and good-natured. Rose's views on the evils of private property were humored if not widely shared, and Offen was happy to share his speaking platform with a bright and articulate woman. Gilbert Vale mentioned Rose favorably in accounts of the exchange, which lasted thirteen weeks, in *The Beacon*, at first referring to Rose as "a Polish lady of great literary attainments," taking care to protect her identity.[136] *The Beacon* gave a more detailed report on a full speech by Rose in October: "The Polish lady gave a most acceptable lecture last Sunday evening at Tammany Hall, on the evils of private property; and notwithstanding the unpopularity of the subject, and the little influence which the lecture apparently made on the audience, many of whom hugged their dollars and looked about with a smile indicating that preaching would not avail; she retained a most attentive audience, who were evidently pleased at the manner of her delivery, and the number of facts introduced, and the many important isolated truths, which she stated."[137]

After making her American speaking debut with the Society of Moral Philanthropists, Rose went on to a distinguished career as a speaker and activist. A central focus of Rose's activism was to secure the property rights of married women in America. In May 1836, Thomas Herttell, a freethinking New York State assemblyman who attended meetings of the Moral Philanthropists, introduced a measure in the State Assembly calling on it to study the issue of married women's property rights.[138] At that time, following English common law, a woman legally surrendered all her property to her husband upon marriage in every state in the Union. Changing the laws on married women's property was an important goal of the US women's movement before the Civil War. Soon after it was introduced, Rose learned of Herttell's legislation, probably from Herttell himself, and she canvassed her Lower East Side neighborhood to collect women's signatures on a petition supporting action on the issue. In an 1877 letter to Susan B. Anthony, she recalled that she succeeded in getting only five signatures on that first petition, but she didn't give up. "I continued sending petitions with increased number of signatures until 1848 and '49 when the Legislature enacted a law which granted to woman the right to keep what was her own," she writes.[139] Her efforts to improve married women's property rights did not end in 1848. She kept lobbying and petitioning until a stronger version of the law was passed in 1860.[140] Although Rose made little progress in creating a society-wide "community of property," she did succeed in making property more communal within marriage. To this day "community property" laws govern marital property in many states.

Collecting signatures was only a small part of what Rose did. She lectured almost continuously in America from 1837 until she and her husband returned to England in 1869. The letter to Anthony lists thirty-four specific cities she spoke in between 1836 and 1848, which is probably only a fraction of the total, and she spoke multiple times in many of those places.[141] Although she was not able to attend the famous 1848 Seneca Falls convention on women's rights, she spoke at the 1850 National Women's Rights Convention and, in her own words, "nearly all the National and State Conventions since until I went to Europe in 1869."[142] She was president of the Fifth National Women's Rights Convention in Philadelphia in 1854.[143] In addition to continuous lecturing on the women's rights circuit, she also spoke at freethought meetings, such as the 1845 "Infidel" Convention in New York and the Hartford Bible Convention,[144] and at antislavery meetings, such as the 1855 New England Anti-Slavery Conventions.[145] And, of course, she also participated yearly in Thomas Paine birthday celebrations. *Mistress of Herself,* Paula Brown Doress-Worters's collection of Rose's speeches and letters, contains eight speeches given at Paine birthday celebrations between 1840 and 1861, some of which will be discussed in greater detail below. Jenny d'Héricourt paints a vivid picture of Rose's life during these busy decades of activism: "Always on the frontlines, for some twenty years she traveled through twenty-three states of the Union, each one several times, leaving the train to speak for two or three hours on the rostrum. Climbing aboard the train to do the same thing in other places. Often sick, unable to eat, she would give three speeches in one day, each one several hours long. One could see her going from city to city, getting petitions signed against laws whose injustice she succeeded in making people understand."[146]

Rose naturally was well known to American-born members of the women's rights movement in her day, including Lucretia Mott, Paulina Kellogg Davis, Elizabeth Cady Stanton, and Susan B. Anthony. Elizabeth Cady Stanton joined her in lobbying for the Married Women's Property Act in New York State, and she was particularly close to Susan B. Anthony, who joined her on a lecture tour in 1854.[147] Anthony helped her overcome objections to her atheism to become elected president of the Fifth National Women's Rights Convention, arguing "that every religion—or none—should have an equal right on this platform."[148] Rose toured with Anthony again in 1855. This time they spoke in central New York State and were joined by pioneering female minister Antoinette Brown Blackwell, with whom Rose had debated on the topic of biblical authority at the Third National Women's Rights Convention.[149] Rose and Brown Blackwell disagreed about the sacred authority of the Bible, but they did agree on women's rights, and worked well together.

Rose also crossed paths with Frances Wright, who was fifteen years her senior. Although Ernestine Rose worked for many of the same goals as Wright, and both were prominent speakers, her personal life contrasted with Wright's in many ways. Rose remained happily married to her husband, William, who supported her causes in every way he could, until his death of a heart attack in 1882.[150] But sadly the couple lost both children they conceived in infancy. Wright's 1830 marriage to William Phiquepal D'Arusmont was, in contrast, unhappy, but she did bear a daughter, Sylva, who lived a full life. William D'Arusmont was a French educator in the Pestalozzian tradition who worked at the School of Industry at New Harmony and supervised the printing of the *New Harmony Gazette* and later *The Free Enquirer*.[151] He had accompanied Wright to Haiti on her quest to find a home for the Nashobans. The couple separated about five years after their daughter was born, and finally divorced in 1850, leaving Wright fighting for her inheritance and earnings against the very laws that she had worked to change.[152] Rose's career was in some ways less dramatic than Wright's, whose ventures took her from Lafayette's parlor to a utopian community in the malarial swamps of Tennessee, but of no less importance. Rose and Wright met in 1839 when they both were speakers at a benefit for Benjamin Offen, who was down on his financial luck, and possibly other times as well.[153] Rose admired Wright, but sided with the Owen family when Wright had a falling out with them over Robert Dale Owen's rejection of her marital overtures.[154] Later in life, Rose wrote of the important contributions to women's rights that Wright had made.[155]

Rose became much more deeply a part of the annual celebrations of Paine's birthday than Wright had been, and she greatly influenced the direction of "the cause" through her yearly toasts and speeches. But she effected an even more fundamental change first. It all began with a declined invitation. William Rose was invited to a Paine birthday celebration in 1839. Ernestine was not invited to the dinner and toast, but only to the ball afterwards, because women were only allowed to join the men for dancing. Ernestine later wrote that she thought the *Rights of Man* did not exclude women," and that if the men were going to exclude the women from dining, they "may as well have the ball without them."[156] Both William and Ernestine declined their invitations and organized an alternative celebration where both men and women could fully participate. Its success led to the abandonment of the "Old-English" style celebrations established by Offen.

The Roses went on to organize a larger mixed-gender Paine birthday in 1840 sponsored by the Society of Socialists. As reported in the *Boston Investigator*, the freethought paper edited by Abner Kneeland, both Ernestine and William offered toasts, and William seems to have sung a song in honor of Paine.[157] Rose's toasts at this gathering were conventional, even if the gathering itself was not, but on later occasions she frequently urged the celebrants to honor Paine by working for the rights and liberty of women and of oppressed and enslaved peoples. Her 1849 Paine birthday address calls attention to the plight of the Irish, suffering under the combined hardships of the potato famine and an oppressive British government, and then moves to the topic of women's rights: "While we gratefully remember all that Thomas Paine has done for the rights of man, we must also remember that to us is left to achieve that greater task—the rights of woman!—without which, even the works of Thomas Paine, I greatly fear, will be useless, for man can never truly be free until woman has her rights as his equal, until she becomes elevated as an intellectual, independent, moral being."[158] In her Paine birthday address of 1850, she took up the cause of Hungary, which had established a democratic republic in 1848 that was crushed by the combined forces of Russia and Austria in 1849, urging those gathered to honor Paine to support the exiled Hungarian leaders Lajos Kossuth and József Bem, and the Italian revolutionary Giuseppe Mazzini.[159] She called on the participants in a Paine birthday celebration in 1855 to sign two petitions, one for a strengthened women's property law and another to give women the right to vote, saying, "Friends, I honor the author of the *Rights of Man*, with the endeavor to promote the rights of woman."[160]

Although she had been speaking and writing for the abolitionist cause since at least the mid-1850s, it was only in the early 1860s that Rose began expressing abolitionist ideas in her Paine birthday speeches. A speech at an 1861 Boston celebration of Paine's birthday took up the issues of slavery and the threat of southern secession after praising Giuseppe Garibaldi's efforts to create a unified Italy under a democratic republican government.[161] A letter she wrote to be read at the Boston Paine birthday the next year concluded, "Let every friend of Thomas Paine resolve, like him, to devote himself to the promotion of human Freedom; and as the greater includes the lesser, remember that the first of rights is the right of man to himself, and in honoring the memory of Thomas Paine proclaim the rights of man without distinction of sex, country, or color."[162] Rose did much to propel the views of those who celebrated Paine's birthdays forward from the Jacksonian vision of universal male, white suffrage and freethought where many had begun toward the acceptance of a far more universal understanding of human rights.

The Infidel and Anti-Sabbath Conventions

Although the United States Moral and Philosophical Society had emerged from a grand meeting of freethinkers in Saratoga Springs in 1836,[163] the freethought movement consisted mostly of local groups holding local meetings until 1845. The Moral and Philosophical Society and the Free Enquirers had many local chapters but no national conventions. The movement was knit together by its national publications and by traveling speakers. Calls for a national "infidel convention" began to appear in *The Beacon* in the early 1840s from writers like Charles Knowlton, who had been deeply involved in organizing the US Moral and Philosophical Society, and William C. Bell. Both hoped a national infidel convention would strengthen the movement.[164] Despite much enthusiasm for the idea of a convention, nothing seemed to actually happen to get one organized until Ernestine Rose and her husband undertook the task in 1845. The presence of the seventy-four-year-old Robert Owen as well as Rose herself drew some five hundred freethinkers to a convention at the Coliseum on Broadway in New York. The gathering, which began on May 3, did not officially adopt the name "infidel convention" until its final day. "Infidel" had been a term of abuse hurled at freethinkers for centuries. Now some argued that freethinkers should proudly flaunt it, but not everyone was easily convinced. Rose made a speech that won over a majority, arguing freethinkers should "show the world that even nicknames can be lived down, or made respectable and fashionable . . . let us adopt it, and make our enemies ashamed of the hour they ever applied it to us."[165] "Give us the name of Infidel," another delegate said, "and we would soon deprive it of all odium and stigma—we could make it so honorable that the other sects would seek to steal it from us!"[166] And so was born the Infidel Society for the Promotion of Mental Liberty. The name echoes the fading memory of Owen's "declaration of mental independence." The group seemed to have a promising beginning, but in actuality antislavery remarks by Samuel Ludvigh, publisher of a German language freethought paper, and other northern freethinkers alienated attendees from the south, who did not return the next year.[167] This and other disputes caused only thirty-four participants to attend the next convention in Palmyra, Ohio. The Infidel Society dissolved after 1847.[168]

The collapse of the Infidel Society did not end freethinkers' efforts to stage national gatherings. In 1848 an Anti-Sabbath Convention was held in Boston by freethinkers and others who opposed laws that enforced the Christian Sabbath on Sunday in much of the country, a practice that endorsed the Sabbath doctrine of many Christians at the expense of freethinkers, Jews, and Seventh Day Adventists.[169] The idea of an infidel convention was reborn in 1857 in Philadelphia when the Infidel Association of the United States was founded, again with the help of Rose's organizational skills. This organization met every year, save 1861, until 1863. It was estimated that the 1860 convention drew two to three hundred people, but attendance fell off sharply after the beginning of the Civil War in 1861 because many members were pressed by war duties, and the strain of the war seems to have finally led to a suspension of activities.[170]

It is convenient to think of the time between 1863 and 1866 as a boundary between the second and the third waves of the American freethought movement, but it was not a period of complete dormancy as between 1810 and 1825. It was more of a lull brought on by the war. The *Boston Investigator* continued to be published, and there is no reason to think that local groups of freethinkers stopped meeting or celebrating Paine's birthday. But the movement stopped growing and lost the ambition to embark on new projects.

Taking Stock of the Second Wave of American Freethought

Although many native-born Americans participated in it, the second wave of American freethought was ignited and sustained by immigrants. It is an open question whether there would have been anything that could be called a freethought movement in America between 1825 and 1863 if not for Benjamin Offen, Robert Owen and Robert Dale Owen, Frances Wright, Gilbert Vale, and Ernestine Rose. Many of these freethinking immigrants were refugees from politically oppressive conditions in Britain. Historian of the Radical Enlightenment, Jonathan Israel, characterized the late eighteenth and early nineteenth centuries in Britain as a time when "republicanism, egalitarianism, comprehensive toleration, and democratic ideals were packaged together as objects of virulent common loathing, principles no one could openly champion without provoking a furious reaction."[171] It is no wonder that people like Benjamin Offen and Gilbert Vale came to America seeking a more tolerant environment. Many of the Owenites, on the other hand, were drawn to America less by the promise of toleration than by the possibility of building utopian societies in the open spaces of the frontier.

The second wave of American freethought saw the intermingling of Paineite and Owenite strains of freethought. The Paineite freethinkers of the northeast in the 1820s and 1830s were outspokenly deistic and antiscriptural, just as Paine had been. They looked to science to improve human life, but their activities retained a religious character, offering a substitute for Christian worship in the form of Sunday morning meetings where they promoted their antiscriptural religious perspectives. Paine even described the Deistical Society as the "Deistical Church" in one of his letters to Fellows.[172] Owenites, in contrast, were much more thoroughly secular in their methods of organization. They put more energy into economic and social reform than prolonged discussion of religion, even though they did not believe in revealed religion any more than the Paineites did. They placed as much stock in social progress as scientific progress. Those who were deists did not belabor the point, and some, like Rose, had gone far beyond deism. In the late 1820s, there is a good argument for viewing Owenite and Paineite freethought as separate movements, but by the time the Owenite Ernestine Rose became a prominent organizer of Paine birthday celebrations, that was no longer true. As Owenites such as Robert Dale Owen, Frances Wright, and Ernestine Rose became involved in Paineite circles, they tended to propagate their social reform agenda—which included ending slavery and promoting the rights of women—and temper the antiscripturalism of the movement. Owenites generally believed there were better ways of spending time than denouncing scripture to audiences who had mostly already rejected it. Younger freethinkers who had grown up in the movement had probably drifted too far from Bible culture to be able to easily produce or avidly consume the kind of scathing and detailed biblical criticism that earlier Paineites had reveled in. One needs to have an extensive knowledge of the Bible in order to engage in Bible critique in the style of *Age of Reason*, so to some extent such critique became a victim of its own success.

Throughout the second wave, freethinkers struggled with the issue of how to label themselves. The Deistical Society of New York had worn its non-Christian theology on its sleeve for all to see. But many of its successors chose names that would fit almost any philanthropic organization. Offen's Society of Moral Philanthropists and Charles Knowlton's United States Moral and Philosophical Society for the General Diffusion of Useful Knowledge are organizations whose names seem to be calculated not to raise any alarm among Christians. The label "deist" was problematic not only because it set some Christians off like a dog whistle but also because it was not a good description of freethinkers who were pantheists (like Abner Kneeland), neo-Epicureans (like Frances Wright), or atheists (like Ernestine Rose). Frances Wright came up with an eloquent solution to the label issue with the phrase "Free Enquirer," which she used both in the title of her paper and the name of her organization, the Society of Free Enquirers. The name is far more inclusive than "deist," and it has deep roots in the history of freethought. *The Free Enquirer* was the name of a periodical published by the English deist Peter Annet in 1761. Indeed, it was this publication that caused his blasphemy conviction. Interestingly, Richard Carlile, a publisher convicted of blasphemy for publishing *Age of Reason* in Britain, reprinted Annet's paper in London in 1826, just a couple years before Wright started using the "Free Enquirer" label, and this may have influenced Wright's naming of her organization.[173] "Free Enquirer" is a label that is inclusive and doesn't ring alarm bells for outsiders but might be recognizable as a code word for freethought by movement insiders. Freethinkers, however, were not so cleverly cautious for the whole of the second wave. Ernestine Rose's two self-proclaimed infidel societies threw caution to the wind with their names, boldly owning a term of ridicule and also creating a big tent for many varieties of freethinkers.

Thomas Paine remained an important common reference point that knit the movement together through the whole of the second wave. Owenites were integrated into networks of Paineite freethinkers through celebrations of Paine's birthday. The often-retold story of Paine's victimization by reactionary Christians allowed freethinkers to understand themselves as an oppressed minority, and new chapters were added to that narrative of victimhood by the convictions of Charles Knowlton and Abner Kneeland. The sense that Paine had been wrongly excluded from the pantheon of American founders gave projects like the building of a Paine memorial extra meaning, for it would in a sense be a memorial to everyone who had been mistreated because of their dissent from orthodox Christianity. In addition, the fact that there were both political and religious dimensions to Paine's thought proved useful in forming alliances with other movements. When Ernestine Rose argued that freethinkers should pay more attention to the rights of women and oppressed and enslaved people, it was *Rights of Man* that she drew on, not *Age of Reason*.

The three great themes of *Age of Reason*—antiscripturalism, science, and separationism—received varying emphasis over the course of the second wave. Offen picked up where Palmer had left off, with strong attacks on biblical authority and Christian doctrine every Sunday morning at Tammany Hall. But this approach began to give way as Owenites gained more influence. Wright's Hall of Science hosted only lectures on nonreligious topics, and Offen's Sunday morning slot at Tammany Hall was taken by Gilbert Vale, who taught at the Hall of Science and substituted scientific lectures for Offen's antibiblical ones. Paineite freethinkers continued to speak about the importance of science, but Wright's Hall of Science may have done more to promote science on a practical level. Separationist discourse was always in the background, but it was not as important as antiscripturalism for the Paineites and not as important as social reform for the Owenites.

The freethought movement built its infrastructure substantially over the course of the second wave. It went from a small and loosely connected network of cells to the nationally coordinated organization of the Society of Free Enquirers, from the locally circulated *Correspondent* to the nationally circulated *Free Enquirer* and *Boston Investigator*. The movement would continue its growth in the third wave. In its next phase it would be driven more by native-born Americans and focus more on church-state separation.

CHAPTER FOUR

The Third Wave of American Freethought

The Golden Age

The freethought movement came back with a roar after the Civil War as new organizations such as the Free Religious Association and the National Liberal League appeared on the scene. Attendance at their conventions and the circulation of their periodicals would grow to dwarf their antebellum predecessors. Separationism, which had been a background component of the movement ever since *Age of Reason*, became a central focus of activity. Because separationism is the most inclusive of the major themes of the freethought movement, its centrality to the third wave allowed for the deepening and expansion of alliances with other movements, helping to create what Susan Jacoby called "the golden age of freethought,"[1] a period that ran from the 1870s into the early twentieth century, corresponding closely to the cultural period called the Gilded Age. During the golden age of freethought, materialistic freethinkers joined together with spiritualists and "free religionists" to campaign for secularism. While the movement's legislative and legal gains were disappointing, its growth was impressive, and it became more publicly visible than ever before. This chapter will describe the golden age of freethought, which corresponds to the movement's third wave.

Origins of the Golden Age: The Free Religious Association, *The Index*, the Christian Amendment, and the Nine Demands of Liberalism

In the final months of the Civil War in 1865, the American Unitarian Association (AUA), composed of churches that had grown out of the Congregationalist tradition and tended toward a Unitarian theology, issued a call for Unitarian churches and societies to send representatives to a national convention in New York City. According to William J. Potter, one of the founding members of the Free Religious Association, that call was "animated by a new spirit of humanity" and consequently, "Among those responding to this call were societies and persons who had previously manifested little or no sympathy with denominational Unitarianism."[2] Among these religious freethinkers were Francis Ellingwood Abbot, a graduate of the Harvard Divinity School whose unorthodoxy had lost him his standing as a Unitarian minister in Dover, New Hampshire,[3] and William Potter, a fervent abolitionist and Congregationalist minister.[4] They went to New York hoping to organize a new "Liberal Church" but were disappointed at the conservatism of the American Unitarian Association, whose 1825 founding documents spoke of Jesus as "Lord and Savior" and had no recognizably Unitarian tenets.[5]

The next year, at a National Conference at Syracuse, they attempted to "amend the Constitution and Preamble [of the AUA] in the interests of wider liberty" but were "emphatically defeated." A group of twenty-five radical Unitarians and fellow travelers who had been disappointed by the outcome at Syracuse gathered in October 1866 at the Boston home of a liberal transcendentalist Unitarian minister named Cyrus A. Bartol and laid plans to form a new religious association that would encourage religious inquiry and place no limits on religious belief.[6] The organization's first president was Octavius Frothingham, a former Unitarian minister who had left the denomination to form the Independent Liberal Church in New York. The leadership of the organization was composed mostly of Unitarians and former Unitarians, but it also included liberal Universalists and Quakers, progressive Jews, freethinkers, and spiritualists.[7] The first public meeting of the Free Religious Association was held on May 30, 1867, at Horticulture Hall in Boston and featured speeches by transcendentalist Ralph Waldo Emerson, Robert Dale Owen, and Lucretia Mott, a feminist and abolitionist with Quaker roots. The hall was filled to capacity by an enthusiastic crowd.[8] The Free Religious Association did not ask its members to renounce any other religious affiliations that they might have. It strove to guard its members' freedom of conscience above all else. Its great hope was to facilitate, in Potter's words, the "ultimate union of all the great faiths of the world in one religion; and this not by the conversion of all the others to any one of the faiths, but by the conversion and education of them all to the perception of a higher realm of truth."[9]

Although the Free Religious Association sponsored lectures and maintained a press and reading room, it was influential on a national level mainly through the periodical that was associated with it, *The Index*, published in Toledo by Francis Ellingwood Abbot, one of its founders. Although Abbot proclaimed that he would speak only for himself in his writings, the paper did regularly have a section devoted to the business of the Free Religious Association, and his theology was characteristic of the views that many in the association held. In his prospectus for *The Index*, Abbot wrote that the paper's aim was to increase both the amount of "pure and genuine religion in the world" and also to increase "freedom in the world": "to destroy every species of spiritual slavery, to expose every form of superstition, to encourage independence of thought and action in all matters that concern belief, character or conduct. It will, in short, be devoted to the cause of FREE RELIGION."[10] The first page of early issues of *The Index* was devoted to lists of "affirmations." Some of these capture the essence of how Abbot understood "free religion": "The great law of Free Religion is the still, small voice in the private soul. The great peace of Free Religion is spiritual oneness with the infinite One."[11] Because it grew out of liberal Christianity, the tone of *The Index* was less antiscriptural than many earlier freethought journals such as *The Prospect* and *The Correspondent*. Abbot stated that, although his journal stood "squarely outside of Christianity, it will yet aim to be just to it, recognizing its excellencies, noting its defects."[12]

January 21, 1871, marked the first appearance in *The Index* of a topic that would become a call to arms for its readership, a notice of an attempt to add a "Christian Amendment" to the US Constitution that would acknowledge the supremacy of God and Jesus Christ over the nation. In a short piece called "The Coming Conflict," Abbot informed his readers that a National Convention in support of a Christian Amendment was being held in Philadelphia and that there were smaller meetings in churches all over the country. "Christianity is mustering its forces for an open war on republican liberty," he warned.[13] In fact, the movement to add a Christian Amendment to the Constitution had been around since 1863, when, animated by the sense that the Civil War was as much a punishment for a godless Constitution as for slavery, the National Reform Association (NRA) had come into being under the leadership of a Presbyterian layman named John Alexander. In that same year it sent a delegation to present a petition for a Christian Amendment to Congress and to President Lincoln, who gave a polite but evasive reply and took no action.[14] Although these early efforts bore no fruit, the NRA was now renewing its efforts in the postwar years. According to a report read at the 1874 convention, in that year the NRA had collected more than 54,000 signatures on a Christian Amendment petition that it planned to once again send to congress.[15]

Driven by the fear that the NRA might be gaining ground politically, *The Index* issued dire warnings about the Christian Amendment in 1871 and 1872, and with them came a countervailing set of demands for secular political reform. Abbot habitually used the word "liberal" to describe his religious perspective, and that label also was applied to the separationist political agenda that he increasingly advocated for. On April 6, 1872, *The Index* printed what became a classic statement of the separationist demands of a resurgent freethought movement, a statement that came to be known as "The Nine Demands of Liberalism." Framed as a response to Christian demands for a Christian Amendment, the demands are as follows:

1. We demand that churches and other ecclesiastical property shall no longer be exempted from just taxation.
2. We demand that the employment of chaplains in Congress, in State legislatures, in the army, navy, and militias, and in prisons, asylums, and all other institutions supported by public money, shall be discontinued.
3. We demand that all public appropriations for sectarian educational and charitable institutions shall cease.
4. We demand that all religious services now sustained by the government shall be abolished; and especially that the use of the Bible in the public schools, whether ostensibly as a text-book or avowedly as a book of religious worship, shall be prohibited.
5. We demand that the appointment, by the President of the United States or by the Governors of the various States, of all religious festivals shall wholly cease.
6. We demand that the judicial oath in the courts and in all other departments of government shall be abolished, and that simple affirmations under the pains and penalties of perjury shall be established in its stead.
7. We demand that all laws directly or indirectly enforcing the observance of Sunday as the Sabbath shall be repealed.
8. We demand that all laws looking to the enforcement of "Christian morality" shall be abrogated, and that all laws shall be conformed to the requirements of natural morality, equal rights, and impartial liberty.
9. In short, we demand that not only in the Constitution of the United States and of the several States, but also in the administration of the

same, no privilege or advantage shall be conceded to Christians or any other special religion; and that whatever changes shall prove necessary to this end shall be consistently, unflinchingly, and promptly made.[16]

This set of separationist demands became the foundation on which the National Liberal League, the largest freethought organization of the golden age, was built. They were a blueprint for completing the disestablishment of religion that had been begun in the Revolutionary era but which had not yet been fully realized.

The Dawn of the Golden Age of Freethought

In his 1894 work, *400 Years of Freethought*, freethought historian Samuel P. Putnam recounts the astonishing growth of the National Liberal League, later renamed the American Secular Union, in the late 1870s through the 1880s, growth to which he had been a firsthand witness. He gives Abbot the credit for getting the ball rolling with "The Nine Demands of Liberalism" and his other calls to arms in *The Index*. "The appeals of Mr. Abbot resulted in the preliminary organization of a few local Liberal societies. October 17, 1875, a few delegates from these societies met in convention in Philadelphia. Mr. Abbot was chosen president."[17] The little convention issued a call for a General Congress of all who sympathized with the goal of the "immediate and absolute secularization of the state" before the American Centennial on July 4, 1876, "for the purpose of organizing a National League, and of promoting the organization of local auxiliary Liberal Leagues throughout the country."[18] The Liberal Congress duly met in Philadelphia on July 1, 1876. This time 170 delegates representing forty different liberal associations were in attendance. Eighteen of the attending organizations were accepted as affiliates of the National Liberal League.[19] The league adopted a constitution that was printed in the July 13 issue of *The Index*. Its first article was: "The general object of the National Liberal League shall be to accomplish the TOTAL SEPERATION OF CHURCH AND STATE; to the end that equal rights in religion, genuine morality in politics, and freedom, virtue, and brotherhood in all human life may be established, protected, and perpetuated."[20]

It was further proposed that the league push for a "Religious Freedom Amendment," to "effect the complete secularization of the government."[21] The National Liberal League was organized along the lines of a political party. It had an executive committee of thirty members, from twenty-nine different states plus the District of Columbia. Its vice presidents in 1876 included freethought orator Robert Ingersoll and women's rights leaders Elizabeth Cady Stanton and Amy Post.[22] At its 1877 convention in Rochester, New York, the league adopted a platform for the 1880 presidential election in a comprehensive list of disestablishmentarian objectives:

1. TOTAL SEPARATION OF CHURCH AND STATE to be guaranteed by amendment of the United States Constitution: including the equitable taxation of church property, secularization of the public schools, abrogation of Sabbatarian laws, abolition of chaplaincies, prohibition of public appropriations for religious purposes, and all other measures necessary to the same general end.
2. NATIONAL PROTECTION FOR NATIONAL CITIZENS in their equal civil, political, and religious rights: to be guaranteed by amendment of the United States Constitution and afforded through the United States courts.
3. UNIVERSAL EDUCATION THE BASIS OF UNIVERSAL SUFFRAGE IN THIS SECULAR REPUBLIC: to be guaranteed by amendment of the United States Constitution requiring every State to maintain a thoroughly secularized public school system, and to permit no child within its limits to grow up without a good elementary education.[23]

The Liberal League grew explosively between 1879 and 1882. The growth of the Liberal League can be tracked by the number of local affiliates that were reported at its Annual Congresses: by 1879 there were 62; by 1880 there were 212; and by 1881 there were 225. The *New York Times* noted one or more freethought conventions every year from 1877 to 1885, and another in 1899. Especially extensive coverage was devoted to the 1883 conventions.[24] George MacDonald, the third editor of a leading freethought journal called *The Truth Seeker*, carefully chronicled the yearly meetings of both national and notable local freethought organizations from 1875 to 1925 in *Fifty Years of Freethought*, leaving a clear record of the diversity and vibrance of the movement.[25]

It is not possible to discuss in detail all the local liberal leagues that came into being across the country in the 1870s through the 1890s. In *400 Years of Freethought* Putnam gives what is probably the most extensive account of them. Among those he mentions are the Chicago Secular Union, the Texas Liberal Association, the California State Liberal Union (of which Putnam himself was president), the Oregon State Secular Union, the Washington State Secular Union (which grew out of the Walla Walla Liberal Club), the For Fairfield Liberal League in Maine, the Ingersoll Secular Society of Boston, the Newark Liberal League, the Friendship Liberal League of Philadelphia, the Pittsburgh Union, and the Ohio Liberal Society. He mentions that thirty to forty liberal clubs had formed in Kansas before 1883 and that multiple liberal clubs formed in Iowa beginning in 1878.[26]

As impressive as the growth of freethought was from 1875 to 1890, it is important to view it in the context of church membership and total population. Freethinkers gathered 200,000 signatures for the release from prison of D. M. Bennett, the founding editor of *The Truth Seeker* who was imprisoned for sending a pamphlet that argued for the right of "sexual self-government" through the US mail.[27] We might take that figure as a rough proxy for the number of freethinkers who were seriously committed to the movement, but not, of course, for the total number of Americans who identified as freethinkers, which is likely three or four times larger, and much less the number of religious doubters. As impressive as 200,000 petition signatures is, this number is dwarfed by the approximately twenty million people who were church members by 1890, although that large sum was only about a third of the US population.[28]

Because I have been tracing the history of freethought in New York State and New York City more closely than elsewhere throughout this book, it seems appropriate to devote a little extra space to the third wave of freethought there. According to Putnam the Manhattan Liberal League was formed in 1869 by D. T. Gardiner.[29] He also mentions the Brooklyn Philosophical Association as a liberal organization.[30] George MacDonald says that his mother founded an organization called the New York Liberal Association around the same time.[31] He also describes an organization called the Fourth New York Liberal League.[32] The first mention of freethought activity in this period in the *New York Times* is a report of a "mass meeting" of the "Free-Thinkers' Association" at the Cooper Institute on January 13, 1874, that was attacked by police.[33] Although no other record of this meeting that I know of is preserved, the organization that staged it may have been the Freethinkers' Association of Central and Western New York, which would draw 2,500 people to its convention in Wayne County in 1877. It was at least five times larger than the largest prewar freethought national convention, and it was only regional in scope. At its 1877 convention the organization approved the following statement of purpose:

First. To stimulate free thought and investigation among the people in relation to their civil, religious, and political rights and encourage the investigation of questions relating to religion, science, and reform, and to that end sustain Freethought speakers, hold Liberal meetings, and circulate Liberal, scientific, and reform papers and periodicals.

Second. To act as an auxiliary to the National Liberal League in its efforts to accomplish the total separation of Church and State, and to organize Local Liberal Leagues in the State in accordance with the provisions of the Constitution of the National Liberal League.[34]

By the next year the organization had restyled itself the New York Freethinkers' Association. Its 1878 convention was held in Watkins, New York (now called Watkins Glen),[35] "in the beautiful grove in the center of the village."[36] Putnam claims that a subsequent convention at Rochester "was without doubt one of the largest and most important Liberal conventions ever held in this country."[37] In sum, going into the 1880s, New York City and Brooklyn seemed to have several liberal clubs between them, and there was also a large and active statewide organization.

It seems unlikely that the Liberal League could have grown so explosively if conditions were not favorable for the spontaneous formation of freethought organizations on the local level. There were a number of background factors at play that aided the rapid growth of the movement in this period. First of all, the ground had been well prepared by antebellum freethinkers. Organizations like the Free Enquirers and publications like the *Boston Investigator* had nurtured cells of freethinkers all across the country, cells that were just waiting to be reawakened and reconnected to a national organization. Additionally, the movement was likely propelled by the fact of scientific progress. Ever since Paine, freethinkers had looked to science to improve human life. Nineteenth-century inventions like the steam locomotive, photography, the telegraph, the telephone, and the lightbulb had clearly shown that it could do so. It became more and more possible to imagine a future where science, and not religion, had solved all the most pressing material and social problems of humankind, as Edward Bellamy did in his 1888 utopian novel *Looking Backward*. Jules Verne and H. G. Wells created the modern genre of science fiction in this environment. And Darwinism now could provide a scientific explanation for all the beautiful adaptations of life on earth, and even for the emergence of humankind. The world could increasingly be understood without reference to a deity, even the distant Creator God of deism.

In addition to the tailwinds of scientific progress, freethought's increased focus on the separation of church and state, as articulated in the Nine Demands of Liberalism, allowed it to attract a broader band of supporters than ever before. People with a very wide range of theological positions, including liberal Christians, spiritualists, Creator God deists, pantheists, agnostics, and atheists could all agree that having a more secular society would be a good thing. Thus, the freethought coalition could increase its numbers. The movement benefited particularly from the rapid growth of spiritualism in the second half of the nineteenth century, as many spiritualists tended toward freethought. (More on this soon!)

The freethought movement benefited from new vocabulary that allowed it to articulate its viewpoints and goals more attractively and precisely. Although all the leaders of the third wave of American freethought were born in America, the movement did import a key piece of vocabulary from Britain: secularism. The term "secularism" was popularized by English freethinker George Holyoake in the 1850s to describe a nonreligious approach to public affairs and individual life.[38] Derived from an ecclesiastical term that meant living in the world rather than in monastic seclusion, "secularism" became an indispensable word in freethought separationist rhetoric. The term "agnostic" also seems to have come into common usage in the second half of the nineteenth century. "Secularist" and "agnostic" offered freethinkers ways to define themselves more precisely than "freethinker" and certainly more attractively than "infidel."

Another factor that may have aided the growth of freethought is a background of fear and anxiety about the role of religion in civic life. The movement benefited not only from liberals' fear that a Christian Amendment might be successful but also from a more widespread anxiety about the possibility of sectarian strife over religion in public schools. Most public education in this period was, de facto, nondenominationally Protestant, and it included prayer, Bible reading, and moral instruction. Catholics had long objected to the Protestant flavor of public education. In the 1840s, Bishop John Hughes in New York and Bishop Francis Kenrick in Philadelphia, among others, protested the use of the King James version of the Bible rather than the approved Catholic translation for Bible readings in school. They also complained that the Catholic perspective on the Bible and history were nowhere reflected in the curriculum.[39] The dispute pitted Protestant, anti-immigrant, nativist "Know-Nothings" against Irish Catholic immigrants haunted by memories of Protestant oppression of Catholics in their homeland. It grew so heated that it sparked the "Bible riots" in Philadelphia in May 1844. Several people, including an eight-year-old boy, were killed and about thirty Catholic homes in the Kensington section of Philadelphia were burned.[40] The failure of Catholic efforts to find religious accommodation in the public schools led them to the founding of separate Catholic school systems in New York, Philadelphia, Baltimore, Boston, and other cities with large Catholic populations.

Thirty years after the Bible riots, the issue of whether Catholic schools should receive state support was still hotly contested. "With all the fervor of religious faith," proclaims a July 1875 editorial in the *New York Daily Tribune*, "many believe that it is a sin to separate religious instruction from popular education. With not less firmness and fervor of conviction, others believe that self-government cannot continue to exist among us unless free, nonsectarian schools are maintained by the State for the education of all its children."[41] In some places, Bible reading and prayer were being removed from schools mainly to appease Catholics. In 1870, in the case of *John D. Minor et al. v. Board of Education*, a Cincinnati school board's ban on prayer and Bible reading in school was barred by the Superior Court of Cincinnati but eventually reinstated when the Ohio Supreme Court reversed the Superior Court's decision.[42] Following the Ohio decision in 1872, school boards in heavily Catholic New York and Chicago suspended Bible reading and religious exercises, followed by school boards in Buffalo and Rochester in 1875.[43] These bans on Bible reading, while warmly supported by liberals, were not enacted to promote secularism for its own sake. They were enacted to stave off sectarian strife between Catholics and Protestants. An 1890 Wisconsin Supreme Court decision ended reading of the King James Bible in the public schools specifically because it was held to violate the rights of conscience of Roman Catholics and others who questioned the accuracy of the King James Bible.[44] The widespread anxiety about sectarian strife fit well with the freethought movement's frequently repeated narrative that organized religion is inherently divisive and that reason and science, not religion, must be the common ground for both civic life and public education. It also gave many who were not themselves freethinkers a reason to support the liberal demand for secular public education.

Freethought and the Blaine Amendment

The freethought movement got an ambiguous gift when President Grant, in his December 7, 1875, message to Congress, called for a constitutional amendment that would stipulate that every state should establish schools to provide a free education to all children, regardless of sex, color, or religion, and "forbidding the teaching in said schools of religious, atheistic, or pagan tenets; and prohibiting the granting of any school funds . . . for the benefit . . . of any religious sect or denomination." In the same message, he warned of the danger of churches accumulating huge amounts of untaxed wealth and called for taxation of church property.[45] The message echoed the words of a speech Grant had given in Des Moines, Iowa, on September 29 that also called for nonsectarian schools and taxes on church property, demanding that America should "Forever keep Church and State entirely separate."[46] On December 14, just one week after Grant's message, US House Representative James Gillespie Blaine of Maine, who had been speaker of the House before Republicans lost the majority in 1874, introduced a constitutional amendment that acted on some of Grant's ideas. It read, in part: "No State shall make any law respecting an establishment of religion or prohibiting the free exercise thereof; and no money raised by taxation in any State for the support of public schools . . . shall ever be under the control of any religious sect."[47] Blaine had his eye on the Republican nomination in the upcoming presidential race and he likely wanted to campaign on the promise of this new constitutional amendment.

Many freethinkers had mixed feelings about what became known as the Blaine Amendment. Although the amendment was a step in the right direction, the problem was that Grant and Blaine were campaigning for nonsectarian schools that would still be hospitable to what passed for nondenominational religious activity such as Bible reading, while freethinkers sought completely secular schools. Freethinkers were also worried about loopholes in Grant's proposed policy on taxation of church property. In a December 16 editorial in *The Index*, Abbot raised both of these concerns:

> While we congratulate the liberal public on President Grant's most important Message, as a signal advance in the right direction. . . . [However,] nothing short of the absolute secularization of the state will now suffice. President Grant recommends that every State shall be required to establish free schools, and that no "sect" shall have any control over them or any share of

the school funds; but he stops short of recommending explicitly that *Protestant worship* in the school be discontinued.... He recommends that "all church property" shall be taxed; but he almost neutralized the recommendation by suggesting the "possible" non-taxation of "church-edifices."

A number of contemporary historians are of the opinion that by taking a stand for nonsectarian schools that would allow nondenominational Protestant religious practices to continue but would block public funding of Catholic schools, Grant and Blaine were catering to anti-Catholic sentiment under the cover of separationist rhetoric.[48] This may be so, but it should also be noted that there was a sizable liberal minority who supported separation of church and state for its own sake, and who backed the Blaine Amendment only with significant reservations, or who did not support it at all, because it was not separationist enough. If anti-Catholicism had been their main motivation, the Blaine Amendment would have made them happy, but it did not.

Ultimately, Abbot found that he could not support the Blaine Amendment, but he recognized that he was living in a politically important moment for the idea of a Religious Freedom Amendment, so he took matters into his own hands and launched a campaign in *The Index* for a much stronger amendment. "ORGANIZE!" commanded the opening headline of the December 23 *Index*. Much of the rest of the front page is taken up with reprints of the Nine Demands of Liberalism and the constitution of the Liberal League. There is also an excerpt of the relevant part of Grant's Des Moines speech and a very strongly worded proposal for a Religious Freedom Amendment.

Not all freethinkers took the course that Abbot did. For some, a step in the right direction, however insufficient, was better than no step at all. Despite the misgivings of freethinkers like Abbot, a rising star of the freethought lecture circuit named Robert Ingersoll signaled his support of Blaine and his amendment by giving a rousing speech nominating Blaine to be the Republican candidate for US president at the party's Cincinnati convention in June 1876. In this speech, considered to be one of Ingersoll's finest efforts in politics, he calls Blaine a "plumed knight" who "marched down the halls of the American Congress and threw his shining lance full and fair against the brazen foreheads of the defamers of his country."[49]

As it turned out, neither Blaine's amendment nor his presidential aspirations got very far. In June, Blaine lost out for the Republican nomination to Rutherford B. Hayes in spite of Ingersoll's fine speech. Then, on August 4, by a vote of 180 to 7, the Democrat-majority House passed a version of Blaine's amendment that had just two differences from the original. It changed "religious sect" to "religious sect or denomination," and it added the following line to the end: "This article shall not vest, enlarge, or diminish legislative power in the Congress."[50] This implied that the only way to enforce the rule would be for the Supreme Court to strike down state laws that violated it. George W. McCrary, a representative from Iowa who supported the Blaine Amendment, felt that the added sentence significantly weakened the amendment, but his views did not prevail. The fact that Democrats passed even this weakened version of the Blaine Amendment would make it difficult for anyone to use the issue against them in the upcoming campaign. And the issue became even more unusable when the Republican-controlled Senate failed to pass a stronger version by the two-thirds supermajority required for a constitutional amendment. The proposed Senate version would have given Congress the authority to pass legislation to enforce the new amendment. It also clarified that Bible reading in school was *not* a sectarian activity and threw in a prohibition on religious tests for public office to sweeten the deal for liberals.[51] But the process stopped dead with the failure of this measure to win the required supermajority.

Despite the failure of the Blaine Amendment to make it out of Congress, the issue of religious sectarian control of public schools remained highly contentious in many areas of the country. At the state level, proponents of nonsectarian public schools almost always won the day. Between 1840 and 1875, nineteen states had already added amendments to their constitutions prohibiting the use of state monies to fund schools under the control or influence of a particular religious sect, and by 1900 sixteen more states had added such amendments.[52] Today, all but thirteen states have Blaine-like provisions in their constitutions.[53] There is good reason to think that state and local liberal leagues played a role in getting the "baby Blaines," as the state Blaine-like amendments are sometimes called, enacted in so many states.

Robert Ingersoll: The Voice of Freethought

No freethinker of the nineteenth century reached more Americans with a positive vision of a secular society than Robert Ingersoll, an orator known as "The Great Agnostic."[54] His fame rested on his oratorical gifts. He was the most prominent orator of an age in which oratory was one of the primary public entertainments. A speech of his was once gushingly described by Mark Twain, a prominent speaker in his own right, as "just the supremest combination of English words that was ever put together since the world began."[55]

Ingersoll was a self-made orator. He was born in the small town of Dresden on the shores of Lake Seneca in upstate New York on August 11, 1833, the youngest of five children. His mother died when he was only a year and a half old, leaving him to be raised by his older siblings and his father, who was a Presbyterian minister with strong abolitionist views. Those views frequently brought him into conflict with his congregations, and those conflicts led to the family relocating many times. The relocations limited the amount of formal education Ingersoll received, so he was largely self-educated. As a teen, he fell in love with the work of Scottish poet Robert Burns and with Shakespeare's plays. In both cases, Ingersoll happened to hear someone reading aloud and was fascinated by the odd sound of the words, which were Scottish dialect in one case (and being read by a Scottish shoemaker!) and Shakespearean English in the other. These books became his constant companions, a "source of perpetual joy," feeding his love of language and fascination with the sound of language.[56]

As a young man, Ingersoll apprenticed in the office of an Illinois attorney, teaching himself enough in the process to pass the bar exam in 1854 and open his own law office with his older brother, Ebon Clark, in a southwestern Illinois settlement called Shawneetown. In 1857 the two relocated to Peoria, a bigger town with more potential clients. Their law practice prospered there. In 1860 he ran as a Democrat to represent Illinois's Fourth Congressional District against incumbent Republican Judge William Kellogg. Lincoln and Douglas had held their famous series of seven debates in the state just two years earlier as they vied for a Senate seat, setting an example that Ingersoll and Kellogg followed. A topic of one of their debates was the Fugitive Slave Law, which compelled the return of slaves who had escaped to free states. Although Ingersoll was a Douglas Democrat who believed that each state and territory should decide for itself on the slavery issue, he came out against the Fugitive Slave Law in the debates while, ironically, Kellogg, the candidate from the party of Lincoln, argued in support of it. One observer of the debates remarked with regard to Ingersoll, "It may be doubted whether there was ever pronounced by any human being so terrific a philippic against human slavery and the Fugitive Slave Law."[57] But Republicans had the edge that year in Illinois, regardless of the positions of individual candidates. Republicans Abraham Lincoln for president, Richard Yates for governor, and Judge Kellogg for Congress all came out on top.[58]

After the Civil War commenced with the bombardment of Fort Sumter, Ingersoll sent a telegram to Governor Yates volunteering to raise a regiment of 1,000 men. When he was successful, he was awarded the rank of colonel and command of the unit, which came to be called the Eleventh Illinois Cavalry. As he was raising the troops, he met and fell in love with a young woman named Eva Parker, the child of a freethinking family headed by Benjamin Weld Parker in Groveland, Illinois. With Ingersoll's deployment approaching, the couple wasted no time in getting engaged and then married on February 13, 1862. In April, the Eleventh Illinois Cavalry took part in the Battle of Shiloh in Tennessee. Then it encamped near Jackson, Tennessee, with the Army of the Tennessee. In December 1862, Ingersoll was sent with 650 men to delay the advance of a Confederate force of about 2,500 that was threatening the Union position at Jackson. His mission was to buy time for reinforcements to arrive. Ingersoll and his men skirmished with Confederate scouting parties for a day and a half before his troops were overrun as they defended two bridges near Lexington. Ingersoll was captured after his horse went down. He was released on parole a few days later, with the condition that he would not rejoin the war. Ingersoll returned to Jackson, where he learned that he and his men had bought enough time for the reinforcements to arrive, and the town had been saved. Soon he was joined by Eva in Jackson, and by the end of June the army accepted his resignation. Ingersoll then returned to Illinois with Eva and went back to practicing law.[59] He supported his brother's successful run for Congress as a Republican in 1863.[60]

His first daughter, Eva Robert Ingersoll, was born in September 1863, and she was followed by a sister, Maud Robert Ingersoll, in November 1864.[61] Ingersoll called his wife and daughters "my holy trinity comprising the only Deity that I worship."[62] Eva is often credited with encouraging Robert to champion the causes of freethought and women's rights. He dedicated his first collection of lectures to her, "a woman without superstition," and by all accounts they remained happily married until Robert's death in 1899.[63]

After the war, Ingersoll tried to get back into politics, but his progress was frustrated by growing public awareness of his agnosticism. Like his brother, he had become a Republican during the war, and, because he was a prominent Republican with a background in law and a brother in the US Congress, he was appointed state attorney general of Illinois in 1867, but that was the last public office he was to hold.[64] In 1868 he made a bid to be the Republican candidate for Illinois State governor but reports of his open religious infidelity doomed his nomination.[65] After that, although he campaigned for many Republican candidates, he never sought office for himself again, choosing to devote himself to his family, his law practice, and his public speaking.

In the 1870s and 1880s, Ingersoll built his reputation as a lawyer and as an orator until he was nationally recognized as a leader in both fields. His 1876 "plumed knight speech" nominating Blaine to be the Republican candidate for president might ultimately have done more for the speaker than the unsuccessful nominee, as it won his wide recognition as a gifted orator. In 1882 and 1883, his legal talents were prominently showcased, in addition to his oratory, as lead attorney for the defense in a sensational government corruption case known as the Star Route scandal. Held in Washington, DC, it was the trial of the decade, followed in newspapers across the country. Eight men including former Senator Steven W. Dorsey and Second Assistant Postmaster General Thomas W. Brady were accused of participating in a scheme in which private mail carriers, contracted by the government to deliver mail along special "star routes" without rail service, conspired with government officials to unreasonably boost their contract pay. The first trial, which ended in September 1882, resulted in two defendants being found not guilty, two guilty, and the jury being divided on the rest. The judge granted requests from both prosecution and defense for a new trial. The second trial, ending in June of 1883, to the astonishment of most of the nation, resulted in all the defendants being found not guilty.[66] Ingersoll gained the reputation of a mercenary legal genius, as attested by a cartoon on the cover of the June 1883 issue of *Puck* magazine that shows him walking out the front of a Washington courthouse with bags of money under his arms while Brady and Dorsey sneak shadily out the back.[67]

Despite his legal prowess, speaking on the lecture circuit came to be Ingersoll's most cherished and most lucrative occupation. The searchable and filterable chronology of Ingersoll's life on the website of the Ingersoll Birthplace Museum provides what is probably the most complete picture of Ingersoll's speaking activities available. As best as can be ascertained from newspaper notices and Ingersoll's letters, he gave approximately 1,345 public lectures and 113 political speeches in his career, making 97 speaking tours.[68] His twelve-volume collected works contain at least thirty-one stand-alone lectures in addition to his most famous legal and political speeches, numerous interviews, editorials, and other writings.[69] The lectures cover a great range of topics from the perspective of secular humanism. Many argue that orthodox religion has been a great burden to humankind, enslaving minds and stunting progress for centuries, and that human advancement has coincided with religion's loss of influence. Speeches in this vein include "The Gods," "The Ghosts," "What Must We Do to Be Saved?"

"Some Mistakes of Moses," "The Great Infidels," "Orthodoxy," "About the Holy Bible," and "Why I Am an Agnostic." Other speeches are biographical commemorations of great figures in literature, politics, and science. Speeches of this type include "Humboldt," "Thomas Paine," "Shakespeare," "Robert Burns," "Abraham Lincoln," "Voltaire," and "Liberty in Literature," which is about Walt Whitman. Still other lectures and speeches are calls for social and political reform. "The Liberty of Man, Woman, and Child" is the foremost of these, championing women's rights and arguing against the disciplinary beating of children.

The best way to understand Ingersoll's appeal is to engage with his speeches. On occasion, Ingersoll could be a masterly painter of pictures with words. In one passage from "The Liberty of Man, Woman, and Child," he literally asks anyone who would beat a child to have a picture taken of themselves, then he describes what that picture would look like, and then moves on to an even more vivid scene of tragic regret:

> I do not believe in the government of the lash, if any one of you ever expects to whip your children again, I want you to have a photograph taken of yourself when you are in the act, with your face red with vulgar anger, and the face of the little child, with eyes swimming in tears and the little chin dimpled with fear, like a piece of water struck by a sudden cold wind. Have the picture taken. If that little child should die, I cannot think of a sweeter way to spend an autumn afternoon than to go out to the cemetery, when the maples are clad in tender gold, and little scarlet runners are coming, like poems of regret, from the sad heart of the earth—and sit down upon the grave and look at that photograph, and think of the flesh now dust that you beat.[70]

More often than he described vivid scenes, Ingersoll told a big, sweeping story of how humanity has emerged from an age of darkness governed by superstition into an age of reason and liberty: a narrative of progress. The people who have led the way have been called infidels, and in past ages they have been jailed, tortured, and burned by the defenders of religion for their beliefs. But as the influence of religion has receded, liberty and progress have increased. In the service of this master narrative of progress, he often recounted instances of the extremes of cruelty and superstition of earlier ages, for example:

> In the time of James the First, a man was burned in Scotland for having produced a storm at sea for the purpose of drowning one of the royal family. A woman was tried before Sir Matthew Hale, one of the most learned and

celebrated lawyers of England, for having caused children to vomit crooked pins. She was also charged with nursing demons. Of course, she was found guilty, and the learned Judge charged the jury that there was no doubt as to the existence of witches, that all history, sacred and profane, and that the experience of every country proved it beyond any manner of doubt.... People were burned for causing frosts in the summer, for destroying crops with hail, for causing cows to become dry, and even for souring beer. The life of no one was secure, malicious enemies had only to charge one with witchcraft, prove a few odd sayings and queer actions to secure the death of their victim. And this belief in witchcraft was so intense that to express a doubt upon the subject was to be suspected and probably executed.[71]

For Ingersoll the belief that the Bible is the word of God and the belief in a hell where a "merciful" God torments human souls for all eternity were just as much superstitions as the belief in witches, and these beliefs could be just as destructive if left unchecked. At the end of the narrative of progress there is a choice to make between the natural and the supernatural, between reason and superstition:

THERE are two ways,—the natural and the supernatural.
    One way is to live for the world we are in, to develop the brain by study and investigation, to take, by invention, advantage of the forces of nature, to the end that we may have good houses, raiment and food, to the end that the hunger of the mind may be fed through art and science.
    The other way is to live for another world that we expect, to sacrifice this life that we have for another that we know not of. The other way is by prayer and ceremony to obtain the assistance, the protection of some phantom above the clouds....
    One way is to be an honest man, giving to others your thought, standing erect, intrepid, careless of phantoms and hells.
    The other way is to cringe and crawl, to betray your nobler self, and to deprive others of the liberty that you have not the courage to enjoy.[72]

Ingersoll frequently used humor to cheer his audiences as he guided them through the narrative of human progress. In the following passage Ingersoll pokes fun at an intelligent design–style argument for the existence of a benevolent God in the tradition of William Paley:

A devout clergyman sought every opportunity to impress upon the mind of his son the fact that God takes care of all his creatures; that the falling sparrow attracts his attention, and that his loving kindness is over all his works. Happening, one day, to see a crane wading in quest of food, the good man pointed out to his son the perfect adaptation of the crane to get his living in that manner. "See," said he, "how his legs are formed for wading! What a long slender bill he has! Observe how nicely he folds his feet when putting them in or drawing them out of the water! He does not cause the slightest ripple. He is thus enabled to approach the fish without giving them any notice of his arrival." "My son," said he, "it is impossible to look at that bird without recognizing the design, as well as the goodness of God, in thus providing the means of subsistence." "Yes," replied the boy, "I think I see the goodness of God, at least so far as the crane is concerned; but after all, father, don't you think the arrangement a little tough on the fish?"[73]

Not long before he died, Ingersoll visited the labs of Thomas Edison in Menlo Park, New Jersey. Edison was a fellow freethinker who became a vice president of the Thomas Paine National Historical Association in the mid-1920s.[74] In Menlo Park, Ingersoll recorded seven short excerpts from his speeches on wax cylinders. Three of these recordings can be listened to on the website of the Ingersoll Birthplace Museum. Beneath the crackling and hissing, one can hear Ingersoll speaking in unhurried, measured, and well-modulated phrases with a slight western accent. On one of the cylinders he recorded his personal creed: "Happiness is the only good. The time to be happy is now. The place to be happy is here. The way to be happy is to make others so."[75] While Ingersoll lived, this was the voice of freethought for a great many Americans.

Factions and Alliances: An Anatomy of Freethought in the Golden Age

In the third wave of American freethought, separation of church and state became a dominant theme, and because this is the most inclusive of the three main themes of American freethought (separationism, antiscripturalism, hope in science) it allowed the movement to attract a greater number of followers into itself and to expand its alliances with other movements. But as a greater diversity of freethinkers swelled the ranks of the movement, factions began to emerge that did not in all instances co-exist in complete harmony.

Eyewitness freethought historian Samuel Putnam wrote that there were three main branches of the freethought movement in his day: the *materialists*, the *free religionists*, and the *spiritualists*. Although all these groups embraced the separationist principles of the Nine Demands of Liberalism, each was a distinct faction.[76] Two of these factions, the free religionists and the materialists, have received some introduction already.

The *materialist* faction of freethought was composed of agnostics, atheists, and materialistic pantheists. They were united in rejecting any form of supernaturalism. They also rejected, or were at least highly skeptical of, the Cartesian dualism which holds that there is a substance called spirit that is distinct from matter. Among their ranks we find Frances Wright, Abner Kneeland, Ernestine Rose, and Robert Ingersoll. The committed materialistic faction of freethought was probably the smallest by numbers in the late nineteenth century, but it was destined to continue growing into the next century.

At the core of the *free religionist* faction was the group of renegade Unitarians that formed the Free Religious Association, whose proceedings were covered by Abbot's *Index*. Free religionists were generally theists who insisted on absolute individual freedom of conscience. Although they were bound by no creed, free religionists were generally Unitarian in believing that Jesus was not a divine being, Universalist in believing that all souls would eventually find salvation from a beneficent God, and often transcendentalist in believing that God pervades all nature and humanity. Free religionists built enduring bridges between the freethought movement and the most liberal religious denominations. Free religionist leaders like Abbot and Frothingham remained active within denominational Unitarianism, lobbying for liberal reform, and eventually they got it. At the National Conference of Unitarians in 1894 at Saratoga Springs a new constitution was agreed upon that defined "practical religion" as "love to God and love to man." The denomination reaffirmed its commitment to adopt no definitive creed and invited "to our working fellowship, any who, while differing from us in belief, are in general sympathy with our spirit and our practical aims."[77] The new constitution paved the way for Unitarianism's eventual fusion with Universalism and embrace even of secular humanists and followers of "nature-based religions" in the twentieth century.

The openness of the most liberal Unitarian churches to accepting even agnostics into their fellowship was dramatically demonstrated in 1896 when Robert Ingersoll visited the People's Church of Kalamazoo, which, in the words of its leader, Reverend Caroline J. Bartlett, offered fellowship "to any honest man entirely irrespective of belief."[78] Ingersoll approved of the church because its objective was "to make people better, kinder, and nearer just by developing the brain and civilizing the heart."[79] Ingersoll declared at a lecture he gave after his visit to the church that "if there were a similar church near my home, I should join it if its members would permit me." At the end of the lecture, Rev. Bartlett, who was in the audience, rose to state that "the People's Church would take pleasure in extending to him the right hand of fellowship."[80] Soon after, she published a sermon entitled, *Why the People's Church of Kalamazoo Would Fellowship Col. Ingersoll.* In it she praises Ingersoll's sincerity while gently chiding him for taking too strong a tone in his attacks on scripture. The People's Church of Kalamazoo still exists today as a Unitarian Universalist congregation.[81] Although free religionists both inside and outside of denominational Unitarianism were extremely progressive in comparison to orthodox Christianity in America, they were theologically conservative in comparison to other factions of freethinkers.

The third, and perhaps most surprising, faction of the freethought movement that Putnam identifies is the spiritualist faction. Because I have said little about spiritualism up to this point in the book, some background is required to understand how spiritualists became part of the freethought movement. Spiritualism was a movement in its own right that gained a large following in America beginning in the 1850s. Although people have believed in spirits and ghosts from time immemorial, a key event that prompted the organization of spirit believers into a movement in America was the rise of sisters Margaretta, Catherine, and Leah Fox to the status of celebrity mediums. In 1848 the Fox family began to hear mysterious rapping noises at night in their newly rented home in Hydesville, New York. Surmising that the sounds were being produced by a specter, the youngest sister, twelve-year-old Kate, asked the spirit to repeat a pattern of claps, and, lo and behold, the pattern was repeated. Then fifteen-year-old Maggie asked the spirit to count with raps, and it did. Their mother asked the spirit the ages of her children, and the spirit answered correctly by a number of raps, including the age of a child that had died. After that, the spirit began to reveal its secrets by answering yes and no questions with raps. Then it was prompted to spell out sentences by rapping at the correct letters as someone recited the alphabet. Soon neighbors were stopping by to ask the spirit questions.[82] Within a few months, the sisters were asked to stage a public séance in nearby Rochester. The phenomenon known as the "Rochester rappings" became a sensation across America after it was picked up by the national press.[83] Kate and Maggie's career as professional mediums had been launched. Soon their much older sister, Leah, discovered that she also had the gifts of a medium, as did quite a number of other young women across the country. As the electric telegraph had been introduced just a few years earlier, the Fox sisters' mode of communication with the spirit world was dubbed the spiritual telegraph.[84]

Numerous investigations into whether any trickery was involved seemed to support the Fox sisters' claim to be in communication with the dead. The seeming genuineness of the sisters' spectral intercourse won many converts to a nebulous system of spiritualist belief, which held that the dead live on in a spirit world, growing wiser and purer with passing ages, and under some circumstances make contact with the living. In the 1880s, Maggie and Kate admitted that the first rappings had been produced as a girlish prank by repeatedly dropping an apple on a string against the wooden floor, and that later, as profiteers and investigators began to surround them, they had learned to produce the noises by surreptitiously dislocating joints.[85] But by the time of these admissions, too many true believers had convinced themselves of the reality of the spirit realm for the movement to be derailed by the confessions of its initiators. Especially after the Civil War, bereaved Americans sought solace in making contact with the spirits of the departed. By the end of the nineteenth century—at which point spiritualism could boast local and national associations, dozens of periodicals, and even spiritualist churches—it is estimated that between four and eleven million Americans identified as spiritualists.[86]

I believe it is safe to say that there were as many or more spiritualists in America during the golden age of freethought as there were free religionist and materialist freethinkers combined. But were spiritualists freethinkers? In many cases the answer is yes. Although some spiritualists remained within traditional religion, as a class, spiritualists dissented from Christian orthodoxy. Most embraced a set of beliefs that was radically Universalist in that the spirits of all the departed continue toward perfection after death, moving into higher and higher spirit realms. Many spiritualists believed that spiritualism was a completely rational system of belief, a modern scientific religion based on the empirical evidence of innumerable séances. The California Spiritualist Association stated that spiritualism was a scientific religion in its very first guiding principle: "Spiritualism is a scientific philosophical religion and embraces the science of life, the philosophy of existence, and the religion of humanity."[87] Conceiving of spiritualism as a scientific religion, many spiritualists fully endorsed freethought's denunciations of the "superstitions" of orthodox Christianity, such as belief in eternal damnation, the divinity of Christ, original sin, and the need for a redeemer. Spiritualists were often skeptical of scripture because scripture was so often used by orthodox Christian preachers to discredit spiritualistic beliefs.[88] In these ways, many spiritualists could be thought of as deists or animistic pantheists who had the additional belief that the living can communicate with the dead. Many people who had been freethinkers before the rise of spiritualism became converts. Among those swept up in the rising tide of spiritualism were both Robert and Robert Dale Owen, and they inspired many who had been involved in Owenite social reform projects to move toward spiritualism.[89] Within spiritualism, women were far more likely to hold positions of power, often as mediums, than in orthodox Christianity, so spiritualism tended to be allied with feminism, as did freethought. Spiritualism was most strongly bound to freethought by spiritualists' recognition that their beliefs were often feared and sometimes hated by orthodox Christians. This led spiritualists to support the separation of church and state, lest Christian disapproval be translated into official persecution. Some Christians equated spiritualism with witchcraft and deployed old biblical injunctions against the practice of witchcraft against spiritualism.[90] Secularism offered spiritualists the best way to stay off the road that led back to Salem.

In a passage from *Fifty Years of Freethought*, MacDonald, writing from his perspective as editor of *The Truth Seeker*, sums up the contribution that spiritualists made to the freethought movement from the perspective of a materialist freethinker:

> The Spiritualists were loyal and practical Secularists. After a manner, it seemed to me, they contributed to the cause a feminine element of rare value. The women who at a Spiritualist gathering[s] were liable to go into a trance and deliver an inspirational address knew how to leave out the spirits when speaking before the Liberal Leagues. *The Truth Seeker* carried a full column of meeting notices, about half of which were Spiritualist. Announcements of deaths were equally impartial. It was deemed no unusual thing to see a death notice begin "passed to spirit life." Twenty-five per cent of the readers of *The Truth Seeker* were Spiritualists.[91]

So deep was the interconnection of spiritualism and freethought that today one of the best internet sources for freethought periodicals is the website of the International Association of the Preservation of Spiritualist and Occult Periodicals.

An event that demonstrated the close connection between spiritualism and freethought even before the Civil War was the Hartford Bible Convention. Taking place over four days at the beginning of June in 1853, the convention was organized by spiritualist leader Andrew Jackson Davis. Born in 1826 before his namesake was even elected president, Davis was working as an apprentice shoemaker in Poughkeepsie, New York, when the town was visited by a traveling mesmerist named Professor Grimes. Grimes revealed the secrets of mesmeric magnetism to the townsfolk, who enthusiastically began to "magnetize" each other. The town's tailor, Mr. Levingston, had the best knack for it. Upon being magnetized by Levingston, Davis discovered he had a gift of clairvoyance that allowed him to diagnose illnesses and prescribe cures as well as any doctor.[92] Soon he went into business as a magnetic healer. After the Rochester Rappings, Davis was able to enlarge his following considerably as the tide of spiritualism rose. His 1847 book, *Principles of Nature*, which he allegedly dictated while in a trance state, reveals him to be a sort of pantheist who saw spirit as a divine essence that permeates all things.[93] Davis moved to Hartford, Connecticut, in the winter of 1850 at the invitation of followers there, and three years later he organized the Hartford Bible Convention. He hoped that Bible-believing local ministers would attend and have a productive discussion with Bible-doubting spiritualists and other skeptics. From the beginning, the local ministers refused to take part, but some eloquent defenders of the Bible were invited speakers at the convention. They were cheered by many of the townspeople who attended, as the anti-Bible speeches were applauded by the spiritualists and their out-of-town guests.[94]

The most prominent figure to join the Hartford spiritualists at the abandoned church where the convention was held was abolitionist leader William Lloyd Garrison, who had become skeptical of the Bible because it was so often used to justify slavery. He introduced several resolutions condemning biblical authority.[95] Many of the most passionate speeches at the convention were delivered by Ernestine Rose. The atheistic feminist was no spiritualist, but, like many materialistic freethinkers, she was happy to make common cause with spiritualists, whose ranks were swelled with women, against biblical literalism and scriptural authority, and in support of social causes like abolition and women's rights. Her speeches, more than any other of the anti-Bible speeches, were met with intense heckling from the townspeople, who had little experience of women making public speeches, let alone radical ones. After Rose's final speech on the convention's fourth day, such pandemonium erupted that the convention needed to adjourn early, and the participants flee. Putnam gives a vivid account of the chaotic scene:

Ernestine L. Rose, amidst hissing and stamping of feet, and whistling in the gallery, and cries of "Go on, go on," undismayed, gave one of her radical lectures. During its delivery the lights were put out, accompanied with renewed hissing and stamping and whistling and drumming with canes. In the utter confusion, hardly any voice could be heard, but the plucky little woman finished her address notwithstanding the opposition and tumult. In closing, amidst deafening applause, she said, "My sisters, the Bible has enslaved you; the churches have been built on your subjugated necks. Do you wish to be free? Then you must trample the Bible, the church, and the priests under your feet!"[96]

Although spiritualists and other freethinkers had made common cause at least from the days of the Hartford Bible Convention, the relationship was not without its tensions. Sometimes materialistic freethinkers could not refrain from debunking phony mediums, and the spiritualists would sometimes react defensively to such attacks. One blow-up between materialism and spiritualism came at the Liberal League convention of 1884. The meeting was held on the grounds of the Cassadaga Lake Free Association, which was a spiritualist organization in far western New York. A spiritualist center exists at that place to this day.[97] Among those who were nominated for the presidency of the Liberal League that year was George Chainey, a Unitarian from England. Chainey went to Cassadaga Lake early to spend some time at the spiritualist camp, and, to the great surprise of all who knew him, had a profound experience that caused his conversion to spiritualism. Still a nominee for president, Chainey delivered an address at the convention full of enthusiasm for his newfound religion but which some took to be derisive of materialism.[98] This address was answered in no uncertain terms by several materialist freethinkers, including Thaddeus Wakeman and Charles Watts, causing a rift between the materialists and the spiritualists.[99] Chainey lost his bid for the presidency, although he would probably not have won out over Robert Ingersoll, who was elected president, in any case. The hard feelings between spiritualists and materialists lingered in some quarters.[100] An editorial in the spiritualist periodical, *Banner of Light*, called for a "divorce" between liberalism and spiritualism in 1885: "Spiritualists offered them [the liberals] the right hand of fellowship in opposing bigotry and superstition, but they have of late ignored it by traducing our mediums in public, in private, and in the columns of their newspapers, and calling us all delusionists!"[101] Notwithstanding the angry rhetoric, the bonds between spiritualism and the rest of freethought were too strong and too practical to quickly dissolve, although over the decades, as evidence against spiritualism mounted, and especially after Harry Houdini's campaign to debunk fraudulent mediums in the 1920s, the bounds did loosen and slip away.[102]

During its golden age, freethought continued the alliance with feminism it had formed before the Civil War, and increasingly this alliance overlapped the spiritualist component of freethought. A figure who is emblematic of this conjunction of feminism, freethought, and spiritualism is Amy Kirby Post, a signer of the famous 1848 Seneca Falls Declaration that championed women's rights and an ardent abolitionist whose home would become a stop on the underground railroad. In the same year that Post attended the Seneca Falls Convention she and her husband, Isaac, became involved with the Fox sisters, who lived quite close to their home in Rochester, New York. Isaac Post was an acquaintance of the Fox family and was called upon for support and advice when the strange phenomena began. It was he who had suggested that the technique of spelling out sentences by rapping at the correct letters as the alphabet was recited be made into a regular mode of spirit communication. Amy Post was among the women who participated in the rather intimate investigation of the sisters' abilities that took place backstage at Corinthian Hall, Rochester, where they made their first public appearance.[103] Both Amy and Isaac Post were convinced by what they saw and heard and were attracted to the spiritualist conception of reality. Isaac began his own practice of channeling the voices of the dead and published a book of communications from the dead in 1852. Both Amy and Isaac had been raised as Quakers but had become too freethinking for all but the most progressive branches of that faith, so it is perhaps not surprising that one of Isaac's most frequent spectral visitors was Elias Hicks, a progressive Quaker leader who passed on in 1830, and whose spirit, as channeled by Isaac, had become much more progressive in the years since his death.[104] Amy Post was very active in freethought circles in addition to being a spiritualist and a women's rights activist. In the year 1878, for instance, she served both as a vice president of the National Liberal League and treasurer of the New York Freethinkers' Association.

Of course, many women who were not spiritualists also were active in freethought associations. Among them were Elizabeth Cady Stanton, organizer of the Seneca Falls Convention and a vice president of the Liberal League;[105] Lucy N. Colman, a vigorous abolitionist and frequent speaker at meetings of the New York State Freethinkers' Association;[106] Matilda Joslyn

Gage, who was for nine years the president of the New York State Woman Suffrage Association and author of *Woman, Church, and State* (1893), which explores the connection of female subjugation and Christianity;[107] Lucretia Mott, who was a vice president of the Free Religious Association;[108] and anarchist feminist freethinker Voltairine de Cleyre.[109]

A project published in the last years of the nineteenth century shows both the ongoing importance of freethought to some feminists, and also how divisive freethought could be among women's rights advocates. In 1895, the first of the two volumes of *The Woman's Bible* appeared. The product of a twenty-five-woman committee headed by Elizabeth Cady Stanton, *The Woman's Bible* was an ambitious project that sought to offer feminist commentary on "those texts and chapters [of the Bible] directly referring to women, and those also in which women are made prominent by exclusion."[110] The project was undertaken, in Stanton's words, because "from the inauguration of the movement for woman's emancipation the Bible has been used to hold her in the 'divinely ordained sphere,' prescribed by the Old and New Testaments."[111] In general, the commentaries of *The Woman's Bible* did not aim to show that nothing in the Bible was divinely inspired, as Paine and his close followers had attempted, but only that those parts of the Bible that degraded women were not divinely inspired. "We have made a fetish of the Bible long enough," wrote Stanton. "The time had come to read it as we do all other books, accepting the good and rejecting the evil it teaches."[112] Despite Stanton's relatively moderate approach to challenging biblical authority, many in the suffrage movement thought it constituted a political liability. In January 1896, two years before the second part of *The Woman's Bible* even appeared, the National American Woman Suffrage Association officially dissociated itself from *The Woman's Bible* at its annual convention. Association president Susan B. Anthony protested, "When our platform becomes too narrow for people of all creeds and of no creeds to stand on it, I myself shall not stand upon it." But regardless, a resolution disavowing *The Woman's Bible* was passed 53–41.[113]

In addition to women's rights, another cause with which freethought was strongly associated was free love. Advocates of free love were critical of the institution of marriage as it existed in their time and thought that individuals should be able to enter into and leave romantic partnerships without state interference or social sanction. Like spiritualism, free love could be a divisive topic among freethinkers. Although almost all advocates of free love were by necessity questioners of traditional religion, there were many freethinkers who were deeply invested in a traditional understanding of marriage and sexual relations. Robert Ingersoll, for instance, rather clearly implied his opposition to free love in his speech "On the Liberty of Man, Woman, and Child": "The unit of good government is the family, and anything that tends to destroy the family is perfectly devilish and infamous. I believe in marriage, and I hold in utter contempt the opinions of those long-haired men and short-haired women who denounce the institution of marriage."[114] But there was a faction of freethinkers, of varying hair lengths, who did question the institution of marriage. Ernestine Rose, while not supporting free love per se,[115] embraced a critique of marriage as a patriarchal institution that, up until the mid-nineteenth century in most states, deprived married women of any independent property or legal standing. "When a woman marries, in almost every sense she dies legally," protested Rose in 1855. "She is in our statute books classed with infants and idiots."[116] Even after the passage of new laws regarding married women's property, feminists such as Victoria Woodhull still argued that marriage limited women's social freedom and scope of civic participation and that conventional marriage was an institution that had outlived its usefulness. "I am conducting a campaign against marriage," pronounced Woodhull in a speech she often delivered in the 1870s. "As a bond to love another until death, it is a fraud upon human happiness."[117]

The appeal of free love extended well beyond the bounds of feminism, and even beyond the bounds of the freethought movement. The earliest hotbeds of free love social experimentation in America were utopian communities. As we saw in chapter 3, New Harmony celebrated the fiftieth anniversary of American independence by declaring marriage one of the "trinity of monstrous evils," alongside private property and irrational systems of religion, that it sought liberation from.[118] Although it is not clear exactly in what ways the inhabitants of New Harmony put the conventions of marriage behind them, Robert Dale Owen did become a prominent advocate for the liberalization of divorce laws later in his life, which was one of the more conservative ways to support the cause of free love.[119] The New Harmony critique of marriage was grounded in both a socialist perspective on private property that took a dim view of a wife's person and possessions being made the property of a husband, and the freethought critique of the orthodox Christianity that proclaimed that this unfair property arrangement was ordained by God.

The justification of free love developed along rather different lines in the utopian community founded by John Humphrey Noyes, whose eventual home was the town of Oneida, New York. As a student at Yale Divinity School in the 1830s, Noyes had a realization that the second coming of Christ had taken place long ago, in about 70 CE, and that the world now existed in a state of regeneration in which the old moral laws did not apply. Taking this as justification to reprogram the moral and social order, Noyes founded a community that permitted free sexual relations between its male and female members provided that men practiced continence—i.e., keeping their seed to themselves—and that all agreed to procreate only with the official blessing of the community elders, who would be matchmakers seeking to eugenically improve the quality of the community's offspring. As it turned out, the community elders seem to have lain a strong priority on Noyes himself fathering a great number of "superior children" by procreating with the most eugenic young women. Noyes was eventually obliged to flee to Canada to avoid answering a statutory rape charge. After Noyes's departure, the economically successful community he founded converted to a joint stock company.[120] The company exists to this day, making fancy flatware that bears the name of Oneida. Freethinkers generally found more to learn from this deeply flawed example of free love in action than in Mormon polygamy, which they condemned almost universally as one-sided free love justified by phony revelation.[121]

Free love had many champions who were not connected to utopian communities. One such was Austin Kent, whose 1857 *Free Love: Or, a Philosophical Demonstration of the Non-exclusive Nature of Connubial Love* was among the earliest treatises to openly support the idea. But no one was more successful in prompting a broad public discussion of it than Victoria Woodhull, a freethinking spiritualist who gained notoriety in the 1870s as a champion of free love. Woodhull's condemnation of marriage and support of free love comes from a distinctly feminist perspective. In her most passionate speech on the topic, "Tried as by Fire," she expresses her views as follows,

> Of all the horrid brutalities of this age, I know of none so horrid as those that are sanctioned and defended by marriage. Night after night there are thousands of rapes committed, under cover of this accursed license; and millions—yes, I say it boldly, knowing whereof I speak—millions of poor, heart-broken, suffering wives are compelled to minister to the lechery of insatiable husbands, when every instinct of body and sentiment of soul revolts in loathing and disgust ... yet marriage is to be held synonymous with morality! I say, eternal damnation sink such morality![122]

Woodhull, whose parents had given her into an unhappy marriage with a much older man when she was just fourteen, believed that inside or outside of marriage, human dignity demands that the heart needs to be free to choose whom to love and how, and should be able to choose anew every day, regardless of what is written in scripture or taught by the church. She promoted this view not only in her speeches but in the first new freethought periodical to appear in New York City after the Civil War, *Woodhull & Claflin's Weekly*.

Woodhull & Claflin's Weekly, *The Truth Seeker*, and the New Freethought Press

Beginning in the 1870s there was an explosion of freethought periodicals to accompany the explosive growth of the movement. The most prominent and most enduring of the new freethought periodicals was called *The Truth Seeker*, founded in 1873 by D. M. Bennett. But before there was *The Truth Seeker*, there was *Woodhull & Claflin's Weekly,* founded by sisters Victoria Woodhull and Tennessee Claflin in 1870, two women who embarked on a journalistic career after becoming the first female stockbrokers on Wall Street.

Woodhull and Claflin led lives with enough unexpected turns to rival any fictional steampunk heroines of today's literature and film. Victoria Woodhull was born in September 1838 in Homer, Ohio, the seventh of ten children. Queen Victoria's coronation had taken place the previous June, perhaps influencing her parents' choice of name. Her sister Tennessee (often written Tennie C.) was born six years later. Her father, Buckman, was a lawyer and speculator who lost the family's modest fortune when Victoria was about three. Her mother, Roxana, was a spiritualist who believed she could commune with the spirit world, but she also attended Christian revivalist meetings. The only contemporaneous biographical account of Woodhull was written by her friend Theodore Tilton in 1871, probably in preparation of her 1872 candidacy for president of the United States. According to this campaign-oriented biography, both the father and the mother beat the children more than was normal for the time. From a young age, like her mother, Victoria believed that she could talk to spirits and felt that she was often guided by the spirit of the ancient Greek orator Demosthenes. When Victoria was just fourteen, her parents gave their consent for her to be wed to a twenty-eight-year-old doctor named Canning Woodhull, a relation of a mayor of New York, Caleb Smith Woodhull. The couple had two children, Byron, who was mentally disabled, and Zulu Maude. According to Tilton's account, the marriage was dreadful for Victoria because of her husband's drunkenness, liaisons with other women, and incapacity to provide a decent home. Victoria began a career as an actress to help make ends meet but then discovered she could earn more by calling on the spirits to heal the sick. She earned enough money in this way to become financially independent and so divorced her husband after the birth of her daughter. She kept the name Woodhull because it was that name by which she was known as a spiritual healer. She soon became close with one Colonel James Harvey Blood, a fellow spiritualist who had served with the Union during the Civil War. She married Colonel Blood in 1866.

In the meantime, Mr. and Mrs. Claflin had set up their youngest daughter, Tennessee, as a medium and had made holding séances into the main family business. According to Tilton, Tennessee had true spiritual gifts, but those gifts had been corrupted by the deceptions of her parents. After her divorce, Victoria rescued young Tennessee from the dishonest family and teamed up with her to work as partners in an honest séance and spiritual healing business.[123] They seemed a likely pair, for by that time the Fox sisters had well established in the public mind that spiritual gifts ran in families and were not infrequently shared by sisters.

Woodhull and Claflin's lives changed course again when, through their spiritual services business, they formed a connection with ultrawealthy transportation magnet Cornelius Vanderbilt. As they won Vanderbilt's trust and affection, they set their sights on a trade even more lucrative than speaking to the dead: finance. With Vanderbilt's help they went into business as stockbrokers in 1869 under the name Woodhull, Claflin and Company. In an interview with the *New York Herald*, they claimed to have made $700,000 by 1870, thriving in the midst of a market crash that wiped out many competitors.[124] On the heels of this success, and with more aid from Vanderbilt, they launched *Woodhull & Claflin's Weekly*. There is not much record of Woodhull, Claflin and Company after the launch of *Woodhull & Claflin's Weekly* and the beginning of Woodhull's career as a lecturer.[125]

Woodhull & Claflin's Weekly was not the tidy little financial paper that Vanderbilt probably imagined it would be. Its banner, beginning October 8, 1870, read, "Progress! Free Thought! Untrammeled Lives!"[126] A good deal of the content of the paper was spiritualistic and feministic, but it also opposed organized religion, and championed workers' rights and free love. It did not reprint the Nine Demands of Liberalism, but it did run editorials calling for the secularization of public schools. It published the first English translation of *The Communist Manifesto* on December 30, 1871.[127] As estimated by *Geo.*

P. Rowell and Co.'s *American Newspaper Directory*, its circulation in 1873 was 1,500. But what the paper lacked in circulation it made up in ambition. The *Weekly* became the party organ of the Equal Rights Party, a small political party organized by Woodhull and Claflin that nominated Woodhull as its candidate for president of the United States at its convention in 1872. Frederick Douglass, the well-known escaped slave who had become a prominent abolitionist, was nominated as her running mate.[128] Douglass was not present at the nominating convention, was not consulted about the nomination beforehand, and does not seem to have acknowledged it.

The eclectic nature of *Woodhull & Claflin's Weekly* can be accounted for by Woodhull's unique spiritualistic brand of freethought, which is perhaps best explained in her lecture "The Religion of Humanity" delivered to the American Association of Spiritualists in 1872 and reprinted in the *Weekly*. In it she made clear that, unlike most freethinkers, she did not believe that religion should remain separate from politics but rather that it was the responsibility of her religion, spiritualism, to act in the political realm. For her, spiritualism was the "religion of humanity," the purest expression of the human religious instinct; a religion that gave the assurance of immortality but abolished the fear of hell; a religion that needed no priests to act as intermediaries with God, and no hierarchal religious organizations, for each person could learn to commune with the spirit world for themselves. It was the responsibility of spiritualism to solve social problems of poverty and injustice.[129] In her own mind, being a spiritualist candidate for president was perhaps even more important than being a female candidate. She may have hoped that her spirits might lend a helping hand in her ambition that a woman named Victoria be head of state on both sides of the Atlantic, but in 1872, the spirits could not deliver even a single electoral vote. They were perhaps more helpful in getting Woodhull elected as president of the American Association of Spiritualists in 1871 and reelected every term through 1876.[130]

Although *The Truth Seeker* would quickly surpass *Woodhull & Claflin's Weekly* as New York's leading freethought paper, its beginnings were less portentous. DeRobigne Mortimer Bennett was born in 1818 in Springfield, New York. A congenitally malformed foot caused him to walk with a limp for his entire life. As a boy he attended a Methodist church with his mother, got a rudimentary education, and began working at a printing press when he was twelve. At fourteen, he was moved by the kindness of some Shakers he encountered and joined their community in New Lebanon, New York. The Shakers continued his education in their school, and he learned something about horticulture and herbalism in service of the community. He thought well of the Shakers his whole life, but in 1846 he and a young woman named Mary Hicks, who had also been taken in by the Shakers, left the celibate religious community to get married. In the following years he supported himself as an apothecary, a seller of shrubs and fruit trees, and the proprietor of a seed business. Curiosity prompted by encounters with freethought literature inspired Bennett to go to New York City to visit Gilbert Vale, the editor of *The Beacon*. Bennett bought twenty volumes of freethought literature from Vale, including *Age of Reason*. As it is recorded in his obituary, "He read and re-read that [*Age of Reason*], saw it was unanswerable, and from a strict churchman, praying twice a day, and asking a blessing at each meal besides, he became an outspoken Freethinker."[131]

Eighteen seventy-three found Bennett in Paris, Illinois, struggling to get a seed-selling business going. For two years he had been hampered by weather that was too dry. After refusing to call on the Lord through prayer for better weather, he became engaged in a debate with a couple of local ministers about the efficacy of prayer. Because the local newspaper's editor would not give him the space to publish his views, he started his own paper. That was *The Truth Seeker*. Its first issue was eight pages long and appeared in September 1873. It contained Bennett's reply to the prayerful ministers of Paris, Illinois, the Nine Demands of Liberalism, and articles such as "Priestcraft and Science Contrasted." Its banner proclaimed that it was devoted to "Science, Morals, Free Thought, Free Enquiry, and the Diffusion of Liberal Sentiments." After his partners forced him to liquidate his seed business, he relocated *The Truth Seeker* to New York City in 1874 and set up an office on the top floor of the Moffat building on Broadway. He quickly fell in with the members of New York's liberal clubs and through them became acquainted with Eugene MacDonald, a young printer he engaged to produce the paper for him. Soon the two were joined in their work by Eugene's younger brother, George.[132] Eugene and George would each in turn succeed Bennett as editor of *The Truth Seeker*. In 1878 *The Truth Seeker* became the de facto organ of the National Liberal League when, at the national convention in Syracuse at the end of October, Francis Abbot, editor of *The Index*, which had covered the league's activities up to that time, led a faction that seceded from the league and henceforth used his paper to report the activities of the short-lived breakaway group.[133] *N. W. Ayer & Son's American Newspaper Annual* put *Truth Seeker*'s circulation at around 8,000 in 1881, but other estimates are far higher.[134] The paper gained a great asset when cartoonist Watson Heston began contributing his comically irreverent and often rude illustrations in 1886. Beginning January 9, 1886, most issues of *Truth Seeker* had one of his cartoons printed quite large at the top of page one. The first one shows a gang of demon-horned clergy—labeled Baptist, Methodist, Presbyterian, and Catholic—blasting a beleaguered Uncle Sam with trumpets to try to get more appropriations from him.

The *Truth Seeker* was the most successful of a large crop of freethought publications that sprang up during the golden age of freethought. Among the American periodicals listed by Putnam in *400 Years of Freethought* are Horace L. Green's *Freethinkers' Magazine*, later renamed *Free Thought Magazine*, which was published from 1882 to 1903, as it merged with *Torch of Reason* to become the *Liberal Review*;[135] James Dickinson Shaw's *Independent Pulpit* out of Waco, Texas;[136] *Secular Thought*, the principal organ of the Canadian freethought movement from 1887 to 1911;[137] the *American Nonconformist* out of Tabor, Iowa;[138] Dr. Jasper Roland Monroe's *Ironclad Age* out of Indianapolis;[139] a San Francisco journal called *Freethought* that Putnam himself ran with George MacDonald until it merged with *Truth Seeker*;[140] the journal *Man* edited by T. C. Leland, which also merged with *Truth Seeker*; the *Radical Review*, which started publishing in Madison, Wisconsin, in 1881, edited by George Schumm;[141] the *Chicago Liberal* edited by Mrs. M. A. Freeman; and Moses Harman's *Lucifer, the Light Bearer*, a journal that promoted sexual liberation in Kansas.[142] There likely were far more freethought periodicals in America than Putnam named. He does not, for instance, mention *Woodhull & Claflin's Weekly*. Because of their free discussions of religion and especially matters concerning sex and reproduction, the editors of some of these freethought periodicals—including Victoria Woodhull, Tennessee Claflin, and D. M. Bennett—found themselves being prosecuted under a new set of federal laws that forbade the distribution of "obscene" materials through the US mail. These laws were generally called the Comstock laws in reference to their primary architect and agent, Anthony Comstock.

Anthony Comstock: Freethought's *Bête Noire*

In the spring of 1872, the New York YMCA Committee for the Suppression of Obscene Literature had a problem, and Anthony Comstock appeared to be the solution. Alarmed by the proliferation of pornography in New York, the YMCA had taken on the mission of protecting young Christian men from immoral words and pictures. Years of work had culminated in the passage of New York State's first anti-obscenity law in 1868, but all subsequent attempts to get the law rigorously enforced had met with frustration.[143] What the committee really needed was an agent of its own who could be trusted to carry out the morally hazardous work of infiltrating dens of iniquity to obtain evidence. Enter Anthony Comstock, a sturdy young man with muttonchop sideburns. Born in 1844, Comstock hailed from Connecticut and had served in the Union Army before moving to Brooklyn in 1867, where he lived with his wife and worked as a salesclerk. After the death of a friend that he blamed on exposure to pornographic material, an inference made possible by the widespread belief that masturbation could sap a person's vital energy even to the point of mortality, he dedicated himself to shutting down purveyors of sexual vice. A letter to the YMCA got him a visit from Morris Ketchum Jesup, the chairman of the New York YMCA board, and a salary to help police enforce the anti-obscenity law. By the end of 1872, Comstock had helped the police seize seven tons of illicit books, 187,600 illicit pictures, and many other articles. But Comstock was only just getting started.[144]

On November 2, 1872, *Woodhull & Claflin's Weekly* published a lengthy article written by Woodhull concerning an extramarital affair between Henry Ward Beecher, a renowned Brooklyn preacher, and Elizabeth Tilton, the wife of Theodore Tilton, his co-editor on the paper *The Independent* and a friend of Woodhull's. Woodhull wrote that she was publishing the material to expose the hypocrisy of those who, like Beecher, denounced her free love outlook in public but followed it in private.[145] In the same issue Claflin wrote an article about the shameful conduct of one Mr. L. C. Challis, who, with a male friend, seduced and bedded two fifteen-year-old girls from Baltimore when they were visiting New York and then kept them at a brothel for their continuing enjoyment. The point of the article was to expose not only this misdeed but also the broader problem of sexual double standards.[146] There was nothing explicit in either of these articles, and nothing that this author finds obscene, except the conduct that is alluded to without being described in detail. Nonetheless, Comstock became determined to have both sisters prosecuted. When state law enforcement declined to act, under an assumed identity Comstock requested that the sisters mail him a copy of the paper. Then he had them arrested for violating a new federal law against sending obscene material through the mail. After a harrowing series of arrests and bail proceedings that caused Woodhull to become seriously ill, she and her sister were acquitted on June 27, 1873, after the judge ruled that the law on obscenity they were being tried under did not cover newspapers.[147] They were acquitted in a separate libel case concerning Claflin's article about

Challis the next year.[148] So, Comstock's first high-profile prosecutorial effort was a bust, but it was only the beginning.

For their part, Woodhull and Claflin were given golden parachutes of a sort by the Vanderbilt family. After the death of Cornelius Vanderbilt in 1877, the Vanderbilt family was eager to get Woodhull and Claflin and all the embarrassing secrets that they knew well out of the way, so they paid them handsomely to leave the country. The sisters cut their ties to America, romantic and otherwise, and took a ship to London. By 1885, both sisters had married wealthy British men. Tennessee even got the use of the title "Lady," because her husband, Francis Cook, was made a baronet less than a year after the wedding.[149] It was a remarkably unlikely conclusion to the story of the women who published the first English translation of *The Communist Manifesto*.

As Woodhull and Claflin were being brought to trial, Comstock went to Washington to lobby for a stronger federal obscenity law. He was successful. On March 3, 1873, Congress passed an act that made it unlawful to send any "book, pamphlet, picture, paper, print, or other publication" that was "obscene, lewd, lascivious" or "of an indecent character" through the US mail, in addition to "any article or thing designed or intended for the prevention of conception or procuring of abortion."[150] Comstock had the word "paper" included with the Woodhull and Claflin case in mind, but this backfired: the judge in the case took the addition of "paper" to the new law to imply that newspapers were not covered by the old one under the heading of "other publication." Even though he inadvertently laid the groundwork for Woodhull and Claflin's acquittal, Comstock now had a law that in the future could and would be applied to papers like *The Truth Seeker*. And his appointment as a special agent of the US Postal Service, another by-product of his trip to Washington, gave him a government title that turned his privately funded crusade to make the world safe for young Christian men into official government business.[151] The federal "Comstock Law" of 1873 was just one of a crop of new anti-obscenity laws, most of which were enacted at the state level, the product of a nationwide anti-obscenity movement.[152]

Comstock's drive to use the new obscenity laws to punish those who violated the tenets of Christianity as he understood it led him to go after no small number of freethinkers, but his most celebrated persecution, and the one that, quite opposite his intentions, did the most to unify and grow the movement, was his campaign against *Truth Seeker* editor D. M. Bennett. On Monday, November 12, 1877, Comstock entered the offices of *The*

Truth Seeker accompanied by a deputy US marshal and displayed two pamphlets that he had ordered from Bennett using an assumed name. The pamphlets were Bennett's own *Open Letter to Jesus Christ*, which consisted of a long series of searching and somewhat irreverent questions to the man who inspired the Christian religion, and a piece of popular nature science by A. B. Bradford called *How Do Marsupials Propagate Their Kind?* It described the fascinating mechanics of pouch-based gestation in opossums and kangaroos. Comstock deemed these works obscene on the grounds that one was blasphemous and the other discussed sex. He charged that Bennett had broken federal law by sending them through the mail, and he had obtained a warrant for Bennett's arrest. As Bennett accompanied Comstock and the deputy marshal to have his bail set, he suggested that members of the Bible Society should also be indicted as the Bible had far more obscene material in it than either of the pamphlets he had mailed. By way of example, he cited "Abraham and his concubine . . . David and Bathsheba and his other wives, the rape of Amnon and his sister Tamar, the adultery of Absalom and his father's concubine, and the extensive operations of Solomon with his seven hundred wives . . ." As they happened to be walking through crowds with women in them, Comstock indicated that he didn't think it was proper to speak of such matters in mixed company.[153] This particular case against Bennett never got to trial because Robert Ingersoll went to Washington and called on the postmaster general to show him copies of the pamphlets that Bennett was charged with selling and appealed to his good judgment about whether they were actually obscene. He also let it be known that he would defend Bennett if the case went to trial. The case was quickly dropped.[154] But Comstock persisted in his efforts to send Bennett to jail.

The next time Bennett was arrested was at the Freethinkers Convention in Watkins, New York, on August 24, 1878. This time he and two colleagues, W. S. Bell and Josephine Tilton, were arrested for selling a pamphlet called *Cupid's Yokes* that had been written by Tilton's brother-in-law, Ezra Heywood. It was a work that defended "the natural right and necessity of sexual self-government," in other words, free love. The content is not explicit nor even sensual. There are no pictures. It is an intellectual defense of the idea that women and men both should be able to make free choices about sex. In the course of making his arguments, Heywood attacks the federal Comstock Law for suppression of necessary public discussions of sexuality, and Comstock himself for his callous attitude toward those he persecutes.[155] This is perhaps the real reason that Comstock singled the book out as obscene and tricked Heywood into mailing him a copy in order to have him arrested and given a two-year prison sentence. Freethought and free love activists rallied to Heywood's defense and secured a rare presidential pardon from Rutherford B. Hayes after Heywood had served six months. It was for selling this book, whose author had been jailed by Comstock and would be pardoned by the president, that Bennett, Tilton, and Bell were arrested. Although the arrest was made by local authorities for violating New York State obscenity laws, it eventually came out that Comstock had orchestrated it by writing to the Watkins YMCA. Although Bennett had to travel back to Watkins a couple times to make court appearances in this case, it was a third arrest, this time for selling *Cupid's Yokes* through the mail, that landed Bennett in jail.[156]

Bennett was not overly sympathetic with the free love position, but he most certainly believed in free speech, so after his arrest in Watkins for selling *Cupid's Yokes* he printed a notice in his paper that he would mail a copy of *Cupid's Yokes* to anyone who sent him fifteen cents.[157] Using another assumed name, Comstock did just that and Bennett was arrested again on December 10, 1878. This time the case did go to trial and although Bennett was ably defended by the brothers Abraham and Thaddeus Wakeman, both prominent freethinking attorneys, Judge Charles L. Benedict, in whose court Comstock had never lost a case, sustained objections against most of their arguments that *Cupid's Yokes* was not obscene, forbidding anything more than short excerpts to be read aloud. Bennett was found guilty.[158] The case was appealed, and the conviction was upheld by a panel of judges that included Benedict. In writing the decision that upheld the conviction, Judge Samuel Blatchford became one of the first judges in the United States to employ the dangerously broad Hicklin test of obscenity. This test, borrowed from the 1868 *Regina v. Hicklin* case in England, held that any work that tended to "deprave and corrupt those whose minds are open to such immoral influences" is obscene.[159] It made no allowance for authorial intent, artistic merit, or the context in which obscene words and phrases were used. This broad standard of obscenity continued to be used by Comstock and his followers to censor any work they believed to be immoral until it was struck down in a 1933 case concerning James Joyce's *Ulysses*.[160] After his conviction was upheld, Bennett was sentenced to thirteen months at Albany Penitentiary. Both Ingersoll and Thaddeus Wakeman appealed to President Hayes to pardon Bennett as he had pardoned Heywood, the author of the book Bennett was convicted of mailing, but this time Comstock had launched his own anti-pardon campaign, calling on prominent clergy to make the case for keeping Bennett in jail. After much soul-searching Hayes decided against a pardon. "While I am satisfied that Bennett ought not to have been convicted," he wrote in his diary, "I am not satisfied that I ought to undertake to correct the mistakes of the courts."[161] Bennett ended up serving eleven months of his sentence.

Bennett's imprisonment had an effect on the freethought movement exactly the opposite of what Comstock and his allies hoped for. Putnam attributes the explosive growth of the National Liberal League in 1880 to an outpouring of sympathy for Bennett. The New York Freethinkers' Association and *The Truth Seeker* gathered 70,000 signatures on a petition to Congress for the repeal of the Comstock laws that year.[162] A group called the National Defense Association was founded in 1878 as a response to Comstock's persecution of Bennett, Heywood, and others; it was to be the legal defense arm of the freethought movement. Its founding articles state: "The objects of this association are to investigate all questionable cases of prosecution under what are known as the Comstock laws state and national and to extend sympathy, moral support, and material aid to those who may be unjustly assailed by the enemies of free speech and free press."[163] It gathered 200,000 signatures in support of a presidential pardon for Bennett and raised large amounts of money for the cause of defending Bennett and other freethinkers.[164]

Because the jailing of Bennett seemed so palpably unjust to the great mass of those who had come to think of themselves as liberals, Comstock proved to be an even more effective *bête noire* for the Liberal League than had been the prospect of a Christian Amendment to the constitution, but exactly what position to take on the Comstock laws became a divisive issue within the growing league. While some argued vigorously that the laws should be repealed, others argued with equal vigor that laws against true obscenity were justified in principle, and that the Comstock laws should be reformed rather than repealed. Francis Abbot, the editor of *The Index* and first president of the National Liberal League was one of those who took the position that the Comstock laws should be reformed rather than repealed. In an editorial published in *The Index* on April 25, 1878, he took issue with the petition to repeal the Comstock laws. Liberals, he writes, "blindly blundered into petitioning for the total repeal of the 'obscene literature' laws ... they will have to pay for their blunder by being held up (falsely, of course) by their opponents everywhere, as defenders of the vile stuff."[165]

The difference between Abbot's position on the Comstock laws from that of Bennett caused a major rift in the Liberal League in 1878. At the League's

Congress in Syracuse in late October, Abbot led a group of about fifty delegates to secede from the league after he lost the election for president to write-in candidate Elizur Wright, a man known to support total repeal of the Comstock laws. Abbot withdrew from the organization, taking eight local affiliates with him and formed the National Liberal League of America. Henceforth, the original organization became known as the National Liberal League of the United States. A similar dispute led to the departure of Robert Ingersoll the following year.[166] Ingersoll, however, returned to the organization and was elected president in 1884, when it made a "new departure" and changed its name to the "American Secular Union."[167] It continued to meet under that name until at least 1911.

Although the rift between Ingersoll and the Liberal League was mended in a few years, Abbot's opposition to Bennett took a bitter turn in 1879 while Bennett was in prison. In 1876, Bennett, during a rough patch in his marriage, had fallen in love with a woman in her thirties who had worked briefly at *The Truth Seeker*. Her name was Hannah Josephine McNellis, described as a petite and chatty woman who had been born an Irish Catholic but who had become a liberal and a spiritualist. The affair remained platonic, but Bennett's attachment to McNellis persisted even after she had left *The Truth Seeker* and caused him to write her a series of love letters before friends convinced him he was being foolish, and he reconciled with his wife. Unfortunately, the love letters fell into the hands of those who did not approve of Bennett's hard line against the Comstock laws. McNellis, after trying unsuccessfully to sell the embarrassing letters back to Bennett, who turned down her offer because he had already confessed everything to his wife, sold them to John C. Bundy, the editor of the *Religio-Philosophical Journal*, a reform-minded but relatively conservative spiritualist paper out of Chicago.[168] Bundy published the letters in the October 25, 1879, issue of his paper. The headline read, "Another Imposter Unearthed. The Would-Be Martyr a Foul-Mouthed Libertine. D. M. Bennett, the Apostle of Nastiness. Professing Devotion to His Wife, He Teaches Free Love."[169] The same article and headline were reprinted in Abbot's *Index* on October 30.[170] In case any of Bennett's readers had missed the exposition of his letters in the *Religio-Philosophical Journal* and *The Index*, Bundy acquired a copy of *Truth Seeker*'s mailing list and sent the October 25 issue of his paper to everyone on it.[171]

Despite all this nastiness, Bennett's reputation was done little long-term harm by the scandal. He admitted in print that he had behaved badly and apologized, while also giving the lie to the falsehoods and misrepresentations in Bundy's account of the affair.[172] When the dust settled, as George MacDonald writes, "Bennett lost no credit. Those who had been his friends remained so still."[173] It might be added that those who had been his readers also remained so still, with possibly some new readers attracted by the sensational scandal. After Bennett was released from prison on April 29, 1880, grand receptions were held in his honor by the National Defense Association, the Fourth Liberal League of New York, and other organizations. The following August, the National Liberal League sent him on a trip to Brussels, Belgium, to represent the organization at the Congress of the Universal Federation of Freethinkers, a major international freethought organization. The reports of international freethought that he sent back to *The Truth Seeker* were eventually collected into one of his most popular books, *The Truth Seeker Abroad* (original title *An Infidel Abroad*).[174]

Bennett was far from being the only freethinker persecuted by Comstock. There were others who came to far greater harm than he did. One of the most tragic cases was that of Ida Craddock, a mystic spiritualist born in 1857 who served as secretary of the American Secular Union from 1889 to 1891.[175] She began her career as an author with a defense of a belly dancing exhibition at the 1893 World's Fair in Chicago that Comstock had attacked as obscene.[176] Soon after, she, in her own mind at least, married the spirit of a childhood friend named Soph who had died years earlier. As she prepared a manuscript explaining her status as the "wife of an angel," her mother, a strictly religious widow who made a living selling a cannabis extract as a cure for a variety of illnesses,[177] decided that Ida was insane and attempted to have her committed to an asylum against her will. Ida fled to London and stayed there until she reconciled with her mother in 1895, after which she returned to the United States and briefly led a Chicago congregation called the Church of Yoga.[178] Purportedly drawing on her experience with her spirit husband, she began to publish sex manuals for married or soon-to-be married people, including *Right Marital Living* (1899) and *The Wedding Night* (1900).[179] These works are explicit, but instructional in character rather than erotic, mainly giving advice on how to make sex as enjoyable for the woman as for the man, albeit from a very Victorian point of view. The instructional nature of these books made no difference to Comstock, who had Craddock arrested for sending them through the mail. An 1899 conviction led to a three-month prison term, which she refused to evade by pleading insanity. After being convicted again in 1902, she committed suicide rather than face a five-year prison term.

Craddock wrote letters to both the public and to her mother before, as she saw it, crossing into the spirit world to be with her Soph. To the public she wrote, "I am taking my own life, because a judge, at the instigation of Anthony Comstock, has decreed me guilty of a crime I did not commit . . . and has announced his intention of consigning me to prison long term."[180] To her mother she wrote, "I will not consent to go to the asylum, as you are evidently planning to have me go. I know this means perpetual imprisonment all my life long, unless I recant my religious beliefs or else hypocritically pretend to do so. I cannot bring myself to consent to any of these three alternatives. I maintain my right to die as I have lived, a free woman, not cowed into silence by another human being."[181]

A special 1878 issue of *The Truth Seeker* gives a list of Comstock's victims up to that point. Among them are George Francis Train, a successful railroad financier who was arrested and jailed in 1872 for publishing a collection of Bible verses that were obscene by the standards of the day. He hoped to get a trial at which it would be ruled that the Bible was obscene, but he was never granted one. John A. Lant was arrested for publishing a freethought journal called *The Sun*. Dr. Edward Bliss Foote was arrested for publishing a book of medical advice for lay people called *Medical Common Sense* that contained advice for married people about fulfilling sex and contraception. Dr. J. Bryon was arrested simply for advertising that a perfume was "bewitching."[182] To these cases reviewed in *The Truth Seeker* in 1878, we should add the later cases of Elmina Slenker, an atheistic novelist whose romantic fiction featuring freethinking women was serialized in *The Truth Seeker*. She was arrested in 1887 for sending letters of sex and marriage advice to private correspondents through the mail.[183] And of course, Margaret Sanger was prosecuted in 1914 for distributing a birth control pamphlet called *Family Limitation*.[184] Comstock's long-term commitment to suppressing freethought and allied causes, while securing many convictions, in the long term only fueled a movement that had long since learned to thrive on persecution.

Charles B. Reynolds's Blasphemy Trial

Although Comstock's persecution of freethinkers remained an ominous background drumbeat as the movement marched on into the twentieth century, Comstock was not the only martyr-maker of his era. The 1887 blasphemy trial of Charles B. Reynolds was prosecuted entirely by local New Jersey authorities, but it won the attention of the mainstream press and generated headlines that were seen across the country. Reynolds was born in New York City in 1832 and preached as a Seventh Day Adventist before converting to what he called "the religion of humanity" in his forties. By 1886 he had become a very prominent freethinker. Since 1884, he had served as chair of the Executive Committee of the American Secular Union.[185] He lectured widely in New York, New Jersey, and Canada that year. *The Truth Seeker* covered an incident where a business had threatened to fire employees who attended his lecture in Jobstown, New Jersey.[186] His lectures included titles like "Sabbath of the Bible," "The Devil Not So Black as He is Painted," and "The Heaven of the Bible." He sometimes appeared with Mrs. Frank C. Reynolds, who is occasionally referred to as his wife.[187] She was the secretary of the New York State Freethought Association and gave a lecture called "Woman's Reasons for the Religion of Humanity."[188]

In March 1886, Reynolds helped organize a chapter of the Secular Union in Boonton, New Jersey, with liberal town councilman James Maxfield and a local family named Booth.[189] On Monday, July 26, Reynolds set up his lecture tent in Boonton, likely at the invitation of the Boonton Secular Union. The several daughters of the Booth family formed a choir that was to begin the lectures with secular hymns. The lecture went smoothly on Monday night, but on Tuesday the lecturer and his audience found the tent surrounded by what were said to be Methodist and Catholic protesters, who heckled attendees and threw some stones at the tent. Although Reynolds was able to finish his lecture, the following day he lodged complaints against some of the more aggressive hecklers and asked the mayor for protection. But that night the mob came back even bigger than before, and a marshal showed up to arrest Reynolds for blasphemy as soon as he started lecturing. The bail of $300 was quickly posted by Maxfield, but Reynolds was told that local authorities could not guarantee his safety. When he tried to resume his lecture, the mob outside made so much noise that it was impossible to continue, and he was forced to tell the audience, which had waited patiently as bail was set and paid, to go home. After the mob started shouting threats against Reynolds, members of the Booth family encircled him and got him through the crowd to safety. Soon after, the mob attacked the tent, causing its collapse. The tent was badly damaged, and Reynolds pressed charges against the mob leaders responsible.[190]

The incident was reported in detail in *The Truth Seeker*, and Reynolds received a huge outpouring of support from the freethought community. Almost every subsequent issue for months announced more contributions to his defense fund. On August 21, Robert Ingersoll, who at the time was serving as the president of the American Secular Union, announced that he would undertake Reynolds's defense at no charge, but still the contributions for defense and tent repair kept pouring in.[191] The September 4 issue of *The Truth Seeker* printed a large Watson Heston cartoon on the front page depicting Reynolds in front of his tent in Boonton tossing pearls to swine marked as Methodists or Catholics as the local Methodist minister and Catholic priest threatened him with cudgels.[192] Reynolds included the cartoon, which was rude but typical of its era, in a pamphlet that he wrote to defend himself, *Blasphemy and the Bible*, which was published in *The Truth Seeker* in two parts before being offered for sale as a pamphlet.[193] Copies of this pamphlet were distributed in Morristown, New Jersey. Some Morristown residents were so incensed by it that they arranged for a second blasphemy indictment of Reynolds related to the content of the pamphlet.[194]

After a series of delays, the trial finally opened on May 19, 1887, in Morristown, the county seat. It was decided that charges related to the Boonton incident would be dropped, likely because the main witnesses against Reynolds were also the leaders of the mob that had attacked him, and that Reynolds would be tried only for the distribution of *Blasphemy and the Bible* in Morristown. From a legal perspective, the situation was much the same as it had been in the Kneeland trial fifty years earlier. New Jersey had passed an antiblasphemy statute in 1796 that had a provision against ridiculing scripture, and the law had been reaffirmed in 1844 and 1874, although it was not known to ever have been used.[195] Reynolds had clearly broken this unused law with his pamphlet. Ingersoll did not even make a show of trying to argue otherwise. He called no witnesses but simply made a three-hour speech to the jury denouncing the law as unjust and unconstitutional. He got right to the point in his opening:

> The question to be tried by you is whether a man has the right to express his honest thought; and for that reason, there can be no case of greater importance submitted to a jury. And it may be well enough for me, at the outset, to admit that there could be no case in which I could take a greater—a deeper interest. For my part, I would not wish to live in a world where I could not express my honest opinions. Men who deny to others the right of speech are not fit to live with honest men. I deny the right of any man, of any number of men, of any church, of any State, to put a padlock on the lips—to make the

tongue a convict. I passionately deny the right of the Herod of authority to kill the children of the brain.[196]

Ingersoll went on to point out how unequivocal the New Jersey constitution's affirmation of the right of free speech is, and how vague and arbitrary the blasphemy law is given the inconsistencies and contradictions of the Bible and Christian doctrine. Eventually, he uses the vagueness of the term "blasphemy" to turn the accusation of blasphemy against Reynolds on its head:

> What is blasphemy? I will give you a definition; I will give you my thought upon this subject. What is real blasphemy?
> To live on the unpaid labor of other men—that is blasphemy.
> To enslave your fellow man, to put chains upon his body—that is blasphemy.
> To enslave the minds of men, to put manacles upon the brain, padlocks upon the lips—that is blasphemy.
> To deny what you believe to be true, to admit to be true what you believe to be a lie—that is blasphemy.
> To strike the weak and unprotected, in order that you may gain the applause of the ignorant and superstitious mob—that is blasphemy.
> To persecute the intelligent few, at the command of the ignorant many—that is blasphemy.
> To forge chains, to build dungeons, for your honest fellow men—that is blasphemy.
> To pollute the souls of children with the dogma of eternal pain—that is blasphemy.
> To violate your conscience—that is blasphemy.
> The jury that gives an unjust verdict, and the Judge who pronounces an unjust sentence, are blasphemers.
> The man who bows to public opinion against his better judgment and against his honest conviction, is a blasphemer.[197]

Naturally, *The Truth Seeker* was very complimentary about what Ingersoll had to say: "Mercilessly, he denounced the law, and with flawless logic showed that if Mr. Reynolds had not the right to express his sentiments, then no man on the Jury had the right to speak his. He touched every chord of the human heart and had the audience with him in every thought."[198]

It would have been a very unusual jury to have completely ignored the judge's clear instruction that the constitutionality of the law was not at issue and attempt to nullify the law with a "not guilty" verdict. But although the jury found Reynolds guilty, they imposed only a minimal sentence of $25 plus expenses, amounting to $75 in total, far less than the year of hard labor Reynolds could have been sentenced to. Ingersoll paid the judgment out of his own pocket on behalf of his client, and Reynolds headed back home the next day. A few months after the trial he received an invitation to lecture for a new chapter of the Secular Union in Walla Walla, Washington. Within two years he moved his family to the new state, where he organized new local chapters of the Secular Union and continued to lecture for the rest of his life.[199]

Ingersoll's speech in defense of Reynolds was remembered by freethinkers as "one of the most eloquent defenses of liberty in the annals of Freethought" through which "the law against blasphemy received its death wound."[200] The trial was covered not only by *The Truth Seeker* but by the *New York Times*, which printed a substantial excerpt of Ingersoll's speech. Freethinkers for a long time asserted that it was the last trial for blasphemy in the United States, a lost battle that won the war. Even after the conviction of Michael Mockus for blasphemy in 1921, it could be asserted that it was the last blasphemy trial south of Maine. Ingersoll made the trial into a symbol of the futility of trying to restrict speech to repress ideas, saying that the trial "will give Mr. Reynolds a congregation of fifty millions of people. And yet it was done for the purpose of stopping a discussion."[201]

Freethinkers Write the History of Freethought

Amid all the sound, fury, and explosive growth of the 1870s and 1880s, the freethought movement became increasingly self-aware, developing an understanding of itself as a movement with deep historical roots. In 1894, Samuel Porter Putnam published a sweeping history called *400 Years of Freethought*. Born in 1838, Putnam became a Congregational minister after serving in the Union Army during the Civil War. By 1871 he had become a Unitarian and after a few more years embarked on a career as a freethought lecturer who ascended to the presidency of the American Secular Union in 1895. I have been liberally quoting *400 Years of Freethought*'s chronicling of the movement's golden age, but it is perhaps equally important to take a step back from the valuable details it provides to observe how Putnam framed the historical progress of freethought for his American contemporaries. The four hundred years the title refers to is the period from 1492 to 1892. Putnam saw Columbus's "discovery" of America as a moment that initiated modern freethought, even though he admits that "Columbus was no freethinker," and that "fifteen millions human beings [Native Americans] perished beneath the cross that waved in his silken banner."[202] Columbus furthered the cause of freethought in spite of himself because his voyage provided Europeans with incontrovertible evidence that the flat earth geography of the Bible was wrong, and, by extension, that the Bible could not be the inerrant word of God. From that point forward, the history of the freethought movement for Putnam runs parallel to the history of European science. Putnam relates the familiar story of scientific progress from the Copernican revolution through Newton to Darwin, praising the contributions to freethought made by Giordano Bruno, an Italian philosopher burned at the stake by the inquisition for proclaiming that space was infinite, in addition to those of such figures as Baruch Spinoza, and Thomas Bacon.

The great theme of *400 Years of Freethought* is that the American freethought political movement is connected to a much broader and deeper movement that has led European civilization away from a stunting dependence on biblical and clerical authority and into an era of scientific discovery and political liberation. It is a message that is perfectly aligned with, but more fully developed than, Robert Ingersoll's metanarrative of how human progress has accelerated as the influence of religion has diminished. While abolition finds only passing mention in Putnam's narrative of progress, he devotes a substantial chapter to how "Woman's Emancipation" has needed to struggle against the forces of Christian orthodoxy in its fight to win equal rights,[203] building on the insights of Sara Underwood's 1876 *Heroines of Freethought* and anticipating *The Woman's Bible*. The overall message that Putnam has for his freethinking readers is that they are participating in a historic struggle for the future of humanity as part of a movement that has made amazing progress over the course of the previous centuries, and is on the verge of greater things still: "Through darkness and struggle; through bloody war; through torture and terror, through superstition, ignorance, and tyranny, Freethought has steadily pushed onward, with true Promethean fire, with the torch of reason, with undaunted face, with unreceding step, until now it leads the world with victorious colors."[204]

The other great chronicle of freethought's golden age is George MacDonald's *Fifty Years of Freethought*, a book that, while it is even richer in the operational details of freethought than Putnam's history, takes a markedly different approach. Where Putnam tells the story of a heroic intellectual and social movement that has been building for four hundred years, MacDonald just tells his own story and the story of the movement as he had personally experienced it. About half of the first volume is a memoir of MacDonald's early life that traces the path that led him from his early experiences as a farmhand in southern New Hampshire to his work at *The Truth Seeker* in New York.

Although freethought historians were now looking further backwards in time for their deepest roots, Thomas Paine retained his privileged position in the movement's history. In Boston, a Paine memorial building was constructed in 1874 and dedicated in 1875. It housed the offices of several freethought organizations, including the *Boston Investigator*.[205] Closer to New York, the Thomas Paine memorial that Gilbert Vale succeeded in having erected at New Rochelle in 1839 proved to be a site that repeatedly drew freethinkers together. D. M. Bennett led efforts to restore the monument that led to an 1881 rededication ceremony at which he and Putnam both spoke.[206] In 1884, the Thomas Paine National Historical Association (TPNHA) was founded by members of the Manhattan Liberal Club to preserve and promote Paine's legacy, a mission that it carries on to this day.[207] It helped to raise money for another monument restoration campaign that culminated in an 1894 event headlined by Robert Ingersoll.[208] The TPNHA broke ground on a new Paine Memorial Building in New Rochelle in 1924 that subsequently served as its headquarters and has since overseen the restoration of Paine's cottage. Paine birthday celebrations continued to be held across the country in this period, and *The Truth Seeker* continued to run nostalgic features on Paine and provide coverage of major Paine commemorative events, such as the two just mentioned. *Age of Reason* continued to be a celebrated foundational text of the movement, and copies were advertised for mail order in every issue of *The Truth Seeker*. "I know nothing that excels this book for propaganda work," wrote M. Rowe of Illinois to the editor of *The Truth Seeker* in 1918 concerning *Age of Reason*. "I have given away scores of copies, and I wish I could flood the United States with them."[209] The most definitive biography of Paine up to that time was published in 1892 by Moncure Conway, an abolitionist Unitarian from Virginia who became president of the TPNHA in 1906.[210]

Black Freethinkers, Eugenics, and the Fate of *The Truth Seeker*

The freethought movement has a mixed overall record regarding race relations. Before and during the Civil War, the movement, as we have seen, had strong ties with abolitionism. But after the war, although some freethinkers worked with groups like the Freedmen's Aid Society, most took little notice of the fate of freed Blacks in the south. The movement did far less to extend the hand of fellowship to freethinking Blacks than to freethinking feminists. Some of the movement's most shameful moments came in the mid-twentieth century when its flagship journal, *The Truth Seeker*, under the influence of eugenic pseudoscience, went through a phase of blatant racism.

Although the extent to which various forms of freethought prevailed among African American intellectuals has been unappreciated due to the marginalization of Blacks in majority white freethought organizations, there have been a number of African American freethinkers who were prominent in the movement. One was Frederick Douglass, who had escaped slavery in 1838 to become the foremost abolitionist of his era. Driven by his loathing for Bible-based defenses of slavery, Douglass drifted slowly from liberal Christianity toward theistic freethought over the course of his public career. In 1874 he was invited to give a speech at a convention of the Free Religious Association by William Potter, one of its founders. Although conflicting engagements compelled Douglass to decline, he voiced support for the organization, writing to Potter in his reply, "Only the truth can make men free, and I trust that your convention will be guided in all its utterances by its light and feel its power."[211] By 1892, Douglass had been elected a vice president of the Free Religious Association and was said to have formed a "deep and lasting" friendship with Robert Ingersoll.[212]

Although Douglass, because of his celebrity status, was sought after by freethought organizations, Black freethinkers were not always offered quite so warm a welcome. When a Black lawyer named Mr. Carr gave an address called "The Negro's Viewpoint of the Negro Question" to the Manhattan Liberal Club in 1903, in which he expressed frustration with the lack of progress toward social and economic equality between Blacks and whites that had been made since emancipation, he met with a range of responses. One Dr. Roberts, an African American who was in the audience, voiced support for Carr's position, but white attendees expressed reservations. A Mr. Perrin argued that Blacks were already legally equal to whites, in New York at least. Another white attendee named Mr. Boulanger asserted that "there really is no race question," while Moncure Conway, a progressive freethinker from a wealthy Virginia family, blamed the lack of progress almost entirely on poor southern whites.[213] Subsequent issues of *The Truth Seeker* carried more pernicious responses to Carr's speech. W. L. Dolphyn and J. M. Benjamin separately defended the south's Jim Crow institutions, and even lynching.[214]

Acceptance of African American freethinkers into white freethought organizations seems to have been hindered not only by white defensiveness about the fairness of existing institutions but also by the general perception that African Americans, as a class, had a high propensity for unreflective religiosity. In 1889, the editor of the *Boston Investigator* declared that African Americans are "apt to be credulous, and easily imposed upon."[215] Eugene MacDonald, the second editor of *The Truth Seeker*, was even more blunt in his racism, writing that "the negro is unquestionably of an inferior race. . . . He is not and never can be the equal of the white race."[216] Although some African Americans did participate in white-dominated freethought organizations—among them David S. Cincore and Hubert Harrison—others practiced freethought on their own or in Black majority groups.[217] For instance, an all-Black group of freethinkers led by W. C. Martin and Dr. Julius Chilcoat came together in March of 1901 to commemorate the life of Robert Ingersoll, who in his later years had become an advocate of stronger civil rights for African Americans.[218] Many of the best-known leaders of the Harlem Renaissance were freethinkers who made their way without the support of the established white majority freethought organizations. As Christopher Cameron shows in *Black Freethinkers: A History of African American Secularism*, Alain Locke, Claude McCay, Langston Hughes, and Zora Neale Hurston can all plausibly be claimed as freethinkers even though they did not belong to any white-dominated freethought organizations.[219]

The scarcity of African American freethinkers within *Truth Seeker*'s community of discourse had the effect of allowing white freethought's pernicious tendency toward eugenics to grow unchallenged. The feminist and free love components of freethought had long been associated with eugenics, and as eugenics became more explicitly racist in the 1920s and 1930s, *The Truth Seeker* followed suit. In its earliest phases, eugenics was understood to be the science of "right generation." The "cardinal doctrine" of eugenics among many freethinking feminists and free love advocates was that "woman must be the sole person to decide when and under what conditions she will give birth to children."[220] Unwanted children would not be properly cared for and would become a burden on society. Therefore, to ensure "right generation," women must be given both sexual education and access to contraception to ensure that all their children would be properly reared. This progressive version of eugenics was unfortunately soon displaced by calls to check the rapid multiplication of the "unfit." Victoria Woodhull is an example of an individual who started off as a free love progressive eugenicist but evolved into a genetic elitist. Her 1891 pamphlet, *The Rapid Multiplication of the Unfit*, opened with the reassuring statement that "there are often greater differences between individuals of the same race than between individuals of different races,"[221] but it goes on to warn about "the rapid multiplication of Negros in America, who at some not far distant day will outnumber and overrun the whites if the rapid increase is not checked."[222] She concludes that "under our present industrial system there is a strong tendency against the survival of the fittest," "the fittest" being understood as the well-educated white people with refined manners who are being out-reproduced by the "lower" classes.[223]

Woodhull's writings about eugenics were tame stuff compared to the books that subsequently shaped the field, such as Madison Grant's *The Passing of the Great Race: Or, The Racial Basis of European History* (1916) and Lothrop Stoddard's *The Rising Tide of Color Against White World-Supremacy* (1921). These books were calls to arms warning that the "superior" Nordic, or Aryan, race was in danger of going extinct through interbreeding with "inferior" races. It was this blatantly racist version of eugenics that came to dominate *Truth Seeker*'s editorial vision when George MacDonald ceded control of the publication to Charles Smith in 1937. This happened because freethinkers had long failed to employ the same skepticism toward pseudoscientific claims that they did toward religious ones. Nineteenth-century issues of *The Truth Seeker* featured advertisements for useless magnetic clothing that was supposed to have health benefits, as well as books on phrenology. Challenges to the legitimacy of such material were never seriously entertained. So, it is not surprising that a good number of freethinkers were taken in by the racist claims of the pseudoscience of eugenics. It would be surprising if many had not been, since much of the legitimate scientific establishment was also taken in. It is now quite difficult to find issues of *Truth Seeker* from years when Smith and his successor James Harvey Johnson were the editors, but it is asserted even by those most sympathetic to the legacy of *The Truth Seeker* that from 1937 to 1988 the publication was rife with "racism, anti-Semitism, white supremacism, eugenics advocacy, and other marginal interests."[224]

Not all freethinkers succumbed to the lure of eugenics. One of a new generation of freethinkers who ultimately pitted himself against eugenics was Clarence Darrow, a defense attorney whose success in seemingly hopeless cases earned him the nickname "Attorney for the Damned."[225] Born to freethinking parents in 1857, he grew up in rural Kinsman, Ohio. "My father was the village infidel," recalls Darrow in his autobiography. "Neither of my parents held orthodox religious views. They were readers of Jefferson, Voltaire, and Paine; both looked at revealed religion as these masters thought."[226] Darrow followed in his parents' footsteps with regard to religion, expressing his own views in such essays as "Why I Am an Agnostic" and "Absurdities of the Bible."[227] As a young man, Darrow admired Robert Ingersoll's principles and his oratory but resolved to invent his own style rather than to imitate.[228] After graduating from law school, Darrow moved from his first practice in the small town of Andover, Ohio, to a position as a lawyer for the Chicago and North-Western Railway Company in Chicago. But he cut ties with the railway company to take on the case of American Railway Union leader Eugene Debs, a man who would be the Socialist candidate for US president in four elections. Darrow went on to become one of the most prominent attorneys in the country, defending labor leaders and defendants who faced the death penalty, which he opposed on principle.

Darrow's earliest public statement bearing on eugenics seemed to put him in the pro-eugenics camp. In 1915 he weighed in on the public controversy that followed the advice of a Chicago doctor named Harry Haiselden not to perform a life-saving operation on a severely deformed infant named Alan Bollinger because such surgery would condemn the child to a life of horrible suffering. The parents agreed to the advice and the baby died five days after it was born. A public debate erupted after the story hit the papers.[229] Darrow, with a surprising number of others, including Helen Keller, made comments supportive of the doctor. Darrow recommended euthanasia for "unfit children" such as baby Bollinger.[230] It is difficult to say if these remarks were motivated by a general support for eugenics or by the belief that people who face a life of unrelenting suffering should be allowed to die. Was he a supporter of eugenics or euthanasia? I would guess the latter, because a decade later Darrow became a staunch critic of the eugenics movement. In a 1925 essay, "The Edwardses and the Jukeses," he mocked eugenicists' claims that some bloodlines were superior to others,[231] and in "The Eugenics Cult," published a year later, he concluded,

> We have no knowledge of what kind of man would be better than the one that Nature is evolving to fit into the environment which he cannot escape. We have neither facts nor theories to give us any evidence based on biology or any other branch of science as to how we could breed intelligence, happiness,

or anything else that would improve the race. We have no idea of the meaning of the word "improvement." We can imagine no human organization that we could trust with the job, even if eugenicists knew what should be done, and the proper way to do it.[232]

As eugenics became associated in the popular mind with the Third Reich from the late 1930s onward, an increasing number of freethinkers came around to Darrow's position, and this left *The Truth Seeker* increasingly isolated in its support of eugenics. During the period of Smith and Johnson's editorships, its subscription list shrank from several thousand to a few hundred. *The Truth Seeker* went from playing a central role in the freethought movement to being an embarrassing vestige of some of the movement's worst tendencies. Then in 1988, Johnson died, leaving a $16 million estate that has helped to revive *The Truth Seeker* as a legacy freethought periodical. It continues to be published today, purged of the offensive content of earlier decades and devoted as much to the positive aspects of the history of the freethought movement as to current issues.[233] The course of the golden age of freethought can be considered to run parallel to the career of *The Truth Seeker*, beginning in the 1870s, growing through the 1890s, and then fading in the first decade of the twentieth century as *The Truth Seeker* descended into a racist tailspin.

Taking Stock of the Golden Age of American Freethought

Several factors combined to cause the explosive growth of freethought in the 1870s and 1880s. First, Francis Ellingwood Abbot, alarmed by the prospect of a Christian Amendment to the US Constitution, unfurled the Nine Demands of Liberalism on the pages of his paper, *The Index*. Abbot can be considered a movement-framing entrepreneur. The Demands, which all concerned achieving a better separation of church and state, became the organizing principles of the National Liberal League. They had the effect of making the broadly inclusive frame of separationism the central theme of freethought, and this, in turn, allowed freethinkers in the Paineite and Owenite traditions to join forces with the radical Unitarians of the Free Religious Association, and also with the vigorous and unorthodox new religion of spiritualism. Although the free religionists, materialists, and spiritualists who bolstered the ranks of the freethought movement in its golden age had extremely diverse and often conflicting theologies, they could all come together on the issue of separation of church and state. "Secularist" became the one identity that all freethinkers shared. Although efforts to add the Blaine Amendment and a Religious Freedom Amendment to the Constitution both failed, freethinkers had good success in securing state-level "baby Blaine" amendments, with the help of more orthodox citizens who feared renewed sectarian strife in public education. Anthony Comstock's persecutions of prominent freethinkers provided a common enemy to all the disparate elements of the movement. It also was a reason for more people to become actively involved in the movement through such activities as signing petitions and giving money to legal defense funds. Throughout this period, issues like free love, the Comstock laws (whether they should be reformed or repealed), and genuineness of spirit phenomena caused tensions and ruptures in the movement but did little to check its momentum. The ebbing of the spiritualist tide coincided with the ending of freethought's golden age, but not with the end of the movement.

On a political level, the freethinkers of the golden age laid the foundations of modern American liberalism. The National Liberal League, founded in 1876, built its platform on the separationist Nine Demands of Liberalism. The original National Liberal League was disbanded in 1885, having been superseded by the American Secular Union, which survived until at least 1911.[234] A new political organization called the National Liberal Party was constituted at a convention of freethinkers in Cincinnati in January 1902. The convention was timed to coincide with Paine's birthday, and Clarence Darrow himself was the principal speaker at the commemorative ceremony. The name "National Liberal Party" was adopted as a compromise between delegates who wanted to revive the old moniker "National Liberal League" and those who favored "National Secular Party."[235] It seems to have reverted to the name "National Liberal League" before 1950, when the Truth Seeker Company published a monograph praising the *McCollum v. Board of Education* Supreme Court decision that ended school-based religious instruction. The monograph was "Endorsed by the National Liberal League."[236] The influence of this "liberal" or "secular" party, founded by freethinkers to promote separation of church and state, is likely the reason that the term "liberal" in American politics today is less associated with classically liberal free trade economic policies, as it is in much of the world, and more associated with the causes espoused by the religiously liberal freethought movement and its sympathizers. In the words of Robert Ingersoll, "*The Age of Reason* has liberalized us all."[237]

Implications for the Current Interpretation of the Establishment Clause

Philip Hamburger's *Separation of Church and State* has little to say about antebellum freethought in its attempt to explain how "separation of church and state" wrongly became part of the tradition of American constitutional law. After discounting Madison's and Jefferson's own words about the meaning of the Establishment Clause and insisting that the apparent silence of the Danbury Baptists regarding Jefferson's letter to them somehow delegitimizes the separationism as a constitutional principle, Hamburger picks up his story with the growth of tensions between Protestants and Catholics in mid-nineteenth-century America. He argues that the cast-off idea of Jeffersonian separationism, after, we must assume, moldering on a pile of rejected constitutional principles for about forty years, was taken up by Protestant American nativists for the purpose of keeping newly arrived Catholic American immigrants down. He states: "If separation has seemed one of the nation's fundamental constitutional and cultural principles, this was because it became popular not in the eighteenth-century struggle to obtain constitutional guarantees of religious freedom, but rather in the nineteenth century movement to impose an aggressively Protestant 'Americanism' on an 'un-American' Catholic minority."[238]

There is much that is true in what Hamburger writes of nineteenth-century anti-Catholicism, but there are also serious difficulties and oversights. Hamburger gives ample demonstration that nativists did invoke "separation of church and state" to prevent Catholics from gaining the kind of control over public institutions that Protestants exercised. The prevailing view of church-state relations in the nineteenth century can be called nondenominationalism. It held that the government could not favor one denomination over another, but not that the government needed to avoid any involvement with religious activity. Nondenominationalism undeniably advantaged Protestants over Catholics because it meant that "denominational" Catholic schools, which used a Catholic translation of the Bible and promoted a Catholic outlook, could not receive government funding, but "nondenominational" Protestant schools, which many public schools in effect were, were eligible for public funding because they did not favor any single Protestant denomination, even though they had students read from a Protestant version of the Bible and say supposedly "nondenominational" prayers. Even though there is evidence that nondenominationalism was deployed evenhandedly to block funding for schools that catered to specific Protestant denominations as well as Catholic schools, the concept of nondenominationalism was structurally anti-Catholic.[239] The nativist American Party, whose members were often referred to as "Know-Nothings," certainly did take advantage of this oh-so-convenient quirk of nondenominationalism. Hamburger's citations from *The American's Text-Book*, by "An American," promoting the views of the American Party are rather convincing on this point.[240]

Despite his valid insights into the politics of nineteenth-century nondenominationalism, Hamburger's argument has some difficulties. Just as he failed to take notice of deists as a group of religious dissenters in the eighteenth century, he mostly fails to take notice of freethinkers in the nineteenth century. Had Hamburger searched the records of antebellum freethought, he would have found a steady stream of separationist discourse that opposed Catholicism in no greater degree than it opposed every other organized religion. Although separationism did not dominate antebellum freethought in the way it dominated golden age freethought, it was a consistent theme. In 1804 Palmer's *Prospect* was already campaigning to end "blue law" restrictions in Connecticut, and between 1828 and 1835 the *Free Enquirer* ran six pieces pertaining to general church-state issues, two pieces calling for an end to all government-supported chaplaincies, eight pieces opposing judicial oaths sworn on the Bible, four pieces opposing laws that restricted normal activities on Sundays, and nine pieces opposing blasphemy laws.[241] All these pieces are separationist in the strong Jeffersonian sense that Hamburger claimed was not supported by any group of religious dissenters between Jefferson's supposedly dead letter to the Danbury Baptists and the nativist appropriation of the theme in the 1840s. The pure separationism freethinkers supported in these writings was far less prejudicial against Catholics than the prevailing norm of nondenominationalism. When it came down to it, most nativists were more nondenominationalist than true separationist. They were just fine with their children reading the King James Bible in school. They just didn't want Catholics to get any of their tax money. Freethinkers, in contrast, didn't want either the Catholic or the Protestant Bible in schools and knew that there is no such thing as a nondenominational prayer. All this makes Hamburger's suggestion that separationism was resurrected by nativists for the express purpose of imposing "aggressively Protestant 'Americanism' on an 'un-American' Catholic minority" insupportable. Not only had separationism never died in freethought discourse, but the legal principle that was being used to keep Catholic schools from benefiting equally from public funds was not true separationism, which would have cut funding to any public school that taught any religious content whatsoever. Nondenominationalism would cut funding to Catholic schools but allow Protestant content to be taught in public schools.

To his credit, Hamburger recognizes that the freethought position on separation of church and state in the 1870s was not anti-Catholic, but his characterization of it as "anti-Christian" fails to consider the fact that, if they had the opportunity, freethinkers would also have opposed the compulsory reading of the Koran in public schools as well as teachers leading students in Jewish prayer.[242] Freethinkers opposed all religious intrusions on public institutions, not just the Christian intrusions. For the record, freethinkers also opposed the Know-Nothings. "It is easier to win a battle than to conquer minds filled with Know-Nothingism," said Ernestine Rose in an 1855 speech at a Paine birthday celebration.[243] She knew this from experience. In addition to being anti-immigrants, the Know-Nothings also strongly opposed the expansion of women's rights, a cause that freethinkers overwhelmingly endorsed.

Another difficulty with Hamburger's imputations about the connection between separationism and anti-Catholicism concerns his ultimate goals. In making his arguments, Hamburger hopes to discredit "separation of church and state" as a constitutional principle and presumably replace it with something more like nineteenth-century nondenominationalism. He claims to do this to right wrongs committed against Catholics. The problem with this stance is that it was not the pure Jeffersonian separationism that was promoted by freethinkers that was prejudicial against Catholics, rather it was the nondenominationalism that Hamburger hopes to resurrect. The very reason separationism began to displace nondenominationalism in the second half of the nineteenth century is that it was a more evenhanded standard for settling sectarian disputes between Protestants and Catholics.[244] Discarding separationism in favor of nondenominationalism in the name of rectifying a wrong against Catholics is like bringing back compulsory boarding school education for Native American children in the name of rectifying the wrongs committed against Native Americans. It just makes no sense at all.

Up Next: The Fourth Wave

Although there is even less discontinuity between the third and fourth waves of freethought than between the second and third, beginning in the 1920s there was a distinct changing of the guard as old freethought organizations disappeared and new ones replaced them. The New York Society of Freethinkers replaced the New York Freethinkers' Association. The First Humanist Society of New York replaced the Free Religious Association. And the American Association for the Advance of Atheism became the first group to organize atheists. These organizations and their successors, the Freethinkers of America, the American Humanist Association, and American Atheists, all took to heart an important lesson of the golden age, namely, that freethought thrives best when it is focused on advancing the separation of church and state. There was also a global change of strategy in the movement. Hamburger is correct in observing that where golden age freethinkers attempted to advance their agenda mainly through legislation, twentieth-century freethinkers pivoted to a legal offensive.[245] Despite successes at the state level, the major golden age legislative efforts to overturn the Comstock laws and secure the passage of a Religious Freedom Amendment failed. In the 1920s freethinkers began pursuing a new strategy that attempted to force legal rulings favorable to their cause through strategic lawsuits. It was this strategy that led to the movement's great successes of the mid-twentieth century. Chapter 5 will chart the surprising advances made during freethought's fourth wave.

CHAPTER FIVE

The Fourth Wave of American Freethought

The Journey to Disestablishment

The 1920s opened with a red scare that sowed fear of atheistic Bolsheviks across the nation, witnessed the passage of uncompromisingly strict immigration laws driven by eugenic anxiety for "the passing of the great [white] race," and experienced a wave of Christian fundamentalism that fueled a campaign to halt the teaching of evolution in public schools. At first glance, it was not a decade that would seem to have been very hospitable to freethinkers. But it was also a decade of unprecedented modernism. Many people felt that the Great War had changed the world forever and that the future would be nothing like the past. As flappers ripped up the old rules of acceptable public sexuality, danced to jazz music, and tried to dodge attempts to legislate morality, a new generation of freethinkers got to work on rejuvenating a movement that had failed to realize its goal through legislation despite being able to make impressive shows of strength. Thanks to their efforts, the movement experienced an unlikely renaissance as new organizations arose to take the place of their fading nineteenth-century counterparts.

An Unlikely Renaissance

In the early 1920s, the New York Freethinkers' Association that had thrived in the 1870s and 1880s was superseded by a new freethought organization, the New York Society of Freethinkers. It was led by Joseph Lewis, a man who took the battle for the separation of church and state to the courts as no one had before. Lewis was born June 11, 1889, in Montgomery, Alabama, one of at least eight children of a Jewish merchant and his wife.[1] Lewis recalled that he was introduced to the writings of Thomas Paine through a volume of Ingersoll's lectures that one of his brothers brought to the family home.[2] Reading Ingersoll's speech on Paine, Lewis was inspired to seek out Paine's works. He abandoned religious orthodoxy of any kind early in life and eventually became an outspoken atheist who happily referred to himself as an "infidel," like Ingersoll and Rose before him.[3] He made his way to the New York area in the early 1920s, accompanied by his first wife, initially working with his brother in the garment industry and then opening his own shirt-making business. He might have been drawn to New York City by its long history of relative hospitality toward freethinkers and infidels, or by opportunities in the garment industry, or both. By 1922 he had become president of the New York Society of Freethinkers.

Lewis and the Society of Freethinkers got their first mention in the *New York Times* in March 1922, with a story about Lewis's threat of legal action after he was forbidden to give a lecture titled "The Bible, Nemesis of Mankind" to the New York University Philosophical Society in the auditorium of Washington Irving High School.[4] Later, City Superintendent William Ettinger justified blocking the lecture by saying that the City Charter indirectly forbade the expression of thoughts "repugnant to [the] Christian community" in city schools. He argued that because the Bible was read in schools, it would cause trauma to Christians if it were also criticized there.[5] Lewis retreated for a while, but he went back on the legal offensive in 1925, after being inspired by Clarence Darrow's participation in a sensational trial where he defended a young Tennessee teacher charged with teaching evolution in a public school. Eventually, Lewis incorporated his organization as the Freethinkers of America. It remained active until his death in 1968.

As the Society of Freethinkers arose to take the place of the New York Freethinkers' Association, so too the Free Religious Association was replaced by the First Humanist Society of New York, an organization that also had its roots in radical Unitarianism. This association, which is alive and well today, traces its history back to 1927, when a group of mostly Unitarian professors at the University of Chicago formed the "Humanist Fellowship" and launched a publication called the *New Humanist*.[6] At about the same time a Unitarian minister named Charles Francis Potter founded the First Humanist Society of New York and explained the humanist perspective in a 1930 book that he wrote with his wife, Clara, *Humanism: A New Religion*. Although Potter proclaimed agnosticism concerning God, agnosticism was not the central thesis of his humanism. Instead, Potter defined "faith in the supreme value and self-perfectibility of human personality" as humanism's most essential tenet.[7] In 1933, Chicago and New York humanists joined others from across the country to produce the first Humanist Manifesto, which affirmed that the universe is "self-existing and not created," that the "traditional dualism of mind and body must be rejected" as well as any "supernatural or cosmic guarantees of human values."[8] In 1941 Chicago humanists led by Unitarian ministers Curtis W. Reese and John H. Dietrich reorganized to form the American Humanist Association.[9] Since its founding, the American Humanist Association has supported separationist causes and today has a robust agenda of legal and legislative initiatives.

As freethinkers reorganized and free religionists were evolving into humanists, a new strain of organized freethought was also emerging: atheism. In 1925, Charles Smith, future editor of *The Truth Seeker*, helped to organize the American Association for the Advancement of Atheism, often just called "the four A's," which promoted junior atheist clubs at colleges and universities across the country and paved the way for the atheist activism of Madalyn Murray O'Hair in the 1960s.[10] If the springing up atheists societies on the campuses of major universities wasn't enough to let the public know that atheists had arrived, then the sensational career of a child prodigy atheist lecturer named Queen Silver must certainly have. In a lecture titled "God's Place in Capitalism" delivered in 1926 when she was just twelve, she observed, "In America, the church controls the State and Capital controls both Church and State. Capital finances religion and god sanctifies capital. The workingman is victimized by both god and gold. One destroys his brain and the other plunders his body." The saying, "Out of the mouths of babes" was never more apt, although young Queen likely was well coached by her mother Grace V. Silver, a prominent socialist lecturer. The 1928 Cecil B. DeMille silent film, *The Godless Girl*, is said to have been inspired by Queen Silver.[11]

Freethinkers looking for a full library of short book titles curated for the discerning secular humanist in the 1920s had all of the Little Blue Books of Emanuel Haldeman-Julius to choose from. In 1919 Haldeman-Julius and his wife Marcet bought the printing presses of the socialist periodical out of Girard, Kansas, called *Appeal to Reason*, which Haldeman-Julius had edited, together with its subscriber list. Five thousand readers of *Appeal to Reason* advanced him five dollars each to receive fifty pocket-sized paperbacks, which were printed and delivered in due course.[12] Thus was born a pioneering line of twenty-five-cent literary works, each assigned a number, intended for the masses. Haldeman-Julius ultimately published 1,914 titles. Many of the books were abridged, and sometimes retitled, classics covering everything from Plato (#96) to Jack London (#30, #148, #152), but in amongst the traditional classics were works such as Paine's *Age of Reason* (#4), lectures by

Robert Ingersoll (#56, #88, #130, #139, #185, #236), Robert Dale Owen's debate with Horace Greeley on divorce (#43), and Clarence Darrow's *Why I Am an Agnostic* (#1500).[13]

The Great Monkey Trial

One of the most sensational trials of the 1920s featured a nationally broadcast showdown between freethinker Clarence Darrow and fundamentalist William Jennings Bryan on the literal truth of scripture. This took place at the trial of John Scopes, a teacher who had volunteered to test the constitutionality of a Tennessee law banning the teaching of evolution in public schools, making headline news across the country in the summer of 1925. The law that the Scopes trial was meant to test was Tennessee's Butler Act, passed on March 13, 1925. This law made it illegal "to teach any theory that denies the story of the Divine creation of man as taught in the Bible, and to teach instead that man has descended from a lower order of animals" in any public school in the state, including universities, and it imposed fines of between $100 and $500. The law quickly came to the attention of American Civil Liberties Union founder Rodger Baldwin. Although the ACLU was to some extent modeled after the Free Speech League, in its early years it had concentrated on the free speech rights of leftist political dissenters and labor leaders rather than on Establishment Clause issues or academic freedom. But the new Tennessee law struck Baldwin as so outrageous that he thought the ACLU needed to be involved. He advertised in the *Chattanooga Times* ACLU support to anyone willing to challenge the law.

Leaders of the small town of Dayton, Tennessee, saw the ACLU offer an invitation to stage a spectacular trial that would put their small town of 1,500 on the map. Businessman George Rappelyea, school superintendent Walter White, and local attorney Sue Hicks recruited John Scopes, a young coach at Rhea High School who sometimes substituted as a biology teacher, to draw an indictment for violating the law. Scopes's motive was mainly to further the cause of academic freedom. It was not hard to violate the law, because the state-approved biology textbook, *Civic Biology: Presented in Problems*, contained a chapter on evolution. On April 24, Scopes showed the class a chart that depicted how humans evolved from animals as part of a review of the state-approved curriculum. As agreed, Rappelyea filed a complaint against him and on May 5, Scopes was nominally arrested, a process that caused only a minor delay in a tennis game he was playing. Town leaders gave the story to the *Chattanooga News* and it was quickly picked up by the Associated Press and soon became a national news item.[14] When the trial began in July 1925, Dayton was packed with newspaper reporters, and the microphones of radio broadcasters had been set up to capture the courtroom action.

Part of the reason the Scopes trial was so sensational was that each side was represented by a celebrity lawyer. Clarence Darrow had volunteered to defend Scopes and William Jennings Bryan played a key role in the prosecution. Bryan was a three-time Democratic presidential candidate who had served as secretary of state under Woodrow Wilson. Well known for his earlier opposition to the gold standard, in the 1920s Bryan had channeled his political energies into a campaign against the teaching of Darwinian evolution. In 1921 he began delivering a lecture called "The Menace of Darwinism," which was also published as a pamphlet. It presented Darwinism in a negative light to many who were unfamiliar with it, aiming to cause a moral panic. Its rhetoric was finely calibrated for mass appeal. For example, "It is better to trust in the Rock of Ages, than to know the age of rocks; it is better for one to know that he is close to the Heavenly Father than to know how far the stars in the heavens are apart."[15] Bryan's anti-evolution rhetoric inspired activists in the emergent fundamentalist movement to introduce forty-five anti-evolution bills in twenty-one different states, and it succeeded in enacting legislation in Oklahoma, Florida, Tennessee, Mississippi, and Arkansas.[16] Bryan's participation in the trial was one of the reasons Darrow agreed to take the case. After he had heard that Bryan would be appearing on behalf of the prosecution in the Scopes trial, he volunteered to serve the defense without fee. "I knew that education was in danger from the source that had always hampered it—religious fanaticism."[17]

As the trial commenced, Judge John Raulston derailed many of Darrow's plans for the defense, including calling expert witnesses on the theory of evolution. In response, Darrow improvised a plan to call Bryan himself to the witness stand to testify on behalf of the Bible. This was highly unorthodox legally. A defense attorney had no right to examine any prosecuting attorney. Nonetheless, Bryan happily agreed to take the stand. Each side hoped to win broad support from the large radio audience.

Darrow's examination of Bryan was set to take place on the afternoon of the seventh day of the trial, Monday July 20. The judge, citing fear that the balcony gallery of the courtroom would give way under the weight of the spectators, ordered that the trial be moved outside that afternoon. So it was in the warm breezes of a July afternoon, on a platform outside the courthouse, with the radio microphones close by, that Darrow questioned Bryan, attempting to show that even an ardent Bible believer couldn't defend the literal truth of Genesis. Darrow proceeded to pepper Bryan with questions about the plausibility of Old Testament events, including Jonah being swallowed by a whale, Joshua making the sun stand still, and the flood survived by Noah and an ark full of animals. Bryan was unable to account for how the sun could appear to stop moving without the disastrous consequences of earth abruptly ceasing to spin. Nor could he say where Cain's wife might have come from if he, Adam, and Eve were the only humans in the world; nor how the snake moved around before being cursed by God to crawl on its belly. Darrow's material had been standard fare in antiscriptural freethought lectures from the time of Paine and Palmer onward, but now it was finding a national radio audience for the first time. Many listened on the radio with minds more open than the Bryan supporters who dominated the courtroom audience. Despite the relentless questioning, Bryan maintained his humor and his composure with only a few lapses. "I want the Christian world to know that any atheist, agnostic, unbeliever can question me any time as to my belief in God, and I will answer him,"[18] he maintained, even though it was his belief in the literal truth of the Bible, not his belief in God, that was being examined. His most disappointing admission for some of his followers was his admission that the "days" of creation spoken of in Genesis might represent whole ages rather than twenty-four-hour days.[19]

The next day, Judge Raulston had Bryan's testimony stricken from the record as not relevant to the issue of the trial, which then moved rapidly toward a conclusion. Wishing Darrow's cross-examination of Bryan to be the last public word of the trial, whether it was in the official record or not, the defense moved to close the trial and actually requested that the jury be instructed to find the defendant guilty. The trial had originally been planned as a mere preliminary to an appeal at the Tennessee Supreme Court, and this move deprived Bryan of the opportunity to make his long-planned closing speech. The jury quickly returned a guilty verdict and Judge Raulston then imposed the minimum $100 fine, a move that turned out to be a procedural mistake.[20]

Both sides proclaimed victory in the trial. The anti-evolutionists had got their guilty verdict, and the defense, which always had greater hopes for a victory on appeal than in the first trial, had reached a broad public with its message through radio and other coverage of the trial.[21]

Just as the fervor over the trial had begun to fade, an unexpected event reignited it. On Sunday July 25, five days after the trial's end, Bryan laid down for a nap after church and never woke up. He had died quietly in his sleep of a stroke.[22] Although Bryan himself had been portraying the Scopes trial as a victory, and his death was not connected to the trial, supporters were quick to portray him as a martyr, and they unleashed a new wave of anti-evolution activity across the nation.[23]

In the long run, the myth of the Scopes trial became more important than its legal consequences. A guilty verdict had always been expected. The real hope was to have the conviction overturned by the Tennessee Supreme Court. The appeal was filed, but the Tennessee Supreme Court did not rule on Scopes's appeal until January 1927. When it finally came, the ruling was not what Scopes and his defense team hoped. Scopes's conviction was overturned on the technical grounds that the jury and not the judge should have decided upon the fine, but the constitutionality of the law Scopes was tried for breaking was upheld.[24] The Tennessee anti-evolution law technically remained in force until its repeal in 1967,[25] just a year before the case of *Epperson v. Arkansas*, in which the US Supreme Court ruled unconstitutional a 1928 Arkansas law modeled on it. But long before then the events of those July days in 1925 had been first retold, and then fictionalized, in ways that portrayed the moral victory of the defense as being more clear cut than it had appeared to many Americans who had originally followed the trial.[26] The process reached its zenith with the release of the film *Inherit the Wind* in 1960, a fictionalized version of the trial in which a local preacher stirs up an angry mob against the fictionalized Scopes and the fictionalized Bryan collapses in the courtroom after being humiliated by the fictionalized Darrow.[27]

Joseph Lewis and the Origins of the Freethought Legal Offensive

One important but little-known consequence of the Scopes trial was the role it played in inspiring Joseph Lewis to continue his own legal campaign to further the separation of church and state, a campaign that, through its strategy and its example (if not through its legal victories), contributed mightily to the significant court victories that were to follow.

As part of the same 1920s wave of fundamentalist enthusiasm that led to attempts to ban the teaching of evolution, public schools across the country began adopting a scheme where students would be released from school during the day to attend religious instruction.[28] One municipality to adopt this technique of religious instruction in early 1925 was Mount Vernon, New York, a town that ironically was just west of Thomas Paine's former farm in Westchester County. Inspired by Darrow's upcoming appearance at the Scopes trial, in June of 1925 Lewis launched a lawsuit designed to test the constitutionality of the Mount Vernon program of religious instruction on school time. He arranged for Lawrence B. Stein, a citizen of Mount Vernon, to bring the suit. He even tried to enlist the support of Darrow for the case. Occupied with the Scopes trial and other matters, Darrow offered moral rather than legal support, but he did declare the Mount Vernon case "as important as the evolution case in Tennessee."[29] The freethinkers won the first round of the battle when Justice Albert H. F. Seeger issued a permanent injunction against the Mount Vernon religious instruction program.[30] Encouraged, Lewis and the Society of Freethinkers filed a similar suit in the town of White Plains, New York, in northern Westchester County. This time Justice Piece H. Russell ordered Frank P. Graves, the state commissioner of education, to present arguments as to why school release programs should be legal anywhere in the state.[31] For a while, it looked as if the freethinkers might succeed in ending school release for religious instruction throughout the State of New York. But the court ultimately found that it was permissible for students to leave school for half an hour per week for religious instruction, and nothing came of their plans to make an appeal.[32]

Although Lewis's challenges to the school release for religious instruction programs in New York State failed to end the practice, they did gain attention for himself and the Society of Freethinkers. This seems to have been all the reward that he needed to keep going. A classic "happy warrior," he continued his freethought legal offensive for another three decades, contending that it was wrong for city-owned and -operated radio station WNYC to broadcast either a Catholic bishop's speech or Yom Kippur music.[33] He also attempted to stop the practice of Bible reading in New York City public schools and in 1956 tried to have the words "under God" removed from the Pledge of Allegiance,[34] to which they had been added in 1954. He also fought a ban on birth control therapy in New York City hospitals.[35]

There was more to Lewis's activism than a string of unsuccessful lawsuits. In 1928 he incorporated the former New York Society of Freethinkers as the Freethinkers of America, and by 1945, as reported by *Time* magazine, the organization had 30,000 members who paid a dollar a year in dues.[36] He acted as president of the organization for the rest of his life. A prolific writer, he had published nineteen books by 1957 and started a publishing company called the Freethought Press Association. He also seems to have been a driving force behind the earlier Truth Publishing Company.[37] In addition to his book on Ingersoll and an edition of Paine's *Age of Reason*, he published *Sexual Problems of Today* by William J. Robinson, MD, a book originally published in 1914 but which remained controversial for its calls to decriminalize the sharing of information about contraception by doctors through the mail, for more humane treatment of prostitutes, a more realistic approach to stopping the transmission of venereal disease, and liberalization of abortion laws.[38] Lewis started a Thomas Paine Memorial Committee, originally to organize a commemoration of the two hundredth anniversary of his birth. He also led an effort to restore Robert Ingersoll's birth house in Dresden, New York, in 1954.[39]

Vashti McCollum vs. The Board of Education

Although Lewis and his Freethinkers of America never had a major legal victory after Mount Vernon, Lewis's legal offensive set an example that others would emulate with much greater success. Lewis had an interesting connection to a landmark US Supreme Court ruling against school-based religious instruction, *McCollum v. Board of Education* (1948). To help him complete the restoration of Robert Ingersoll's birthplace house in 1954, Lewis enlisted the aid of a Rochester-based freethinking couple: Arthur and Ruth Cromwell.[40] The Cromwells had a grown daughter they had named Vashti, after the first wife of a Persian king in the book of Esther. The biblical Vashti is known for courageously defying her husband (Esther 1:9–22).[41] While Vashti's mother described her daughter's biblical namesake as "the first exponent of women's rights," a reporter covering the trial called her "the first recorded exponent of free thinking among women."[42]

The biblically literate Cromwells had become involved in what their daughter referred to as the "Freethinkers' Society," after she had left home to attend college. Vashti's son, Dannel, identifies the group as the Rochester Society of Freethinkers, which Vashti's father, Arthur, founded in 1938, probably as an affiliate of Lewis's organization.[43] Of her father, Vashti wrote, "He began to read Voltaire and Ingersoll and Tom Paine and developed his views as a rationalist."[44] Vashti became familiar with freethought mostly through conversations with her parents.

Vashti McCollum began her college education at Cornell on a scholarship in 1929 at the age of seventeen, but needed to leave after two years when the funding ran out due to the onset of the Depression. Within a year, she resumed her education at the more affordable University of Illinois. Before graduating, she married a young professor from Cornell named John McCollum, whom she habitually refers to as "Pappy" in her memoir. He was the eldest son from a large family of Arkansas farmers who had developed a strong distaste for the fundamentalist Christianity he had been raised on. The couple settled in Champaign, where John was able to find employment as an assistant professor in agriculture, and they had three boys: James Terry (1934), Dannel (1937), and Errol (1940). Vashti finished her degree in political science in 1944. She would earn a master's degree from the same institution in 1957.[45]

McCollum had come to espouse the separationist principles adopted by her parents strongly enough that, during the 1943–1944 school year, when her oldest son, James, came home from school with a permission slip to sign for an in-school religious instruction program, she refused. She had been warned of the advances recently made by school-based religion programs by her father, whose freethought group was caught up in the campaign against them.[46] After some months, she relented and let her son attend, only to discover that the program "wasn't a course in ethics or morals or tolerance or good behavior" but was rather "a complete religious indoctrination, abounding in faith and miracles."[47] Again, she withdrew him. But now, during religious instruction, which took place in the school itself (unlike the New York program that Lewis had opposed, which excused students from school to attend religious instruction off campus), James was made to sit alone in a tiny room where musical instruments were stored, or a hallway. He was the only student not taking religious instruction in the school and other children teased him badly enough that one day in February of 1945 he went home in tears. That determined Vashti McCollum to file a lawsuit. A sympathetic Unitarian Universalist minister named Phil Schug put her in touch with a civil liberties organization called the Chicago Action Committee, which undertook to fund the suit.[48]

McCollum's "Bible trial" began on Monday, September 10, 1945, about a month after atomic fire had obliterated Hiroshima and Nagasaki, and a week and a day after Japan's formal surrender. Held at the Champaign County courthouse in Urbana, the trial attracted so much attention that at one point McCollum characterized it as a "three ring circus."[49] Letters from both opponents and supporters poured in, and one reporter suggested that many in the large crowds who attended the trial had come "to have a look at a woman atheist."[50] One man, who has no other connection to the case, came to exemplify a common misperception among fundamentalists when he approached the team defending the school board and offered to be a witness, saying, "I'm here to testify for the Lord." He was politely turned away with the comment "I'm sorry sir, but the Lord is not on trial here today."[51]

The trial, held before three Illinois circuit judges who would decide the case, lasted four days. Schug, the Unitarian Universalist minister who had first helped McCollum find financial backing, sat with her through the whole thing. Dannel McCollum calls him one of the "unsung heroes" of the case.[52] As the McCollum family waited for the decision, things got worse for them in their neighborhood. As Halloween approached, Christian tricksters began writing "Atheist" on their home and car and gangs of teenagers assembled in the dark of night to sing "Onward Christian Soldiers" outside their house. On Halloween, Vashti opened the door to give candy to what she thought were late trick-or-treaters only to be barraged with rotten vegetables and mud by a mob of Christian youth.[53] When McCollum and her team returned to the courtroom on January 26, 1946, the Reverend Schug was optimistic, but in fact the journey had just begun. The judges found that because James McCollum had not been required to take a religion class, his rights had not been violated.[54] Not long after the trial, another boy, without any provocation, punched James in the face for his role in the trial.[55] James moved to another school and the case moved to the Illinois Supreme Court, where again the judges ruled against McCollum.[56] Again McCollum appealed the decision. On June 2, 1947, the US Supreme Court agreed to hear the case.[57] The hearing date was set for December 8.[58]

Appealing to the Highest Court

The *McCollum* case unquestionably reached the US Supreme Court at an opportune moment, landing there toward the beginning of a period in which Hugo Black, an Alabama senator who had been appointed to the court by Franklin Roosevelt in 1937, was beginning a decades-long process of reinforcing a strongly separationist interpretation of the Establishment Clause and bringing state and local laws into line with it. In the previous year, Black had authored an opinion that was one of the most important of his career: *Everson v. Board of Education*. It set the stage for *McCollum v. Board of Education* and subsequent cases. The peculiar features of the case, however, had prevented it from yet being recognized as a fundamental advance for separationist principles.

Everson v. Board of Education would have been a challenging case for any justice, and it held at least one uniquely personal challenge for Black. The plaintiff, Arch Everson, executive director of the New Jersey Taxpayer Association, had brought a lawsuit against the public schools of Ewing Township, New Jersey, because they had established a busing program that served not only the public school children of the district but also the private and Catholic school children. Philip Hamburger plausibly characterizes the case as seeking to continue the long-standing pattern of denying public funding to denominational Catholic schools while granting it to nondenominational Protestant schools.[59] After the court heard the case argued in November 1946, opinion was divided among the justices. Justices Black and Stanley Reed, together with Chief Justice Fred Vinson thought that the New Jersey law should be upheld because it benefited the children and not the religious schools themselves. It was therefore not in violation of the Establishment Clause. However, Establishment Clause hardliners Felix Frankfurter and Wiley Rutledge contended that letting the New Jersey busing program stand would open the door to direct public aid to religious schools. Chief Justice Vinson assigned Black the task of writing an opinion that would uphold the busing program, but it was touch and go for some time about whether it would be the majority or the dissenting opinion. Every time Black wrote a draft, Rutledge countered with a draft of an opposing opinion that Black used as a basis for revision. Back and forth they went. Black wrote six drafts and Rutledge eight. The less committed justices switched from one side to the other as the opinions evolved.[60]

Whatever the outcome of *Everson* was to be, it was destined to be consequential. This was because *Everson* was to be the first case to "incorporate" the Establishment Clause, making the court's decision as applicable to state and local laws as it was to federal laws. The process of "incorporating" the Bill of Rights had begun in 1925 with *Gitlow v. New York*. In that case, the Supreme Court upheld the conviction of Benjamin Gitlow under New York's Criminal Anarchy Statute of 1902 for distributing anarchist literature. In the process it asserted that because the Fourteenth Amendment (1868) guarantees that US citizens cannot be "deprived of liberty without due process of law," state laws must be in conformity with First Amendment guarantees of free speech and freedom of the press.[61] This ruling began the process of the "selective incorporation" of rights contained in the US Constitution into state law, which previously had not been required to conform to federal law.

The Supreme Court first incorporated the Free Exercise clause of the First Amendment in the 1940 *Cantwell v. Connecticut* case, where it upheld the right of a Jehovah's Witness to go door to door preaching without a state solicitor's license.[62] Now *Everson v. Board of Education* presented an opportunity to incorporate the Establishment Clause in addition to the Free Exercise Clause. But how could that be done while upholding the Ewing busing program?

Beyond the challenge of writing an opinion that would incorporate the Establishment Clause while at the same time exempting the New Jersey busing program from it, there was an episode in Black's past that made the terrain of the *Everson* case personally challenging for him. Black had arrived at the Supreme Court in 1937 with the credentials of a Roosevelt loyalist but also a shocking skeleton in his closet, a skeleton that wore a pointy white hood and robes. Born in 1886 in rural central Alabama, Black had been only twenty when he was admitted to the bar in 1906. An impressive performance in a case that he argued on behalf of an African American convict who had been forced to continue working in a labor gang past his sentence earned him a judicial appointment to the police court in Birmingham in 1911.[63] Black was elected to the US Senate in 1926. After Franklin Roosevelt became president in 1932, Black became his fierce defender, backing every New Deal program he had the opportunity to. This loyalty earned him an appointment to the Supreme Court, which had previously blocked a number of Roosevelt's New Deal programs.[64] The fly in the honey of Black's political career was the fact that he had joined the Ku Klux Klan in 1923 in an effort to build support for his Senate run in Alabama.[65] Although he resigned two years later before entering the Senate, rumors of his past membership almost derailed the Senate confirmation of his Supreme Court appointment. There is no record of Black endorsing the Klan's most extreme positions, but he does seem to have harbored suspicions of the Catholic Church as an institution. And that was just the difficulty with *Everson v. Board of Education*, a case that threatened valuable state aid to Catholic school children. After Black's confirmation to the Supreme Court, he had worked hard at damage control, giving a radio address where he disavowed racism, anti-Semitism, and anti-Catholicism.[66] He also very deliberately, it seems, hired a Jew, a Catholic, and an African American to his staff.[67] Now what would he do, all these years later, with a case that sought to stop the busing of Catholic school children in the name of "separation of church and state"? Critics might say that his support of the program was only to demonstrate his break with the Klan. But if he changed his mind and opposed the program, it would likely be attributed to a continuing Klannish anti-Catholicism. Tensions were raised by the fact that the 1940 *Cantwell v. Connecticut* decision, written by Justice Owen Roberts and supported unanimously by the court, had upheld the right of a Jehovah's Witness to engage in anti-Catholic speech in a Catholic neighborhood on Free Exercise grounds. Would separation of church and state cases always go against Catholics?

Emerging from tensions between Establishment Clause moderates and hardliners on the court, and from Black's struggles to live down his past connection to the KKK, the *Everson* opinion combined the strongest legal affirmation of the separationist principle that the court had ever produced, with the finding that the New Jersey busing program did not violate that principle. To get that job done, Black turned to the history of the Establishment Clause, tracing its roots to Madison's *Memorial and Remonstrance Against Religious Assessments* and Jefferson's Virginia Statute for Religious Freedom. He found that in colonial America, religious "dissenters were compelled to pay tithes and taxes to support government-sponsored churches whose ministers preached inflammatory sermons . . . against dissenters." This practice of compelling religious dissenters to financially support ministers who attacked them for their beliefs "became so commonplace as to shock the freedom-loving colonials into a feeling of abhorrence. . . . It was these feelings which found expression in the First Amendment."[68] Thus, for Black, because of the particular abhorrence of being forced by law to support a religion in which one does not believe, the Establishment Clause is designed to protect the citizens of the United States from being compelled to support *any* religious institution. Consequently, neither state nor the federal governments "can pass laws which aid one religion, aid all religions, or prefer one religion over another. . . . No tax in any amount, large or small, can be levied to support any religious activities or institutions. . . . In the words of Jefferson, the clause against establishment of religion by law was intended to erect 'a wall of separation between church and State.'"[69]

Black's interpretation of the First Amendment was strongly separationist. There is not the slightest hint of Joseph Story's nondenominationalist approach, which held that the First Amendment was intended only to "exclude all rivalry among Christian sects" and did not require a "wall of separation" between church and state. Not only does Black's opinion assert a strongly separationist interpretation of the Establishment Clause, it also clearly asserts that it applies in the states as well as to the federal government. But having asserted both a separationist interpretation of the Establishment Clause and the jurisdiction to enforce that interpretation in state and local law, Black says the New Jersey busing program is not in violation of it because busing is a public welfare program that is offered to all children regardless of their religion. "The First Amendment has erected a wall between church and state," Black wrote in conclusion. "That wall must be kept high and impregnable. We could not approve the slightest breach. New Jersey has not breached it here."[70] The four justices who dissented from the ruling loved what Black had written about the meaning of the Establishment Clause but did not agree that the busing program should be exempt. "Neither so high nor so impregnable today as yesterday is the wall raised between church and state by Virginia's great statute of religious freedom and the First Amendment," wrote Rutledge in his dissent.[71] Thus it was that a singularly important decision for separation of church and state was at first viewed as weakening it.

The *Everson* decision was announced on February 10, 1947, just a couple weeks after Vashti McCollum lost her appeal at the Illinois Supreme Court, and about four months before the US Supreme Court agreed to hear her case. McCollum's description of press reaction to the decision shows that Catholic publications generally approved of it, while Protestant publications saw the decision as actually weakening the separation of church and state.[72] McCollum was inclined to agree with the latter opinion. At the time, she saw the dissenting justices as more likely to be on her side than those in the majority, including Black. "I felt that at least we had four men on our side," she wrote. "Our job was to convince the other five."[73] The hearing in Washington, DC, on December 8 seemed to go well. McCollum wrote that she was "lost in admiration at the thorough and complete way in which the United States Supreme Court reviews a case . . . I was in wonderful spirits by the end of the hearing."[74] She and her team returned to Illinois in an optimistic mood.

The *McCollum* decision was easier for Black and the court than *Everson* had been, but there were still disagreements. The case was not haunted by the legacy of discrimination against Catholics as *Everson* had been, and the use of school property for religious instruction seemed a clear violation of the Establishment Clause to eight of the nine justices from the start. But there was disagreement about whether the strong separationist language of *Everson* should be invoked in the decision. Black, who had again been assigned to write the opinion, stood up for his previous decision and refused to write an opinion that did not refer to it.[75] In this way, the phrase that Jefferson had used in his letter to the Danbury Baptists became a fixture of constitutional law. "As we said in the *Everson* case," wrote Black, "... the First Amendment has erected a wall between Church and State which must be kept high and impregnable. Here not only are the State's tax-supported public school buildings used for the dissemination of religious doctrines. The State also affords sectarian groups an invaluable aid in that it helps to provide pupils for their religious classes through use of the State's compulsory public school machinery. This is not separation of Church and State."[76]

By March 8, 1948, when the *McCollum* decision was announced, James McCollum had moved in with his mother's freethinking parents in Rochester, New York, to avoid unwanted attention. A paper quoted James as saying, "I knew Mom was right" when he learned the outcome of his case.[77] A photograph taken the day after the decision shows Vashti McCollum, now a spritely woman in her thirties, beaming as she reads the newspaper headline announcing her victory.[78] The case was over, but her career as a much-sought-after speaker on the separation of church and state was just beginning. Vashti McCollum was elected to be the first female president of the American Humanist Association in 1962.[79]

Ironically, even though the *McCollum* opinion clearly forbade the use of school resources for religious instruction, the White Plains school release for religious instruction programs that Joseph Lewis had put so much energy into opposing in the 1920s survived the ruling because the religious instruction did not take place on school property.[80] The legal battle was already in the past when Vashti's parents, Arthur and Ruth Cromwell, undertook the restoration of Ingersoll's birth home with Lewis, who was no doubt happy to be working with the parents of a woman who had achieved such a victory for separationist principles. Lewis lived on until 1968. He died one morning of a heart attack as he was working in the offices of the Freethought Press Association in New York. He was seventy-nine years old.[81] He had lived to see the end of school religious instruction, school prayer, and Bible reading at school, goals that it had been his life's work to achieve.

McCollum v. Board of Education was among the earliest of a series of Supreme Court rulings that remade the judicial landscape of the United States in the mid-twentieth century with regard to church-state issues. Until *McCollum* it was unclear that future Supreme Court decisions would employ and extend the precedent of *Everson*. *McCollum* did employ *Everson* as a precedent and indicated what the future would bring. After *McCollum* there came

Burstyn v. Wilson, which ended the censorship of speech that some might consider sacrilegious or blasphemous in 1952; *Torcaso v. Watkins*, which ended religious tests for public office in 1961; *Engel v. Vitale*, which ended school prayer in 1962; *Abington School District v. Schempp*, which ended school-based Bible reading in 1963; *Epperson v. Arkansas*, which ruled laws that forbade the teaching of evolution in public schools unconstitutional in 1968; and *Lemon v. Kurtzman*, which in 1971 forbade public funds from being used to pay the salaries of teachers at private religious schools and which established the influential "Lemon Test" for Establishment Clause legal issues. These decisions did not realize quite all the goals set forth in the Nine Demands of Liberalism, but they realized far more than had been achieved in the movement's previous 150 years of existence.

This series of Supreme Court decisions is referred to by constitutional law scholars as the "third disestablishment." Steven K. Green sees the state-level disestablishment of the Revolutionary era and passage of the First Amendment as the "first disestablishment." The "second disestablishment" was, for him, a process that occurred over the course of the nineteenth century as nondenominationalism proved inadequate to the task of mediating tensions between Protestants and Catholics. And the "third disestablishment" is the series of twentieth-century court decisions that began with *Everson* and *McCollum*.[82] Collectively, these decisions did away with the nineteenth century's nondenominationalist interpretation of the Establishment Clause and replaced it with the principle of separationism, which demanded that government not only should avoid favoring one religion over another but also that it should avoid all entanglement with religion.

Taking Stock of the Fourth Wave of American Freethought

The 1920s saw the birth of new freethought organizations that would endure and grow to support the movement through the rewarding years of the third disestablishment. These organizations included the New York Society of Freethinkers, the First Humanist Society of New York, and the American Association for the Advance of Atheism. These organizations and their successors, the Freethinkers of America, the American Humanist Association, and American Atheists, learned from nineteenth-century freethought's discovery that the movement thrives most vigorously when it is focused on advancing the separation of church and state. Acting on this principle, the next generation of freethinkers launched a series of lawsuits that would bring about the third disestablishment. Joseph Lewis, inspired by the role that Clarence Darrow was to play in the Scopes trial, pioneered the legal strategy of challenging laws and practices that violate separationist principles, adding a critical element to the repertoire of the freethought movement. This set the stage for Vashti McCollum and the other plaintiffs in the great legal proceedings of the third disestablishment to push forward.

I contend that the third disestablishment would have been unimaginable without the freethought movement. The third disestablishment was not a spontaneous evolution of constitutional law driven by the internal dynamics of American jurisprudence but rather the result of a century and a half of freethought pressure and agitation. The plaintiffs in all the lawsuits that brought about the third disestablishment had a strong belief that they had a constitutionally protected right not to be discriminated against for either religious belief or nonbelief, and that government and public institutions at all levels were constitutionally bound to promote neither any one religion nor religion in general. Throughout the nineteenth century, lawsuit after lawsuit had shown that this belief was more aspirational than settled, but the freethought movement, looking forward to the day when the ideals of Paine's *Age of Reason* would be realized, kept it alive until more favorable historical circumstances arose. And arise they did. A century and a half of struggle to complete a robust disestablishment of religion in the United States came to fruition when the freethought legal offensive entered a period in which sympathetic Supreme Court justices used the due process guarantees of the Fourteenth Amendment to bring state and local laws into conformity with a strongly separationist interpretation of the Establishment Clause.

Implications for the Current Interpretation of the Establishment Clause

In *Separation of Church and State,* Philip Hamburger spends considerable time sharing the results of his investigation of Hugo Black's connections to the KKK. Those connections are real and undeniable. Black was a member of the KKK from 1923 to 1925 and even campaigned at Klan events in an effort to win the Alabama senatorial Democratic primary. Hamburger plausibly argues that the main thing that the generally liberal Black shared with the Klan was a suspicion of the Catholic Church, and he implies, less plausibly, that Black supported "the separation of church and state" for the same reason that the Klan did. (Yes, the Klan *did* support "separation of church and state"!) The reason that the Klan supported what it called "separation of church and state," as it had been interpreted for the previous hundred years, was that it could be used to keep denominational Catholic institutions from benefiting from public funds in the same way that nondenominational Protestant institutions did. Hamburger means for us to believe that Black very intentionally enshrined the KKK's anti-Catholic ideas about "separation of church and state" in American constitutional law. He frames the *Everson* decision as one that *appeared* to give relief to Catholics by allowing the Ewing busing program to stand, while *actually* installing anti-Catholic "separation of church and state" into constitutional law in the same decision. Here is how he puts it (the quotations are from the Klan oath): "Black had an opportunity to make separation of church and state the unanimous standard of the Court while reaching a judgement that would undercut Catholic criticism.... Black had long before sworn, under the light of flaming crosses, to preserve 'the sacred constitutional rights' of 'free public schools' and 'separation of church and state.'"[83] The conclusion we are intended to draw is that "separation of church and state" should be abandoned as a principle of constitutional law because it is a bad, anti-Catholic principle sneaked in through the back door of the Supreme Court by a KKK member.

The problem with Hamburger's line of reasoning here is that what the Klan meant by "separation of church and state" and what Black wrote about that topic in the *Everson* decision are demonstrably as different as night and day. *Principles and Purposes of the Knights of the Ku Klux Klan, Outlined by an Exalted Cyclops of the Order* clearly states the Klan's views on separation of church and state circa 1920. "The Klan stands for law and order, freedom of speech, freedom of the press and freedom of conscience, for the free public school, separation of church and state, white supremacy and Protestant Christianity," writes the anonymous "cyclops" who assembled this document.[84] He elaborates on what "separation of church and state" meant to him a few pages later:

> The preservation of American ideals and the Christian religion depends upon the early creation in the children of this nation of a reverence for and an undying faith in God's holy word. That this reverence and faith may be indelibly stamped upon the minds of the children, the Bible must be read and explained to them daily, during their early school years. The Knights of the Ku Klux Klan believe that the free public schools should be the vehicle for this Bible reading and instruction, and that no atheist, infidel, skeptic, or non-believer should be allowed to teach in the public schools. The Klan does not contend for sectarian instruction in the Bible, but asks that it be read and explained from the broad viewpoint of its divine origin and inspiration.[85]

By way of contrast, here is what Black wrote about separation of church and state in the *Everson* decision:

> The "establishment of religion" clause of the First Amendment means at least this: neither a state nor the Federal Government can set up a church. Neither can pass laws which aid one religion, aid all religions, or prefer one religion over another. Neither can force nor influence a person to go to or to remain away from church against his will or force him to profess a belief or disbelief in any religion. No person can be punished for entertaining or professing religious beliefs or disbeliefs, for church attendance or non-attendance. No tax in any amount, large or small, can be levied to support any religious activities or institutions, whatever they may be called, or whatever form they may adopt to teach or practice religion. Neither a state nor the Federal Government can, openly or secretly, participate in the affairs of any religious organizations or groups, and vice versa. In the words of Jefferson, the clause against establishment of religion by law was intended to erect "a wall of separation between church and State."[96]

I don't think one needs to be a highly discerning legal scholar to see that what the Klan says about separation of church and state and what Black says about it are strongly contradictory. In the Klan document, "separation of church and state" has been co-opted into a Christian nationalist agenda that would enshrine the Bible as a staple of public education and bar anyone with non-Christian beliefs from teaching in public school. This is in stark contradiction to Black's opinion that "no tax in any amount . . . can be levied to support any religious activities" and "no person can be punished for entertaining or professing religious beliefs or disbeliefs." Black himself extended the logic of *Everson* to end school-based religious instruction in the *McCollum* case (1948), to end religious tests for public office in *Torcaso v. Watkins* (1961), and to end school prayer in *Engel v. Vitale* (1962). Black's colleague Justice Thomas Clark employed Black's precedent to end Bible reading in *Abington School District v. Schempp* (1963). If the Christian nationalists of the Klan thought they were getting a friend on the Supreme Court when Hugo Black took the bench, the *Everson* decision should have left them reaching beneath their pointy white hoods to scratch their heads and thinking, "With a friend like this, who needs enemies?" If it is undeniable that Hugo Black was a member of the KKK in the early '20s, it is also undeniable that the version of "separation of church and state" that he brought into constitutional law was not the Klan version. Instead, it will make the Klan's Christian nationalist agenda impossible to achieve for as long as it stands. Those who work against it are helping the Klan and other Christian nationalist organizations achieve their goals.

As this is the last time in the book that I will be discussing Hamburger's arguments in detail, it is probably a good place to summarize my critique. There is much good scholarship in the 514 pages of Hamburger's book. Only someone with his perspective would have discovered how deeply the idea of "separation of church and state" became part of the ideology of nativist and even, surprisingly, Christian nationalist groups. But Hamburger has mistaken distorted repetitions of the original idea of separationism for the idea itself. The original idea was to keep all religion apart from government. Not just Catholicism. Not just Christianity. All religion. Hamburger's gifts as a scholar allow him to tell a plausible-sounding story about how an idea that Madison made it a priority to enshrine in the Constitution, and Jefferson hit upon a clever phrase for describing, ended up in KKK indoctrination materials. Although this is a topic that merits investigation, I notice that Hamburger did not spend 514 pages investigating how "freedom of the press," "freedom of conscience," and "free public school" also ended up in KKK indoctrination materials. For some reason it is only the presence of "separation of church and state" in KKK discourse that interests him.

To explain the presence of "separation of church and state" in KKK indoctrination materials, Hamburger tells a long story. Despite its length, Hamburger's story has only three main plot points, and each of them is problematic.

Plot point one: "The constitutional authority for separation is without historical foundation."[87] Hamburger tries to establish this by first demonstrating that the phrase "separation of church and state" is nowhere in the Constitution but rather is an interpretation of the Establishment Clause that Jefferson voiced in his letter to the Danbury Baptists. This is a fact that most bright high school students know. It proves nothing. No separationist has ever contended that the words "separation of church and state" are in the Constitution, only that "separation of church and state" is a good description from an authoritative source of what the Establishment Clause meant to Jefferson and Madison. Next, Hamburger argues that "the Danbury Association . . . acted as if the correspondence [with Jefferson] had never taken place" by which he infers that the Baptists didn't agree with Jefferson.[88] I have countered that after the Baptists had sent John Leland and a 1,200-pound cheese to thank Jefferson, they might have felt that no further reply was necessary.

Further, Leland and other Baptists expressed more separationist beliefs than Hamburger gives them credit for. But even if it is conceded that the Baptists might not have been in complete agreement with Jefferson, it is unclear why that disagreement would negate the legitimacy of Jefferson's words about the meaning of the Establishment Clause. "Separation of church and state" is what Jefferson thought the Establishment Clause meant, so that is one of its original meanings regardless of what the Baptists thought.

Beyond this, Hamburger ignores vital evidence about what the Establishment Clause meant to its author, James Madison. Jefferson's ideas about the Establishment Clause are, from a certain perspective, secondary to the words of Madison as a guide to interpreting it. In the House debate that followed the introduction of the Establishment Clause, Madison said that it meant, among other things, that Congress must not "compel men to worship God in any manner contrary to their conscience."[89] This certainly must mean both that a Jew must not be compelled to acknowledge the divinity of Jesus and also that an atheist must not be compelled to accept the existence of God. Madison demonstrated what this interpretation entailed in his "Detached Memoranda," where he wrote that he believed the existence of congressional chaplains to be a "violation . . . of Constitutional principles."[90] Even though the specific phrase "separation of church and state" belongs to Jefferson and not Madison, Madison's separationist principles went beyond even the separationism that has been enacted to this day, for we still have congressional chaplains. Madison clearly intended that the Establishment Clause should forbid the government to pay anyone to practice or promote any variety of religion. To say that the separationist interpretation of the Establishment Clause is without historical foundation is to ignore the words of its primary author.

Plot point two: "In the mid-nineteenth century, nativists adopted the idea [of separationism] against Catholics who were presumptuous enough to demand the same legal rights as Protestants. . . . Eventually, as adherents of liberal theology came to fear all ecclesiastical authority, these liberals developed a more secular version of separation."[91] In the second act of his story, Hamburger asks us to believe that "separation of church and state" was resurrected by nativists for the purpose of keeping Catholic hands off Protestant tax revenue and only later was taken up by principled liberals advocating for a more secular society. The reverse is actually true. As I have shown, separationist items were present even in Elihu Palmer's *Prospect* in the first decade of the nineteenth century and were a regular feature of

Frances Wright's *Free Enquirer* in the 1820s and '30s. Separationism was part of American freethought from the very beginning, going back to Paine's *Age of Reason*. Nativists appropriated the concept for their own purposes by linking it to a nondenominationalist interpretation of the Establishment Clause, with which most freethinkers did not agree. Because of their differences with nativists on topics like women's rights, nativists and freethinkers were mostly at odds. To blame freethinkers for the havoc nativists wreaked with their distorted understanding of "separation of church and state" is like giving someone a ticket for speeding after their car had been stolen because the thief broke the speed limit while escaping.

Plot point three: "Black had long before sworn, under the light of flaming crosses, to preserve 'the sacred constitutional rights' of 'free public schools' and 'separation of church and state.'"[92] In the final act of his story, Hamburger asks us to believe that Justice Hugo Black, formerly a KKK member, enshrined the anti-Catholic, nativist principle of "separation of church and state" into constitutional law because of his sympathies with Klan anti-Catholicism. This position, as I have just argued, ignores the deep differences between how the Klan understood "separation of church and state" and what Black wrote about it in *Everson*, and it ignores the fact that *Everson*'s overturning of the nondenominationalist interpretation of the Establishment Clause brought the Klan's Christian nationalist agenda to a screeching halt. If one wants to get an idea of what drove Black's *Everson* decision, rather than looking to Black's renounced Klan membership, it might be better to look to his friendship with Unitarian minister Arthur Powell Davies, who performed Black's second marriage and once gave a sermon entitled "The God of the Atheist," in which he sympathetically quoted Robert Ingersoll.[93]

Like many key political phrases, the Establishment Clause probably never had a single original meaning but was thought to mean different things by the different factions that supported it. All these meanings should be available to contemporary constitutional interpretation. The separationist interpretation of the Establishment Clause, so well articulated in Jefferson's letter to the Danbury Baptists, is unquestionably among its original meanings. Hamburger has tried to discredit the separationist position not only by falsely claiming it is "without historical foundation" but also by dwelling on some of the nefarious characters who have used the phrase "separation of church and state." There is no doubt that such characters employed "separation of church and state" for nefarious purposes, but the fact that the KKK promoted what it understood to be "separation of church and state" does not diminish the legitimacy or correctness of the separationist interpretation of the Establishment Clause any more than the Klan's support for what it understood as "free speech" diminishes the importance of that fundamental right.

In conclusion, I have to wonder if Hamburger has ever really pondered the consequences of ending separationism. Does he seek to bring back nondenominationalism, which truly has been used against Catholics, or does he seek to go even further and allow government to directly support all religious groups so long as it treats them equally? It may be possible that evenhanded support for all religions might avoid nasty occurrences like the Bible riots that have plagued past attempts to use the government to promote religion, but Hamburger offers no clues about what it might look like. If the state evenhandedly supported all Protestant denominations, Catholicism, all varieties of Judaism, all varieties of Islam, all varieties of Buddhism, Hinduism, Jainism, Sikhism, all Native American religious traditions, Humanism, Wiccanism, Spiritualism, Santeria, and all the other religious communities active in America, would all these groups live in greater peace, harmony, and prosperity than they do now? Or is it more likely that some of these denominations would be favored over others, or at least that there would be the perception of favoritism, and that such real or perceived favoritism would lead to new resentments? Would all the members of all these religious groups be happy with their tax dollars going to support each and every other variety of religion, or would some groups begin to claim that other religions are not true religions and so should not get any support? Would advocates of small government and tax fairness be happy with a government subsidy for any group that proclaims itself a religion? In a situation where government funding could be obtained by religious groups just for existing, there is a strong likelihood that there would be spurious claims of religiosity made for the sole purpose of getting money. It would be necessary for the government to distinguish between true and false religions, but who would decide what is a true support-worthy religion and what is not? Would the support status of some controversial religious groups become dependent on which political party holds power?

Because of the high degree of religious pluralism in America, and because Americans so deeply love to fight over who is entitled to what when anyone is entitled to anything, stepping back from separationism would likely have very serious consequences. And those consequences are not limited to funding squabbles. Just as the overturn of *Roe v. Wade* reactivated almost overnight antiquated abortion restrictions in many states, an overturn of *Everson*'s separationist interpretation of the Establishment Clause could lead to the reactivation of numerous unrescinded laws that discriminate against religious minorities. Article One, Section Four of the current Pennsylvania State Constitution, for instance, reads, "No person who acknowledges the being of a God and a future state of rewards and punishments shall, on account of his religious sentiments, be disqualified to hold any office or place of trust or profit under this Commonwealth." The strong implication of this provision is that people who do not acknowledge the existence of God and a future state of rewards and punishments *can* be disqualified from holding public office. The only thing that currently prevents public office holders from being required to swear an oath affirming their belief in God, heaven, and hell in my home state of Pennsylvania is the 1961 *Torcaso v. Watkins* decision, which is in turn dependent on the 1947 *Everson* decision. A Supreme Court repudiation of *Everson* thus could lead to the partial disenfranchisement not only of atheists and agnostics in Pennsylvania and similar states, but also of Universalists and others who do not believe that a benevolent God would ever condemn any soul to an eternity of torture. Nowhere in Hamburger's book does he even begin to address these consequences of abandoning the separation of church and state.

CONCLUSION

Freethought Today and Tomorrow

American freethought continues to be a viable movement today. There are presently as many national freethought organizations as there were during the golden age, if not more. The American Humanist Association, as we have seen, can trace its roots back to the freethought resurgence of the 1920s. But many others are newer. Americans United for the Separation of Church and State was founded in 1948 with the original name Protestants and Other Americans United for the Separation of Church and State. Although it was created by progressive mainline Protestants, it has since expanded its base. As an organization, it is more committed to separationism than freethought per se, and might best be thought of as an ecumenical religious organization that includes liberal believers from many faith traditions as well as nonreligious people.[1] American Atheists was founded in 1963 by Madalyn Murray O'Hair with the help of a donation from *Truth Seeker* editor Charles Smith.[2] The Center for Inquiry has its roots in a 1976 gathering of academics and science professionals, including Carl Sagan, Isaac Asimov, and B. F. Skinner, who aimed to create an organization that would debunk the pseudoscientific claims of astrologers and UFO enthusiasts as well as promote secularism.[3] In 2006 evolutionary biologist Richard Dawkins established the Richard Dawkins Foundation as a division of the Center for Inquiry to teach the value of science and advance secularism. The Council for Secular Humanism, a subsidiary of the Center for Inquiry, runs the Robert Ingersoll Birthplace Museum. The Freedom from Religion Foundation was founded in 1978 and bills itself as "the nation's largest freethought association with more than 39,000 freethinkers: atheists, agnostics and skeptics of any pedigree."[4] The Freethought Society evolved out of the Freethought Society of Greater Philadelphia in 2010 and focuses more on community-building activities than many other organizations.[5] The Secular Coalition for America is an umbrella organization founded in 2002 that represents twenty-one member organizations, including American Atheists, the American Humanist Society, the American Ethical Union, the Freethought Society, the Center for Inquiry, Black Nonbelievers, Ex-Muslims of North America, Hispanic American Freethinkers, Humanistic Judaism, Secular Woman, Military Atheists, and the Secular Student Alliance.[6] There are many more American freethought organizations on the local level, and many international organizations as well.

In addition to the civic organizations just reviewed, some religious organizations also have a good claim to be part of the contemporary freethought movement. Being a member of a Unitarian Universalist congregation, the author can speak of some aspects of this tradition from experience. The present Unitarian Universalist Association was organized in 1961 with a formal merger of Unitarian and Universalist Associations and is composed of more than one thousand congregations. Unitarian Universalists, or UUs for short, do not subscribe to any specific creed but instead promise to try to live by seven ethical principles:

1. The inherent worth and dignity of every person;
2. Justice, equity and compassion in human relations;
3. Acceptance of one another and encouragement to spiritual growth in our congregations;
4. A free and responsible search for truth and meaning;
5. The right of conscience and the use of the democratic process within our congregations and in society at large;
6. The goal of world community with peace, liberty, and justice for all; and,
7. Respect for the interdependent web of all existence of which we are a part.[7]

Many congregations have recently also subscribed to a racial justice principle individually.

UU congregations welcome people from all religious backgrounds, including atheists, agnostics, secular humanists, and neo-pagans (commonly referred to as followers of "earth-based religions" in UU discourse). Services include readings from historic and contemporary literature that liturgists hope congregants will find meaningful. Bible readings are rare. Sermons generally contain ethical messages and spiritual inspiration but only occasionally mention God or Christ. Christian sacraments have been replaced with symbolic rituals of fairly recent invention, like flower communion, where congregants exchange flowers, and the gathering of waters, where everyone can contribute water to the supply that will be used in blessings throughout the year. The story of Jesus's birth is read and even reenacted by children at Christmas, but it is framed as a traditional Christian story, not as gospel truth. A chalice has replaced the cross as the denominational symbol. A 1998 survey found that 46% of UUs identify as humanists, while only 9.5% identify as Christians.[8]

If ever there was a denomination of freethinkers, it is Unitarian Universalism, but other liberal Protestant groups have a similar claim. Progressive Quakers and Swedenborgians also follow religions without set creeds, and, even though they are more definitively theistic than UUs, they seem to have at least as much room for freethought as did historical deists.[9] Among non-Christian traditions, Humanistic and Reconstructionist Judaism, Sufism (especially in the tradition of the Inayati Order), and Zen Buddhism have much of the spirit of freethought, if somewhat more adherence to traditional ritual forms and/or spiritual disciplines than many liberal Christian and post-Christian groups.[10] And of course, people in many other faith traditions also practice freethought in contradiction to the official teachings of their religions.

In the United States there are perhaps 50,000 to 100,000 people who are actively involved with a freethought civic organization, and perhaps 900,000 who participate in a religious tradition that is officially hospitable to freethought (about 200,000 Humanistic and Reconstructionist Jews; 200,000 UUs; perhaps 200,000 Zen and other Progressive Buddhists; about 80,000 Quakers; plus others).[11] This means that about one million people or about 0.3% of the population has formal ties with a civic or religious organization that welcomes freethought. This number is truly dwarfed by the 22.8% of the population (almost 75.7 million people) who are religiously nonaffiliated (aka "nones"), including about 13.3 million professed agnostics, and 10.3 million atheists. It can be speculated that a fair number of the non-atheist, non-agnostic "nones," representing about 15% of the total US population, could be described as deists.[12] Clearly, there are vastly more freethinkers in the United States than are formally involved with the organizations that could be said to constitute the freethought movement. This means that the movement has huge growth potential under the right conditions.

Lessons from the Past

Freethinkers of today and tomorrow would do well to take a few lessons from the movement's past. One is that, of the three movement frames whose usage has been traced through the course of freethought's history (antiscripturalism, scientific hope, and separationism), separationism seems to have had by far the most success in helping to define and advance movement goals. A separationist political agenda became a cornerstone of the movement's collective identity in the 1870s and remains so today. Antiscripturalism was a predominant theme in the first and second waves of freethought, but the popularity of the movement expanded by leaps and bounds after the Nine Demands of Liberalism became its rallying cry. I suspect that a focus on separationism is even more strategically sound today than it was in the nineteenth century. It is the glue that holds together the alliance between a-religious organizations like the Freedom from Religion Foundation and the liberal but ecumenically religious organizations like Americans United for the Separation of Church and State.[13]

Science continues to have its champions and to need more, but the public is now generally aware that science can bring revolutionary improvements to human life in a way it was not when Paine wrote *Age of Reason*. The defense of science is one of the Secular Coalition for America's key policy areas, but in practical terms this amounts to defending scientific research and education against religiously motivated threats, and this in turn usually amounts to a defense of church-state separation.

As for antiscripturalism, it seems unlikely that any American who today believes in the literal truth of the Bible is unaware that many other Americans disagree with them on that point. While serious questioning of the use of biblical texts to justify contemporary moral pronouncements and policy claims may be warranted, generalized and sustained attacks on the divine authority of the Bible in the style of *The Age of Reason* might do more harm than good by giving biblical literalists additional reason to think of themselves as an oppressed minority. Freethinkers would do better to give the Bible a respected place among humanity's other sacred books, recognizing them all as having deep cultural meaning, and aiding efforts to bring their interpretation into line with contemporary scientific and ethical standards. If Paine had taken this sort of attitude toward the Bible in *Age of Reason*, would freethought have perhaps been more successful? It is hard to say.

A second lesson from the history of freethought is that the movement has thrived on internal tolerance and external alliances. If early nineteenth-century freethinkers had allowed theological disputes between Creator God deists and pantheists to divide the movement, they would have been finished before they began. They might have gotten even further if they had allowed Swedenborgians like John Hargrove, who did not interpret the Bible literally, into the fold. The golden age of freethought was underwritten by a remarkable alliance between theistic free religionists, materialistic agnostics and atheists, and spiritualists who believed the spirits of the dead could return to guide the living. Although freethought's external alliances have at times caused internal tensions, by and large, freethought has benefited from its partnerships with the feminist, labor rights, abolition, free speech, free love, and birth control movements. Its involvement with the eugenics movement serves as a cautionary tale about the dangers of choosing the wrong alliances. Likely allies in the current political landscape are those concerned for reproductive and LGBTQ rights, feminism, and the defense of the recommendations of science about global warming and public health issues like vaccination.

It should also be remembered that freethought has benefited greatly from the contributions of religious people and organizations. Many freethought lecturers—including Elihu Palmer, Abner Kneeland, and Charles Reynolds—started out as Christian preachers, and spiritualists and Unitarians have played key roles in the movement's history. Contemporary freethought would do well to continue and expand its connections with liberal religion. Additionally, most civic and religious organizations currently in the freethought movement do not appear to have memberships in which BIPOC people (Black, Indigenous, and People of Color) are represented in positions that correspond to their representation in the overall population. Given freethought's previous unfortunate overlap with the eugenics movement and its failure to ally with Black freethinkers, it is both a special responsibility of the movement and a strategically good move to find ways to build bridges to freethinkers who have backgrounds that are currently underrepresented in the movement. The Secular Coalition has done well in developing a diverse group of member organizations.

A final lesson concerns the fragility of secularism. It is important to remember that the third disestablishment consisted of a series of Supreme Court legal rulings and did not involve any landmark legislation. Much of the work of contemporary freethought organizations like the Secular Coalition, the Freedom from Religion Foundation, and the American Humanist Association involves advancing a similar legally centered agenda. Over the years, freethinkers have had little success in securing the passage of legislation that reaffirms the will of state and national legislatures to support these legal victories. Politicians remain hesitant about opposing the interests of organized religion. As we have seen with the *Dobbs* decision overturning *Roe v. Wade*'s abortion protections, in the absence of legislation affirming court decisions, what the judicial giveth, the judiciary can taketh away. It perhaps does not now seem likely that key Supreme Court decisions that have forbidden prayer and Bible reading in public schools and invalidated laws that require that public officials take religious oaths, criminalize blasphemy and sending information about birth control through the mail, and forbid the teaching of evolution will be overturned. But just a few years ago it did not seem likely that *Roe v. Wade* would be overturned. The 2022 *Kennedy v. Bremerton* Supreme Court ruling has already started to chip away at the 1962 precedent of *Engel v. Vitale*. In the final weeks that I have spent working on this manuscript, Louisiana passed a law requiring the display of the Ten Commandments in public school classrooms. Although the law will almost certainly face legal challenges, its supporters claim that the *Kennedy v. Bremerton* decision is a signal that the court will uphold it. Failure to pass legislation that positively affirms third disestablishment Supreme Court decisions has made the legal victories that are at the foundation of the present regime of secularism vulnerable.

There is mounting pressure to turn the clock back on the advance of secularism. In the present time, about a quarter of Americans believe that the Bible is the "actual word of God" (as opposed to writing inspired by God, or a collection of fables and myths).[14] About 20% fit the definition of Christian nationalists proposed by sociologists Andrew L. Whitehead and Samuel L. Perry,[15] believing that the United States was created to be a Christian nation governed by Christian laws and Christian people. The website of the Christian Liberty Party, a party with chapters in Alabama, Idaho, Maine, and Washington, states the Christian nationalist position succinctly: "As worshipers of the one true God, we boldly proclaim God's Lordship over politics. He alone is sovereign over all things. His Word is Truth, and to Jesus Christ has been given all authority in heaven and on earth. This is truly the foundation of political liberty."[16] Christian nationalist organizations like

Capitol Ministries, Project Blitz, and the Wallbuilders are working diligently to realize their vision of a Christian America by weakening the separation of church and state, limiting reproductive rights and the rights of LGBTQ citizens, and changing the teaching of history and science in public schools through legislative interference. They have secured powerful allies like antiseparationist legal scholar Philip Hamburger, Speaker of the House Mike Johnson, and Supreme Court justice Clarence Thomas. There is no doubt that contemporary freethinkers have much work to do if they wish to maintain the separation of church and state, prevent the censorship of history and science to conform with narrow religious views, and avert the curtailment of civil liberties on religious grounds.

The American freethought movement had its roots in the viral popularity of Paine's *Age of Reason* in the 1790s, so it is perhaps fitting to close the circle and conclude with a reflection on the meaning of "the Age of Reason" today. Many people today would identify "the Age of Reason" with the Enlightenment and the eighteenth century, a time when prominent intellectuals argued that governments, commerce, science, medicine, and even religion needed to be reorganized on a more rational basis. But in the 1790s Paine wrote of the Age of Reason as an age that was still to come. As Paine's experience shows, the Enlightenment did not always treat those who championed its most characteristic ideals in a very enlightened way. In 1793, Paine thought that the Age of Reason might be dawning, but the 1790s did not turn out to be the Age of Reason that Paine dreamed of. Progress toward the true Age of Reason has been slow. We are now, despite a few recent backward steps, much closer to living in an Age of Reason than Paine was. The "rights of man," have become "human rights," and a lot more humans are legally recognized as having them than in the past, including the descendants of those humans who were enslaved in Paine's time. The half of humanity that could not vote and did not have full property rights in Britain and America in Paine's time now has those rights in much of the world. Even if science has not displaced traditional theology for most people, it has made staggering advances that have given us greater power to do good or evil than Paine could ever have imagined. We have truly made great progress toward an Age of Reason.

But this is still not yet *the* Age of Reason. How could we give such a name to an age that can foresee that its greenhouse gas emissions will alter the planetary climate, causing widespread death and disaster, but can't take the actions necessary to avert the catastrophe? Despite the progress we have made, we live in an age of increasing income inequality, eroding civil rights, dangerous extremism, and rampant misinformation. The true Age of Reason must still lie in the future if is ever to be at all. It is a dream we must keep working to achieve.

NOTES

Bibliographic Note

As much as possible, I have tried to use sources that are easily accessible on the internet so that those who are interested may consult them with just a few keystrokes. In the notes, I employ the following abbreviations to indicate common internet sources:

> GB = Google Books, available from any Google search using the Books filter
> IA = Internet Archive, available at https://archive.org/details/texts
> HT = HathiTrust, available at https://www.hathitrust.org/
> TPNHA = Thomas Paine National Historical Association, where a timeline of all Thomas Paine's writings can be found at https://www.thomaspaine.org/timeline.html
> WTP = Moncure Daniel Conway, ed., *The Writings of Thomas Paine*, vols. 1, 2, 3, and 4 (New York: G. P. Putnam's Sons, 1894 to 1896). Citations will appear in the following format to include volume and page number: WTP 4, 22. All volumes can be freely accessed through the following HathiTrust page: https://catalog.hathitrust.org/Record/009832797/Home

I provide the full web addresses only of sources that are not easily found using a simple search on these platforms. This is an endnote-only style book that will give a full citation of the first instance of every source in each chapter and shortened citations for sources previously cited in the same chapter.

Introduction

1. Thomas Jefferson, *The Writings of Thomas Jefferson*, vol. 10: *1816–1826*, Paul Leicester Ford, ed. (New York: G. P. Putnam's Sons, 1892), 220. Available from GB.
2. WTP 4, 22.
3. Joseph Story, *Commentaries on the Constitution of the United States: With a Preliminary Review of the Constitutional History of the Colonies and States, Before the Adoption of the Constitution*, vol. 3 (Boston: Hilliard, Gray, and Company, 1833), 726.
4. Story, *Commentaries on the Constitution*, 728.
5. Walter Lippmann, *A Preface to Morals* (New York: Macmillan Company, 1929/1982), 8.

6. Anthony Collins, *A Discourse of Free-thinking: Occasion'd by the Rise and Growth of a Sect Call'd Free-thinkers* (London, 1713), 4–5. Available from GB.

7. Craig Allen Smith, Charles J. Stewart, and Robert E. Denton, *Persuasion and Social Movements*, 5th ed. (Long Grove, IL: Waveland Press, 2007), 24. For a compact overview of the social movements research tradition, see Michael Lienesch, *In the Beginning: Fundamentalism, the Scopes Trial, and the Making of the Antievolution Movement* (Chapel Hill: University of North Carolina Press, 2007), 4–6.

8. Lorenz von Stein seems to have introduced the phrase in his 1850 work, *Geschichte der socialen Bewegung in Frankreich von 1789 bis auf unsere Tage* (Leipzig: Berlag von Otto Wigand, 1850). The title translates as *History of the Social Movement in France from 1789 to Our Day*. For commentary, see Charles Tilly and Lester J. Wood, *Social Movements, 1768–2008* (Boulder, CO: Paradigm Publishers, 2009), 5–6.

9. For a review of New Social Movement Theory, see Suzanne Staggenborg, *Social Movements*, 3rd ed. (New York: Oxford University Press, 2022), 25–28.

10. For a review of Collective Behavior Theory and Political Process Theory, see Staggenborg, *Social Movements*, 15–18; 20–23.

11. See Alberto Melucci, "The Process of Collective Identity," in *Social Movements and Culture*, Hank Johnston and Bert Klandermans, eds. (Minneapolis: University of Minnesota Press, 1995), 41–63. For a broader perspective on collective identity in social movements, see Scott A. Hund and Robert A. Benford, "Collective Identity, Solidarity, and Commitment," in *The Blackwell Companion to Social Movements*, David A. Snow, Sarah A. Soule, and Hanspeter Kriesi, eds. (Hoboken: Wiley-Blackwell, 2008), 433–57.

12. David A. Snow and Robert D. Benford, "Ideology, Frame Resonance, and Participant Mobilization," *International Social Movement Research* 1 (1988): 197–219. For an overview of the literature on framing in social movements, see Paul Almeida, "The Framing Process," in *Social Movements: The Structure of Collective Mobilization* (Oakland: University of California Press, 2019), 80–100.

13. Tilly and Wood, *Social Movements, 1768–2008*, 4. One of Tilly's most extended and insightful discussions of repertoires can be found on pages 266–68 of Charles Tilly and Sidney Tarrow, "Conclusion: From Interactions to Outcomes in Social Movements," in *How Social Movements Matter*, Charles Tilly, Marco Giugni, and Doug McAdam, eds. (Minneapolis: University of Minnesota Press, 1999), 253–70. For a broader overview of literature on movement repertoires, see Verta Taylor and Nella Van Dyke, "'Get up, Stand Up': Tactical Repertoires of Social Movements," in *The Blackwell Companion*, 262–93.

14. On movement waves, see Ruud Koopmans, "Protest in Time and Space: The Evolution of Waves of Contention," in *The Blackwell Companion*, 19–46. Also see Alice Mattoni and Emiliano Treré, "Media Practices, Mediation Processes, and Mediatization in the Study of Social Movements," *Communication Theory* 24, no. 3 (August 2014): 256–57.

15. Sidney Warren, *American Freethought, 1860–1914* (New York: Columbia University Press, 1943).

16. Albert Post, *Popular Freethought in America, 1825–1850* (New York: Octagon Books, 1974).

17. Amanda Porterfield, *Conceived in Doubt: Religion and Politics in the New American Nation* (Chicago: University of Chicago Press, 2012).

18. Eric R. Schlereth, *An Age of Infidels: The Politics of Religious Controversy in the Early United States* (Philadelphia: University of Pennsylvania Press, 2013).

19. Leigh Eric Schmidt, *The Church of Saint Thomas Paine: A Religious History of American Secularism* (Princeton, NJ: Princeton University Press, 2021).

20. Leigh Eric Schmidt, *Village Atheists: How America's Unbelievers Made Their Way in a Godly Nation* (Princeton, NJ: Princeton University Press, 2016).

21. Fred Whitehead and Verle Muhrer, *Freethought on the American Frontier* (Buffalo, NY: Prometheus Books, 1992).

22. Christopher Cameron, *Black Freethinkers: A History of African American Secularism* (Evanston, IL: Northwestern University Press, 2019).

23. Harvey J. Kaye, *Thomas Paine and the Promise of America* (New York: Hill and Wang, 2005); Susan Jacoby, *Freethinkers: A History of American Secularism* (New York: Harry Holt and Company, 2004).

24. Tilly and Wood, *Social Movements, 1768-2008*, 49.

25. Philip Hamburger, *Separation of Church and State* (Cambridge, MA: Harvard University Press, 2002), 483.

26. See, for instance, Scott Yenor, "Hamburger, Philip; Separation of Church and State," *Perspectives on Political Science* 32, no. 2 (Spring 2003): 108; Mark G. Toulouse, "Separation of Church and State," *Church History* 73, no. 4 (2004): 885-87; Hunter Baker, "Separation of Church and State," *Journal of Church and State* 46, no. 4 (2004): 904-905.

Chapter 1 • Prelude to American Freethought

1. This passage may be found in Elias Boudinot, *The Age of Revelation; or, The Age of Reason Shewn to be an Age of Infidelity* (Philadelphia: Asbury Dickins, 1801), xii. Available from GB.

2. On Boudinot's life, see George Boyd, *Elias Boudinot: Patriot and Statesman, 1740-1821* (Westwood, CT: Greenwood Publishing, 1969). Also see Jonathan J. Den Hartog, "Advocating 'Public Righteousness': Elias Boudinot and the Transformation of Federalist Religion," in *Patriotism and Piety: Federalist Politics and Religious Struggle in the New American Nation* (Charlottesville: University of Virginia Press, 2015), 93-115.

3. This passage may be found in WTP 4, 21-22.

4. Gregory Claeys, *Thomas Paine: Social and Political Thought* (Boston: Unwin Hyman, 1989), 33; David Freeman Hawke, *Paine* (New York: Harper and Row, 1974), 326; Jack Fruchtman, Jr., *Thomas Paine and the Religion of Nature* (Baltimore: Johns Hopkins University Press, 1993), 53-54. Paine spoke favorably of the Theophilanthropic Society in a letter to Thomas Erskine, who prosecuted Thomas Williams for selling *Age* in England. See WTP 4, 231-35.

5. See Claeys, *Thomas Paine*, 191; John Keane, *Tom Paine: A Political Life* (Boston: Little, Brown, 1995), 396; and Herbert M. Morais, *Deism in Eighteenth Century America* (New York: Russell & Russell, 1934), 121.

6. See Morais, *Deism*, 130-38. Also see Kristen Fischer, *American Freethinker: Elihu Palmer and the Struggle for Religious Freedom in the New Nation* (Philadelphia: University of Pennsylvania Press, 2021), 96-101; 222-350. On the history of American

deism in general, see Morais, *Deism*, and Kerry S. Walters, *The American Deists: Voices of Reason and Dissent in the Early Republic* (Lawrence: University of Kansas Press, 1992), G. Adolf Koch, *Republican Religion: The American Revolution and the Cult of Reason* (New York: Holt, 1933), and James Turner, *Without God, without Creed: The Origins of Unbelief in America* (Baltimore, MD: Johns Hopkins University Press, 1985), 35–113.

7. On the publication runs, see John Keane, *Tom Paine*, 396. On the reception in Britain and the trial of Williams, see Claeys, *Thomas Paine*, 188.

8. Turner, *Without God, without Creed*, 73.

9. See Jonathan I. Israel, *The Enlightenment That Failed: Ideas, Revolution, and Democratic Defeat, 1748–1830* (Oxford: Oxford University Press, 2019), 689. Henry May actually went a little further than Israel does in acknowledging *Age of Reason*'s continuing influence in America in *The Enlightenment in America* (New York: Oxford University Press, 1976), 176. He writes that "Paine's version" of "Revolutionary Enlightenment . . . was defeated in its pure form," but "it left major effects on the culture, including the religious culture, of nineteenth-century America." He does not, however, trace what those effects were.

10. Craig Nelson, *Thomas Paine: Enlightenment, Revolution, and the Birth of Modern Nations* (New York: Viking, 2006), 14; Keane, *Tom Paine*, 3.

11. There are conflicting views on this point. Paine's friend and biographer Clio Rickman claims that Joseph was disowned by the Quakers because of his marriage outside the faith. See *The Life of Thomas Paine* (London, 1819), 33: available on GB. But Keane points out that Joseph was registered as a Quaker when he was buried, *Tom Paine*, 17. Paine himself wrote of his father's Quaker faith. See WTP 4, 62.

12. Keane, *Tom Paine*, 25–28.

13. Paine writes of this episode in *The Rights of Man*. See WTP 2, 462.

14. Rickman, *Life of Thomas Paine*, 12–15.

15. Rickman, *Life of Thomas Paine*, 15.

16. WTP 1, 84–85.

17. See David C. Hoffman, "Paine and Prejudice: Rhetorical Leadership through Perceptual Framing in 'Common Sense,'" *Rhetoric and Public Affairs* 9, no. 3 (2006): 375.

18. Keane, *Tom Paine*, 138–41.

19. WTP 1, 170.

20. Jett Conner has pointed out that, although nearly all biographies of Paine repeat the story that the first *American Crisis* was read to Washington's troops before they crossed the Delaware, the only identifiable source for this claim is James Cheetham's 1809 *The Life of Thomas Paine* (New York: Southwick and Pelsue, 1809), 32. Cheetham was not an eyewitness and cites no source for his claim. There is no account of the event from Paine, Washington, or any of the soldiers who participated in the crossing. See Jett Conner, "The American Crisis before Crossing the Delaware?" *Journal of the American Revolution*, February 25, 2015: https://allthingsliberty.com/2015/02/american-crisis-before-crossing-the-delaware/, accessed October 20, 2023.

21. Keane, *Tom Paine*, 248–54.

22. For an in-depth exploration of Paine's bridge-building project, see Edward G. Gray, *Tom Paine's Iron Bridge: Building a United States* (New York: W. W. Norton and Company, 2016).

23. For an English translation of *The Declaration of the Rights of Man and Citizen*, see John Hall Stewart, *A Documentary Survey of the French Revolution* (New York: Macmillan Company, 1951), 113–15. For original, see Philip B. J. Buchez and Prosper C. Roux, *Histoire parlementaire de la révolution française, Tome Onzième* [vol. 11] (Paris: Paulin, 1834–38), 404–406. Available from HT.

24. Edmund Burke, *Reflections on the Revolution in France and on the Proceedings of Certain Societies in London Relative to that Event: In a Letter Intended to Have Been Sent to a Gentleman in Paris, The Third Edition* (London: J. Dodsley, 1790): 88. Available from GB.

25. For a fuller discussion of Wollstonecraft's reply to Burke, see Lyndall Gordon, *Vindication: A Life of Mary Wollstonecraft* (New York: HarperCollins, 2005), 139–43 in the Kindle edition.

26. Keane, *Tom Paine*, 307; Gray, *Tom Paine's Iron Bridge*, 143. In a letter from November 1791, Paine wrote the following to his old friend John Hall back in America about the success of the work, claiming 16,000 copies sold in England, 40,000 in Ireland, and 1,000 in Scotland. See Thomas Paine to John Hall, November 25, 1791, available from TPNHA: https://thomaspaine.org/letters/other/to-john-hall-november-25-1791.html, accessed June 11, 2024.

27. "Copy of a Proclamation, dated at the Queen's House this 21st Day of *May 1792*" is recorded in the *House of Lords Journal* 39 (May 1792): 21–30. It is available from British History Online: https://www.british-history.ac.uk/lords-jrnl/vol39/pp431-458, accessed June 11, 2024.

28. An original copy of this broadside, published by James Aitken, is held by the British Museum: BM Satires 8152. An image of this broadside is figure 2 in Ian Haywood's "The Spectropolitics of Romantic Infidelism: Cruikshank, Paine, and *The Age of Reason*," *Romanticism and Victorianism on the Net* 54 (May 2009). Available online at: https://www.erudit.org/en/journals/ravon/2009-n54-ravon3401/038758ar/, accessed June 11, 2024.

29. This letter is held at the British Museum. Keane cites it as F. Paine to "Dear Daughter," Thetford, July 27, 1774, 47.6.12.105, British Museum. See Keane, *Tom Paine*, 595, note 198.

30. For an account of one such rally, see Robert I. Wilberforce and Samuel Wilberforce, *William Wilberforce, The Life of William Wilberforce, in Five Volumes*, vol. 2, 2nd ed. (London: John Murray, 1839), 5. Available from GB. For other cases of symbolic violence against Paine, see Keane, *Tom Paine*, 338–39.

31. WTP 3, 98.

32. WTP 3, 98.

33. See Sandrine Berges, "Sophie de Grouchy on the Cost of Domination in the *Letters on Sympathy* and Two Anonymous Articles in *Le Républicain*" 98, no. 1 (2015): 103. Also see Keane, *Tom Paine*, 316–19.

34. Simon Schama, *Citizens: A Chronical of the French Revolution* (New York: Vintage Books, 1989), 639–44; William Doyle, *The Oxford History of the French Revolution* (Oxford: Oxford University Press, 1989), 197–200.

35. WTP 3, 124.

36. Keane, *Tom Paine*, 367.

37. WTP 3, 125. The comments of Paine's hecklers are recorded in the Conway edition version of Paine's speech.

38. Doyle, *The Oxford History of the French Revolution*, 196; Ian Davidson, *The French Revolution* (New York: Pegasus Books, 2016), 143.

39. On the expulsion and arrest of the Girondins, see Doyle, *The Oxford History of the French Revolution*, 234–35; Davidson, *The French Revolution*, 154–63.

40. For a translation of the Law of Suspects, see Stewart, *Documentary Survey*, 477–79. For the French text, see Buchez and Roux, *Histoire parlementaire*, vol. 29, 109–10.

41. Doyle, *The Oxford History of the French Revolution*, 253.

42. Doyle, *The Oxford History of the French Revolution*, 253; Davidson, *The French Revolution*, 198.

43. Davidson, *The French Revolution*, 191; Donald Greer, *The Incidence of Terror During the French Revolution: A Statistical Interpretation* (Gloucester, MA: Peter Smith, 1966), 25–30.

44. WTP 1, 76–79.

45. In 1816, Adams wrote to a friend, "As I understand the Christian Religion, it was, and is, a Revelation. But how has it happened that Millions of Fables, Tales [and] Legends have been blended with both Jewish and Christian Revelations that have made them the most bloody Religions that ever existed?" See John Adams and Charles Francis Adams, *The Works of John Adams, Second President of the United States, with a Life of the Author, Notes and Illustrations*, vol. 10 (Boston: Little, Brown, and Company), 235. On John Adams's religious views, see Steven Waldman, "John Adams: The Angry Unitarian," in *Founding Faith: Providence, Politics, and the Birth of Religious Freedom in America* (New York: Random House, 2008), 33–39.

46. John Adams and Charles Francis Adams, *The Works of John Adams*, vol. 2, 508.

47. WTP 4, 65. There is a chance that the sermon Paine heard might have been Caleb Fleming's *An Essay to State the Scripture-Account of Man's Redemption by the Death of Christ*. It was published in 1745 in London when Paine was eight years old. (This sermon is available through the Eighteenth Century Collections Online database.)

48. For an overview of the concept of natural theology and its relationship to revealed religion, see Peter Byrne, *Natural Religion and the Nature of Religion: The Legacy of Deism* (London: Routledge, 1989), 1–21.

49. For a fuller account of Paine's encounter with Martin and Ferguson, see David C. Hoffman "'The Creation We Behold': Thomas Paine's *The Age of Reason* and the Tradition of Physico-Theology," *Proceedings of the American Philosophical Society* 157, no. 3 (September 2013): 289–92.

50. James Ferguson, *Astronomy Explained upon Sir Isaac Newton's Principles, and Made Easy to Those Who Have Not Studied Mathematics* (London, 1756). Available from GB: http://books.google.com/books?id=Ji1cAAAAQAAJ&dq, accessed June 11, 2024.

51. See John R. Millburn. *Benjamin Martin: Author, Instrument-Maker, and "Country Showman"* (Leyden: Noordhoff International Publishing, 1976), 441.

52. Benjamin Martin, *A Plain and Familiar Introduction to the Newtonian Philosophy, in Six Sections* (London, 1751). Available from the Eighteenth Century

Collections Online. A nearly identical 1754 edition is available from GB: http://books.google.com/books?id=arsAAAAAMAAJ&dq, accessed June 11, 2024.

53. Benjamin Martin, *A Panegyrick* [sic] *on the Newtonian Philosophy. Shewing the Nature and Dignity of the Science, and Its Absolute Necessity to the Perfection of Human Nature, etc.* (London, 1749), 14. Available from the Eighteenth Century Collections Online.

54. WTP 4, 63.

55. WTP 4, 66.

56. On physico-theology, see Hoffman "'The Creation We Behold,'" 284–88.

57. In *Tom Paine: A Political Life*, 45–49, John Keane notes a Sandwich tradition which has it that Paine belonged and preached to a local Methodist congregation. The main evidence to support this claim is a footnote in *The Journal of the Rev. John Wesley*, vol. 8, Nehemiah Curnock, ed. (London: Epworth Press, 1938), 31. The note refers to an anonymous 1906 article titled "The White Cliffs of Dover: Methodism in the Great Fortress," in the *Methodist Recorder and General Christian Chronicle* (August 19, 1906), p. 9, and no further. Both the article and the note claim that Benjamin Grace, Paine's employer, brought Paine with him to worship at the Methodist chapel and that Paine would sometimes lead the service if the circuit minister was unavailable. Keane introduces confirmatory evidence for a portion of this account: an inscription inside the front cover of a 1746 edition of Wesley's *Sermons for Several Occasions*, vol. 1, that is currently at the Methodist Archive and History Center at the Drew University Library, in New Jersey. The inscription says that Paine read sermons from the volume on occasions when a preacher was not available. See Keane, *Tom Paine*, 544n29. Vikki Vickers offers further commentary on Paine's Methodism in *"My Pen and My Soul have Ever Gone Together": Thomas Paine and the American Revolution* (New York: Routledge, 2006), 92.

58. This letter is discussed in Edward H. Davidson and William J. Scheick's *Paine, Scripture and Authority: "The Age of Reason" as Religious and Political Ideal* (Bethlehem, PA: Lehigh University Press, 1994), 28–29. For the text of the letter, see Désirée Hirst's *Hidden Riches: Traditional Symbolism from the Renaissance to Blake* (London: Eyre & Spottiswoode, 1964), 11–12.

59. On the possible influence of American deists on Paine, see Hoffman, "'The Creation We Behold,'" 292–95.

60. For a fuller account of this discovery and piecing together of the two surviving copies of *Le Siècle de la Raison*, see David Hoffman and Claudia Carlos, "Thomas Paine's *Le Siècle de la Raison, ou Le Sens Commun Des Droits De L'Homme*: Notes on a Curious Edition of *The Age of Reason*," in *New Directions in Thomas Paine Studies*, Scott Cleary and Ivy Linton Stabell, eds. (New York: Palgrave Macmillan, 2016), 133–37.

61. For a more detailed account of church-state relations in France over this period, see Hoffman and Carlos, "Thomas Paine's *Le Siècle de la Raison*," 139–40.

62. WTP 2, 327. Unless otherwise noted, emphasis in quotations is in the original.

63. WTP 4, 23.

64. Translation by Claudia Carlos from the French text: *Serons-nous moins chrétiens, mes neveux, je vous le demande; ma foi, la vôtre, sera-t-elle moins vive & moins ferme, parce que le chef visible de l'église cessera de grossir son trésor temporel de notre*

numéraire; parce que le clergé Français sera notre pensionnaire, au lieu d'être notre riche oppresseur . . . See Hoffman and Carlos, "Thomas Paine's *Le Siècle de la Raison*," 141.

65. This is from Paine's third "Letter to American Citizens," written in 1802. See WTP 3, 396–97.

66. Quoted by Moncure Daniel Conway in *The Life of Thomas Paine: With a History of His Literary, Political and Religious Career in America, France and England*, vol. 2, 3rd ed. (New York: G. P. Putnam, 1892): 115. Available through HT.

67. On this decree, see Michel Vovelle, *The Revolution against the Church: From Reason to the Supreme Being*, Alan Jose, trans. (Columbus: Ohio State University Press, 1991): 179–80. This work was originally published as *1793: la révolution contre l'Eglise: de la raison à l'être supreme* in 1988.

68. Vovelle, *The Revolution against the Church*, 63–66.

69. A 1793 engraving entitled *"Fête de la Raison: le décadi 20 brumaire de l'an 2.e de la République française . . ."* is one of numerous visual representations of feasts of reason at the Bibliothèque nationale de France. Available from Gallica: https://gallica.bnf.fr/ark:/12148/btv1b6950572f?rk=21459;2, accessed May 10, 2024. For more on dechristianization, see Doyle, *The Oxford History of the French Revolution*, 260–61; Schama, *Citizens*, 778.

70. Michel Vovelle works out the geographic distribution of the Cult of Reason by examining the origins of some eight hundred archived addresses related to it. See *The Revolution against the Church*, 98–105; 189. Mona Ozouf puts Revolutionary Feasts of Reason into the context of the larger role played by feasts and festivals in the French Revolution in her landmark study, *Festivals and the French Revolution*, Alan Sheridan, trans. (Cambridge, MA: Harvard University Press, 1988): 97–102. Originally published in 1976 as *La Fête révolutionnaire, 1789-1799*.

71. On Fouché's dechristianization campaigns, see Davidson, *The French Revolution*, 259; Schama, *Citizens*, 777.

72. Marie-Joseph de Chénier and François-Jean Dusausoir, *Office des décades, ou Discours, hymnes et prières en usage dans les temples de la raison* (Paris: Dupart, 1793-1794). Available through Gallica: https://gallica.bnf.fr/ark:/12148/bpt6k484344/f6.item, accessed February 15, 2021.

73. Charles A. Gliozzo argues for the importance of earlier French philosophers for the dechristianization movement in "The Philosophes and Religion: Intellectual Origins of the Dechristianization Movement in the French Revolution," *Church History* 40, no. 3 (1971): 273–83.

74. WTP 4, 240.

75. WTP 4, 205.

76. See, for instance, Alfred Owen Aldridge, *Man of Reason: The Life of Thomas Paine* (Philadelphia: J. P. Lippincott, 1959), 229; A. J. Ayer, *Thomas Paine* (New York: Atheneum, 1988), 141; and Davidson and Scheick, *Paine, Scripture and Authority*, 70.

77. WTP 4, 88.

78. WTP 4, 85.

79. John Toland, *Pantheisticon: or the Form of Celebrating the Socratic-Society* (London: Sam Paterson, 1751), 18. Available from GB: https://www.google.com/books/edition/Pantheisticon_or_the_Form_of_Celebrating/-PIGAAAAcAAJ?hl=en&gbpv=0, accessed May 10, 2024.

80. Thomas Woolston, *A Discourse on the Miracles of Our Saviour, The Second Edition* (London, 1727), 3. Available from GB, accessed May 10, 2024, http://books.google.com/books?id=Uc5bAAAAQAAJ.

81. WTP 4, 91.

82. WTP 4, 22.

83. WTP 4, 22–23.

84. *Platform of the National Liberal League for the Presidential Election of 1880: Adopted at Rochester, N.Y., Oct. 26, 1877* (Boston: National Liberal League, 1877), 1. Available from GB.

85. WTP 4, 23.

86. WTP 4, 91.

87. WTP 4, 34.

88. Numbers 31:18. WTP 4, 102.

89. WTP 4, 162.

90. WTP 4, 24.

91. WTP 4, 27.

92. WTP 4, 43.

93. For a more detailed account of Paine's arguments against the authority of scripture, see David Hoffman, "Cross-Examining Scripture: Testimonial Strategies in Thomas Paine's *The Age of Reason*," *Rhetorica. A Journal of the History of Rhetoric* 31, no. 3 (2013): 261–95.

94. Benjamin Offen, *A Legacy, to the Friends of Free Discussion: Being a Review of the Principal Historical Facts and Personages of the Books Known as the Old and New Testament; With Remarks on The Morality of Nature* (Boston: J. P. Mendum, 1851), viii; vii. Available on GB.

95. WTP 4, 83.

96. WTP 4, 55.

97. For a fuller account of Paine's positive deism and relationship to physico-theology, see Hoffman, "'The Creation We Behold,'" 281–303.

98. A. Owen Aldridge, "Natural Religion and Deism in America before Ethan Allen and Thomas Paine," *The William and Mary Quarterly* 54, no. 4 (1997): 835–48.

99. Ethan Allen, *Reason, the Only Oracle of Man: Or, A Compendious System of Natural Religion* (Boston: J. P. Mendum, 1854), 5, 3. Available from GB.

100. D. Driscol, "The Temple of Reason," Available online: https://www.loc.gov/resource/rbpe.1130010e/?st=text, accessed September 18, 2021.

101. Frances Wright, *Course of Popular Lectures, as Delivered by Frances Wright, in New York, Philadelphia, Baltimore, Boston, Cincinnati, St. Louis, Louisville, and Other Cities Towns and Districts of The United States, with Three Addresses on Various Public Occasions, and A Reply to The Charges Against the French Reformers Of 1789* (New York, 1829), 74. This volume is available on GB, but note the date has been incorrectly listed as 1820 due to the smudged printing of the 9 in 1829.

102. Robert Ingersoll, *Lectures of Col. R. G. Ingersoll, Latest* (Chicago: Rhodes and McClure Publishing Company, 1898), 460. Available on GB.

Chapter 2 • The First Wave of American Freethought

1. *The Examiners Examined; Being a Defence of "The Age of Reason"* (New York, 1794), 16. This work had previously been attributed to Elihu Palmer but is no longer generally believed to have been written by him. A digital transcript of this work is available through the Evans Early American Collection at the University of Michigan: https://quod.lib.umich.edu/e/evans/N20543.0001.001?rgn=main;view=fulltext, accessed September 11, 2021. The file can also be accessed through the "Online Books by Elihu Palmer" page at the University of Pennsylvania: http://onlinebooks.library.upenn.edu/webbin/book/lookupname?key=Palmer%2C%20Elihu%2C%201764%2D1806.

2. Charles Blount, *The Oracles of Reason* (London, 1693), 198. Available on GB.

3. Full text of "An Act for Exempting their Majestyes Protestant Subjects dissenting from the Church of England from the Penalties of certaine Lawes" is published in *Statutes of the Realm*, vol. 6: *1685-94*, ed. John Raithby (London: Dawsons of Pall Mall, 1819), 74-76. The volume is available digitally from GB, HT, and British History Online.

4. A 1696 London printing by Sam Buckley is available on GB. For a gloss on this work, see Henning Graf Reventlow, *The Authority of the Bible and the Rise of the Modern World*, John Bowden, trans. (Philadelphia: Fortress Press, 1984), 295-301.

5. Full texts of "An Act for the more effectual suppressing of Blasphemy and Profaneness" is published in *Statutes of the Realm*, vol 7: *1695-1704*, 409.

6. For this history of the birth of the Socinian Church in Poland, see Charles A. Howe, *For Faith and Freedom: A Short History of Unitarianism in Europe* (Boston: Skinner House Books, 1997), 61-78.

7. Howe, *For Faith and Freedom*, 135-42.

8. Nye's *Brief History* was printed in London and is available on GB. See Howe, *For Faith and Freedom*, 143, for context. Also see Nye's, *The Doctrine of the Holy Trinity, and the Manner of our Saviour's Divinity; As They Are Held in the Catholic Church, and the Church of England* (London, 1701). Available through the Eighteenth Century Collections Online database.

9. Howe, *For Faith and Freedom*, 131-34.

10. Howe, *For Faith and Freedom*, 152-54.

11. An 1871 edition of this work, published in London by the British and Foreign Unitarian Association, is available on GB.

12. Volume 4 of this work, printed in Birmingham by Pearson and Rollason in 1786, is available on GB.

13. The edition printed in London by J. Johnson in 1777 is available on GB. For context, see Robert E. Schofield, *The Enlightened Joseph Priestley: A Study of His Life and Work from 1773 to 1804* (University Park: Pennsylvania State University Press, 2004), specifically the chapter "Matter and Spirit," 59-76.

14. Jonathan I. Israel, *The Enlightenment That Failed: Ideas, Revolution, and Democratic Defeat, 1748-1830* (Oxford: Oxford University Press, 2019), 8.

15. Israel, *The Enlightenment That Failed*, 54.

16. Leslie Stephen and Sidney Lee, eds., *Dictionary of National Biography*, vol. 15 (London: Oxford University Press, 1917), 369, available on GB.

17. *Encyclopedia Britannica*, vol. 3, 11th ed. (Cambridge: Cambridge University Press, 1910), 918-19, available on GB.

18. Sidney Lee, ed., *Dictionary of National Biography*, vol. 56 (New York: MacMillan, 1898), 438–42, available on GB.

19. A Society of Gentlemen, *The Biographical Dictionary or Complete Historical Library* (London: F. Newbery, 1780), 764–66, available on GB.

20. *British Biography: Or, an Accurate and Impartial Account of the Lives and Writings of Eminent Persons in Great Britain and Ireland*, vol. 9 (London: R. Goadby, 1778), 48–54, available on GB.

21. Sidney Lee, ed., *Dictionary of National Biography*, vol. 2 (London: Smith, Elder and Company, 1885), 9–10, available on GB.

22. Joseph Priestley, *Memoirs of the Rev. Dr. Joseph Priestley to the Year 1795* (London: Several Unitarian Societies, 1809), 105–106, available on GB.

23. Barry Coward, *The Stuart Age: England 1603–1714*, 2nd ed. (London: Longman, 1994), 294.

24. Charles II, 1662, "An Act for the Uniformity of Publique Prayers and Administrac[i]on of Sacraments & other Rites & Ceremonies and for establishing the Form of making ordaining and consecrating Bishops Priests and Deacons in the Church of England.," in *Statutes of the Realm*, vol. 5: 1628–80, ed. John Raithby (1819), 364–70.

25. Charles II, 1661, "An Act for the Well Governing and Regulating of Corporations," in *Statutes of the Realm*, vol. 5: 1628–80, ed. John Raithby (1819), 321–23.

26. See "Test Acts," in *The Encyclopaedia Britannica: A Dictionary of Arts, Sciences, Literature and General Information*, vol. 26, 11th ed. (New York: Encyclopedia Britannica, 1911), 665–66.

27. Samuel Rawson Gardiner, "The Conventicle Act," in *Student's History of England: From the Earliest Times to 1885*, vol. 2 (London: Longmans, Green and Company, 1892), 588.

28. William and Mary, 1688, "An Act for Exempting their Majestyes Protestant Subjects dissenting from the Church of England from the Penalties of Certaine Lawes [Chapter XVIII. Rot. Parl. pt. 5. nu. 15.]" in *Statutes of the Realm*, vol. 6: 1685–94, 74–76.

29. For a narrative summary of religious freedom and establishment in the colonial era, see Steven K. Green's "Early Colonial Period" in *Inventing a Christian America: The Myth of the Religious Founding* (Oxford: Oxford University Press, 2015), 23–44. For another such summary, see Michael W. McConnell, "Establishment and Disestablishment at the Founding, Part I: Establishment of Religion," *William and Mary Law Review* 44, no. 5 (April 2003): 2105–2208. For a compendium of colonial and state law concerning religion, see Neil H. Cogan, *The Complete Bill of Rights: The Drafts, Debates, Sources, and Origins*, 2nd ed. (Oxford: Oxford University Press, 2015), 13–49.

30. For the original text, see Cogan, *The Complete Bill of Rights*, 30.

31. For an account of Baptist persecution in Virginia, see Steven Waldman, *Founding Faith: Providence, Politics, and the Birth of Religious Freedom in America* (New York: Random House Publishing Group, 2008), 100–106.

32. Michael Joseph Canavan, "Where Were the Quakers Hanged in Boston? A Paper Read Before the Bostonian Society, May 17, 1910" (Boston: Bostonian Society, 1911). Available on HT.

33. For a narrative account of Revolutionary and post-Revolutionary disestablishment, see Green, "The Early Federal Period," in *Inventing a Christian America*, 188–98.

For a compendium of colonial and state law concerning religion, see Cogan, *The Complete Bill of Rights*, 13–49.

34. For an account of the political maneuvering needed to defeat Henry's bill, see Waldman, *Founding Faith*, 113–25.

35. See David Barton, *America's Godly Heritage* (Aledo, TX: WallBuilder Press, 1993); David Barton, *The Jefferson Lies: Exposing the Myths You've Always Believed about Thomas Jefferson* (Nashville, TN: Thomas Nelson, 2012); Michael Medved, "Big Lie #3: The Founders Intended a Secular, Not a Christian, Nation," in *The 10 Big Lies about America: Combating Destructive Distortions about Our Nation* (New York: Three Rivers Books, 2008), 72–94; Rick Saccone, *Our Godly Heritage: From William Penn to Donald Trump* (Meadville, PA: Christian Faith Publishing, Incorporated, 2019).

36. In addition to the books by Waldman and Green that have already been cited, see Sam Haselby, *The Origins of American Religious Nationalism* (Oxford: Oxford University Press, 2015), and John Fea, *Was America Founded as a Christian Nation? A Historical Introduction*, rev. ed. (Louisville, KY: Westminster John Knox Press, 2016).

37. *Franklin*: In his autobiography, Franklin writes that when he was a young man, "Some books against Deism fell into my hands . . . they wrought an effect on me quite contrary to what was intended by them; for the arguments of the Deists which were quoted to be refuted appeared to me much stronger than the refutations; in short, I soon became a thorough Deist." Benjamin Franklin, *Autobiography*, 55–56, available on GB. On Franklin's religious views, see Waldman, *Founding Faith*, 18–26; also see Thomas S. Kidd, *Benjamin Franklin: The Religious Life of a Founding Father* (New Haven, CT: Yale University Press, 2017). *Jefferson*: In a letter to his nephew Peter Carr giving advice about his course of academic study, Jefferson gives the following advice about the study of religion: "Shake off all the fears and servile prejudices under which weak minds are servilely crouched. Fix reason firmly in her seat, and call to her tribunal every fact, every opinion. Question with boldness even the existence of a god; because, if there be one, he must more approve the homage of reason, than that of blindfolded fear." *The Papers of Thomas Jefferson*, vol. 12: *7 August 1787–31 March 1788*, ed. Julian P. Boyd (Princeton, NJ: Princeton University Press, 1955), 14–19. Available online from founders.archives.gov: https://founders.archives.gov/documents/Jefferson/01-12-02-0021, accessed February 4, 2022. In addition, Jefferson prepared for his personal use versions of the Bible with all references to supernatural events cut out of it, commonly referred to as "Jefferson's Bible." The surviving copy of the Jefferson Bible, formally, *The Life and Morals of Jesus of Nazareth Extracted Textually from the Gospels* is at the Smithsonian National Museum of American History. The Smithsonian publishes a facsimile version of it, and a translation into English is available on GB: *The Jefferson Bible: The Life and Morals of Jesus of Nazareth Extracted Textually from the Gospels* (St. Louis: Thompson Publishing Company, 1902). For a full discussion, see Peter Manseau, *The Jefferson Bible: A Biography* (Princeton, NJ: Princeton University Press, 2020). It is less commonly known, but perhaps just as important, that Jefferson worked on a translation from the French of another popular work about deism, *The Ruins: Or, Meditation on the Revolutions of Empires: and The Law of Nature*, with its author, Constantin François de Chassebœuf, the comte de Volney, frequently referred to just

as Volney, who visited him at Monticello. The work was called *Les Ruines, ou méditations sur les révolutions des empires* in the original French. See Jefferson's letter to Volney dated March 17, 1801, in *The Papers of Thomas Jefferson*, vol. 33: *17 February–30 April 1801*, ed. Barbara B. Oberg (Princeton, NJ: Princeton University Press, 2006), 341–42. Available online from founders.archives.gov: https://founders.archives.gov/documents/Jefferson/01-33-02-0289, accessed February 4, 2022. For more on Jefferson's religious views, see Waldman, *Founding Faith*, 72–85. *Ethan Allen*: Ethan Allen was the commander of a militia known as the Green Mountain Boys during the Revolutionary War. Later in life he published a deistic work titled *Reason, The Only Oracle of Man, Or, A Compendious System of Natural Religion* (Bennington, VT: Haswell & Russell, 1784), available on GB. Allen was not so central a figure in the founding movement as Franklin or Jefferson, but his work attests to the presence of deistic sentiments in the wider populace of the colonies.

38. The full text of the treaty is available from Yale Law School: https://avalon.law.yale.edu/18th_century/bar1796t.asp, accessed February 4, 2022. The passage in question occurs in Article 11 of the treaty. Historian Frank Lambert argues that the language in Article 11 is intended mainly to reassure the Muslim rulers of Tripoli that the United States, as a sovereign nation, had no religious objection to the treaty. But it should also be taken into consideration that the author of the treaty, Joel Barlow, was a close friend of Paine's who had overseen the publication of the first part of *The Age of Reason* in 1794, two years before he drafted the treaty. I think it is probable that Barlow inserted the language of Article 11 in order to get a definitive statement that the United States is not a Christian nation into the public record, but that the treaty was approved by the Senate and signed by Federalist president John Adams exactly because the language could be viewed as nothing more than an assurance to the Muslim rulers of Tripoli, as Lambert argues, and as Barlow probably foresaw. See Frank Lambert, *The Founding Fathers and the Place of Religion in America* (Princeton, NJ: Princeton University Press, 2010), 11.

39. These, and other writings bearing on religious freedom and the separation of church and state, are collected in Forrest Church, ed., *The Separation of Church and State: Writings on a Fundamental Freedom by America's Founders* (Boston, MA: Beacon Press, 2004): "Memorial and Remonstrance against Religious Assessments," 56–71; and Jefferson's "Virginia Statute for Religious Freedom," 72–77; in addition to his Letter to the Danbury Baptist Association, 124–30.

40. Thomas Jefferson, *The Writings of Thomas Jefferson: Being His Autobiography, Correspondence, Reports, Messages, Addresses, and Other Writings Official and Private*, edited by Henry Augustine Washington (Washington, DC: Taylor & Maury, 1853), 45. Available on GB.

41. Jefferson, *Writings*, 45.

42. Church, *Separation of Church and State*, 61, 68.

43. Church, *Separation of Church and State*, 74.

44. For an account of the religious practices of the Continental and Confederation Congresses, see Green, *Inventing a Christian America*, 173–78.

45. Church, *Separation of Church and State*, 138–39.

46. See Madison's "Proclamation of Day of Fasting and Prayer," July 9, 1812. Available online from the Miller Center at the University of Virginia: https://

millercenter.org/the-presidency/presidential-speeches/july-9-1812-proclamation-day-fasting-and-prayer, accessed February 5, 2022.

47. For a review of the religious belief of a broad range of "founders," see Green, *Inventing a Christian America*, 130–53.

48. *The Debates and Proceeding of the Congress of the United States*, vol. 1 (Washington, DC: Gales and Seaton, 1834), 757–58.

49. John Leland, *The Rights of Conscience Inalienable, etc.*, in *The Writings of the Late Elder John Leland: Including Some Events in His Life*, edited by L. F. Greene (New York: G. W. Wood, 1845), 181. Available on GB.

50. Leland, *The Rights of Conscience*, 182.

51. Leland, *The Rights of Conscience*, 183.

52. Leland, *The Rights of Conscience*, 183.

53. Mark D. McGarvie, "Disestablishing Religion and Protecting Religious Liberty in State Laws and Constitutions (1776–1833)," in T. Jeremy Gunn and John Witte Jr., eds., *No Establishment of Religion: America's Original Contribution to Religious Liberty* (Oxford: Oxford University Press, 2012), 93–94.

54. Alfred F. Young, *Liberty Tree: Ordinary People and the American Revolution* (New York: New York University Press, 2006), 473–74.

55. Philip Sheldon Foner, *The Democratic-Republican Societies, 1790–1800: A Documentary Sourcebook of Constitutions, Declarations, Addresses, Resolutions, and Toasts* (Westport, CT: Greenwood Press, 1976), 258, 22; Eugene P. Link, *Democratic-Republican Societies, 1790–1800* (New York: Columbia University Press, 1942), 6–11; François Furstenberg, *When the United States Spoke French: Five Refugees Who Shaped a Nation* (New York: Penguin, 2015), 42–43; Simon P. Newman, "Paine, Jefferson, and Revolutionary Radicalism in Early National America," in *Paine and Jefferson in the Age of Revolutions*, Simon P. Newman and Peter S. Onuf, eds. (Charlottesville: University of Virginia Press, 2013), 71–94.

56. Elias Boudinot, *The Age of Revelation; or, The Age of Reason Shewn to be an Age of Infidelity* (Philadelphia: Asbury Dickins, 1801): xx. Available on GB. Circulation details are from Alfred F. Young, *Liberty Tree*, 473. Young obtained information about American editions of *Age of Reason* from Charles Evans's *American Bibliography: A Chronological Dictionary of All Books, Pamphlets, And Periodical Publications Printed In the United States of America From the Genesis of Printing In 1639 Down to And Including the Year 1820*, vols. 9–14 (Chicago: Blakely Press, 1903).

57. The source of this claim is Moses Hoge's "Letter from Shepherd's-Town," dated August 12, 1799. This letter is preserved in John Blair Hoge's, *Life of Moses Hoge*, pp. 97–98. This is according to James H. Smylie, who quotes Moses Hoge via John Hoge in "Clerical Perspectives on Deism: Paine's *The Age of Reason* in Virginia," *Eighteenth-Century Studies* 6, no. 2 (1972): 219n67.

58. This is according to a letter from Paine to B. F. Bache, dated September 20, 1795, available from the Castle-Bache microfilm collection at the American Philosophical Society Library, cited in Patrick W. Hughes, "Irreligion Made Easy: The Reaction to Thomas Paine's *The Age of Reason*," in *New Directions in Thomas Paine Studies*, Cleary and Stabell, eds. (New York: Palgrave Macmillan, 2016): 114, 128n23.

59. Lyman Beecher, *Autobiography, Correspondence, Etc., of Lyman Beecher, D.D.*, vol. 1 (New York: Harper & Brothers, 1864), 43.

60. Gregory Claeys, *Thomas Paine: Social and Political Thought* (Boston: Unwin Hyman, 1989), 191–92.

61. John H. Spencer, *A History of Kentucky Baptists: From 1769 to 1885, Including More Than 800 Biographical Sketches*, vol. 1 (Cincinnati: J. R. Baumes, 1885), 499–501.

62. Benjamin Franklin, *Autobiography of Benjamin Franklin* (Chicago: R. R. Donnelley and Sons, 1903), 84–85.

63. Janice Stagnitto Ellis, Barbara Clark Smith, Harry Rubenstein, and Thomas Jefferson, *The Jefferson Bible, Smithsonian Edition: The Life and Morals of Jesus of Nazareth* (Washington, DC: Smithsonian, 2011); Thomas Jefferson, *Notes on the State of Virginia* (Boston: Lilly and Wait, 1832), 166.

64. Fea, *Was America Founded as a Christian Nation?*, 179–80.

65. *Massachusetts Spy*, November 19, 1772. For commentary, see A. Owen Aldridge, "Natural Religion and Deism in America before Ethan Allen and Thomas Paine," *William and Mary Quarterly* 54, no. 4 (1997): 835–48.

66. Ethan Allen, *Reason, the Only Oracle of Man: Or, A Compendious System of Natural Religion* (Boston: J. P. Mendum, 1854). The publication misfortune is described in the "Introduction," which has no page numbers.

67. Rodney Stark and Roger Finke, "American Religion in 1776: A Statistical Portrait," *Sociological Analysis* 49, no.1 (1988): 39–51. Also see Mark C. Carnes, John A. Garraty, and Patrick J. Williams, *Mapping America's Past: A Historical Atlas* (New York: H. Holt, 1996), 50–51.

68. Timothy Dwight, *Travels in New-England and New-York*, vol. 4 (London: William Baynes and Son, 1823), 353–69.

69. Spencer, *A History of Kentucky Baptists*, 220.

70. See Sidney G. Tarrow, *Power in Movement: Social Movements and Contentious Politics*, 3rd ed. (Cambridge: Cambridge University Press, 2011/1994), 160; 165–67.

71. Writing from a Resource Mobilization perspective, John McCarthy and Mayer Zald describe how "social movement organizations" may arise when skilled professionals choose to become "movement entrepreneurs" and build new organizations with a social purpose. See John D. McCarthy and Mayer N. Zald, "Resource Mobilization and Social Movements: A Partial Theory," *American Journal of Sociology* 82, no. 6 (1977): 1212–41. Also see Suzanne Staggenborg, "The Consequences of Professionalization and Formalization in the Pro-Choice Movement," *American Sociological Review* 53, no. 4 (1988): 585–605.

72. The most important narrative source for details about Palmer's life is John Fellows, "Memoir of Mr. Palmer," a very short biographical sketch based on Fellows's recollections of his friend printed at the beginning of a posthumously published collection of Palmer's writings. See John Fellows and Elihu Palmer, *Posthumous Pieces by Elihu Palmer* (London: R. Carlile, 1824), 3–10, available on GB. Fellows states that Palmer was born "near Norwich," Connecticut. Research on cemetery headstone markers and in Congregational Church records allowed Kirsten Fischer to pinpoint Palmer's birth in the village of Scotland. See Kirsten Fischer, *American Freethinker: Elihu Palmer and the Struggle for Religious Freedom in the New Nation* (Philadelphia: University of Pennsylvania Press, 2021), 253n2. Some biographies of Palmer mistakenly report that he is from the country, rather than the village, of Scotland.

73. Fischer, *American Freethinker*, 33; Fellows and Palmer, *Posthumous Pieces*, 4–5.

74. Fischer, *American Freethinker*, 36. See the listing for Elihu Palmer in the *Catalogue of the Officers and Members of the United Fraternity, Dartmouth College* (Concord: Asa McFarland, 1840), 9. Available on GB.

75. Fischer, *American Freethinker*, 35; Baxter Perry Smith, *The History of Dartmouth College* (Boston: Houghton, Osgood and Company, 1878), 84.

76. Fellows and Palmer, *Posthumous Pieces*, 5–6.

77. This is according to James Riker's 1852 *The Annals of Newtown, in Queens County, New-York: Containing Its History from Its First Settlement, Together with Many Interesting Facts Concerning the Adjacent Towns; Also, a Particular Account of Numerous Long Island Families Now Spread Over this and Various Other States of the Union* (New York, D. Fanshaw, 1852), 332–33. Available on GB. Also see Fischer, *American Freethinker*, 69.

78. *The Augusta Chronicle and Gazette of the State*, July 25, 1789, p. 3, col. 3. Available from Georgia Historic Newspapers: https://gahistoricnewspapers.galileo.usg.edu/lccn/sn82015220/, accessed September 10, 2021.

79. *The Augusta Chronicle and Gazette of the State*, July 18, 1789, p. 2, col. 3. Available from Georgia Historic Newspapers: https://gahistoricnewspapers.galileo.usg.edu/lccn/sn82015220/, accessed September 10, 2021.

80. Fischer, *American Freethinker*, 80–84.

81. Fischer, *American Freethinker*, 93–96.

82. *National Gazette*, March 15, 1792, p. 159, bottom of the fourth column. Available from the Library of Congress's digital collections: https://chroniclingamerica.loc.gov/lccn/sn83025887/1792-03-15/ed-1/seq-3/, accessed September 10, 2021.

83. Fellows and Palmer, *Posthumous Pieces*, 6; Fischer, *American Freethinker*, 91–92.

84. Fellows and Palmer, *Posthumous Pieces*, 7; Fischer, *American Freethinker*, 124–25.

85. Fellows and Palmer, *Posthumous Pieces*, 7; Fischer, *American Freethinker*, 127–31.

86. For details of Fellows's life, see George L. Stevens, "John Fellows: Minor American Deist" (master's thesis, University of Maryland, 1956), 6–17. Among the interesting primary sources cited by the modestly titled but very helpful thesis is a May 1821 letter to William Lee in which Fellows describes his military experience and career (pp. 6–8), said to be in the Military Records Division of the National Archives, Washington, DC.

87. A 1794 edition of *Age of Reason* printed in New York by "T. and J. Swords for J. Fellows" opens with a notice from district clerk Robert Troup, which says that John Fellows laid claim to proprietary rights to *Age of Reason* on June 17th, 1794. This edition is available through Gale Primary Sources: Eighteenth Century Collections Online. A letter from Paine to Fellows dated January 20, 1797, acknowledges an earlier letter from Fellows that informed Paine he had entered the copyright. The letter is available from the TPNHA: https://www.thomaspaine.org/works/letters/other/to-colonel-john-fellows-january-20-1797.html, accessed June 27, 2023.

88. All these titles except *Examiners Examined* can be found in the Gale Primary Sources: Eighteenth Century Collections Online database and list J. Fellows as the underwriter of the printing expenses. Advertisements at the end of the John

Fellows edition of *Age of Reason* list a number of other books that Fellows had an interest in. The title page of *Examiners Examined* also lists J. Fellows as the underwriter.

89. Fischer, *American Freethinker*, 132.
90. Fischer, *American Freethinker*, 137.
91. Fellows and Palmer, *Posthumous Pieces*, 8.
92. Fellows and Palmer, *Posthumous Pieces*, 11.
93. Fellows and Palmer, *Posthumous Pieces*, 11–12.
94. Fischer, *American Freethinker*, 211; Sidney I. Pomerantz, *New York: An American City, 1783–1803*, 2nd ed. (Port Washington, NY: Ira J. Friedman, 1938), 389; G. Adolf Koch, *Religion of the American Enlightenment* (New York: Thomas Crowell Company, 1933), 103. On Denniston's relation to the Clinton family, see Thomas N. Baker, "Speculations on the Genealogy of Deism in New York, 1700–1850," *New York History* 89, no. 1 (2008): 50–51.
95. Fischer, *American Freethinker*, 212–13; Eric R. Schlereth, *An Age of Infidels: The Politics of Religious Controversy in the Early United States* (Philadelphia: University of Pennsylvania Press, 2013), 132–34.
96. Fischer cites a letter from John Fellows to Horatio Gates dated July 11, 1798, as evidence for Palmer's residence at Powell's house. The letter is held by the New York Historical Society. See Fischer, *American Freethinker*, 273n4.
97. Fellows and Palmer, *Posthumous Pieces*, 8.
98. Elihu Palmer, *Principles of Nature; Or, A Development of the Moral Causes of Happiness and Misery Among the Human Species* (New York, 1801), 1–2.
99. Palmer, *Principles of Nature*, 6–7.
100. Palmer, *Principles of Nature*, 77.
101. Palmer, *Principles of Nature*, 266.
102. Palmer refers to d'Holbach as Mirabaud, the pseudonym by which he was known at the time. See Palmer, *Principles of Nature*, 251.
103. Palmer, *Principles of Nature*, 253.
104. Fellows and Palmer, *Posthumous Pieces*, 3–4.
105. Fischer, *American Freethinker*, 232.
106. The first issue of the first volume is dated December 10, 1803. Available on GB. Page 8 gives notice of Palmer's lecture at 6 p.m. on Sunday.
107. Schlereth, *Age of Infidels*, 112–16; Fischer, *American Freethinker*, 191–92.
108. *Temple of Reason*, November 8, 1800, p. 1.
109. The broadside is titled, "The Temple of Reason, A Quarto Paper. To be Published every Saturday Morning, in New-York: By D. Driscol" and is dated October 4, 1800. It is held by the Library of Congress and is available online: https://www.loc.gov/resource/rbpe.1130010e/?st=text, accessed September 15, 2021.
110. *Prospect: Or, View of the Moral World*, December 10, 1803, p. 2. Available on GB.
111. To Thomas Clio Rickman, March 8, 1803. The text of this letter is available on the website of the TPNHA: https://thomaspaine.org/letters/other/to-thomas-clio-rickman-march-8-1803.html: accessed June 8, 2021. On the fervor surrounding Paine's arrival in Baltimore, see David Freeman Hawke, *Paine* (New York: W. W. Norton, 1974), 353–58; John Keane, *Tom Paine: A Political Life* (New York: Grove Press, 1995), 455–63.

112. *New-York Evening Post*, January 10, 1803, p. 2, col. 3. Available through www.nyshistoricnewspapers.org, accessed June 8th, 2021.

113. WTP 3, 393.

114. James Cheetham, a hostile biographer of Paine, describes his reception in Washington as "cold and forbidding," *The Life of Thomas Paine* (London: Reprinted for A. Maxwell, 1817; original: 1809), 119, available on GB. However, a Federalist senator from New Hampshire named William Plumer was appalled by the fact that Paine appeared to have free run of the White House when he called on President Jefferson there in December of 1802. See *Life of William Plumer* by Plumer's son, William Plumer, Jr. (Boston: Phillips, Sampson, 1857), 241–43, available on GB, in which a letter to Judge Smith describing the incident is reprinted. This account is likely truer than Cheetham's. See Keane, *Tom Paine*, 469–70, 610, nn. 41 and 42.

115. This incident is discussed by Keane (*Tom Paine*, 480), who cites Moncure Daniel Conway's biography of Paine, *The Life of Thomas Paine; with a History of his Literary, Political and Religious Career in America, France, and England*, vol. 2 (London: Putnam, 1892), 327n. Conway in turn quotes an account of the incident from the *Trenton True American*. The Trenton Historical Society lists a paper with that title that started publishing in 1801 but does not have any issues prior to 1860.

116. Thomas Paine to George Clinton, May 4, 1807. The text of this letter is available on the website of the TPNHA: https://thomaspaine.org/letters/other/to-george-clinton-may-4-1807.html, accessed June 10, 2021. This incident is described in most all Paine biographies including Conway, *The Life of Thomas Paine*, vol. 2, 379–84; Keane, *Tom Paine*, 520–21; Hawke, *Paine*, 387–88.

117. This is according to Marguerite de Bonneville's reminiscences of Paine written up shortly after his death. They were later edited and partially rewritten by William Cobbett but left unpublished. Moncure Conway included this manuscript as appendix A to his *Life of Thomas Paine*. See Conway, *The Life of Thomas Paine*, vol. 2, 448.

118. Paine discusses the Theophilanthropic Society in his 1797 "Letter to Mr. Erskine," WTP 4, 331–35.

119. Fellows and Palmer, *Posthumous Pieces*, 8.

120. See "To Colonel John Fellows January 20, 1797." The text of this letter is available on the website of the TPNHA: https://thomaspaine.org/letters/other/to-colonel-john-fellows-january-20-1797.html, accessed September 15, 2021.

121. Gilbert Vale, *The Life of Thomas Paine*, 7th ed. (New York, 1853), 12.

122. *Prospect: Or, View of the Moral World*, February 18, 1804, pp. 83–85. Conway includes eighteen pieces in his collection of Paine's "Prospect Papers" (WTP 4, 304–55) but a number of them have recently been disattributed to Paine, according to the TPNHA: https://thomaspaine.org/essays/religion/prospect-papers.html, accessed September 16, 2021.

123. "To Col. John Fellows, July 9, 1804." The text of this letter is available on the website of the TPNHA: https://thomaspaine.org/letters/other/to-col-john-fellows-july-9-1804.html, accessed September 15, 2021.

124. The account given by Gilbert Vale (*Life of Thomas Paine*, 148–49) is supported by Paine's letter, "To John Fellows, April 22, 1805." The text of this letter is available on the website of the TPNHA: https://thomaspaine.org/letters/other/to-john-fellows-april-22-1805.html, accessed September 16, 2021.

125. Elihu Palmer, *Principles of Nature: Or, A Development of the Moral Causes of Happiness and Misery Among the Human Species*, 3rd ed. (New York: 1806), 225. Available on GB.
126. Palmer, *Principles of Nature*, 179.
127. Palmer, *Principles of Nature*, 230–31.
128. WTP 4, 240.
129. WTP 4, 83.
130. Palmer, *Principles of Nature*, 168.
131. Palmer, *Principles of Nature*, 173.
132. On Stewart's life, see Fischer, *American Freethinker*, 150–67; 229–32. An important source for Stewart's connection to the group is a letter from John Fellows to Julius Ames held by the New York Historical Society. It was also noted in the diary of Alexander Anderson, MD. See Frederic Martin Burr, *Life and Works of Alexander Anderson, M.D.: The First American Wood Engraver* (New York: Burr Brothers, 1893), 176. Available on GB.
133. John Stewart, *The Revelation of Nature, with the Prophesy of Reason* (New York, "fifth year of intellectual existence"), 6. Available on GB.
134. Stewart, *Revelation of Nature*, xxxiii–xxxiv.
135. John Hargrove, *The Temple of Truth: Or a Vindication of Various Passages and Doctrines of the Holy Scriptures* (Baltimore: Warner and Hanna, 1801), 4–5. Available on GB.
136. Hargrove, *Temple of Truth*, 6.
137. For more about this episode, see Fischer, *American Freethinker*, 198–205.
138. *Prospect: Or, View of the Moral World*, December 10, 1803, p. 8.
139. *Prospect: Or, View of the Moral World*, December 17, 1803, p. 6.
140. *Prospect: Or, View of the Moral World*, February 25, 1804, p. 92.
141. John Wood, *A Full Exposition of the Clintonian Faction, and the Society of the Columbian Illuminati. With an Account of the Writer of the Narrative, and the Characters of His Certificate Men, as Also Remarks on Warren's Pamphlet* (Newark, 1802), 22. Available on GB.
142. See, for instance, John Robison, *Proofs of a Conspiracy: Against All the Religions and Governments of Europe, Carried on in the Secret Meetings of Free Masons, Illuminati, and Reading Societies*, 4th ed. (New York: G. Forman, 1798). Also see Jean Joseph Mounier, *On the Influence Attributed to Philosophers, Free-masons, and to the Illuminati, on the Revolution of France* (London: W. and C. Spilsbury, 1801), who claims to take a more evenhanded view. Both titles available on GB.
143. For a more detailed account of the episode, see Fischer, *American Freethinker*, 210–12, and Schlereth, *Age of Infidels*, 132–36.
144. A letter from Elihu Palmer to Robert Hunter dated September 6, 1805, held at the New York Public Library, is quoted by John Keane, *Tom Paine*, 513.
145. Fellows says he died in the "winter of 1805" of pleurisy (*Posthumous Pieces*, 8), but Fischer dates the death March 31, 1806, after extensive archival research (*American Freethinker*, 238; 291, nn. 30 and 32).
146. Fischer, *American Freethinker*, 235.
147. Many of the details in the following section can be found in "Thomas Paine: A Sketch of His Life and Character" by Marguerite de Bonneville, edited by William

Cobbett, which is published at the end of Moncure Daniel Conway's *The Life of Thomas Paine*. For this detail, see Conway, *The Life of Thomas Paine*, vol. 2, 447.

148. This can be gleaned from Paine's will, where he says the north part of the farm is "now in the occupation of Andrew A. Dean." See WTP 4, 508.

149. For de Bonneville's account, see Conway, *The Life of Thomas Paine*, vol. 2, 447–48. Keane discusses with incident and quotes a letter from Thomas Paine to William Carver dated January 16, 1805, which is not included in the letters collected on the website of the TPNHA. See Keane, *Tom Paine*, 505–506. The letter is, however, given in full in Conway's *Life of Thomas Paine* (vol. 2, 341–42). Conway examined records that convinced him that Paine did not press charges, although this is in disagreement with de Bonneville's account, which says Derrick was acquitted. Also see the "Letter to the Editor regarding Thomas Paine," *New-York Spectator*, February 3, 1806, posted in the Virtual Archives of Westchester County. Note the piece is incorrectly titled "July 15" although the text says February 3. Available at: https://www.westchesterarchives.com/HT/muni/newRoch/spectator.htm, accessed September 19, 2021.

150. "To Andrew Dean, August 15, 1806." The text of this letter is available on the website of the TPNHA: https://thomaspaine.org/letters/other/letter-to-andrew-dean-august-15-1806.html, accessed September 20, 2021. The original is at the Library of Harvard University.

151. Vale, *Life of Thomas Paine*, 149.

152. This is from a letter from Jarvis to C. B. King, dated May 2, 1807, quoted in Harold E. Dickson, "Day vs. Jarvis: With Notes on the Early Years of John Wesley Jarvis," *The Pennsylvania Magazine of History and Biography* 63, no. 2 (1939): 187. Requoted in Keane, *Tom Paine*, 522. Vale also notes that Paine lived with Jarvis, who was still alive when he drafted his biography of Paine. See Vale, *Life of Thomas Paine*, 149.

153. Conway, *The Life of Thomas Paine*, vol. 2, 453–54.

154. Gilbert Vale wrote his life of Paine in the years just before its first publication and still had access to living eyewitnesses of Paine's final days. He took great care to soundly discredit persistent rumors of a deathbed conversion. To do so he obtained the testimony of Mr. Amasa Woodsworth, who owned the house Mrs. de Bonneville rented for Paine in Greenwich Village. See Vale, *Life of Thomas Paine*, 156–57.

155. Conway, *The Life of Thomas Paine*, vol. 2, 455.

156. See Paine's will in WTP 4, 507–509.

157. It is said in some places that Benjamin Bonneville's explorations of the American west in the 1830s are the basis for Washington Irving's novel *The Adventures of Captain Bonneville, Digest from his Journal* (1837). Of course, Irving is famous for writing amusing half-truths with only partial basis in history, so perhaps such claims should be further investigated.

158. Stevens, *John Fellows*, 62.

159. On *The Theophilanthropist*, see G. Adolf Koch, *Republican Religion: The American Revolution and the Cult of Reason* (New York: Holt, 1933), 168–84. On the toast, see Koch, *Republican Religion*, 298.

160. Everson v. Board of Education, 330 U.S. 1 (1947), p. 330 US 16. Available from Justia: https://supreme.justia.com/cases/federal/us/330/1/#F2/8, accessed May 16, 2024.

161. Philip Hamburger, *Separation of Church and State* (Cambridge, MA: Harvard University Press, 2002), 481.
162. Hamburger, *Separation of Church and State*, 65–73.
163. Hamburger, *Separation of Church and State*, 101–107.
164. Hamburger, *Separation of Church and State*, 111–26.
165. Joseph Story, *Commentaries on the Constitution of the United States: With a Preliminary Review of the Constitutional History of the Colonies and States, Before the Adoption of the Constitution*, vol. 3 (Boston: Hilliard, Gray, and Company, 1833), 728.
166. Hamburger, *Separation of Church and State*, 105.
167. *Debates and Proceeding of the Congress of the United States*, vol. 1, 757–58.
168. Church, *Separation of Church and State*, 138–39.
169. Hamburger, *Separation of Church and State*, 177.
170. Hamburger, *Separation of Church and State*, 61, 166n41.
171. Hamburger, *Separation of Church and State*, 164–65.
172. For Leland's account of this episode, see John Leland, *The Writings of the Late Elder John Leland: Including Some Events in His Life*, edited by L. F. Greene (New York: G. W. Wood, 1845), 32. Available on GB. Also see James H. Hutson's "Thomas Jefferson's Letter to the Danbury Baptists: A Controversy Rejoined," which contains a useful report on an FBI analysis of the many edits Jefferson made to his letter, *William and Mary Quarterly* 56, no. 4 (1999): 775–90.
173. Hamburger, *Separation of Church and State*, 156–57.

Chapter 3 • The Second Wave of American Freethought

1. Moncure Daniel Conway, *Thomas Paine: A Celebration, Delivered in the First Congregational Church, Cincinnati, Ohio, January 29, 1860* (Cincinnati, 1860), 5. Available on GB.
2. "The Development of American Religion: An Interpretive View," in *Encyclopedia of American Religions*, 7th ed., edited by J. Gordon Melton (Farmington Hills, MI: Gale, 2003), 10.
3. William Peter Strickland, *History of the American Bible Society from Its Organization to the Present Time* (New York: Harper & Brothers, 1849), 20.
4. See *A Brief History of the American Tract Society, Instituted at Boston, 1814* (Boston: T. R. Marvin, 1857). Available on GB.
5. "Cheethem [sic] and his Tory Paper," in the *Public Advertiser*, September 26, 1807. The text is available on the website of the TPNHA: https://thomaspaine.org/essays/american-politics-and-government/cheethem-and-his-tory-paper.html, accessed October 1, 2021.
6. James Cheetham, *Life of Thomas Paine* (London: Reprinted for A. Maxwell, 1817; original: 1809), xxvii. Available on GB.
7. Gilbert Vale, *The Life of Thomas Paine*, 7th ed. (New York, 1853), 153. Available on GB. Vale includes a rich account of Cheetham's trial and conviction for libel, complete with speech extracts, in the preface of *Life of Thomas Paine*, 5–13.
8. Gustavus Myers, *The History of Tammany Hall* (New York: Gustavus Myers, 1901), 32–34. Available on GB.
9. For the full text of the act, see H. T. Dickenson, ed., *Constitutions of the World from the Late 18th Century to the Middle of the 19th Century*, vol. 1: *Constitutional*

Documents of the United Kingdom 1782–1835 (München, Germany: K. G. Saur Verlag, 2005), 31–39.

10. For a full account of the trial, see Daniel Isaac Eaton and John Prince Smith, *Trial of Mr. Daniel Isaac Eaton, for Publishing the Third and Last Part of Paine's Age of Reason: Before Lord Ellenborough, in the Court of King's Bench, Guildhall, March 6, 1812: Containing the Whole of His Defense, and Mr. Prince Smith's Speech in Mitigation of Punishment* (London: Daniel Isaac Eaton, 1812). Available on GB.

11. *Black Dwarf*, January 21, 1818, vol. 2, no. 3, p. 39 in T. J. Wooler, ed., *The Black Dwarf*, vol. 2 (London: T. J. Wooler, 1818). Available on GB.

12. Gregory Claeys, *Thomas Paine: Social and Political Thought* (Abingdon, UK: Unwin Hyman, 1989), 211.

13. For instance, Edward Royle describes how leading British reformers were brought together at a Paine birthday celebration at the Hall of Science in London on January 30, 1848. See Royle, *Victorian Infidels: The Origins of the British Secularist Movement, 1791–1866* (Manchester: University of Manchester Press, 1974), 95. Also see Iain McCalman, *Radical Underworld: Prophets, Revolutionaries and Pornographers in London, 1795–1840* (Cambridge: Cambridge University Press, 1988), 197; James S. Epstein, *Radical Expression: Political Language, Ritual, and Symbol in England, 1790–1850* (Oxford: Oxford University Press, 1994), 158.

14. Carol A. Kolmerten, *The American Life of Ernestine L. Rose* (Syracuse, NY: Syracuse University Press, 1999), 40. On Offen's life, see Tom Flynn, ed., *The New Encyclopedia of Unbelief* (Amherst, NY: Prometheus, 2007), 581.

15. DeRobigne Mortimer Bennett, *The World's Sages, Thinkers and Reformers: Being Biographical Sketches of Leading Philosophers, Teachers, Skeptics, Innovators, Founders of New Schools of Thought, Eminent Scientists, Etc.* (New York: Truth Seeker Company, 1876), 695. Available on GB.

16. Benjamin Offen, *A Legacy, to the Friends of Free Discussion: Being a Review of the Principal Historical Facts and Personages of the Books Known as the Old and New Testament; With Remarks on The Morality of Nature* (Boston: J. P. Mendum, 1851), vii. Available on GB.

17. *The Correspondent*, January 20, 1927 (vol. 1, no. 1), p. 1. Links to five volumes of *The Correspondent* can be found on HT: https://catalog.hathitrust.org/Record/010304762, accessed June 12, 2024.

18. *The Correspondent*, January 20, 1927 (vol. 1, no. 1), pp. 2–6.

19. *The Correspondent*, February 2, 1928 (vol. 3, no. 2), p. 23.

20. Offen, *A Legacy*, vii.

21. *The Free Enquirer*, February 9, 1833 (vol. 5, no. 16), p. 123, cols. 1–2. Links to all volumes of *The Free Enquirer* and its precursors, including the *New Harmony Gazette*, can be found on HT: https://catalog.hathitrust.org/Record/100113187, accessed June 12, 2024.

22. *The Correspondent*, February 2, 1928 (vol. 3, no. 2), pp. 23–25; *The Correspondent*, February 7, 1929 (vol. 5, no. 3), pp. 42–45; *The Free Enquirer*, February 20, 1830 (vol. 2, no. 17) p. 131, col. 2 to 134, col. 2—this issue gives the transcription of a speech delivered at a Paine birthday at New Hartford, New York; *The Free Enquirer*, February 12, 1831 (vol. 2, no. 16), p. 128, cols. 1–2. Other papers' published accounts of Paine

birthday celebrations in this period are the *Workingman's Advocate* (New York), *The Beacon* (New York), and the *Cleveland Liberalist* (Cleveland). A summary of a number of such accounts can be found on the website of Popular Freethought: https://popularfreethought.wordpress.com/browse-by-subject/thomas-paines-birthday-celebrations/, accessed October 11, 2021.

23. Robert Owen, *The Life of Robert Owen Written by Himself: With Selections from His Writings and Correspondence* (London: Effingham Wilson, 1857), 1–56; 60. Available on GB. There is a dearth of recent biographies of Owen. Ian Donnachie's *Robert Owen: Social Visionary* (Edinburgh: Truckwell Press, 2000) claims to be the first new biography in fifty years. Also see George Douglas Howard Cole's 1925 *Life of Robert Owen*, which was given a new introduction by Margaret Cole in 1965 (London: Frank Cass & Company, 1965).

24. Robert Owen, *A New View of Society*, 3rd ed. (London: Longman, Hurst, Rees, Orme, and Brown, 1817), 91. Available on GB.

25. See Owen's "Address Delivered at New Lanark on Opening the Institution for the Formation of Character on the 1st of January 1816," included in Owen, *The Life of Robert Owen*, 337–60.

26. Owen, *The Life of Robert Owen*, 63.

27. Owen, *The Life of Robert Owen*, 87–97.

28. See Robert Owen, *Observations on the Effect of the Manufacturing System: With Hints for the Improvement of Those Parts of it Which Are Most Injurious to Health and Morals,* 2nd ed. (London: Longman, Hurst, Rees, Orme, and Brown, 1817). Available on HT.

29. Robert Owen, "Report to the County of Lanark," in *A New View of Society and Other Writings* (London: J. M. Dent, 1927), 245–98, see especially 267–92. Available on GB.

30. Robert Owen, "Address Delivered at the City of London Tavern," in *A New View of Society and Other Writings*, 216.

31. Robert Owen, "A New View of Society: Essays on the Formation of Character, Fourth Essay" and "Report to the County of Lanark," in *A New View of Society and Other Writings*, 67; 280.

32. For Robert Dale Owen's account of the founding of New Harmony, see Robert Dale Owen, *Twenty-seven Years of Autobiography: Threading My Way* (New York: G. W. Carleton & Company, 1874), 239–44. Available on GB. For a far more scholarly account of the rise and fall of New Harmony than I am able to give here, see Arthur Eugene Bestor, *Backwoods Utopias: The Sectarian and Owenite Phases of Communitarian Socialism in America, 1663–1829* (Philadelphia: University of Pennsylvania Press, 1950), 133–201. Available on the IA. For a briefer account, see Mark Holloway, *Heavens on Earth: Utopian Communities in America 1680–1880*, 2nd ed. (New York: Dover, 1966), 101–16; 88–95; on the Rappites, see Holloway, *Heavens on Earth*, 88–95.

33. Bestor, *Backwoods Utopias*, 82–87.

34. *New Harmony Gazette*, October 1, 1825, p. 2, col. 3, to p. 3, col. 3.

35. *New Harmony Gazette*, February 15, 1826, 1825, p. 162, col. 1 to p. 163, col. 1.

36. On New Harmony's open chapel policy, see *New Harmony Gazette*, December 21, 1825, p. 102, col. 2.

37. For a more detailed account of Owen's religion, see Robert A. Davis, "Robert Owen and Religion," in *Robert Owen and His Legacy*, Noel Thompson and Chris Williams, eds. (Cardiff: University of Wales Press, 2011), 91–112.

38. Bestor, *Backwoods Utopias*, 176–201. For Robert Dale Owen's account of life in New Harmony and the causes of the experiment's failure, see Robert Dale Owen, *Twenty-seven Years of Autobiography*, 285–90. Other important primary sources for information on life in New Harmony and the unraveling of the community include a series of letters by William Pelham, editor of the *New Harmony Gazette*, to his son. These are reproduced in Harlow Lindley, ed., *Indiana as Seen by Early Travelers: A Collection of Reprints from Books of Travel, Letters and Diaries Prior to 1830* (Indianapolis: Indiana Historical Commission, 1916), 360–417. Available on GB. Also, Paul Brown, *Twelve Months in New Harmony: Presenting a Faithful Account of the Principal Occurrences Which Have Taken Place There Within That Period* (Cincinnati, 1927).

39. For more detail, see the section on Frances Wright below.

40. On Owen's relationship to the co-op movement, see Cole, *Life of Robert Owen*, 254–75.

41. The first issue of the *New Harmony Gazette*, dated October 1, 1825, lists distributors in these and other cities. See p. 1, col. 2.

42. *The Free Enquirer*, March 4, 1829 (2nd ser., vol. 1, no. 19), p. 152, col. 3.

43. Albert Post, *Popular Freethought in America, 1825–1850* (New York: Octagon Books, 1974), 40.

44. *The Free Enquirer*, July 12, 1826, p. 330, col. 2.

45. *New Harmony Gazette*, July 12, 1826, p. 330, col. 2.

46. *New Harmony Gazette*, July 12, 1826, p. 330, col. 3.

47. For a compilation of items from *The Free Enquirer* between 1828 and 1835, see "Free Enquirer," in *Popular Freethought: A Guide to the Periodic Writings of American Infidels, 1825–1865*. Available online: https://popularfreethought.wordpress.com/browse-by-title/free-enquirer-1828-1835/, accessed March 21, 2022.

48. See Frances Wright's autobiography, written in the third person, *Biography, Notes, and Political Letters of Frances Wright D'Arusmont* (Dundee, Scotland: J. Myles, 1844), 3–6. Available on GB. Wright is an astonishingly understudied figure. The most recent full biography of her is Celia Morris's *Fanny Wright: Rebel in America* (Chicago: University of Illinois Press, 1984). Two books from the 1990s offer more partial views. Susan Kissel's *In Common Cause: The "Conservative" Frances Trollope and the "Radical" Frances Wright* (Bowling Green, OH: Bowling Green State University Press, 1993) compares Wright with her friend and fellow writer Frances Trollope. Elizabeth Ann Bartlett's *Liberty, Equality, Sorority: The Origins and Interpretation of American Feminist Thought* (Brooklyn: Carlson Publishing, 1994) has one chapter devoted to Wright. There is a serious need for critical editions of Wright's works and assessments of her place not only in the history of feminism but more broadly in intellectual history.

49. From a letter by James Wright, Jr. to John Pinkerton, August 14, 1795, among the Pinkerton Papers at the National Library of Scotland. Quoted by Morris in *Fanny Wright*, 5.

50. Wright, *Biography*, 4.

51. Wright, *Biography*, 6.

52. Wright, *Biography*, 6.

53. Morris, *Fanny Wright*, 7.
54. Wright, *Biography*, 5.
55. Wright, *Biography*, 10.
56. See Jonathan Israel, *The Enlightenment That Failed: Ideas, Revolution, and Democratic Defeat, 1748–1830* (Oxford: Oxford University Press, 2019), 75–96.
57. Wright, *Biography*, 10–11.
58. Morris, *Fanny Wright*, 27–30; 39.
59. Morris, *Fanny Wright*, 49–52.
60. Wright, *Biography*, 13.
61. Morris, *Fanny Wright*, 75.
62. Wright, *Biography*, 13; Morris, *Fanny Wright*, 78–85.
63. Wright discusses her impressions of Economy and New Harmony in *Biography*, 23–27.
64. Wright, *Biography*, 27–28.
65. See Wright's letter to Jefferson dated July 26, 1825, and Jefferson's reply dated August 7, 1825. Both are available online from the National Archives, Founders Online: https://founders.archives.gov/documents/Jefferson/98-01-02-5411 and https://founders.archives.gov/documents/Jefferson/98-01-02-5449, accessed October 25, 2021.
66. Morris, *Fanny Wright*, 109.
67. Morris, *Fanny Wright*, 136.
68. Morris, *Fanny Wright*, 141–43.
69. An 1850 edition of this book is available from GB, but the title has been altered to appeal to Wright's detractors: *Fanny Wright Unmasked by Her Own Pen: Explanatory Notes, Respecting the Nature and Objects of the Institution of Nashoba, and of the Principles Upon Which It Is Founded* (New York, 1850). Wright's text does not seem to have been altered, though.
70. Sometime in 1828 English travel writer Frances Milton Trollope visited Wright at Nashoba and published an account of it, including a sketch of the compound, in her book *Domestic Manners of the Americans*. See vol. 1, 3rd ed. (London: Whittaker, Treacher, & Company, 1832), 38–42. Trollope had met Wright when Wright returned to Europe in 1927 and had found her plans for Nashoba inspiring, but she was surprised by how rustic the reality was.
71. Morris, *Fanny Wright*, 211.
72. Morris, *Fanny Wright*, 171.
73. The full speech is reprinted in the July 9, 1828, issue of the *New Harmony Gazette*, ser. 1, vol. 3, no. 37, pp. 289–91. The quotation is from p. 291, near the top of col. 1.
74. Trollope, *Domestic Manners*, vol. 1, 98.
75. Morris, *Fanny Wright*, 172; Trollope, *Domestic Manners*, vol. 1, 94–96.
76. The full title of Wright's collected lectures from this period lists all these places: *Course of Popular Lectures, as Delivered by Frances Wright, in New York, Philadelphia, Baltimore, Boston, Cincinnati, St. Louis, Louisville, and Other Cities Towns and Districts of The United States, with Three Addresses on Various Public Occasions, and A Reply to The Charges Against the French Reformers Of 1789* (New York, 1829). This volume is available on GB, but note the date has been incorrectly listed as 1820 due to the smudged print of the 9 in 1829.

77. On Wright's appearance at a Paine birthday in 1838 in Cincinnati, see Kenneth W. Burchell, "Birthday Party Politics: The Thomas Paine Birthday Celebrations and the Origins of American Democratic Reform," in Ronald F. King and Elsie Begler, eds., *Thomas Paine: Common Sense for the Modern Era* (San Diego: San Diego State University Press, 2007), 182–83. Burchell cites a passage from the *Boston Investigator* reprinted in *The Beacon*, on February 24, 1838.

78. Kolmerten, *American Life*, 34. Kolmerten cites an account in *The Beacon* on January 26, 1839, that tells of Wright's appearance at the Tammany gathering of the Society of Moral Philanthropists.

79. Wright, *Course of Lectures*, 80.

80. Wright, *Course of Lectures*, 74.

81. See Mary B. Whitcom, "Abner Kneeland: His Relation to Early Iowa History," *Annals of Iowa, A Historical Quarterly*, vol. 6, 3rd ser. (Des Moines: Iowa State Historical Department, Division of Historical Museum and Archives, 1903), 344. Available on GB.

82. For Robert Dale Owen's recollections of Frances Wright, see Robert Dale Owen, *Twenty-seven Years of Autobiography*, 298–304; 307–308. Owen pays particular attention to the Nashoba experiment and their transatlantic voyage. He recalls that Wright introduced him to Lafayette.

83. *The New Harmony and Nashoba Gazette, or, The Free Enquirer*, 2nd ser., vol. 1, issue 1, p. 1.

84. *The Free Enquirer*, 2nd ser., vol. 1, issue 19, p. 145.

85. The acquisition is announced March 25, 1829, issue of *The Free Enquirer*, 2nd ser., vol. 1, issue 22, p. 174, second col.

86. *The Free Enquirer*, 2nd ser., vol. 1, issue 24, p. 192, third col.

87. *The Free Enquirer*, 2nd ser., vol. 1, issue 24, p. 187, third col. to 187, first col.

88. Wright, *Course of Lectures*, 207.

89. Charles Williams Windship, *Discourse on Religion and Doctrines: Delivered Before the First Society of Free Enquirers, in Boston, November 15, 1829* (Boston: Amos B. Parker, 1829). Available on GB.

90. Frances Wright, "Speech Concerning the Sunday Mails," delivered at the New York Hall of Science, October 18, 1829. Reprinted in *The Free Enquirer*, vol. 2, issue 1, p. 2, second col. to p. 4, second col.

91. Thomas Skidmore, *The Rights of Man to Property! Being a Proposition to Make it Equal Among the Adults of the Present Generation, and to Provide for Its Equal Transmission to Every Individual of Each Succeeding Generation on Arriving at the Age of Maturity* (New York: A. Ming, 1829), 67. Available on GB.

92. This paragraph summarizes the findings of Frank T. Carlton, "The Workingmen's Party of New York City: 1829–1831," *Political Science Quarterly* 22, no. 3 (September 1907): 401–15. Carlton cites the *Working Man's Advocate*, a paper published by George E. Evens that was closely associated with the party, for many details about party dynamics and platform, particularly the October 31, 1829, issue, which published the party's platform just ahead of the election.

93. *The Free Enquirer*, vol. 5, issue 16, p. 124, second col. to third col.

94. *The Free Enquirer*, vol. 5, issue 16, p. 124, third col. Richard Carlile was jailed in England for publishing *Age of Reason*, and Robert Taylor was a freethinking former

English clergyman known as "the devil's chaplain" to his opponents. Peter Cooper was the Unitarian founder of the progressive Cooper Union school.

95. See Charles Knowlton, *The Fruits of Philosophy, or, the Private Companion of Young Married People*, reprinted from the American edition, 3rd ed. (London: J. Watson, 1841). Available on GB.

96. On the influence of deism on Ballou, see Oscar Fitzalan Safford, *Hosea Ballou: A Marvellous Life-story* (Boston: Universalist Publishing House, 1890), 74, available on GB; Daniel Dulany Addison, *The Clergy in American Life and Letters* (London: Macmillan, 1900), 141–44, available on GB; Ernest Cassara, "Hosea Ballou," in *The Dictionary of Unitarian and Universalist Biography* (Dedham, MA: Unitarian Universalist Historical Society, 2006), available online: https://web.archive.org/web/20060608085635/http://www.uua.org/uuhs/duub/articles/hoseaballou.html, accessed March 26, 2022.

97. Ballou published the series of letters that, for a time, brought Kneeland back to Universalism as *A Series of Letters in Defence of Divine Revelation in Reply to Rev. Abner Kneeland's Inquiry into the Authenticity of the Same* (Boston: H. Bowen, 1820). Available on GB.

98. For the detail of Kneeland's life, see "Abner Kneeland" in *The Dictionary of Unitarian and Universalist Biography* (Dedham, MA: Unitarian Universalist Historical Society, 2006), available online: https://web.archive.org/web/20060609220021/http://www.uua.org/uuhs/duub/articles/abnerkneeland.html, accessed March 26, 2022. Also see Samuel Porter Putnam, *400 Years of Freethought* (New York: Truth Seeker Company, 1894), 755–56, available on GB; Ruth A. Gallaher, "Abner Kneeland—Pantheist," *The Palimpsest* 20, no. 7 (1939): 209–225, available online: https://pubs.lib.uiowa.edu/palimpsest/article/id/24557/, accessed March 28, 2022.

99. Roderick S. French, "Liberation from Man and God in Boston: Abner Kneeland's Free-Thought Campaign, 1830–1839," *American Quarterly* 32, no. 2 (1980): 203.

100. French, "Liberation from Man and God in Boston," 204–210.

101. The text is from Kneeland's account of his own trial, *An Introduction to the Defence of Abner Kneeland, Charged with Blasphemy: Before the Municipal Court, in Boston, Mass. at the January Term in 1834* (Boston, 1834), 37–38, available on GB.

102. See Theron Metcalf and Horace Mann, eds., *The Revised Statutes of the Commonwealth of Massachusetts, Passed November 4, 1835* (Boston: Dutton & Wentworth, 1836), 741. Available on GB. The full text reads: "If any person shall willfully blaspheme the holy name of God by denying, cursing, or contumeliously reproaching God, his creation, government, or final judging of the world, or by cursing or contumeliously reproaching Jesus Christ, or the Holy Ghost, or by cursing or contumeliously reproaching the holy word of God contained in the holy scriptures, or exposing them to contempt and ridicule, he shall be punished by imprisonment in the state prison not more than two years, or in the county jail not more than one year, or by fine not exceeding three hundred dollars, and may also be bound to good behavior."

103. *The Constitution, Or Frame of Government, for the Commonwealth of Massachusetts: Agreed on by the Delegates of the People, in Convention, Begun and Held at Cambridge on the First Day of September 1779, and Continued, by Adjournments, to the Second Day of March 1780, Afterwards Ratified by the People, and Took Place on the 25th Day of October, 1780* (Worcester, MA: Isaiah Thomas, 1787), 6–7. Available on GB.

104. For a full account of these trials, including the speeches of the defense and prosecution, the judges' charges, and the juries' verdicts, see John Davison Lawson, ed., "The Trial of Abner Kneeland for Blasphemy, Boston, Massachusetts, 1835," in *American State Trials: A Collection of the Important and Interesting Criminal Trials Which Have Taken Place In the United States From the Beginning of Our Government to the Present Day*, vol. 13 (St. Louis: Thomas Law Books, 1921), 450–575. Available on HT.

105. Lawson, "The Trial of Abner Kneeland," 532–33.

106. Gallaher, "Abner Kneeland—Pantheist," 216.

107. Octavius Pickering, ed., *Massachusetts Reports: Cases Argued and Determined in the Supreme Judicial Court of Massachusetts*, vol. 20 (Boston: H. O. Houghton and Company, 1864), 221. Available on GB: https://www.google.com/books/edition/Massachusetts_Reports/LQEQAAAAYAAJ?hl=en&gbpv=0, accessed March 28, 2022. Note that Google mislabels it volume 37.

108. Quoted in Gallaher, "Abner Kneeland—Pantheist," 217.

109. French, "Liberation from Man and God in Boston," 220–21. For detail about Kneeland's final years in Iowa, see Margaret Atherton Bonney, "The Salubria Story," *The Palimpsest* 56, no. 2 (1975), 34–45, available online: https://pubs.lib.uiowa.edu/palimpsest/issue/9856/info/, accessed March 28, 2022. A rather nice tribute to Kneeland's life and journey to Iowa can be found on the Our Iowa Heritage website: https://bollerfamily.org/our-iowa-heritage-welcome-to-salubria/, accessed March 28, 2022.

110. See William Cobbett, *The Soldier's Friend: Or, Considerations on the Late Pretended Augmentation of the Subsistence of the Private Soldiers* (London: J. Ridgway, 1792). Available on GB. For details of Cobbett's life, see the autobiography completed by his sons after his death, William Cobbett (and James Cobbett and John Cobbett), *The Life of William Cobbett, Dedicated to His Sons* (Philadelphia: E. L. Carey and A. Hart, 1835). Available on GB.

111. Cobbett, *Life*, 56–57.

112. William Cobbett, *Observations on the Emigration of Dr. J. Priestley, and on the Several Addresses Delivered to Him on his Arrival at New York* (Philadelphia/London: 1794). Available on GB but wrongly attributed to Joseph Priestley.

113. Cobbett, *Life*, 69–70.

114. See William Cobbett, *Observations on the Character and Motives of Paine in the Publication of His "Age of Reason," By William Cobbett; With an Authentic Account of his Death Bed* (T. Knott, 1819); *Observation on Paine's "Age of Reason," by William Cobbett* (T. Knott, 1819). The original publication of these eight-page pamphlets is likely in the late 1790s or very early 1800s. Available on GB.

115. Cobbett, *Life*, 75–84.

116. Cobbett, *Life*, 91–105.

117. See Cobbett's open letter "To Lord Viscount Folkestone, on the Proceedings In Parliament During the Session Of 1819, Relative to the Paper Money," printed in the *Political Register* September 1819, reproduced in William Cobbett, James Cobbett, and John Cobbett, *Selections from Cobbett's Political Works: Being a Complete Abridgement of the 100 Volumes which Comprise the Writings of "Porcupine" and the "Weekly Political Register,"* vol. 5 (London: A. Cobbett, 1835), 420–31. Available on GB.

118. *Cobbett's Weekly Political Register*, November 13, 1819, vol. 35, no. 12, p. 383. In *Cobbett's Weekly Political Register*, vol. 35 (London: Wm. Jackson, 1820). Available on GB.

119. James Watson, *A Brief History of the Remains of the Late Thomas Paine, from the Time of their Disinterment in 1819, by the Late William Cobbett, M.P. Down to the Year 1846* (London: J. Watson, 1847), 5–8. Available on GB, but wrongly attributed to Thomas Paine.

120. Moncure Daniel Conway, "The Adventures of Thomas Paine's Bones." The text is available on the website of the TPNHA: www.thomaspaine.org/aboutpaine/the-adventures-of-thomas-paine-s-bones-by-moncure-conway.html, accessed October 17, 2021. Original text in the TPNHA Collection.

121. Heather Thomas, "The Bones of Thomas Paine," article posted on the website of the Library of Congress, https://blogs.loc.gov/headlinesandheroes/2019/04/the-bones-of-thomas-paine/, accessed October 17, 2021. For a book-length account of the saga of Paine's bones, see Paul Collins, *The Trouble with Tom: The Strange Afterlife and Times of Thomas Paine* (New York: Bloomsbury, 2005). For an interesting account of how similar the quest to find Paine's remains became to a quest for religious relics, see Leigh Eric Schmidt, *The Church of Saint Thomas Paine: A Religious History of American Secularism* (Princeton, NJ: Princeton University Press, 2021), 23–70.

122. Bennett, *The World's Sages*, 698.

123. Samuel Porter Putnam, *400 Years of Freethought* (New York: Truth Seeker Company, 1894), 526. Available on GB.

124. See the notice in *The Free Enquirer*, January 8, 1831, vol. 3, issue 11, p. 87, lower part of the third col.

125. See Albert Schrauwers, "Tilting at Windmills: The Utopian Socialist Roots of the Patriot War, 1838–1839," *Labour/Le Travail* 79 (2017): 63.

126. A notice of these lectures is published in *The Beacon*, May 20, 1837, vol. 1, issue 29, p. 272, second col. At the end of the same column, the United States Moral and Philosophical Society is named as the publisher of *The Beacon*, printed at G. W. & A. J. Matsell's bookstore, 479 Pearl Street. This issue of *The Beacon* is available through EBSCO's American Antiquarian Society (AAS) Historical Periodicals Collection: Series 2 Database.

127. Gilbert Vale's *The Life of Thomas Paine* includes a sketch of the monument and letters pertaining to its construction as an appendix (pp. 190–92).

128. The only two other sympathetic biographies were both published in England in 1819. They were Thomas Clio Rickman's *Life of Thomas Paine* (London: B. D. Cousins, Helmet, Court & Strand, 1918) and W. T. Sherwin's *Memoirs of the Life of Thomas Paine* (London: R. Carlile, 1819). Both are available on GB.

129. George Lippard, *Washington and His Generals: Or, Legends of the Revolution* (Philadelphia: T. B. Peterson, 1847), 443. Available on GB.

130. Charles Hammond, *Light from the Spirit World: The Pilgrimage of Thomas Paine and Others to the Seventh Circle in the Spirit World* (Rochester: D. M. Dewey, 1852). Available on GB.

131. J. R. Cole, *History of Tolland County, Connecticut, Including Its Early Settlement and Progress to the Present Time: A Description of Its Historic and Interesting Localities;*

Sketches of Its Towns and Villages; Portraits of Some of Its Prominent Men, and Biographies, vol. 1 (New York: W. W. Preston & Company, 1888), 121.

132. Vale, *Life of Thomas Paine*, 12.

133. The closest thing to an autobiographical account of Rose's life is the biographical sketch published by French feminist writer Jenny d'Héricourt in 1856 based on personal conversations or interviews with Rose that took place when Ernestine and her husband visited Europe that year. See "Madame Rose," in *La Revue Philosophique et Religieuse* 5 (1856): 129–39, available on GB. This quotation is from the English translation with commentary of "Madame Rose" by Paula Doress-Worters, Jane Pincus, et al., "Madame Rose: A Life of Ernestine L. Rose as told to Jenny P. d'Hericourt," *Journal of Women's History* 15, no. 1 (Spring 2003): 183–201. This particular quotation appears on p. 190 of the translation in *Journal of Women's History*, with the original text appearing on p. 130 of *La Revue Philosophique et Religieuse*.

134. See "A Defense of Atheism" in Paula Doress-Worters, ed., *Mistress of Herself: Speeches and Letters of Ernestine L. Rose, Early Women's Rights Leader* (New York: Feminist Press at the City University of New York, 2008), 295–300.

135. In addition to d'Héricourt's Madame Rose, this account of Rose's early life draws on Kolmerten, *American Life*, 1–20; Doress-Worters, "Introduction: Ernestine L. Rose, Early Women's Rights Advocate," in *Mistress of Herself*, 1–8; and Bonnie S. Anderson, *The Rabbi's Atheist Daughter: Ernestine Rose, International Feminist Pioneer* (New York: Oxford University Press, 2017), 11–44.

136. *The Beacon*, June 3, 1837, quoted in Kolmerten, *American Life*, 34.

137. *The Beacon*, October 14, 1837, quoted in Kolmerten, *American Life*, 34.

138. See Anderson, *The Rabbi's Atheist Daughter*, 47–48; Kolmerten, *American Life*, 31. Herttell published a written version of his 1837 speech advocating for the bill in 1839: *Remarks Comprising in Substance Judge Herttell's Argument in the House of Assembly of the State of New-York: In the Session of 1837, in Support of the Bill to Restore to Married Women "the Right of Property," as Guaranteed by the Constitution of this State* (New York: Henry Durell, 1839), available on GB. On Herttell's opposition to daily prayer in the legislature, and unlikely support for a controversial minister, see James S. Kabala, "'Theocrats' vs. 'Infidels': Marginalized Worldviews and Legislative Prayer in 1830s New York," *Journal of Church and State* 51, no. 1 (2009): 79–80.

139. From "Letter to Susan B. Anthony, January 9, 1877," published in Doress-Worters, *Mistress of Herself*, 348. For a legal review of the history of married women's property acts in the United States, see Richard H. Chused, "Married Women's Property Law: 1800–1850," *The Georgetown Law Journal* 71 (1982): 1359–1425.

140. Rose included the full text of the 1860 New York State Married Women's Property Act in a letter to the editor of the *Boston Investigator*, published April 11, 1860, and reprinted in Doress-Worters, *Mistress of Herself*, 255–59.

141. "Letter to Susan B. Anthony, January 9, 1877," 348.

142. "Letter to Susan B. Anthony, January 9, 1877," 348. *Mistress of Herself* contains Rose's speeches from the first (1850) through fifth (1854), seventh (1856), and tenth (1860) National Women's Rights Conventions. It also contains speeches at the

1853 New York State Women's Rights Convention and speeches from the National Convention of Loyal Women of the Republic (1863).

143. Doress-Worters, *Mistress of Herself*, 179.

144. For the texts of these speeches, see Doress-Worters, *Mistress of Herself*, 69–70 and 135–44.

145. For the text of this speech, see Doress-Worters, *Mistress of Herself*, 187–93.

146. Doress-Worters, Pincus, et al., "Madame Rose," 194; for original French see *La Revue Philosophique et Religieuse* 5 (1856): 135.

147. See an excerpt from Anthony's diary describing the tour in Doress-Worters, *Mistress of Herself*, 169–75.

148. Ida Husted Harper, *The Life and Work of Susan B. Anthony: Including Public Addresses, Her Own Letters and Many from Her Contemporaries During Fifty Years*, vol. 1 (Indianapolis: Bowen-Merrill Company, 1898), 121.

149. See Doress-Worters, *Mistress of Herself*, 123–30.

150. Anderson, *The Rabbi's Atheist Daughter*, 162.

151. For the story of how D'Arusmont came to New Harmony as part of "the boatload of knowledge," see Donald E. Pitzer, "William Maclure's Boatload of Knowledge: Science and Education into the Midwest," *Indiana Magazine of History* 94, no. 2 (1998): 110–37.

152. Morris, *Fanny Wright*, 183–87.

153. Anderson, *The Rabbi's Atheist Daughter*, 52.

154. See Rose's December 1844 letter to Robert Owen in Doress-Worters, *Mistress of Herself*, 65–67.

155. See Rose's letter to the editor of the *Boston Investigator* dated March 28, 1860, and published April 11, 1860, reprinted in Doress-Worters, *Mistress of Herself*, 255–59. Wright is discussed specifically on p. 258.

156. See Anderson, *The Rabbi's Atheist Daughter*, 54. For the quote, she cites a letter from Rose published in the *Boston Investigator*, February 9, 1881, on p. 2.

157. The full February 19, 1840, *Boston Investigator* article is reprinted in Doress-Worters, *Mistress of Herself*, 59–61.

158. The speech was published in the *Boston Investigator*, February 21, 1849, and is reprinted in Doress-Worters, *Mistress of Herself*, 72–74.

159. The speech was published in the *Boston Investigator*, March 6, 1850, and is reprinted in Doress-Worters, *Mistress of Herself*, 75–79.

160. The speech was published in the *Boston Investigator*, February 14, 1855, and is reprinted in Doress-Worters, *Mistress of Herself*, 181–83.

161. The speech was published in the *Boston Investigator*, February 20, 1861, and is reprinted in Doress-Worters, *Mistress of Herself*, 291–94.

162. The letter was published in the *Boston Investigator*, February 5, 1862, and is reprinted in Doress-Worters, *Mistress of Herself*, 301–302.

163. "Liberal Convention," *Boston Investigator*, August 19, 1836, p. 2. Citation from *Popular Freethought: A Guide to the Periodic Writings of American Infidels, 1825–1865*. Available online: https://popularfreethought.wordpress.com/browse-by-subject/conventions/, accessed March 23, 2022. Also see Post, *Popular Freethought in America*, 116, 160–62.

164. *Popular Freethought: A Guide to the Periodic Writings of American Infidels, 1825–1865* lists the following articles calling for a national convention: W. C. Bell, "Infidel Convention," *Boston Investigator*, Aug. 31, 1842, p. 1; "Infidel Convention," *The Beacon* (Third Series), January 7, 1843, pp. 63–64; Charles Knowlton, "Infidel Convention," *Boston Investigator*, May 31, 1843, p. 1; William C. Bell. "Infidel Convention," *The Beacon* (Third Series), December 2, 1843; William C. Bell, "Infidel Convention," *The Beacon* (Third Series), March 2, 1844, pp. 127–28; "Judge [Thomas] Herttell on a Convention," *The Beacon* (Third Series), September 14, 1844: 345–46. See these and more references online: https://popularfreethought.wordpress.com/browse-by-subject/conventions/, accessed March 22, 2022.

165. Quoted in Anderson, *The Rabbi's Atheist Daughter*, 58. Information about the convention comes from p. 57 of the same source. For the full text of one of the speeches given by Rose at this convention, see Doress-Worters, *Mistress of Herself*, 69–70.

166. Quoted from the convention proceedings in Post, *Popular Freethought in America*, 166.

167. "The Late Convention," *The Beacon* (Third Series), August 16, 1845, pp. 279–80. Citation from *Popular Freethought: A Guide to the Periodic Writings of American Infidels, 1825–1865*. Available online: https://popularfreethought.wordpress.com/browse-by-subject/conventions/, accessed March 23, 2022.

168. Anderson, *The Rabbi's Atheist Daughter*, 59.

169. See Henry Martyn Parkhurst, *Proceedings of the Anti-Sabbath Convention: Held in the Melodeon [Boston], March 23d and 24th* (Boston: Order of the Convention, 1848). Available on GB.

170. *Popular Freethought: A Guide to the Periodic Writings of American Infidels, 1825–1865* lists the following articles that report on the "infidel conventions" of 1857–1861: "The Philadelphia Liberal Convention," *Boston Investigator*, November 4, 1857, p. 2; "Minutes of the Infidel Convention," *Boston Investigator*, January 13, 1858, p. 2; "Reason for Organization and Declaration of Principles," *Boston Investigator*, May 5, 1858, p. 4; "Minutes of the Proceedings of the Infidel Convention, Held in Philadelphia, Monday and Tuesday, Oct. 4th and 5th, 1858," *Boston Investigator*, November 10, 1858, pp. 1 & 4; "Minutes of the proceedings of the Infidel Convention, Held in Philadelphia, Oct. 3d and 4th, 1859," *Boston Investigator*, October 26, 1859, pp. 210–11; "A Letter from Mrs. E. L. Rose, to the National Infidel Convention," *Boston Investigator*, November 23, 1859, p. 242; "The Infidel Convention of 1860," *Boston Investigator*, October 17, 1860, p. 204; "Minutes of the Proceedings of the Infidel Convention," *Boston Investigator*, October 31 and November 14, 1860, pp. 218–19, 226–27, and 235; "Minutes of the Proceedings of the Infidel Convention, held in Chapman Hall, Boston, May 27, 1862," *Boston Investigator*, June 4, 1862, p. 35; "Minutes of the Proceedings of the Infidel Convention, Held at Mercantile Hall, Summer Street, Boston, on Wednesday, May 27, 1863," *Boston Investigator*, June 10–17, 1863, pp. 34–35, 38–39, 43, and 46. Available online: https://popularfreethought.wordpress.com/browse-by-subject/conventions/, accessed March 23, 2022. For a fuller account of antebellum national freethought organizations, see Post, *Popular Freethought in America*, 160–70.

171. Israel, *The Enlightenment That Failed*, 664.

172. Thomas Paine to John Fellows, July 9, 1804. Available on the website of the TPNHA: https://www.thomaspaine.org/works/letters/other/to-col-john-fellows-july-9-1804.html, accessed June 10, 2024.

173. Peter Annet, *The Free Enquirer* (London: R. Carlile, 1761/1826). Available on GB.

Chapter 4 • The Third Wave of American Freethought

1. Susan Jacoby, *Freethinkers: A History of American Secularism* (New York: Holt, 2004), 36.

2. William James Potter, *The Free Religious Association: Its Twenty-five Years and Their Meaning: An Address for the Twenty-fifth Anniversary of the Association, at Tremont Temple, Boston, May 27th, 1892* (Boston: Free Religious Association of America, 1892), 8. Available on GB.

3. Abbot was forced to stop preaching in the Dover Unitarian Church by a minority of congregants who brought a lawsuit against him for being insufficiently Christian to preach there. See Hale v. Everett 53 N.H. 9 (1868) in Isaac Grant Thompson, *The American Reports: Containing All Decisions of General Interest Decided in the Courts of Last Resort of the Several States with Notes and References*, vol. 16 (San Francisco: Bancroft-Whitney, 1876), 82–192. Available on GB. On Abbot, also see *Lamb's Biographical Dictionary of the United States*, vol. 1 (Boston: James H. Lamb Company, 1900), p. 1 of the Supplement. Available on GB. For a contemporary book-length treatment, see Sydney E. Ahlstrom and Robert Bruce Mullin, *The Scientific Theist: A Life of Francis Ellingwood Abbot* (Macon, GA: Mercer University Press, 1987).

4. See Francis Abbot's "Biographical Sketch" of William James Potter in William James Potter and Francis Ellingwood Abbot, *Lectures and Sermons* (Boston: G. H. Ellis, 1895), v–lxxvii. Available on GB.

5. *Constitution and Circular of the American Unitarian Association* (Boston: Office of the Christian Register, 1825), 6. Available on GB.

6. Potter, *The Free Religious Association*, 8–10.

7. Francis Abbot, "The Origin of the Association," *The Index, A Weekly Paper*, January 1, 1870, p. 7, col. 3. Links to all volumes of *The Index* from 1870 to 1886 can be found on HT: https://catalog.hathitrust.org/Record/000534293, accessed June 12, 2024.

8. Potter, *The Free Religious Association*, 14.

9. Potter, *The Free Religious Association*, 22.

10. Francis Abbot, "Prospectus," *The Index*, January 1, 1870, p. 5, col. 1.

11. Francis Abbot, "Prospectus," *The Index*, January 1, 1870, p. 1, col. 3.

12. Francis Abbot, "Prospectus," *The Index*, January 1, 1870, p. 5, col. 1.

13. Francis Abbot, "The Coming Conflict," *The Index*, January 21, 1871, p. 20, col. 2.

14. *Proceedings of the National Convention to Secure the Religious Amendment of the Constitution of the United States: Held in Pittsburg, February 4, 5, 1874. With an Account of the Origin and Progress of the Movement* (Philadelphia: Christian Statesman Association, 1874), 4–8. Available on GB.

15. *Proceedings of the National Convention*, 80. For a fuller account of the movement for a Christian amendment to the Constitution, see Morton Borden, "The Christian Amendment," *Civil War History* 25, no. 2 (June 1979): 156–67. William Henry Herndon made the case that Lincoln himself was a freethinker in his famous 1892 biography, *Abraham Lincoln: The True Story of a Great Life*.

16. Francis Abbot, "The Nine Demands of Liberalism," *The Index*, April 6, 1872, p. 108, col. 1 to p. 109, col. 1.

17. Samuel Porter Putnam, *400 Years of Freethought* (New York: Truth Seeker Company, 1894), 528. Available on GB.

18. Putnam, *400 Years of Freethought*, 528.

19. Putnam, *400 Years of Freethought*, 528.

20. "The Constitution," *The Index*, July 13, 1876, p. 325, col. 1.

21. "The Constitution," *The Index*, July 13, 1876, p. 325, col. 1.

22. *Platform of the National Liberal League for the Presidential Election of 1880: Adopted at Rochester, N.Y., Oct. 26, 1877* (Boston: National Liberal League, 1877), 2–3. Available on GB.

23. *Platform of the National Liberal League*, 1. Also see coverage of the convention in *The Truth Seeker*, "The Rochester Liberal Congress," November 3, 1877 (vol. 4, no. 44), pp. 347–49. Most volumes of *The Truth Seeker* from 1773 to 1895 can be found on the website of the International Association for the Preservation of Spiritualist and Occult Periodicals: http://iapsop.com/archive/materials/truthseeker/, accessed June 12, 2024.

24. In addition to the 1877 *New York Times* article cited above, see "Free-Thinkers' Convention," *New York Times*, July 21, 1878, p. 2, col. 7; "Free-Thinkers in Convention," *New York Times*, September 23, 1879, p. 5, col. 2; "Freethinkers in Convention," *New York Times*, September 3, 1880, p. 1, col. 6; "The Freethinkers Convention," *New York Times*, September 7, 1880, p. 2, col. 5; "Free-Thinkers in Convention," *New York Times*, September 3, 1881, p. 5, col. 2; "Freethinkers Adjourn," *New York Times*, September 5, 1881, p. 2, col. 6; "Free-Thinker's Convention," *New York Times*, August 24, 1882, p. 4, col. 7; "The Freethinkers' Convention," *New York Times*, August 29, 1883, p. 5, col. 4; "The Freethinkers' Gathering: Organizing the Rochester Convention—A Lecture on The Clergy," *New York Times*, August 30, 1883, p. 5, col. 7; "Convention of Freethinkers: Papers And Addresses Before The Rochester Gathering," *New York Times*, August 31, 1883, p. 2, col. 6; "The Freethinkers' Convention," *New York Times*, September 1, 1883, p. 1, col. 7; "Platform of The Freethinkers: A Liberal and Sympathetic Declaration of Principles," *New York Times*, September 2, 1883, p. 2, col. 5; "Helping Infidelity," *New York Times*, September 2, 1883, p. 6, cols. 5–6; "The Freethinkers Go Home," *New York Times*, September 3, 1883, p. 4, col. 7; "The National Liberal League," *New York Times*, September 19, 1883, p. 4, col. 5; "Freethinkers in Convention," *New York Times*, December 28, 1883, p. 1, col. 5; "The Freethinkers' Convention," *New York Times*, December 29, 1883, p. 2, col. 1; "The Freethinkers' Convention," *New York Times*, January 1, 1884, p. 2, col. 3; "The Freethinkers' Convention," *New York Times*, January 30, 1884, p. 4, col. 6; "Freethinkers' Convention," *New York Times*, August 8, 1884, p. 2, col. 6; "Freethinkers' Convention," *New York Times*, March 24, 1885, p. 5, col. 5; "Views of Freethinkers: Advocating Separation of Church and State And 'Liberty,'" *New York Times*, September 14, 1885, p. 1, col. 7; "Freethinkers Listen to Addresses," *New York Times*, November 19, 1899, p. 10, col. 7.

25. See George E. MacDonald, *Fifty Years of Freethought: Being the Story of the "Truth Seeker," with the Natural History of Its Third Editor*, vols. 1 and 2 (New York: Truth Seeker Company, 1929 and 1931). Nearly every chapter of this work covering

the period after 1882 ends by describing significant events in the freethought movement during the period covered by the chapter, including important freethought meetings. Chapter 23 of vol. 1, for instance, records a meeting of the National Secular Union in Ohio and the Oregon Secular Union in Portland in 1890 (pp. 519 and 521), and chapter 24 notes the meetings of "sixteen liberal societies" in 1891 (p. 531).

26. For Putnam's full account of local liberal leagues across the United States and Canada, see *400 Years of Freethought*, 566–86.

27. Putnam, *400 Years of Freethought*, 539.

28. Sidney Warren, *American Freethought, 1860–1914* (New York: Columbia University Press, 1943), 26. See also *Compendium of the Eleventh Census, Part Two* (Washington, DC: Government Printing Office, 1894), 265. For a more detailed treatment of nineteenth-century church membership statistics, see Roger Finke and Rodney Stark, "Turning Pews into People: Estimating 19th Century Church Membership," *Journal for the Scientific Study of Religion* 25, no. 2 (1986): 180–92.

29. Putnam, *400 Years of Freethought*, 569–70.

30. Putnam, *400 Years of Freethought*, 571.

31. MacDonald, *Fifty Years of Freethought*, vol. 1, 168–69.

32. MacDonald, *Fifty Years of Freethought*, vol. 1, 89.

33. "The Free-Thinkers: Mass-Meeting at Cooper Institute," *New York Times*, January 13, 1874, p. 8, col. 3.

34. *The Proceedings and Addresses at the Freethinkers' Convention Held at Watkins, N.Y., August 22nd, 23rd, 24th, and 25th '78* (New York: D. M. Bennett, 1878), 5–6. Available on GB.

35. *The Proceedings and Addresses at the Freethinkers' Convention*, 5–6. The *New York Times* also briefly noted the convention, although it is erroneously represented as taking place "near Wolcott," New York. "A Free-Thinkers' Society," *New York Times*, August 21, 1877, p. 5, col. 4.

36. *The Proceedings and Addresses at the Freethinkers' Convention*, 11.

37. Putnam, *400 Years of Freethought*, 549.

38. See George Jacob Holyoake, *Principles of Secularism Briefly Explained* (London: Holyoake & Company, 1859).

39. Carl F. Kaestle, *The Evolution of an Urban School System: New York City, 1750–1850* (Cambridge, MA: Harvard University Press, 1973), 148–58.

40. See *A Full and Complete Account of the Awful Riots in Philadelphia* (Philadelphia: John Perry and Henry Jordan, 1844. Available online from the Library of Congress: https://www.loc.gov/item/01010559/. Also see Vincent P. Lannie and Bernard C. Diethorn, "For the Honor and Glory of God: The Philadelphia Bible Riots of 1840," *History of Education Quarterly* 8, no. 1 (1968): 44–106. Note that the title of this otherwise useful piece incorrectly dates the riots to 1840 rather than 1844.

41. *New York Daily Tribune*, July 8, 1875, p. 4, col. 3. Digital copy available online from the Library of Congress: https://chroniclingamerica.loc.gov/data/batches/dlc _inform_ver01/data/sn83030214/00206531228/1875070801/0072.pdf, accessed July 25, 2023.

42. For the arguments and opinions in the original Cincinnati case, see *The Bible in the Public Schools: Arguments in the Case of John D. Minor et al. Versus the Board of*

Education of the City of Cincinnati et al. (Cincinnati: R. Clarke & Company, 1870). Available on GB. For arguments and opinion in the Ohio Supreme Court case, see *The Bible in the Public Schools: Opinion and Decision of the Supreme Court of Ohio, in the Case of John D. Minor et al., vs. the Board of Education of the City of Cincinnati et al.* (Cincinnati: R. Clarke and Company, 1873). Available on GB.

43. Steven K. Green, "The Blaine Amendment Reconsidered," *American Journal of Legal History* 36, no. 1 (1992): 47.

44. See A. H. Wintersteen, "Supreme Court of Wisconsin. State ex rel. Weiss et al. v District Board of School-Dist. No. 8 of the City of Edgerton," *The American Law Register* 38, no. 5 (1890): 286–330.

45. *Congressional Record: Containing the Proceedings and Debates of the Forty-Fourth Congress*, 1st sess., vol. 4 (Washington, DC: Government Printing Office, 1876), 175. Available from Hein Online: https://home.heinonline.org/content/.

46. A portion of Grant's speech is reproduced in *The Index*, December 23, 1875, p. 601, col. 2.

47. *Congressional Record . . . of the Forty-Fourth Congress*, 1st sess., vol. 4, 205.

48. See, for instance, F. William O'Brien, "The Blaine Amendment 1875–1876," *University of Detroit Law Journal* 41, no. 2 (December 1963): 147–50; Ward M. McAfee, "The Historical Context of the Failed Federal Blaine Amendment of 1876," *First Amendment Law Review* 2, no. 1 (Winter 2003): 1–22.

49. Robert Green Ingersoll, *The Ghosts: And Other Lectures* (Washington, DC: C. P. Farrell, 1878), 224–25.

50. *Congressional Record . . . of the Forty-Fourth Congress*, 1st sess., vol. 4, 5189.

51. *Congressional Record . . . of the Forty-Fourth Congress*, 1st sess., vol. 4, 5580; the results of the vote can be found on p. 5595.

52. See Lemon v. Kurtzman, 403 U.S. 602 (1971), p. 647. Footnote 3/6 on p. 661 gives citations of all the state constitutions that have Blaine amendments. Available online at: https://supreme.justia.com/cases/federal/us/403/602/#F3/6, accessed July 26, 2023.

53. See "Blaine Amendments in State Constitutions" on the website Ballotpedia: https://ballotpedia.org/Blaine_amendments_in_state_constitutions, accessed July 27, 2023.

54. For a recent full biography of Ingersoll, see Susan Jacoby, *The Great Agnostic: Robert Ingersoll and American Freethought* (New Haven, CT: Yale University Press, 2013).

55. Mark Twain, *Mark Twain's Letters*, vol. 1, Albert Bigelow Paine, ed. (New York: Harper and Brothers, 1917), 371. Available on GB.

56. See Robert Ingersoll, "Speech at the Lotos Club Dinner in Honor of Anton Seidl," given in New York on February 2nd, 1895, in *The Works of Robert Ingersoll in Twelve Volumes*, vol. 12: *Miscellany* (New York: Dresden Publishing, 1901), 172–73.

57. Eugene V. Debs, "Recollections of Ingersoll," *Pearson's Magazine* 37, no. 4 (April 1917): 302. Also see Orvin Prentiss Larson, *American Infidel: Robert G. Ingersoll* (New York: The Citadel Press, 1962), 46–47.

58. For a more detailed account of Ingersoll's politics during this period, see Donald E. Angel, "Ingersoll's Political Transition: Patriotism or Partisanship?" *Journal of the Illinois State Historical Society* 59, no. 4 (1966): 354–83.

59. Larson, *American Infidel*, 48–68. The roster of the Eleventh Illinois Cavalry can be viewed at: https://civilwar.illinoisgenweb.org/civilwar/fs/cav011-fs.html, accessed August 3, 2023. Details about the unit's service history may be viewed at https://www.nps.gov/civilwar/search-battle-units-detail.htm?battleUnitCode =UIL0011RC, accessed August 3, 2023.

60. Larson, *American Infidel*, 73–75. See the brief entry on Ebon Clark Ingersoll in United States, *A Biographical Congressional Directory, 1774 to 1903: The Continental Congress: September 5, 1774, to October 21, 1788, Inclusive* (Washington: Government Printing Office, 1903), 615. Available on HT.

61. Larson, *American Infidel*, 85.

62. Larson, *American Infidel*, 103.

63. The dedication, "To Eva A. Ingersoll, my wife, a woman without superstition . . ." can be found in the 1878 edition of Ingersoll's *The Gods and Other Lectures* (Washington, DC: C. P. Farrell Publisher, 1878).

64. Larson, *American Infidel*, 86.

65. Larson, *American Infidel*, 92–93.

66. Larson, *American Infidel*, 173–80. The verdict of the first trial was reported on the front page of the *New York Times*, September 12, 1882: "A Disappointing Verdict: Miner and Rerdell the Only Ones Found Guilty," p. 1, col. 7. The verdict of the second trial was reported on the front page of the *New York Times*, June 15, 1883. "Not Guilty as Indicted: The Members of The Star Route Ring Acquitted," p. 1, col. 1.

67. The illustration is captioned "The Result of the Star Trials" and is on the cover of the June 20, 1883, issue of *Puck* magazine. It is viewable on the website of the Library of Congress: https://www.loc.gov/item/2012645483/, accessed August 4, 2023.

68. This chronology can be found at the following address: https://chronology .secularhumanism.org/, accessed August 4, 2023.

69. The definitive collection of Ingersoll's work is often called "The Dresden Edition" because it was produced by the Dresden Publishing Company, named after the small town where Ingersoll was born. Its full citation is *The Works of Robert G. Ingersoll in Twelve Volumes* (New York: The Dresden Publishing Company, 1902). An online edition can be accessed at https://www.gutenberg.org/files/38813/38813-h /38813-h.htm#Alink0011, accessed August 4, 2023. It can also be found on the HT website: https://catalog.hathitrust.org/Record/012224350, accessed August 4, 2023.

70. Ingersoll, *Works*, vol. 1, 375.

71. Ingersoll, *Works*, vol. 4, 435–56.

72. Ingersoll, *Works*, vol. 3, 399–400.

73. Ingersoll, *Works*, vol. 1, 41–42.

74. See the "History" section of the "About Us" page of the TPNHA website: https://www.thomaspaine.org/pages/about-us.html, accessed October 1, 2023.

75. The recordings can be heard at the following web address: https:// secularhumanism.org/Ingersoll-museum/audio-recordings-of-robert-green -Ingersoll/, accessed August 5, 2023.

76. Putnam, *400 Years of Freethought*, 549.

77. These lines are from the preamble to the new constitution adopted by the Unitarian National Convention, September 26, 1894, quoted in *The Free Church Record* 2, no. 6 (December 1894): 223. Available on HT. Also see George Willis Cooke,

Unitarianism in America: A History of Its Origin and Development (Boston: American Unitarian Association, 1910), 228–30.

78. Letter from Caroline J. Bartlett to Eugene M. MacDonald, editor of *The Truth Seeker*, January 23, 1896, reprinted in Eugene Montague MacDonald, *Col. Robert G. Ingersoll as He Is: A Complete Refutation of His Clerical Enemies' Malicious Slanders* (New York: Truth Seeker Co., 1896), 106. Available on HT.

79. Letter from Robert G. Ingersoll to the Editor of the New York *Journal*, January 12, 1896, reprinted in MacDonald, *Col. Robert G. Ingersoll as He Is*, 107.

80. For this exchange, see Caroline J. Bartlett, *Why the People's Church of Kalamazoo Would Fellowship Col. Ingersoll* (Kalamazoo, MI: Young Men's Union of the People's Church, 1896), 4. A digital copy of this valuable record can be downloaded from Duke University Libraries: https://repository.duke.edu/dc/books/a319ecf8-9b41-4570-8229-852ee18fe7f2, accessed September 21, 2023. For contemporary historical commentary on this incident, see Leigh Eric Schmidt, *The Church of Saint Thomas Paine: A Religious History of American Secularism* (Princeton, NJ: Princeton University Press, 2021), 113–17.

81. See its website: https://peopleschurch.net/, accessed September 21, 2023.

82. The signed statements of the Fox family and their neighbors were published before the end of 1848 as *A Report of the Mysterious Noises Heard in the House of Mr. John D. Fox, in Hydesville, Arcadia, Wayne County, Authenticated by the Certificates, And Confirmed by the Statements of the Citizens of That Place and Vicinity* (Rochester, NY: E. E. Lewis, 1848), available on the IA. Other early accounts by true believers include Eliab Wilkinson Capron, *Modern Spiritualism: Its Facts and Fanaticisms, Its Consistencies and Contradictions* (Boston: Bela Marsh, 1855), 33–87; and Emma Hardinge Britten, *Modern American Spiritualism: A Twenty Years' Record of the Communion Between Earth and the World of Spirits* (New York: Self-Published, 1860/1870), 36–55. My account is based more closely on that in Reuben Briggs Davenport, *The Death-blow to Spiritualism: Being the True Story of the Fox Sisters, as Revealed by Authority of Margaret Fox Kane and Catherine Fox Jencken* (New York: G. W. Dillingham, 1888), 81–95. This account, in which the Fox sisters admitted fraud, was endorsed by Maggie and Kate Fox the year that it was published. However, their admission was later recanted. There is much recent scholarly literature on nineteenth-century spiritualism and its origins. See, for instance, Molly McGarry, *Ghosts of Futures Past: Spiritualism and the Cultural Politics of Nineteenth-Century America* (Berkeley: University of California Press, 2008).

83. For an example of an early mention in a New York paper, see "More About the 'Knockings,' The Rochester Spirits—a Scene," *New York Daily Tribune*, June 29, 1850, p. 5, col. 6. Available online from the Library of Congress: https://www.loc.gov/resource/sn83030213/1850-06-29/ed-1/?sp=5, accessed September 27, 2024. LOC is open access.

84. McGarry, *Ghosts of Futures Past*, 10. One of the most prominent spiritualist periodicals was called the *Spiritual Telegraph*. Many issues are available from the International Association for the Preservation of Spiritualist and Occult Periodicals: http://iapsop.com/archive/materials/spiritual_telegraph/, accessed September 8, 2023.

85. Davenport, *Death-blow to Spiritualism*, 90.

86. Casey Cep, "Why Did So Many Victorians Try to Speak with the Dead?" *New Yorker*, May 24, 2021. Available online: www.newyorker.com/magazine/2021/05/31

/why-did-so-many-victorians-try-to-speak-with-the-dead#, accessed September 9, 2023. For a detailed count of the increasing number of spiritualist meetings and lecturers in the second half of the nineteenth century, see David K. Nartonis, "The Rise of 19th-Century American Spiritualism, 1854–1873," *Journal for the Scientific Study of Religion* 49, no. 2 (2010): 361–73.

87. Quoted in *Proceedings of the Fourth Annual Convention of the National Spiritualists' Association* (Washington, DC: National Spiritualists' Association, 1896), 124. Available on GB. The California Declaration of Principles was quoted as the National Spiritualists' Association debated what statement of principle it should adopt. It is worth noting that some argued that no reference to science should be made, as science was too narrow to encompass spiritualism.

88. For an example of a Christian sermon that describes spiritualism as "wicked," see Edward Peter Barrett, *"Spiritualism," A Sermon* (London: Elliot Stock, 1872), available on GB.

89. Robert Dale Owen's 1871 *The Debateable Land Between this World and the Next* (London: Trubner and Company, 1871—available on GB) is a systematic exposition and defense of spiritualism addressed to mainstream Protestants, which argues that spiritualism is a new Reformation.

90. An 1865 broadside by Alfred Gale uses Bible verses against witchcraft to condemn spiritualism and blames spiritualism for the Civil War. Available online from the Library of Congress: https://www.loc.gov/resource/rbpe.10004600/, accessed September 11, 2023.

91. MacDonald, *Fifty Years of Freethought*, vol. 1, 360–61.

92. See Davis's autobiography, *The Magic Staff: An Autobiography of Andrew Jackson Davis* (New York: J. S. Brown & Company, 1857), 12–14; 204–12. Available on GB.

93. Andrew Jackson Davis, *The Principles of Nature, Her Divine Revelations, and a Voice to Mankind* (Boston: Colby & Rich, Banner Publishing House, 1847). Available on GB.

94. For Davis's account of the convention, see Davis, *The Magic Staff*, 455–57. For a full transcript of the convention, see *Proceedings of the Hartford Bible Convention, Reported Phonographically by Andrew J. Graham* (New York: The Committee, 1854), available on the website of the International Association for the Preservation of Spiritualist and Occult Periodicals: http://iapsop.com/ssoc/1854__graham__ _proceedings_of_the_hartford_bible_convention.pdf, accessed September 11, 2023. Davis called the convention to order, is listed as the first of the participants on the public invitation, and delivered the first speech. *Proceedings*, 9–26. For an academic account of Davis's Hartford years, see Robert W. Delp, "A Spiritualist in Connecticut: Andrew Jackson Davis, the Hartford Years, 1850–1854," *New England Quarterly* 53, no. 3 (1980): 345–62.

95. *Proceedings*, 339.

96. Putnam, *400 Years of Freethought*, 524–25. The speech Putnam quotes was actually given at the end of the third day of the convention. *Proceedings*, 267–79. But Rose also delivered the last speech on the fourth day that precipitated a near-riot among the Bible supporters. *Proceedings*, 369–71.

97. For more detail, visit the website of Fellowships of the Spirit: https://www.fellowshipsspirit.org/, accessed September 11, 2023.

98. For the full text of the speech, see George Chainey, "Through Day to Night, and Night to Day," *The Truth Seeker*, September 20, 1884, pp. 600–601, col. 1.

99. See "The Close of the Convention," *The Truth Seeker*, September 20, 1884, pp. 594–95; 598, cols. 1–2.

100. See George MacDonald's account of the convention in *Fifty Years of Freethought*, vol. 1, 361–62.

101. Quoted by MacDonald in *Fifty Years of Freethought*, vol. 1, 386.

102. On Houdini's campaign against spiritualism, see Bryan Greene, "For Harry Houdini, Séances and Spiritualism Were Just an Illusion," *Smithsonian Magazine*, published online October 28, 2021. Available online: https://www.smithsonianmag.com/history/for-harry-houdini-seances-and-spiritualism-were-just-an-illusion-180978944/, accessed October 5, 2023. Also see Houdini's pamphlet, *Houdini Exposes the Tricks Used by the Boston Medium "Margery" to Win the $2500 Prize Offered by the Scientific American: Also a Complete Exposure of Argamasilla, the Famous Spaniard who Baffled Noted Scientists of Europe and America with His Claim to X-ray Vision* (New York: Adams Press, 1924). Available on GB.

103. Capron, *Modern Spiritualism*, 69–74; 90–97; Britten, *Modern American Spiritualism*, 36–46; McGarry, *Ghosts of Futures Past*, 121.

104. Isaac Post, *Voices from the Spirit World: Being Communications from Many Spirits* (Rochester, NY: Charles H. McDonnell, 1852), 22–27, 28–30, 91–94, 152–56.

105. *Platform of the National Liberal League*, 3; *Proceedings and Addresses at the Freethinkers' Convention*, 18, 54–55, 112–16, 121–22; *Proceedings at the Eighth Annual Meeting of the Free Religious Association* (Boston: Free Religious Association, 1875), 6. Available on the IA. On Stanton's evolution as a freethinker, see Annie Laurie Gaylor, Women without Superstition, *"No Gods, No Masters": The Collected Writings of Women Freethinkers of the Nineteenth and Twentieth Centuries* (Madison, WI: Freedom from Religion Foundation, 1997), 103–11.

106. On Colman, see Gaylor, *Women without Superstition*, 177–78.

107. See Matilda Joslyn Gage, *Woman, Church, and State: A Historical Account of the Status of Woman Through the Christian Ages: with Reminiscences of the Matriarchate* (New York: Truth Seeker Company, 1893). Available on GB.

108. On Lucretia Mott, see Carol Faulkner, *Lucretia Mott's Heresy: Abolition and Women's Rights in Nineteenth-Century America* (Philadelphia: University of Pennsylvania Press, 2011).

109. See Paul Avrich, *An American Anarchist: The Life of Voltairine de Cleyre* (Princeton, NJ: Princeton University Press, 1978).

110. Elizabeth Cady Stanton et.al., "Part One," in *The Woman's Bible: A Classic Feminist Perspective* (Mineola, NY: Dover Publications, 2002/1895), 5.

111. Stanton, *The Woman's Bible*, 7.

112. Elizabeth Cady Stanton et.al., "Part Two," in *The Woman's Bible: A Classic Feminist Perspective* (Mineola, NY: Dover Publications, 2002/1898), 8.

113. "*The Woman's Bible* Repudiated," in "Part Two" of *The Woman's Bible: A Classic Feminist Perspective* (Mineola, NY: Dover Publications, 2002/1898), 215–27.

114. Ingersoll, *Works*, vol. 1, 375.

115. Rose denies supporting free love in a letter to the editor of the *New York Times* dated June 29, 1858. For full text, see Paula Doress-Worters, ed., *Mistress of*

Herself: Speeches and Letters of Ernestine L. Rose, Early Women's Rights Leader (New York: Feminist Press at the City University of New York, 2008), 244–45.

116. Quoted from "Testimony Before Select Committee of the New York Assembly, February 18, 1855." For full text, see Doress-Worters, *Mistress of Herself*, 185.

117. From Victoria C. Woodhull, "Tried as by Fire; Or, the True and the False, Socially," in *Selected Writings of Victoria Woodhull: Suffrage, Free Love, and Eugenics*, edited by Cari M. Carpenter (Lincoln: University of Nebraska Press, 2010), 215.

118. *The Free Enquirer*, July 12, 1826, p. 330, col. 2. Links to all volumes of *The Free Enquirer* and its precursors can be found on HT: https://catalog.hathitrust.org/Record/100113187, accessed June 12, 2024.

119. For a debate about divorce between Robert Dale Owen and Horace Greeley, a freethinker who took a dim view of free love and anything related to it, see Horace Greeley and Robert Dale Owen, *Divorce: Being a Correspondence Between Horace Greeley and Robert Dale Owen* (New York: Robert M. DeWitt, 1860). Available on GB.

120. For a brief account of Noyes and the community he founded, see "Oneida" in Mark Holloway, *Heavens on Earth: Utopian Communities in America, 1680–1860* (New York: Dover, 1966), 179–97. For a current book-length account, see Anthony Wonderley, *Oneida Utopia: A Community Searching for Human Happiness and Prosperity* (Ithaca, NY: Cornell University Press, 2017). For the fullest primary account of the doctrines of the Oneida community, see John Humphrey Noyes et al. *Bible Communism: A Compilation from the Annual Reports and Other Publications of the Oneida Association and Its Branches; Presenting, In Connection with Their History, a Summary View of Their Religious And Social Theories* (Brooklyn: Office of the Circular, 1853). Available on HT. See pp. 57–62 and 127–28 in particular. For Noyes's original defense of communistic or complex marriage and an account of the community's first experience of these practices, see John Humphrey Noyes, "History of The Battle Ax Letter," and George W. Noyes, "Beginnings of Complex Marriage," in Taylor Stoehr, *Free Love in America: A Documentary History* (New York: AMS Press, 1979), 495–99; 501–509.

121. For freethought perspectives on Mormonism, see MacDonald, *Fifty Years of Freethought*, vol. 1, 362–63.

122. Woodhull, "Tried as by Fire," 218–19.

123. Woodhull and Claflin's lives, up to this point, can be extrapolated from Tilton's account. See Theodore Tilton, *Victoria C. Woodhull: A Biographical Sketch* (New York: The Golden Age, 1871), 1–35. For a detailed academic biography, see Amanda Frisken, *Victoria Woodhull's Sexual Revolution: Political Theater and the Popular Press in Nineteenth-Century America* (Philadelphia: University of Pennsylvania Press, 2011). Also see Mary Gabriel, *Notorious Victoria: The Uncensored Life of Victoria Woodhull—Visionary, Suffragist, and First Woman to Run for President* (Chapel Hill, NC: Algonquin Books, 1998); Myra MacPherson, *The Scarlet Sisters: Sex, Suffrage, and Scandal in the Gilded Age* (New York: Twelve, 2014); and Victoria C. Woodhull, *Selected Writings of Victoria Woodhull: Suffrage, Free Love, and Eugenics*, Cari M. Carpenter, ed. (Lincoln: University of Nebraska Press, 2010).

124. See "The Queens of Finance: A New Phase of the Woman's Rights Question," *New York Herald*, January 22, 1870, p. 10, col. 3. Digital copy available through the Library of Congress.

125. Vanderbilt's original support of *Woodhull & Claflin's Weekly* is discussed by Woodhull in "An Open Letter" to Vanderbilt requesting more support in 1875. See Victoria Woodhull, "An Open Letter," *Woodhull & Claflin's Weekly*, April 3, 1875, pp. 4–5. This and most other issues of *Woodhull & Claflin's Weekly* can be found on the website of the International Association for the Preservation of Spiritual and Occult Periodicals: http://iapsop.com/archive/materials/woodhull_and_claflins_weekly/, accessed August 13, 2023.

126. *Woodhull & Claflin's Weekly*, October 8, 1870, p. 1.

127. *Woodhull & Claflin's Weekly*, December 30, 1871, pp. 3–7; 12–13.

128. See "Official Report of the Equal Rights Convention," *Woodhull & Claflin's Weekly*, May 25, 1872, pp. 3–9.

129. Victoria Woodhull, "The Religion of Humanity," *Woodhull & Claflin's Weekly*, November 2, 1872, pp. 2–7.

130. Frisken, *Victoria Woodhull's Sexual Revolution*, vii–ix.

131. "Obituary. D. M. Bennett," in *The Truth Seeker*, December 16, 1882, p. 786, col. 3. For a good book-length biography of D. M. Bennett, see Roderick Bradford, *D. M. Bennett: The Truth Seeker* (Amherst, NY: Prometheus Books, 2006).

132. For George MacDonald's account of the founding of *The Truth Seeker*, see *Fifty Years of Freethought*, 141–44.

133. An account of the fractious convention of 1878 can be found in *The Truth Seeker*, November 2, 1878, pp. 696–97; 692–93.

134. In "The Tale of *The Truth Seeker*," an article on the website of the Center for Inquiry dated September 13, 2018, Tom Flynn put the highest circulation of *The Truth Seeker* at 50,000, although his sources of information are not clear. Available online: https://centerforinquiry.org/blog/the-tale-of-the-truth-seeker/, accessed August 8, 2023. One possible source is a passage from the obscenity trial of D. M. Bennett, where it is stated that *The Truth Seeker* has 50,000 readers. See Samuel B. Hinsdale (Court Reporter), *Trial of D. M. Bennett, in the United States Circuit Court, Judge Charles L. Benedict, Presiding, New York, March 18, 19, 20, and 21, 1879: Upon the Charge of Depositing Prohibited Matter in The Mail* (New York: The Truth Seeker, 1879), 144. Available on HT.

135. For issues and details, see the *Freethinkers' Magazine* archive on the website of the International Association for the Preservation of Spiritual and Occult Periodicals: http://iapsop.com/archive/materials/freethinkers_magazine/, accessed August 7, 2023.

136. See Shaw's biography on the website of the Texas State Historical Association: https://www.tshaonline.org/handbook/entries/shaw-james-dickson, accessed August 7, 2023.

137. On *Secular Thought*, see Ramsay Cook, *The Regenerators: Social Criticism in Late Victorian English Canada* (Toronto: University of Toronto Press, 1985), 52. Available from the IA.

138. See the entry in the Library of Congress catalogue: https://www.loc.gov/item/sn87057974/, accessed May 29, 2024.

139. On Monroe and *Ironclad Age*, see Clifton J. Phillips, *Indiana in Transition: The Emergence of an Industrial Commonwealth, 1880–1920* (Indianapolis: Indiana Historical Society Press, 1968), 461. Available from the IA.

140. This and all the other journals in this paragraph are mentioned in *400 Years of Freethought* on pp. 651–56.

141. The first volume of *Radical Review* is available on GB.

142. See the biography of Moses Harman on the website of the Kansas Historical Association: https://www.kshs.org/kansapedia/moses-harman/12080, accessed August 7, 2023.

143. For the text of the law, see "An Act for the Suppression of the Trade in and Circulation of Obscene Literature, Illustrations, Advertisements, and Articles of Indecent or Immoral Use, and Obscene Advertisements of Patent Medicines," *Laws of the State of New York: Passed at the Session of the Legislature* (Albany: Van Benthuysen & Sons Steam Printing House, 1868), 856–58. Available on GB. On the activities of the New York YMCA to suppress vice, see Amy Werbel, *Lust on Trial: Censorship and the Rise of American Obscenity in the Age of Anthony Comstock* (New York: Columbia University Press, 2018), 53–55.

144. Werbel, *Lust on Trial*, 51–59.

145. See Victoria Woodhull, "The Beecher-Tilton Scandal Case," *Woodhull & Claflin's Weekly*, November 2, 1872, pp. 9–13.

146. Tennessee Claflin, "The Philosophy of Modern Hypocrisy—Mr. L. C. Challis the Illustration," *Woodhull & Claflin's Weekly*, November 2, 1872, pp. 13–14.

147. Werbel, *Lust on Trial*, 60–63; 74. Also see Helen Lefkowitz Horowitz, "Victoria Woodhull, Anthony Comstock, and Conflict over Sex in the United States in the 1870s," *Journal of American History* 87, no. 2 (2000): 403–34. For an account of Woodhull's arrest, see "Arrest of Mrs. Victoria C. Woodhull at the Cooper Institute Last Night," *New York Times*, January 10, 1873, p. 5, col. 3. For the fullest account of the trial, see "The Great Vindication Scheme Exploded," *Woodhull & Claflin's Weekly*, July 12, 1873, pp. 8–9. Also see "Woodhull and Claflin Free," *The Sun*, June 28, 1873, p. 3, col. 5. Digital images of *The Sun* are available through the Library of Congress.

148. "The Woodhull Libel: Acquittal of the Defendants," *New York Times*, March 15, 1874, p. 3, col. 7.

149. MacPherson, *The Scarlet Sisters*, 255–75.

150. "An Act for the Suppression of Trade in and Circulation of Obscene Literature and Articles of Immoral Use," in *The Statutes At Large and Proclamations of The United States of America, From March 1871 to March 1873, And Treaties and Postal Conventions*, vol. 17, George P. Sanger, ed. (Boston: Little, Brown, and Company, 1873), 598–600. Available on GB.

151. Werbel, *Lust on Trial*, 75.

152. For a review of state-level anti-birth control and anti-obscenity laws passed in the Comstock era, see J. C. Ruppenthal, "Criminal Statutes on Birth Control," *Journal of Criminal Law and Criminology* 10, no. 1 (1919), 48–61. Available online: https://scholarlycommons.law.northwestern.edu/cgi/viewcontent.cgi?article=1616&context=jclc, accessed August 13, 2023.

153. See Bennett's own account of his arrest: D. M. Bennett, "It Has Come at Last," *The Truth Seeker*, November 17, 1877, p. 365, cols. 1–3. Also see Bradford, *D. M. Bennett*, 116–21.

154. Hinsdale, *Trial of D. M. Bennett*, iv. Also see MacDonald, *Fifty Years of Freethought*, vol. 1, 227.

155. For Heywood's criticism of Comstock, see "National Gag Law," in *Cupid's Yokes: Or, the Binding Forces of Conjugal Love* (Princeton, MA: Co-Operative Publishing, 1876), 10–12. Available online through the International Association for the Preservation of Spiritualist and Occult Periodicals: http://iapsop.com/ssoc/1877__heywood___cupids_yoke.pdf, accessed August 31, 2023.

156. For Bennett's account of the arrest, see "Another Arrest," *The Truth Seeker*, August 31, 1878, p. 552, col. 1. Also see Bradford, *D. M. Bennett*, 131–43.

157. "Cupid's Yokes," *The Truth Seeker*, September 7, 1878, p. 569, col. 3.

158. For a full transcription of the trial, see Hinsdale, *Trial of D. M. Bennett*.

159. For the full text of the appeal decision, see Samuel Blatchford, *Reports of Cases Argued and Determined in the Circuit Court of the United States for the Second Circuit*, vol. 16 (New York: Baker, Voorhis and Company, 1880), 338–75. Available on GB. The first reference to *Regina v. Hicklin* occurs on p. 366. For more background on the Hicklin obscenity test, see Katherine Mullin, "Unmasking *The Confessional Unmasked*: The 1868 Hicklin Test and the Toleration of Obscenity," *English Literary History (ELH)* 85, no. 2 (2018): 471–99.

160. United States v. One Book Called "Ulysses," 5 F. Supp. 182 (S.D.N.Y. 1933). Available online from Justia: https://law.justia.com/cases/federal/district-courts/FSupp/5/182/2250768/, accessed September 1, 2023.

161. Rutherford B. Hayes, *Diary and Letters of Rutherford Birchard Hayes*, vol. 3: *1865–1881* (Columbus: Ohio State Archaeological and Historical Society, 1922), 562. Available on GB.

162. Putnam, *400 Years of Freethought*, 528–29.

163. Putnam, *400 Years of Freethought*, 538.

164. Putnam, *400 Years of Freethought*, 539.

165. Francis Abbot, *The Index*, April 25, 1878, p. 193, col. 3.

166. For the debate between Thaddeus Wakeman and Ingersoll that led to Ingersoll's resignation from the National Liberal League, see *The Truth Seeker*, October 2, 1880, pp. 635–37; 640.

167. Putnam, *400 Years of Freethought*, 529; 533.

168. MacDonald, *Fifty Years of Freethought*, 251–54. Also see Bradford, *D. M. Bennett*, 215–32.

169. *Religio-Philosophical Journal*, October 25, 1879, p. 1. Available from the International Association for the Preservation of Spiritualist and Occult Periodicals: http://iapsop.com/archive/materials/religio-philosophical_journal/, accessed September 6, 2023.

170. *The Index*, October 30, 1879, p. 519.

171. MacDonald, *Fifty Years of Freethought*, vol. 1, 252.

172. Bennett's explanation and apology can be found in the November 22, 1879, issue of *The Truth Seeker*.

173. MacDonald, *Fifty Years of Freethought*, vol. 1, 254–55.

174. MacDonald, *Fifty Years of Freethought*, vol. 1, 274–81. Also see Bradford, *D. M. Bennett*, 233–67.

175. On Craddock's appointment as secretary, see MacDonald, *Fifty Years of Freethought*, 491. Also see Vere Campbell, *Sexual Outlaw, Erotic Mystic: The Essential Ida Craddock* (San Francisco: Weiser Books, 2010), 22–23; Leigh Eric Schmidt,

Heaven's Bride: The Unprintable Life of Ida Craddock, America Mystic, Scholar, Sexologist, Martyr, and Madwoman (New York: Basic Books, 2010), 50.

176. See "The Danse du Ventre," in Campbell, *Sexual Outlaw, Erotic Mystic*, 7–20.

177. See Campbell, *Sexual Outlaw, Erotic Mystic*, xxii.

178. Schmidt, *Heaven's Bride*, 113–19, 91–92; Campbell, *Sexual Outlaw, Erotic Mystic*, 24–25.

179. See the full text of these works in Campbell, *Sexual Outlaw, Erotic Mystic*, 178–203, 204–15.

180. Campbell, *Sexual Outlaw, Erotic Mystic*, 235.

181. Campbell, *Sexual Outlaw, Erotic Mystic*, 232. Clark Bell, a lawyer with whom Craddock consulted on her legal case, supports his professional opinion that she should have used the insanity defense, in his essay "Ida Craddock and Anthony Comstock," in Clark Bell, *Medico-Legal Studies*, vol. 8 (New York: Medico-Legal Journal, 1906), 47–51. Available on GB.

182. For these and other cases, see "Working of the Comstock Laws," *The Truth Seeker*, January 19, 1878, pp. 36–39, and 42.

183. On the Slenker case, see Leigh Eric Schmidt, "The Obscene Atheist: Or, The Sexual Politics of Infidelity," in *Village Atheists: How America's Unbelievers Made Their Way in a Godly Nation* (Princeton, NJ: Princeton University Press, 2016), 210–48. Also see Gaylor, *Women without Superstition*, 237–39.

184. On the Sanger case, see Werbel, *Lust on Trial*, 297–99. Also see Gaylor, *Women without Superstition*, 401–406.

185. For the details of Reynolds's life, see Putnam, *400 Years of Freethought*, 792–94; also see the biography on the Freethought Trail website: https://freethought-trail.org/profiles/profile:reynolds-charles-b/, accessed March 28, 2022. Reynolds is listed as the chair of the American Secular Union Executive Committee in *The Truth Seeker*, September 11, 1886, p. 580, col. 1.

186. For the Jobstown incident, see *The Truth Seeker*, January 2, 1886, p. 5, col. 3; *The Truth Seeker*, January 9, 1886, p. 21, col. 2.

187. It is hard to explain why she is called Mrs. Frank Reynolds and not Mrs. Charles Reynolds if she is his wife. They both are listed as living in Rochester, New York, and then both listed as living in North Parma, New York. Perhaps she is a sister-in-law.

188. A handbill promoting the lectures of Ex-Reverend Charles B. Reynolds and Mrs. Frank C. Reynolds in Hornellsville, New York, March 20–21, 1886, lists these titles. The handbill is in the collection of the Robert Green Ingersoll birthplace museum. Available online: https://freethought-trail.org/historical-events/event:lectures-by-rev-and-mrs-c-b-reynolds/, accessed March 28, 2022. Mrs. Frank C. Reynolds is listed as having been elected secretary of the New York State Freethinkers' Association in *The Truth Seeker*, September 18, 1886, p. 597, col. 2. Both Charles B. and Mrs. Frank C. Reynolds are listed as residents of North Parma, New York.

189. *The Truth Seeker*, March 6, 1886, p. 148, col. 3.

190. "Reynolds Arrested for Blasphemy," *The Truth Seeker*, August 7, 1886, pp. 504–505. Also see "On Trial for Blasphemy: Col. Ingersoll's Defense of Charles B. Reynolds. History of the Events Which Created Such Intense Excitement in Two New-Jersey Towns," *New York Times*, May 20, 1887, p. 8, cols. 4–5.

191. "Mr. Ingersoll Will Defend Mr. Reynolds," *The Truth Seeker*, August 21, 1886, p. 537, col. 1.

192. *The Truth Seeker*, September 4, 1886, p. 561.

193. "Blasphemy and the Bible," *The Truth Seeker*, October 9, 1886, pp. 646–47; "Blasphemy and the Bible—Continued," *The Truth Seeker*, October 16, 1886, pp. 658–59. The pamphlet's publication is first announced on p. 665 of this issue, bottom of col. 3.

194. "Blasphemy. Reynolds Indicted for the Crime of Libeling a Ghost," *The Truth Seeker*, October 30, 1886, pp. 696–97; "On Trial for Blasphemy: Col. Ingersoll's Defense of Charles B. Reynolds. History of the Events Which Created Such Intense Excitement in Two New-Jersey Towns," *New York Times*, May 20, 1887, p. 8, cols. 4–5.

195. J. B. W. "Christianity and the Law," *New Jersey Law Journal* 2, no. 10 (1879): 295, available on GB; "Blasphemy and the Original Meaning of the First Amendment," *Harvard Law Review* 135, no. 2 (December 2021): n. 33, available online: https://harvardlawreview.org/2021/12/blasphemy-and-the-original-meaning-of-the-first-amendment/, accessed March 28, 2022. The judge, Francis Child, told the jury the history of the New Jersey blasphemy statute in his instruction to them. See *The Truth Seeker*, May 28, 1887, p. 345, col. 2. The text of the version of the statute current in 1887 is quoted in the *New York Times* article cited in the previous note, "On Trial for Blasphemy."

196. Robert Green Ingersoll and Isaac Newton Baker, *Trial of C. B. Reynolds for Blasphemy, At Morristown, N.J., May 19th And 20th, 1887* (New York City: C. P. Farrell, 1899), 3. Available on HT.

197. Ingersoll, *Trial of C. B. Reynolds*, 67–68.

198. "Convicted and Fined," *The Truth Seeker* of May 28, 1887, p. 344, cols. 2–3.

199. Putnam, *400 Years of Freethought*, 793–94.

200. Putnam, *400 Years of Freethought*, 793.

201. Ingersoll, *Trial of C. B. Reynolds*, 14–15.

202. Putnam, *400 Years of Freethought*, 22, 19.

203. Putnam, *400 Years of Freethought*, 476–516.

204. Putnam, *400 Years of Freethought*, 11.

205. Putnam, *400 Years of Freethought*, 527.

206. "Rededication of Paine's Monument," in *The Truth Seeker*, June 4, 1881, p. 356, col. 3 to p. 357, col. 1, accessed September 30, 2023.

207. See the extract of the minutes of the first meeting of the TPNHA quoted by Gary Berton, a contemporary secretary of the TPNHA, in "The Thomas Paine National Historical Association: Freethought, Anarchism, and the Struggle for Free Speech, Part I," *The Truth Seeker* 141 (September 2014): 19.

208. "In Memory of Paine," *The Truth Seeker*, June 9, 1894, p. 356, col. 2 to p. 360, col. 2.

209. "Paine's 'Age of Reason' Still Potent," *The Truth Seeker*, July 6, 1918, p. 429, col. 2.

210. See the "History" section of the "About Us" page of the Thomas Paine National Historical Association website: https://www.thomaspaine.org/pages/about-us.html, accessed October 2, 2023. For Conway's own account of his life, see Moncure Daniel Conway, *Autobiography: Memories and Experiences of Moncure Daniel Conway in Two Volumes* (Boston: Houghton, Mifflin and Company, 1904).

211. "Frederick Douglass to William Potter, May 15, 1874," full text quoted in Frederic May Holland, *Frederick Douglass: The Colored Orator* (Toronto: Funk & Wagnalls, 1891), 334–35.

212. William James Potter, *The Free Religious Association: Its Twenty-five Years and Their Meaning: An Address for the Twenty-fifth Anniversary of the Association, at Tremont Temple, Boston, May 27th, 1892* (Boston: Free Religious Association of America, 1892), 2. Available on GB. For more on Douglass's evolution toward freethought, see William L. Van Deburg, "Frederick Douglass: Maryland Slave to Religious Liberal," in Anthony Pinn, *By These Hands: A Documentary History of African American Humanism* (New York: NYU Press, 2001), 83–100; Christopher Cameron, *Black Freethinkers: A History of African American Secularism* (Evanston, IL: Northwestern University Press, 2019), 26–34.

213. Mr. Carr, "The Negro's Viewpoint of the Negro Question," *The Truth Seeker*, May 23, 1903, 326–27. For discussion, see Cameron, *Black Freethinkers*, 36–38.

214. W. L. Dolphyn, "Must Lynch Them," *The Truth Seeker*, October 30, 1903, p. 634, and J. M. Benjamin, *The Truth Seeker*, December 12, 1903, p. 790. For commentary, see Cameron, *Black Freethinkers*, 38.

215. "Colored Freethinkers," *Boston Investigator*, July 17, 1889, 5, cited in Nathan Alexander, *Race in a Godless World: Atheism, Race, and Civilization, 1850–1914* (Manchester: Manchester University Press, 2019), 250, n34.

216. Eugene MacDonald, "The Negro Problem," *The Truth Seeker*, March 7, 1903, 148, cited in Cameron, *Black Freethinkers*, 183n68.

217. On Cincore and Harrison, see Cameron, *Black Freethinkers*, 34–35 and 84–89.

218. "Negros Praised Him: What Prominent Colored Men of Washington Said About Robert G. Ingersoll," *The Truth Seeker*, April 20, 1901, p. 246. Cited in Cameron, *Black Freethinkers*, 182n61.

219. Cameron, *Black Freethinkers*, 43–80.

220. Jonathan Mayo Crane, "Reproduction of the Unfit," *American Journal of Eugenics* 1, no.1 (July 1907): 17.

221. Victoria Claflin Woodhull, *The Rapid Multiplication of the Unfit* (London: Women's Anthropological Society of America, 1891), 1. Available on GB.

222. Woodhull, *Rapid Multiplication*, 18.

223. Woodhull, *Rapid Multiplication*, 22.

224. See Tom Flynn, "The Tale of *The Truth Seeker*," on the website of the Center for Inquiry, published September 13, 2018. Available online: https://centerforinquiry.org/blog/the-tale-of-the-truth-seeker/, accessed October 5, 2023. Tom Flynn was the executive director of the Council for Secular Humanism at the time of his death in August 2021, a man who had devoted much of his career to preserving the legacy of the freethought movement.

225. John A. Farrell incorporated this memorable phrase into the title of his book *Clarence Darrow: Attorney for the Damned* (New York: Vintage, 2011).

226. Clarence Darrow, *The Story of My Life* (New York: Da Capo Press, 1932), 14.

227. These essays are collected in *The Agnostic Lawyer: Clarence Darrow Explains His Disbelief in God, Christianity, and the Bible* (Walnut, CA: Mount San Antonio College, 2016).

228. Darrow, *The Story of My Life*, 381.

229. For a more detailed account of the incident and its aftermath, see Martin S. Pernick, *The Black Stork: Eugenics and the Death of Defective Babies in American Medicine and Motion Pictures Since 1915* (Oxford: Oxford University Press, 1996), 3–12.

230. *Washington Post*, November 18, 1915, p. 1, col. 6.

231. Clarence Darrow, "The Edwardses and the Jukeses," *The American Mercury*, October 1925, 147–57. Available on HT.

232. Clarence Darrow, "The Eugenics Cult," *The American Mercury*, May 1926, 129–37. Available on HT.

233. Flynn, "The Tale of *The Truth Seeker*."

234. A 1911 pamphlet entitled, *The American Secular Union: Its Principles, Purposes and Demands and State Secularization of Government*, by Fritz Mauthner, Jacob Kendrick Upton, Will Herberg, and Nathaniel Bradstreet Shurtleff (Boston: Damrell and Upham, 1911) is listed on GB.

235. The debate about the name and the convention are described in an article, "The Cincinnati Liberal Congress," by John Maddock in *Freethought Magazine* 20 (March 1902): 159–65. Available on GB.

236. Frank Swancara, *The Separation of Religion and Government: The First Amendment, Madison's Intent, And the McCollum Decision: A Study of Separationism in America* (New York: Truth Seeker Company, 1950). Available at HT. The endorsement is on the title page.

237. Robert G. Ingersoll, *Lectures of Col. R. G. Ingersoll, Latest* (Chicago: Rhodes and McClure Publishing Company, 1898), 455. Available on GB.

238. Philip Hamburger, *Separation of Church and State* (Cambridge, MA: Harvard University Press, 2002), 191.

239. Steven Green presents evidence that a Common Council of New York City, which was charged with judging requests of public funding for schools, rejected a funding request from the Methodist Charity School in 1831 because it violated the state constitution, but it granted funds to a Catholic orphan asylum, reasoning that it was not primarily an educational institution. See Green's "The 'Second Disestablishment,'" in T. Jeremy Gunn and John Witte, *No Establishment of Religion: America's Original Contribution to Religious Liberty* (Oxford: Oxford University Press, 2012), 295–97.

240. Hamburger, *Separation of Church and State*, 236.

241. See *Prospect: Or, View of the Moral World*, June 9, 1804, vol. 1, issue 27, pp. 211–14 and September 1, 1804, vol. 1, issue 39, pp. 326–27. Available on GB. See the following articles in *The Free Enquirer*. On church-state separation in general: "Religion a State Engine," December 3, 1828, p. 46; "A Meeting of Free Men," August 19, 1829, p. 339; "Address delivered at the New York Hall of Science the 18th October 1829," October 31, 1829, pp. 1–5; "Memorial," February 4, 1832, pp. 119–20. On chaplains employed by government: "Report of the Select Committee of the Several Memorials Against Appointing Chaplains to the Legislature" [in two parts], May 19, 1832, pp. 234–36, May 26, 1832, pp. 244–45; "Chaplains. Remarks of Mr. Herttell," February 2, 1833, pp. 116–17. On Bible oaths: "Honesty," December 10, 1828, pp. 52–53; "Communications," June 19, 1830, pp. 271–72; "Connecticut Religious Freedom Bill," June 19, 1830, p. 272; "New Fangled Doctrine," June 26, 1830, pp. 278–79; "Right of Conscience," December 18, 1830, pp. 63–64; "Tammany Hall," February 23, 1833, pp. 143–44; "Competency of a Witness," September 14, 1833, p. 375;

"Rights and Competency of Witnesses. Speech of Mr. Herttell," May 17, 1835, pp. 156–57. On Sabbath laws: "U.S. Senate Committee Report Submitted by Senator Richard M. Johnson of Kentucky Concerning the Several Petitions Submitted on the Subject of the Sunday Mails," November 19, 1828, pp. 30–31; "Liberty of the Citizen," January 21, 1829, pp. 102–103; "Public Outrage," September 30, 1829, p. 391; "Sunday Mail Question," March 27, 1830, pp. 169–72. On blasphemy laws: "Re-Establishment of the Tribunal of the Holy Inquisition in Boston, Mass., in the Year of Our Lord, 1834!!!" January 19, 1834, p. 97; "The Defence of Abner Kneeland," February 9, 1834, p. 125; "My Philosophical Creed," February 9, 1834, p. 126; "The Item," February 9, 1834, p. 127; "The Indictment of the Editor for Blasphemy," February 16, 1834, p. 134; "Kneeland's Sentence," February 23, 1834, p. 134; "Trial for Blasphemy," March 30, 1834, p. 181; "Trial of the Editor," June 8, 1834, p. 264; "To the Hon. Judge Wilde," January 25, 1835, pp. 30–31.

242. Hamburger, *Separation of Church and State*, 302.

243. See Doress-Worters, *Mistress of Herself*, 182.

244. This is especially evident in the reasoning behind an 1869 Ohio Supreme Court decision about Bible reading in Cincinnati public schools that is reviewed by Green. The court was forced to conclude that religious matters were "not within the realm of human government" by the impossibility of finding a version of the Bible acceptable to both Protestants and Catholics. See Green, "The 'Second Disestablishment,'" 291–92.

245. Hamburger, *Separation of Church and State*, 285 and 335.

Chapter 5 • The Fourth Wave of American Freethought

1. "Joseph Lewis, Publisher, Dead; Crusader for Atheism Was 79," *New York Times*, November 5, 1968, p. 47, cols. 2–3.

2. Mary Braggiotti explores Lewis's devotion to Paine in "A Paine-inspired Quest for Knowledge," *New York Post*, September 5, 1945. She writes, "He first became acquainted with his idol [Paine] through a large volume of R. G. Ingersoll's lectures brought into the house by an older brother."

3. Lewis wrote a book on Paine arguing that Paine was, in spirit at least, the true author of the Declaration of Independence: *Thomas Paine: Author of the Declaration of Independence* (New York: Freethought Press, 1947). He published a collection of Ingersoll's "gems," *Ingersoll the Magnificent* (New York: Freethought Press, 1957), and in the early 1950s, led the effort to restore the house he was born in. Books available on GB.

4. "Attack on Bible in School Is Banned," *New York Times*, March 30, 1922, p. 36, col. 2.

5. "Cannot Deride Bible in Schools," *New York Times*, April 9, 1922, p. 31, col. 6.

6. For a short version of the history of the American Humanist Association, see the "Our History" page of the association's website: https://americanhumanist.org/about/our-history/, accessed October 9, 2023. For a more detailed and fully documented account, see William F. Schulz, *Making the Manifesto: The Birth of Religious Humanism* (Boston: Skinner House Books, 2002), 15–53. Available on GB.

7. Charles Francis Potter and Clara Cook Potter, *Humanism: A New Religion* (New York: Simon and Schuster, 1930), 14. Available on the IA.

8. For the text of the manifesto, see Schulz, *Making the Manifesto*, xxv–xxviii.

9. American Humanist Association, see the "Our History" page of the association's website: https://americanhumanist.org/about/our-history/, accessed October 9, 2023.

10. See Bryan F. Le Beau, *The Atheist: Madalyn Murray O'Hair* (New York: New York University Press, 2003), 3. For two sample press references to junior atheist clubs in the 1920s, see "Rochester Students Form Atheist Society: Thirteen in University Organize as 'Damned Souls' to 'Abolish Belief in God,'" *New York Times*, March 4, 1926, p. 23, col. 8; "Starts Yale Atheist Club: Freeman Hopwood Is Not Satisfied With Freethinkers' Society," *New York Times*, May 12, 1926, p. 19, col. 2.

11. For a brief essay on Queen Silver's life, see "Queen Silver" on the website of the Freedom from Religion Foundation: https://ffrf.org/ftod-cr/item/14705-queen-silver, accessed October 9, 2023. For a book-length biography, see Wendy McElroy, *Queen Silver: The Godless Girl* (Amherst, NY: Prometheus Books, 2000). For an accessible collection of archival materials, including many issues of Queen Silver's magazine, see https://www.queensilver.org/, accessed October 9, 2023. The quotation from "God's Place in Capitalism" is taken from the text of the speech included in McElroy's *Queen Silver*, p. 215. Also see Annie Laurie Gaylor, *Women without Superstition, "No Gods, No Masters": The Collected Writings of Women Freethinkers of the Nineteenth and Twentieth Centuries* (Madison, WI: Freedom from Religion Foundation, 1997), 457–59.

12. See R. Alton Lee, *Publisher for the Masses, Emanuel Haldeman-Julius* (Lincoln: University of Nebraska Press, 2017), 93–99.

13. For a list of Little Blue Books held by Kent State University, see https://www.library.kent.edu/special-collections-and-archives/haldeman-julius-publications-little-blue-books#series1, accessed October 25, 2023.

14. For Scopes's account of these events, see John Thomas Scopes and James Presley, *Center of the Storm; Memoirs of John T. Scopes* (New York: Holt, Rinehart and Winston, 1967), 55–62. Scopes's arrest was reported in the *New York Times*, May 7, 1925, although it was not exactly a front-page item. See "Arrest Evolution Teacher: Tennessee Authorities Start Test Case Under New Law," p. 40, col. 3. Also see Edward Larson, *The Summer for the Gods: The Scopes Trial and America's Continuing Debate over Science and Religion* (Cambridge, MA: Harvard University Press, 1997), 88–92.

15. William Jennings Bryan, *The Menace of Darwinism* (New York: Fleming H. Revell Company, 1921), 22. Available on GB.

16. Michael Lienesch, *In the Beginning: Fundamentalism, the Scopes Trial, and the Making of the Antievolution Movement* (Chapel Hill: University of North Carolina Press, 2007), 115.

17. Clarence Darrow, *The Story of My Life* (Boston: Da Capo Press, 1932/1996), 249.

18. See *The World's Most Famous Court Trial, Tennessee Evolution Case: A Complete Stenographic Report of the Famous Court Test of the Tennessee Anti-evolution Act, at Dayton, July 10 to 21, 1925, Including Speeches and Arguments of Attorney* (Cincinnati: National Book Company, 1925), 300. Available on GB. The full cross-examination runs from p. 284 to 304. See references to Jonah (p. 285), Joshua (pp. 284–85), the flood (pp. 288–89), Caine's wife (p. 302), and the snake (p. 304).

19. *World's Most Famous Court Trial*, 299.

20. Lienesch, *In the Beginning*, 165–66; Larson, *Summer for the Gods*, 191–93.

21. Lienesch, *In the Beginning*, 166.
22. Lienesch, *In the Beginning*, 167.
23. Lienesch, *In the Beginning*, 168; 173–74.
24. Lienesch, *In the Beginning*, 169; "Scopes Goes Free, But Law Is Upheld," *New York Times*, January 16, 1927, p. 1, col. 2, p. 28.
25. "Tennessee Ending Its 'Monkey Law,'" *New York Times*, May 17, 1967, p. 49, col. 8.
26. Lienesch and Larson both point to Frederick Lewis Allen's *Only Yesterday: An Informal History of the 1920s* (New York: Harper, 1964/1931), 163–71, as a book that popularized the Scopes trial as a confrontation between enlightened science and benighted fundamentalism. See Lienesch, *In the Beginning*, 203–204; Larson, *Summer for the Gods*, 225–30.
27. The film was based on a play with the same title by Jerome Lawrence and Robert E. Lee (not the general) first staged in 1955. See Lienesch, *In the Beginning*, 217–18.
28. "Schools and Religious Instruction," *New York Times*, June 24, 1925, p. 16, col. 5.
29. "Darrow Offers Aid to Freethinkers," *New York Times*, June 11, 1925, p. 2, col. 4.
30. "Use of School Time for Religion Barred," *New York Times*, June 23, 1925, p. 1, col. 6.
31. "Fight School Time to Teach Religion," *New York Times*, January 17, 1926, p. 16, col. 1.
32. "School Dismissal for Religion Legal," *New York Times*, April 25, 1926, p. 1, col. 3. This series of events is also discussed by George MacDonald in *Fifty Years of Freethought: Being the Story of the "Truth Seeker," with the Natural History of Its Third Editor* (New York: Truth Seeker Company, 1929 and 1931), vol. 2, pp. 615–67.
33. "Wants WNYC to Ban Religious Service: Freethinker Protests on Yom Kippur Music," *New York Times*, September 17, 1926, p. 8, col. 6; "Renews Radio Protest: Joseph Lewis Opposes Use of WNYC for Catholic Bishop's Speech," *New York Times*, September 21, 1926, p. 9, col. 4.
34. "Pledge's 'Under God' Is Opposed in Court," *New York Times*, November 10, 1956, p. 40, col. 5.
35. "Dr. Jacobs Sued on Birth Control: Freethinkers Asking Court to Lift Ban on Therapy in Municipal Hospitals," *New York Times*, August 19, 1958, p. 56, col. 1.
36. "Religion: The Enemy of God," *Time* magazine, November 11, 1935. Available online: http://content.time.com/time/subscriber/article/0,33009,848192-1,00.html, accessed May 27, 2022.
37. The page before the title page of *Ingersoll the Magnificent* lists all of Lewis's publications through 1957. Many of Lewis's earlier titles were issued by Truth Publishing Company.
38. On the legal woes brought on by the publication of *Sexual Problems of Today*, see Jay A. Gertzman, *Bookleggers and Smuthounds: The Trade in Erotica, 1920–1940* (Philadelphia: University of Pennsylvania Press, 2011), 25–26. A copy of *Sexual Problems of Today*, published by Truth Publishing Company, is available on GB: William J. Robinson, *Sexual Problems of Today*, 10th ed. (New York: Truth Publishing Company, 1921/1914).

39. Braggiotti, "A Paine-inspired Quest for Knowledge." Also see the "Restorations" section on the page "Robert Green Ingersoll Birthplace Museum" on the website of the Freethought Trail: https://freethought-trail.org/trail-map/location:robert-green-Ingersoll-birthplace-museum/, accessed May 27, 2022.

40. The caption of a photo from the early 1950s of the Ingersoll birth house identifies two figures in front of the house as Arthur and Ruth Cromwell, explains that they were Lewis's "primary agents" for restoration work on the house, and notes that they are the parents of Vashti McCollum. The photo, identified as the property of the Ingersoll Committee, is available online: https://en.wikipedia.org/wiki/Joseph_L._Lewis#/media/File:Arthur_and_Ruth_Cromwell_at_Ingersoll_house,_1950s.jpg, accessed, May 28, 2022.

41. Vashti McCollum tells the story of her early life in her memoir, *One Woman's Fight* (Garden City, NY: Doubleday & Company, 1951), 9–16. Also see Gaylor, *Women without Superstition*, 463–64.

42. McCollum, *One Woman's Fight*, 12; the reporter is quoted in Dannel McCollum, *The Lord Was Not on Trial: The Inside Story of the Supreme Court's Precedent-setting McCollum Ruling* (Silver Springs, MD: Americans for Religious Liberty, 2008), 39. A PBS documentary about Vashti McCollum's quest for constitutional separation of church and state titled *The Lord Is Not on Trial Here Today* was released in 2010. It was directed by Jay Rosenstein and won a Peabody Award, according to the Internet Movie Database.

43. McCollum, *The Lord Was Not on Trial*, 1.

44. McCollum, *One Woman's Fight*, 14.

45. McCollum, *The Lord Was Not on Trial*, 14, 247.

46. Arthur Cromwell had written a pamphlet titled "Rationalism vs. Religious Education in the Public Schools" that is included as an exhibit in her 1947 appeal to the US Supreme Court. See *Transcript of Record, Supreme Court of the United States, October Term 1947, No. 90*. Filed May 15, 1947 (Washington, DC: Judd & Detweiler Inc., June 26, 1947), 17–44. Available online on GB: https://www.google.com/books/edition/Records_and_Briefs_of_the_United_States/6tBej5uGc1gC?hl=en&gbpv=0, accessed May 28, 2022. Note that this item is mislabeled on Google Books as having been published in 1832. Arthur Cromwell also published *Memoirs of a Freethinker* in 1964.

47. McCollum, *One Woman's Fight*, 19.

48. McCollum, *One Woman's Fight*, 23, 28–29.

49. McCollum, *One Woman's Fight*, 59.

50. McCollum, *The Lord Was Not on Trial*, 39.

51. McCollum, *The Lord Was Not on Trial*, 39.

52. McCollum, *The Lord Was Not on Trial*, xiv.

53. McCollum, *One Woman's Fight*, 81–82.

54. McCollum, *The Lord Was Not on Trial*, 130.

55. McCollum, *One Woman's Fight*, 156–58.

56. McCollum, *The Lord Was Not on Trial*, 145.

57. McCollum, *One Woman's Fight*, 160.

58. McCollum, *One Woman's Fight*, 169.

59. Philip Hamburger, *Separation of Church and State* (Cambridge, MA: Harvard University Press, 2002), 455–56.

60. Roger K. Newman, *Hugo Black: A Biography* (New York: Pantheon Books, 1994), 361–62. Available from the IA.
61. Gitlow v. New York, 268 U.S. 652 (1925), available online: https://supreme.justia.com/cases/federal/us/268/652/, accessed February 21, 2022.
62. Cantwell v. Connecticut, 310 U.S. 296 (1940), available online: https://supreme.justia.com/cases/federal/us/310/296/#tab-opinion-1936772, accessed May 25, 2024.
63. Newman, *Hugo Black*, 27–30.
64. Newman, *Hugo Black*, 234–35.
65. Newman, *Hugo Black*, 91–92. For a full exposition of Black's connections to the Klan, see Hamburger, *Separation of Church and State*, 422–34.
66. Newman, *Hugo Black*, 257–60.
67. Todd C. Peppers, "Justice Hugo L. Black, His Chambers Staff, and the Ku Klux Klan Controversy of 1937," published April 27, 2021, available on the website of the Supreme Court Historical Society: https://supremecourthistory.org/scotus-scoops/justice-hugo-black-ku-klux-klan-controversy-1937/, accessed May 24, 2024.
68. Everson v. Board of Education, 330 U.S. 1 (1947), available online: https://supreme.justia.com/cases/federal/us/330/1/#F2/8, accessed May 25, 2024.
69. Everson v. Board of Education, 330 U.S. 1 (1947), available online: https://supreme.justia.com/cases/federal/us/330/1/#F2/8, accessed May 25, 2024.
70. Everson v. Board of Education, 330 U.S. 1 (1947), available online: https://supreme.justia.com/cases/federal/us/330/1/#F2/8, accessed May 25, 2024.
71. Everson v. Board of Education, 330 U.S. 1 (1947), available online: https://supreme.justia.com/cases/federal/us/330/1/#F2/8, accessed May 25, 2024.
72. McCollum, *One Woman's Fight*, 149–50.
73. McCollum, *One Woman's Fight*, 154.
74. McCollum, *One Woman's Fight*, 172, 175.
75. Newman, *Hugo Black*, 364–65.
76. McCollum v. Board of Education, 333 U.S. 203 (1948), available online: https://supreme.justia.com/cases/federal/us/333/203/#tab-opinion-1939314, accessed May 25, 2024.
77. McCollum, *One Woman's Fight*, 183.
78. The photo is reproduced in McCollum, *The Lord Was Not on Trial*, 152.
79. See the "Our History" page of the website of the American Humanist Association: https://americanhumanist.org/about/our-history/, accessed October 25, 2023.
80. "3 Faiths File Brief for Released Time," *New York Times*, June 17, 1948, p. 27, col. 8.
81. "Joseph Lewis, Publisher, Dead; Crusader for Atheism Was 79," *New York Times*, November 5, 1968, p. 47, cols. 2–3.
82. See Steven Green, *The Second Disestablishment: Church and State in Nineteenth-Century America* (Oxford: Oxford University Press, 2010), 12.
83. Hamburger, *Separation of Church and State*, 462.
84. Exalted Cyclops, *Principles and Purposes of the Knights of the Ku Klux Klan, Outlined by an Exalted Cyclops of the Order* (No Place: No Publisher, 1920), 4, available online from the University of Maine Digital Commons: https://digitalcommons.library.umaine.edu/cgi/viewcontent.cgi?article=1071&context=paul_bean_papers, accessed May 28, 2024.

85. Exalted Cyclops, *Principles and Purposes*, 8.

86. Everson v. Board of Education, 330 U.S. 1 (1947), available online: https://supreme.justia.com/cases/federal/us/330/1/#F2/8, accessed May 25, 2024.

87. Hamburger, *Separation of Church and State*, 481.

88. Hamburger, *Separation of Church and State*, 165.

89. *The Debates and Proceedings of the Congress of the United States*, vol. 1 (Washington: Gales and Seaton, 1834), 757–58.

90. James Madison, "Detached Memoranda," in Forrest Church, ed., *The Separation of Church and State: Writings on a Fundamental Freedom by America's Founders* (Boston: Beacon Press, 2004), 138–39.

91. Hamburger, *Separation of Church and State*, 481.

92. Hamburger, *Separation of Church and State*, 462.

93. On the marriage and Black's friendship with Davies, see Newman, *Hugo Black*, 466. Although I have not been able to find it in the major collections of his work, there is a reference to Davies's sermon "The God of the Atheist" in his biography on the website of All Souls Church in Washington, DC, the Unitarian Universalist church where Davies was a minister for many of the years that Black served on the Supreme Court. Available online: https://all-souls.org/rev-a-p-davies/, accessed May 29, 2024.

Conclusion

1. See the "Our History" page on the website of Americans United for the Separation of Church and State: https://www.au.org/about-au/history/, accessed October 14, 2023.

2. See the "History" page on the website of American Atheists: https://www.atheists.org/about/history/, accessed October 14, 2023.

3. See "The History of CFI" page on the website of the Center for Inquiry: https://centerforinquiry.org/about/the-history-of-cfi/, accessed October 14, 2023.

4. See the "About the Freedom from Religion Foundation" page on the website of the Freedom from Religion Foundation: https://ffrf.org/about, accessed October 14, 2023.

5. See the "Welcome from Margaret Downey" page on the website of the Freethought Society: https://www.ftsociety.org/2010/06/28/welcome-to-the-free-thought-societys-website/, accessed October 14, 2023.

6. See the "Member Organizations" page on the website of the Secular Coalition for America: https://secular.org/about/members/, accessed October 14, 2023.

7. See "The Seven Principles" page on the website of the Unitarian Universalist Association: https://www.uua.org/beliefs/what-we-believe/principles, accessed October 14, 2023.

8. William F. Schulz, *Making the Manifesto: The Birth of Religious Humanism* (Boston: Skinner House Books, 2002), xiii–xiv. Available on GB.

9. On Quaker beliefs, see "What Do Quakers Believe?" on the Quakers.org website: https://quaker.org/faith-and-practice/, accessed October 14, 2023. On Swedenborgians, see the "Beliefs" page of the website of the Swedenborgian Church of North America: https://swedenborg.org/explore/beliefs/#, accessed October 14, 2023.

10. On Humanistic Judaism, see the "What Is Humanistic Judaism?" page on the website of Society for Humanistic Judaism: https://shj.org/meaning-learning/what-is

-humanistic-judaism/, accessed October 14, 2023. On Inayati Sufism, see the "Objects of the Inayatiyya" page on the inayatiyya.org website: https://inayatiyya.org/teachings/objects-of-the-inayatiyya/, accessed October 14, 2023.

11. On the number of Humanistic and Reconstructionist Jews: According to a Pew report of the Jewish population of the United States in 2020, there are 5.8 million Jews, and 4% come from a branch of Judaism other than Orthodox, Conservative, or Reform. These other branches are mainly Humanistic and Reconstructionist. Four percent of 5.8 million comes out to 232,000. See "Jewish Americans in 2020" (Washington, DC: Pew Research Center, 2021), 50, 57. Retrieved from https://www.pewforum.org/wp-content/uploads/sites/7/2021/05/PF_05.11.21_Jewish.Americans.pdf, accessed October 14, 2023. Data on the number of Unitarian Universalists are from the report "UUA Membership Statistics, 1961–2020," on the website of the Unitarian Universalist Association: https://www.uua.org/data/demographics/uua-statistics, accessed October 15, 2023. The figure on Zen Buddhism is a guess, grounded in the fact that there are about 1.5 million Buddhists in the United States, but that within that population, many varieties of Buddhism are represented. For Buddhism figures, see the report "The American Religious Landscape in 2020" on the website of the Public Religion Research Institute: https://www.prri.org/research/2020-census-of-american-religion/, accessed October 15, 2023. On Quaker numbers, see the "About Quakers" page on the website of the Friends General Conference: https://www.fgcquaker.org/quakerism/, accessed October 15, 2023.

12. These statistics about the distribution of religious identities in the United States are taken from the Pew Research Center's "Religious Landscape Study": https://www.pewresearch.org/religion/religious-landscape-study/, accessed October 15, 2023. The population numbers were arrived at by multiplying the population percentages given in that report by a current total US population of 332 million.

13. For a summary of the Secular Coalition's pro-science agenda, see the "Science" page on the group's website: https://secular.org/key-issue/science/?_ga=2.148284343.1822131806.1697462226-1776731864.1697462226, accessed October 16, 2023.

14. "In Depth Topics A to Z: Religion," available online from Gallup: https://news.gallup.com/poll/1690/Religion.aspx, accessed June 2, 2022.

15. Andrew L. Whitehead and Samuel L. Perry, *Taking America Back for God: Christian Nationalism in the United States* (New York: Oxford University Press, 2020), 35–38.

16. Quoted from the "Explicitly Christian" section of the Christian Liberty Party homepage: https://sites.google.com/site/christianlibertyparty/, accessed January 30, 2022.

INDEX

Abbot, Francis Ellingwood, 11, 13, 131–34, 140–41, 149, 162, 168–69, 182, 253n3. See also *The Index*

Abington School District v. Schempp (1963), 204, 207

abolition, 5, 9, 14, 88, 98, 177, 217; Garrison and, 153; Ingersoll and, 143, 174; Ludvigh and, 126; Owenites and, 128; Putnam and, 176; Ernestine Rose and, 120, 122, 124, 129; Frances Wright and, 97, 99, 102–6, 110

Adams, John, 29–30, 55, 57, 61–62, 73, 82, 226n45, 233n38

Adams, John Quincy, 91

African Americans: Black freethinkers, 177–80, 217; history of secularism and, 8–9; Jim Crow institutions, 178. See also abolition

The Age of Reason (Paine), 29–48; John Adams and, 30; American reception of, 16, 59–64, 80; antiscripturalism in, 40–44, 59, 128–29, 216; atheism and, 38–40; background to Paine's writing, 19, 28–29; Bennett and, 162; Boudinot and, 15–16, 89; British publication and reception of, 16–17, 60, 73, 116, 119; compared to Palmer's *Principles of Nature*, 70–71; contemporary reflection on meaning of, 219–20; deism and, 11, 13, 16, 29–30, 38, 40, 47, 61, 86; Democratic-Republicans and, 48; Eaton's addendum to, 92; Fellows as American publisher, 67, 74; French earlier version (*Le Siècle de la Raison*), 33–37, 39; French reception of, 16; launching freethought movement, 4–5, 13, 110, 177; Leland and, 58; liberal legacy of, 183; in Little Blue Books series, 190; Martin and Ferguson's lectures and, 19, 30–32, 45; natural theology and, 30–32; Palmer and, 70; scientific hope frame and, 44–46, 99, 107, 129; separationist frame and, 41–42, 129–30, 210; in two parts, 33

agnostics, 6; Darrow and, 181, 191; Ingersoll as "The Great Agnostic," 46, 142, 144; Charles Potter and, 189; scientific hope frame and, 46; third wave and, 138, 217; Unitarians and, 149; use of terms, 2, 138; US population of, 215; UUs and, 214

Aldridge, A. Owen, 45

Allen, Ethan, 45, 55, 57, 62, 233n37

American Association for the Advance of Atheism, 187, 190, 204

American Association of Spiritualists, 161

American Atheists, 187, 204, 213–14

American Bible Society, 16, 89–90

American Civil Liberties Union, 191

American Ethical Union, 214

American Humanist Association, 4, 187, 189–90, 203–4, 213, 218

American Humanist Society, 214

American Revolutionary era: debates on state constitution reform and, 82; deist leaders of, 48, 55–57, 62, 67; "first disestablishment" and, 53–59, 134, 204; Paine and, 20–21, 24, 27, 78. See also specific Revolutionary leaders

American Secular Union, 134, 169, 183

Americans United for the Separation of Church and State, 4, 42, 213, 216

American Unitarian Association, 130–31

Anglicans, 18–19, 34, 52–54

Annet, Peter, 3, 41, 51, 128
Anthony, Susan B., 122–23, 156
antiscriptural frame, 6; Bible knowledge required, 128; Darrow in Scopes trial and, 193; first wave and, 216; Ingersoll and, 147, 150; Paine's *Age of Reason* and, 40–44; Paine's legacy, 44, 80, 127; Palmer's *Principles of Nature* and, 70; second wave and, 93, 99, 127–29, 216; spiritualists and, 152; today's beliefs and, 216
atheists, 6; freethought movement and, 2; growth of societies, 190; d'Holbach and, 75; Lewis and, 189; Paine's *Age of Reason* and, 38–40; Ernestine Rose and, 120, 123, 128; scientific hope frame and, 42; Silver and, 13; third wave and, 138, 217; US population of, 215; UUs and, 214. *See also* American Atheists

Backus, Isaac, 42, 58
Baldwin, Rodger, 191
Ballou, Hosea, 111, 247n97
Baptists, 42, 52, 54, 58–59, 84–86, 89, 163. *See also* Danbury Baptists
Barlow, Joel, 35–36, 67, 74, 233n38
Bartlett, Caroline J., 149–50
The Beacon, 80, 117–18, 121, 125, 162
Beecher, Henry Ward, 164
Beecher, Lyman, 60–61
Bell, William C., 125
Bell, W. S., 166–67
Bellamy, Edward, 137
Benedict, Charles L., 167
Bennett, DeRobigne Mortimer (D. M.), 136, 159, 161–63; love letters to former employee, 169; obscenity prosecution of, 165–68; *Open Letter to Jesus Christ*, 166; at rededication of Paine's New Rochelle monument, 177; *The Truth Seeker Abroad*, 170
Bentham, Jeremy, 94, 101–2
Bible: availability, increase in, 89–90; "Bible riots" (Philadelphia 1844), 139, 211; deism and, 40; flat earth geography of, 176; Jefferson's personal edit of, 62, 232n37; King James version in public schools, 138–39; opposition to governmental promotion of, 84; reason applied to, 3; respect for, 216; Unitarians and, 50; as Word of God, 6, 53,

218. *See also* antiscriptural frame; public schools
Biddle, John, 50–51
Bill of Rights, 59–60, 82; Fourteenth Amendment incorporating application to states, 199. *See also specific amendments and clauses*
birth control and contraception, 111, 118, 171, 179, 195–96, 217–18
Black, Hugo, 10, 81, 83, 198–203, 205–7, 210
Black Nonbelievers, 214
Blaine, James Gillespie, and Blaine Amendment, 140–42, 145, 183
Blake, William, 24
blasphemy laws and prosecutions, 4, 10, 218; *Burstyn v. Wilson* (1952) ending, 204; in England, 49, 51–53, 128; Kneeland and, 110–15, 247n102; Reynolds and, 171–75; in US, 59, 93
Blount, Charles, 48–49
blue laws. *See* Sunday laws
Boston Investigator, 88, 112, 115, 124, 126–27, 129, 137, 177, 179
Boudinot, Elias, 15–16, 57, 60, 89; *The Age of Revelation*, 15
Brissot, Jacques Pierre, 25–27
Britain/England: blasphemy laws and prosecutions in, 49, 51–53, 128; Church of England, 18, 53–54; Conventicle Act (1664), 53; Corporation Act (1661), 53; deism in, 49; freethinkers as refugees from (second wave), 127; Glorious Revolution (1688), 49; Licensing Act's expiration (1695), 49; Robert Owen as British utopian socialist, 88, 93–95; Paine birthday celebrations originating in, 91–92, 242n13; Paine's *Age of Reason*, reception of, 16, 60, 73, 116, 119; Paine's remains taken to England by Cobbett, 116–17; Paine working on bridge project in, 21–22; Priestley as Unitarian leader in, 50; proposed monument to Paine in, 115–16; republicanism in, 127; "secularism" as term originated in, 138; sedition charges against Paine and his departure for France, 23–24; Seditious Meetings Act (1795), 92; Test Acts (1663 and 1673), 53; Toleration Act (1688/1689), 49, 52–53; Uniformity Act (1662), 52–53. *See also* War of 1812

Brooklyn Philosophical Association, 136
Bryan, William Jennings, 191–94
Bundy, John C., 169–70
Burke, Edmund, 22
Burstyn v. Wilson (1952), 204
Butler Act (Tennessee 1925), 191

California Spiritualist Association, 151
Calvinists, 64–65, 111
Cameron, Christopher: *Black Freethinkers*, 8–9, 179
Cantwell v. Connecticut (1940), 200–201
Carlile, Richard, 110, 128, 246n94
Carroll, Daniel, 57, 83
Carver, William, 74–75, 78, 90, 92, 117, 119
Cassadaga Lake Free Association, 154
Catholics: anti-Catholicism and relations with Protestants, 10, 139, 141, 184–85, 204, 206, 209; Black and, 200–201, 205; colonial and state treatment of, 18, 54; French Revolution's anticlerical sentiment, 33–34, 37–38, 41, 89; Klan and, 205–6, 210; Reynolds threatened by, 172–73; school-related issues, 138–39, 199, 202; in *Truth Seeker* cartoon, 163
Center for Freethought Equality, 4
Center for Inquiry, 5, 213–14
Chainey, George, 11, 154
Cheetham, James: *Life of Thomas Paine*, 89–91, 224n20, 238n114
Chénier, Marie-Joseph de, 37
"Christian Amendment" (proposed), 132–33, 138, 168, 182
Christianity: fundamentalism, 188, 192, 194, 198; government privileging of, 2, 6, 47–48; liberal Christianity and third wave, 132–33, 138; nationalist groups and agenda, 1, 55, 207–8, 210, 218; Paine's call to replace with scientific deism, 11, 70, 118; redemption theology, 30, 39; revealed religion and, 30. *See also* public office; public schools
Christian Liberty Party, 218
Church of England. *See* Anglicans
church-state relations. *See* nondenominationalism; separationism
Claflin, Tennessee, 12, 159–65
clandestine activities of deists and other religious rationalists, 5–6, 47, 51–52, 63, 80, 87

Clark, Thomas, 207
Clinton, George, 69, 74, 77
Cobbett, William, 115–18
Collective Behavior Theory, 6
collective identity formation, 6
Collins, Anthony, 3, 40
Colman, Lucy N., 155
Comstock, Anthony, and Comstock laws (1873), 163–71, 183; Hicklin test of obscenity and, 167; New York YMCA and, 163–64, 167; prosecution of D. M. Bennett, 165–68; prosecution of Ida Craddock, 170–71; prosecution of others for "obscene" publications, 171; repeal versus reform of laws, 168, 187
Congregationalists, 42, 54, 58–59, 65, 82, 112, 130
Congress, US: chaplains, 56, 83, 98, 133, 135, 185, 209; debate over First Amendment, 57
Congress of the Universal Federation of Freethinkers, 170
Constitution, US: Article VI, Clause 3, 54–55; "Christian Amendment" proposed, 132–33, 138, 168, 182; "Religious Freedom Amendment" proposed, 134, 141, 183, 187. *See also* Bill of Rights; *specific amendments and clauses*
Conway, Moncure Daniel, 11, 88, 117, 177–78
The Correspondent, 80, 92–93, 98, 129, 132
Council for Secular Humanism, 213
Craddock, Ida, 12–13, 170–71, 265n181
Cromwell, Arthur and Ruth, 196, 203

Danbury Baptists, Jefferson's letter to (1802), 10, 55–56, 59, 81, 84–86, 184–85, 203, 208–10
Darrow, Clarence, 180–83; enlightenment brought into twentieth century by, 17; Scopes trial, 189, 191–95, 205; "Why I Am an Agnostic," 181, 191
Darwinism, 137, 176, 192, 204, 218
Davies, Arthur Powell, 210, 274n93
Davis, Andrew Jackson, 12, 153
Dawkins, Richard, 213
de Bonneville, Marguerite, and family, 79–80, 90, 238n117
deism and deists: American Revolutionary leaders and, 48, 55–57, 62, 80, 86; as blasphemy, 52; Blasphemy Act (Britain 1697)

deism and deists (cont.)
and, 49; as clandestine activity pre-1794, 5–6, 47, 51–52, 63, 80; compared to Unitarians and other dissenters, 50–52; core tenet of, 48; defined, 16; dormant years following deaths of Paine and Palmer, 86–87, 89–91; in England, 49; European origins of, 48; Franklin and, 232n37; freethought movement and, 1–2; French Revolution and, 16, 37–38; Jefferson and, 85; natural theology and, 32; Robert Owen and, 96; Paine's *Age of Reason* and, 11, 13, 16, 29–30, 38, 40, 47, 61, 86; Radical Enlightenment and, 51; revival of Paineite deism, 17, 87, 127; scientific deism of Paine, 11, 46, 70; third wave and, 138; transformation into open social movement, 63–64, 80; US population involved in, 16, 63, 215

Deistical Society of New York: Clintonians as members, 77; Federalists targeting, 77, 80; formation of, by Palmer and Fellows, 48, 63–72, 74; in freethought movement, 4; non-Christian theology of members, 75–76, 128; offshoots of, 88, 106; Paine and, 48, 72–80, 127; Paine's birthday celebrations growing out of, 91–92; Palmer's lectures, 44, 68, 75, 78; science as universal cause of, 76–77; Sunday morning meetings, 11, 67–69, 81, 127, 129

Deist Society of Philadelphia, 63, 66

Democratic-Republicans (Jeffersonians), 48, 60–62, 64; John Quincy Adams and, 91; anti-British stance of, 116; deism and, 61, 64, 69, 77, 80; Paine and, 60; separation of church and state as American ideal for, 82, 84–85

Denniston, David, 69, 77

Derrick, Christopher, 78, 240n149

Diderot, Denis, 38, 40

disestablishment, 2, 5, 53–55; Baptist call for, 58–59; "first disestablishment" of Revolutionary era and passage of First Amendment, 53–59, 134, 204; Jefferson's vision of, 55–56; "second disestablishment" of nineteenth century, 10, 204; "third disestablishment" of Supreme Court cases, 10, 204–5, 217–18. *See also* separationism

dissenters: Blasphemy Act (1697) criminalizing, 49; colonial tolerance, variations in, 53–54; freethought movement beginning with, 11–12; non-Anglican Protestants as, 18; religiosity as important element of freethought movement, 12; state support for worship, issue of, 49, 201; Toleration Act (1688/1689) decriminalizing, 49; use of term, 52. *See also* deism and deists; Quakers

divorce law liberalization, 157

Dobbs v. Jackson Women's Health Organization (2022), 218

Doress-Worters, Paula Brown, 122–23

Douglass, Frederick, 161, 178

Driscol, Dennis, 72, 76

Duché, Jacob, 32

Eaton, Daniel Isaac, 92

Emerson, Ralph Waldo, 114, 131

Engel v. Vitale (1962), 204, 207, 218

Enlightenment, 16–17, 55, 219. *See also* Radical Enlightenment

Epicurus, 49, 101. *See also* neo-Epicureans

Epperson v. Arkansas (1968), 194, 204

Establishment Clause: applicable to states, 201–2; Black and, 201–2, 207; congressional debate on language, 57; federal in scope only, 54; fourth wave implications for current interpretation of, 205–12; Jefferson on, 55–56, 59, 184, 208–10; Lemon Test (from *Lemon v. Kurtzman*), 204; Madison as author of, 81, 83–85, 184, 209; nondenominationalist interpretation of, 82–83, 210; public aid to religious schools and, 199–202; Story on Christian privilege, 2; third wave implications for current interpretation of, 184–86. *See also* separationism

establishment of religion: Anglican Church and, 53–54; Madison on, 56; Paine's opposition to, 34. *See also* Establishment Clause

eugenics, 158, 178–82, 188, 217

evangelical religion, 16–17, 89–91

Everson v. Board of Education (1947), 81, 83, 198–204, 206–7, 210, 212

evolution, teaching of, 188, 191–94, 204, 218

The Examiners Examined; Being a Defense of "The Age of Reason" (anonymous), 47, 67, 230n1
Ex-Muslims of North America, 214

Faustus Socinus, 50
Federalists, 48, 61–62, 69, 72–73, 77–78, 80, 82, 91, 116
Fellows, John: clandestine deism of, 87; as deistic follower of Paine, 16; Deistical Society of New York created by Palmer and, 48, 74; Offen and, 92; *On the Character and Doctrines of Jesus Christ*, 67; Paine and, 67, 78, 119; Palmer and, 67–69, 71; *The Theophilanthropist* (journal), 80; Vale and, 117
feminism, 5, 14, 88, 98, 110, 129, 155–57, 217; eugenics and, 179; spiritualism and, 152; *Woodhull & Claflin's Weekly* and, 160
Ferguson, James, 19, 30–32, 45
First Amendment, 47, 53–57, 83, 199. *See also* Establishment Clause; freedom of speech; Free Exercise Clause
First Humanist Society of New York, 187, 189, 204
first wave, 7–8, 11–12, 47–87; American reception of Paine's *Age of Reason*, 59–64; background (before *Age of Reason*), 48–52; Deistical Society of New York and, 64–80; end of era, 80–81; Hamburger on era, 81–86; Revolutionary disestablishment and, 53–59. *See also* dissenters
Fischer, Kirsten, 64
Fouché, Joseph, 37
Fourteenth Amendment, 199, 205
fourth wave, 8, 12, 188–212; atheism and, 190; Establishment Clause, implications for current interpretation of, 205–12; *Everson* (1947) and, 198–203; Haldeman-Julius's publications and, 189–90; Lewis and origins of legal offensive, 194–96; *McCollum* (1948) and, 196–98; organizational renaissance, 188–90, 204; Scopes trial and, 191–94
Fox sisters (Margaretta, Catherine, and Leah), 150–51, 155, 160, 258n82
Franklin, Benjamin, 19–20, 32, 45, 52, 55–57, 62, 232n37

Freedom from Religion Foundation, 4, 42, 213, 216, 218
freedom of religion. *See* Establishment Clause; Free Exercise Clause; Religious Freedom Amendment
freedom of speech: National Defense Association as protector of, 168; New Jersey constitution on, 174; state laws and, 199. *See also* blasphemy laws; Comstock, Anthony, and Comstock laws; First Amendment; obscenity laws
Free Enquirer, 3, 80, 88, 98, 106–7, 129, 210; Annet's paper in London as precursor, 3, 128; on church-state issues, 185; originally *New Harmony Gazette*, 97, 106; on Paine birthday celebration (1833), 110
Free Exercise Clause, 54, 57, 59, 200–201
free love, 98, 156–58, 160, 166, 183, 217
Free Press Association, 4, 93
free religionist faction of third wave, 148–50, 182, 217
Free Religious Association, 11, 130–32, 149, 178; successors of, 187, 189
Free Speech League, 4
freethinkers and free thought movement: Black freethinkers, 177–80, 217; branches in third wave, 148–49; defined, 2–3; first wave, 7–8, 12, 47–87; fourth wave, 8, 12, 188–212; four waves of activity, 7–8; "infidels" as term for, 126, 128, 138; linking to movements of feminism, labor, and abolition, 88, 98–99, 129; Paineite and Owenite strains merged, 127; Palmer and, 64, 69; sacrifice for cause of, 111, 129; second wave, 8, 12, 88–129; as social movement, 4–6; terminology, 2–3, 138; third wave (golden age), 3, 130–87; tolerance and alliances of, 130, 148–59, 217; US population involved in, 215. *See also* deism and deists; disestablishment; first wave; fourth wave; second wave; third wave
Freethinkers' Association of Central and Western New York, 136–37
Freethinkers' Association of New York. *See* New York Freethinkers' Association
Freethinkers of America, 4, 187, 189, 195–96, 204
Freethought Press Association, 196
Freethought Society, 5, 213–14

French Revolution, 24–29; American sympathies with, 61, 99; anticlerical sentiment of, 33, 37–38, 41, 89; calendar revised, 98; Civic Constitution of the Clergy, 33–35, 41; Cordeliers Club and, 26, 28; Cult of Reason and Feasts of Reason, 16, 18, 37, 105, 228n70; dechristianization and, 37–39, 106, 228n73; *The Declaration of the Rights of Man and Citizen*, 22, 60; deism and, 16, 37–38; execution of Louis XVI, 27; first wave sparked by, 8; Girondins and, 25–28; illuminati secret societies blamed for, 77; Jacobins and Jacobin Club, 25–27, 38, 91; Law of Suspects (1793), 28; Montagnards and, 25–28; National Convention, 24–28, 33, 39; Paine and, 13, 21–22, 24–28, 33–40, 60, 76; Paris Commune and, 26–27; republicanism and, 8, 24, 26, 72; the Terror, 28, 35–36, 39, 60, 76

Freneau, Philip, 69

Frothingham, Octavius, 131, 149

Fugitive Slave Law debate, 143

fundamentalism. *See* Christianity

Gage, Matilda Joslyn, 155–56

Gardiner, D. T., 136

Garrison, William Lloyd, 114, 153

Gitlow v. New York (1925), 199

God. *See* antiscriptural frame; Bible; deism and deists

Grace, Benjamin, 32, 227n57

Grant, Ulysses S., 140–41

Greeley, Horace, 191, 261n119

Green, Steven K., 10, 53, 55; "first disestablishment," 204; "second disestablishment," 10, 204; "third disestablishment," 10, 204

Haldeman-Julius, Emanuel, and Little Blue Books, 190–91

Hamburger, Philip (*Separation of Church and State*): on Black's *Everson* decision, 210; Christian nationalist organizations and, 219; on first wave era, 81–86; on freethought movement, 10–11; on nineteenth-century anti-Catholicism, 184–86; on public funding of religious schools, 199; on separation of church and state law argument, 205–6, 208–10

Hammond, Charles, 119

Hargrove, John, 76, 217

Hartford Bible Convention (1853), 122, 152–54

Hayes, Rutherford B., 141, 167–68

Hébert, Jacques, 27–28

Helvétius, Claude-Adrien, 38, 40

Henry, Patrick, 54–55, 57

d'Héricourt, Jenny, 120, 123, 250n133

Herttell, Thomas, 122, 250n138

Heston, Watson, 162–63, 173

Heywood, Ezra: *Cupid's Yokes*, 166–68

Hicklin, Regina v. (Eng. 1868), 167

Hicklin test of obscenity, 167

Hicks, Elias, 155

Hispanic American Freethinkers, 214

d'Holbach, Baron (pseud. Mirabaud), 38, 40, 71, 75, 120

Holland, religious dissenters in, 50–51

Holyoake, George, 138

Houston, George, 92–93, 99, 117. *See also The Correspondent*

humanists, 3, 189–91, 213–15; Ingersoll and, 145; Unitarianism and, 149, 189. *See also* American Humanist Association

The Index, 131–34; editorial on Comstock laws (1878), 168; Free Religious Association and, 149; on Grant's proposal for nonsectarian schools and taxes on church properties, 140–41; "The Nine Demands of Liberalism" published in, 13, 130, 133–34, 138, 141, 149, 162, 182–83, 204, 216

Infidel Association of the United States, 4, 126, 128–29

Infidel Convention (1845), 122, 125–26

infidels and infidelity: *Age of Reason* and, 15, 48, 60–63, 89; Darrow and, 181; infidel clubs, 63; Ingersoll and, 144, 146; Klan on, 206; Kneeland blasphemy trial and, 114; Leland on, 58; Lewis and, 189; Paine and, 72–73, 80, 107; politicization of, 48, 62, 72–73, 80, 91; Second Great Awakening and, 89; Story and, 2; use of term, 3, 88, 126, 128–29, 138, 189

Infidel Society for the Promotion of Mental Liberty, 4, 126, 128–29

Ingersoll, Robert, 142–48; antiscriptural stance of, 147, 150; background of, 143–45;

Blaine Amendment and, 141; as civil rights advocate for African Americans, 179; Darrow and, 181; Davies and, 210; as defense attorney in Star Route scandal, 145; Douglass and, 178; Edison and, 148; free love and, 157; influence of, 17, 183, 196; Ingersoll Birthplace Museum (Dresden, NY), 148, 196, 203, 213; "The Liberty of Man, Woman, and Child" (speech), 146, 157; in Little Blue Books series, 191; as materialist, 149; National Liberal League and, 135; obscenity prosecution of D. M. Bennett, 166–67; oratory skills and lectures of, 142, 145–48; Paine and, 177, 188–89; as president of National Liberal League/American Secular Union, 154, 169, 173; Reynolds defended by, 173–75; scientific hope frame and, 45–46, 176

International Association of the Preservation of Spiritualist and Occult Periodicals, 152

Israel, Jonathan I., 17, 51, 127, 224n9

Jacoby, Susan: *Freethinkers*, 9, 130
Jarvis, John Wesley, 78–79, 119
Jay, John, 57, 89
Jefferson, Thomas: Bible, personal edit of, 62, 232n37; deism and belief in God, 1, 32, 52, 55–57, 62, 85, 232n37; Democratic-Republicans and, 48; influence of, 181; letter to Danbury Baptists (1802), 10, 55–56, 59, 81, 84–86, 184–85, 203, 208–10; letter to Waterhouse (1822), 1; *Notes on the State of Virginia*, 62; Paine and, 21, 32, 73, 238n114; presidency and presidential campaigns, 72, 82; as secretary of state, 25; on separation of church and state (*see* letter to Danbury Baptists, *above*); Tammany Society and, 69; as US minister to France, 21; Virginia Statute for Religious Freedom by, 55–56, 201; Frances Wright and, 102–3

Jeffersonians. *See* Democratic-Republicans

Jesus Christ, divinity of, 32, 40, 43, 50–51, 53–54, 56, 62, 65–67, 72, 113, 149, 151, 158, 166, 215, 218

Jews and anti-Semitism, 3, 18, 126, 131, 180, 200; Humanistic Judaism, 12, 214–15, 275n11; Reconstructionist Judaism, 215, 275n11

Johnson, James Harvey, 180, 182
Joyce, James, 167

Kaepernick, Colin, 7
Kaye, Harvey J., 9
Kennedy v. Bremerton School District (2022), 11, 218
Kent, Austin, 158
Kentucky, 61, 63, 89
Kirkbride, Joseph, 73–74
Kneeland, Abner, 11, 110–15, 124, 128–29, 149, 173, 217, 247n97
Knowlton, Charles, 111, 118, 125, 128–29
Know-Nothings, 139, 185–86
Ku Klux Klan, 10, 200–201, 205–11

Lafayette, Marquis de, 22, 25, 102–3, 246n82
Lant, John A., 171
Lanthenas, François-Xavier, 33
Law, William, 32
legal challenges in fourth wave, 7–8, 12, 187; Lewis as leader of, 13, 189, 194–96; Supreme Court cases, 196–204, 207, 212, 218
legislative reforms, failure to achieve, 187, 218
Leland, John, 42, 58–59, 85–86, 208–9; *The Rights of Conscience Inalienable*, 58, 84
Lemon v. Kurtzman (1971), 204
lessons learned, 216–20
Lewis, Joseph: background of, 188–89; enlightenment brought into twentieth century by, 17; legal offensive led by, 13, 189, 194–96, 203–5; Paine's influence on, 188–89, 269nn2–3; as president of Freethinkers of America, 195; as president of New York Society of Freethinkers, 188–89
LGBTQ rights, 217, 219
Liberal Leagues, 4, 134–37; 1875 little convention, 134; 1876 Liberal Congress, 134; 1878 convention, 162; 1879 to 1882 Annual Congresses, 135; 1884 convention, 154
Lincoln, Abraham, 132, 143, 253n15
Lindsey, Theophilus, 50
Lippard, George, 118–19
Louis XVI (French king), 22, 25–27, 33
Louisiana schools and Ten Commandments, 218
Lucretius, 49–50, 101
Ludvigh, Samuel, 126

MacDonald, Eugene, 162, 179
MacDonald, George E., 135–36, 162–63, 170, 180; *Fifty Years of Freethought*, 3, 135, 152, 176–77
Madison, James, 56–57, 74, 81, 83–85, 184, 208–9; *Memorial and Remonstrance against Religious Assessments*, 55–56, 201
Manhattan Liberal Club, 177–78
Manhattan Liberal League, 136
Marat, Jean-Paul, 26–27
marriage liberalization, 98, 157. *See also* free love
married women's property rights, 157; NY Married Women's Property Act (1860), 120, 122–23, 250n140
Martin, Benjamin, 19, 30–32, 45
materialists, 38, 148–49, 154, 182, 217
May, Henry, 17, 224n9
McClure, William, 95–96
McCollum, Vashti: background of, 196–98, 203; US Supreme Court case on separation of church and state (see *McCollum v. Board of Education*)
McCollum v. Board of Education (1948), 4, 183, 196–98, 202–5, 207
McGready, James, 89
Melucci, Alberto, 6
Meslier, Jean, 38, 40
Methodists, 32, 89, 163, 172–73, 227n57
Military Atheists, 214
Mill, James, and son John Stuart, 101
Minor v. Board of Education (1870, on appeal 1872), 139
Mockus, Michael, 175
Monroe, James, 36, 39, 102
Morris, Gouverneur, 36, 74
Mott, Lucretia, 123, 131, 156
movement framing, 6, 41–47. *See also* antiscriptural frame; scientific hope frame; separationism
movement repertoires, 6–7
movement waves: defined, 6–7; four waves of freethought (*see* freethinkers and free thought movement)

Napoléon, 73, 79–80, 102
Nashoba community, 103–4, 246n82
National American Woman Suffrage Association, 156
national days of prayer, 57, 84

National Defense Association, 4, 168, 170
National Liberal League, 42, 69, 130, 134–37, 155, 168–69, 182–83; D. M. Bennett and, 170; restructuring, 169, 183. *See also* Liberal Leagues; *and later name (American Secular Union)*
National Liberal Party, 183
National Reform Association, 132–33
National Women's Rights Convention (1850 & 1854), 122–23
nativism of nineteenth century, 10, 12, 139, 184, 209
natural theology and philosophy, 19, 30–32, 45, 48
nature's divinity, 30, 38, 45, 49, 113, 149
Néez (French citizen) and Paine's *Le Siècle de la Raison*, 33–35
neo-Epicureans, 49–51, 77, 101, 128
New Harmony Gazette, 97–98, 106
New Harmony utopian community, 93, 95–99, 102–6, 157
New Jersey blasphemy cases against Charles Reynolds, 171–75, 266n195
New Rochelle (NY): Paine Memorial Building as headquarters of TPNHA, 177; Paine's funeral in, 79; Paine's reburial and monument in, 117–18, 177
Newtonian science/philosophy, 19, 31, 176
New York: Married Women's Property Act (1860), 120, 122–23, 250n140; YMCA and anti-obscenity law, 163–64
New York Freethinkers' Association, 3–4, 137, 155, 168, 189; Convention (1878), 136, 166; successor of, 187–88
New York Liberal Association, 136
New York Society of Freethinkers, 187–89, 204
Nine Demands of Liberalism, 13, 130, 133–34, 138, 141, 149, 162, 182–83, 204, 216
nondenominationalism, 83, 141, 184–86, 199, 201, 204, 206, 210–11
Noyes, John Humphrey, 157–58
Nye, Stephen, 50

obscenity laws and prosecution, 163, 165–70. *See also* Comstock, Anthony, and Comstock laws
Offen, Benjamin: antiscriptural frame and, 44, 107; fundraiser for, 124; Houston and, 93; *A*

Legacy to the Friends of Free Discussion (lecture), 44; move to America, 92, 127; Paine birthday celebrations started in US by, 92, 124; Paine's influence on, 44, 99, 129; Palmer's deistic movement and, 14; Ernestine Rose and, 118; second wave and, 8, 88, 91–93, 127; Society of Moral Philanthropists and, 44, 92, 121, 128; Vale and, 117; Frances Wright and, 105

O'Hair, Madalyn Murray, 190, 213

Owen, Robert (father): blaming religion for social ills, 95, 98; as British utopian socialist, 88, 93–95; contemporary cooperatives derived from ideas of, 97; "declaration of mental independence" and, 98–99, 104, 126; as industrialist, 93–94; Infidel Convention (1845) and, 126; Kneeland and, 112; on marriage liberalization, 98; move to America, 95, 127; New Harmony, Indiana, as site of social experiment, 95–96; *The New Harmony Gazette* and, 97–98; Ernestine Rose and, 120; as second wave freethinker, 93–99, 127; spiritualism and, 11–12, 152; utopian agricultural vision of, 94–95; Frances Wright and, 101–3

Owen, Robert Dale (son), 95; divorce law liberalization and, 157; Free Religious Association and, 131; in Little Blue Books series, 191; *The New Harmony Gazette* and, 97, 106; as second wave freethinker, 127; spiritualism and, 152; as spiritualist, 11–12; Workingmen's Party and, 108–9; Frances Wright and, 103, 106, 108–9, 124, 246n82

Owenites, 88, 93–99, 121, 127–29, 152, 182

Paine, Thomas: John Adams and, 29; anti-Paine propaganda and rallies, 23–24, 73–74; background of, 18–29, 32; biographies of, 115, 249n128; Bonneville family and, 79–80; Brissot and, 25; in Britain for bridge project, 21–22; Burke refuted by, 22; Cheetham and, 89; Deistical Society of New York and, 48, 72–80; Democratic-Republican clubs and, 60; Derrick's attempt to kill, 78; drunkenness, unfounded allegations of, 110; Federalists targeting, 62, 72–73, 80; first wave ending with death of, 8, 80; fleeing Britain for revolutionary France, 24; Franklin and, 19–20, 32, 45; French Revolution and imprisonment of, 13, 21–22, 24–28, 33–40, 76; funeral in New Rochelle, 79; Hamburger on, 85; health decline and death of (1809), 77–79, 240n154; influence and legacy of, 9, 13, 17–18, 99, 109–10, 129, 177, 181, 196, 224n9; Jefferson and, 21, 32, 73, 238n114; Lafayette and, 22; letter to Samuel Adams (1802), 38; Lewis and, 188–89; Lippard on, 118; monuments to commemorate, 115–17, 129, 177; Offen and, 44, 99, 129; opposition to deism of, 17; Palmer and, 16, 69–70, 74–75; posthumous attacks on, 90–91; reburial and monument in New Rochelle, 117–18, 177; on religious belief as public matter, 107–8; remains taken to England by Cobbett, 117; return to America as media event (1802), 72; among Revolutionary-era deists, 55–57; as Revolutionary propagandist, 1, 20–21, 24–25; in Revolutionary War troops, 20–21, 224n20; sedition charges in Britain against and departure for France, 23–24; on separation of church and state, 84; voting rights and, 74, 78–79; women's rights and, 125

Paine, Thomas, writings by: *The American Crisis* (essays), 20–21, 224n20; *Common Sense* (pamphlet), 20, 22–23, 29, 60, 118; *Decline and Fall of the English System of Finance*, 67, 116; *Rights of Man*, 21–24, 33–34, 60, 62, 72–73, 99, 118, 124, 129, 225n26. See also *Age of Reason*

Paine birthday celebrations, 14, 91–93, 127; British origin of, 91–92, 242n13; Offen starting in US, 17, 91–92, 124; people toasted at as carrying on Paine's legacy, 110; Ernestine Rose and, 120, 122–25, 128, 186; second wave and, 8, 80, 88, 91–92, 129; third wave and, 177, 183; Frances Wright and, 105

Palmer, Elihu, 11, 13, 129, 230n1; antiscriptural frame and, 44, 107; background of, 64–67, 217, 235n72; death of (1806), 77–78, 239n145; deism and, 11, 14, 16, 72; Deistical Society of New York created by, 48, 64–72, 74; Democratic-Republicans and, 77; disestablishment and, 59; lectures at deistical

Palmer, Elihu (*cont.*)
societies, 44, 66, 68–69, 78, 92; Paine and, 16, 69–70, 74–75; *Principles of Nature*, 69–71, 74–75; Ernestine Rose compared to, 120. See also *The Prospect*
Palmer, Mary, 75, 78, 80
pantheists, 6; Deistical Society and, 72, 128; Kneeland and, 111–12, 128; materialism and, 38, 149; Palmer and, 71; Radical Enlightenment and, 51; as religious dissenters, 49; scientific hope frame and, 46; spiritualism and, 152–53; third wave and, 138
Penn, William, 54, 119
Pennsylvania: Charter of Privileges, 54; Constitution on religious test for public office, 212; disestablishment in, 54
Pitt, William, 23, 73
Pledge of Allegiance, 195
Polish Brethren, 50
Political Process Theory, 6
Porterfield, Amanda, 8
Post, Albert, 8
Post, Amy Kirby, 12, 135, 155
Post, Isaac, 12, 155
Potter, Charles Francis, 189
Potter, William J., 11, 130–31, 178
Presbyterians, 65, 89, 132, 163
Priestley, Joseph, 24, 50–51, 116
The Prospect, 71–72, 74, 76–78, 80, 98, 132, 185, 209
public office, religious tests for, 4, 10, 59, 84, 218; Article VI of US Constitution prohibiting, 54; non-Anglicans banned from, 18; in Pennsylvania, 54; *Torcaso v. Watkins* (1961) ending, 204, 207
public schools: *Abington School District* (1963) ending school-based Bible reading, 204, 207; busing costs of private and parochial school children, public funding used for, 199; *Engel* (1962) ending school prayer, 204, 207; evolution, teaching of, 188, 191–94, 204, 218; free and universal education, 109, 140; Klan's desire to enshrine Bible in, 207; *Lemon* (1971) prohibiting public funds to be used for religious school teacher salaries, 204; prayer/Bible reading/religious instruction in, 3, 10–11, 59, 138–42, 160, 195, 218, 269n244; release of pupils for religious instruction, 194–95, 197; secularization of, 139–40, 160; Ten Commandments displayed in Louisiana schools, 218
Putnam, Samuel Porter, 148–50, 168, 175, 177; *400 Years of Freethought*, 3, 134–37, 153–54, 163, 175–76

Quakers, 12, 18–19, 27, 52, 54, 131, 155, 215, 224n11

race relations: freethought movement and, 177–82; racial justice principle, 214. See also abolition; African Americans
Radical Enlightenment, 17, 51–52, 87, 101, 127
Rapp, George, 95–96
Raulston, John, 192–93
"Religious Freedom Amendment" (proposed), 134, 141, 183, 187
religious pluralism, 1, 54, 211
religious revivalism. See Second Great Awakening
repertoires of action, 6–7
republicanism: in Britain, 127; in France, 8, 24, 26, 72. See also Democratic-Republicans
Resource Mobilization Theory, 6
Reynolds, Charles B., 11, 217; blasphemy trials of, 171–75
Richard Dawkins Foundation, 213
Rickman, Thomas "Clio," 80, 91, 224n11, 249n128
Robespierre, Maximilien, 26, 28, 35–36, 39
Robinson, William J., 196
Roe v. Wade (1973), 212, 218
Rose, Ernestine, 13–14, 88, 120–29; advocate of women's rights and NY Married Women's Property Act and, 120, 122–23, 250n140; atheism and, 120, 123, 128; deism and, 127; free love and, 157, 260n115; Infidel Association of the United States and, 126, 128–29; on Know-Nothings, 186; as materialist, 149; spiritualism and, 153–54, 259n96; Frances Wright and, 123–24
Rose, William, 121, 123–24, 126
Ruggles, People v. (1811), 114
Rush, Benjamin, 67, 116
Rutledge, Wiley, 199, 202

Sanger, Margaret, 171
Schlereth, Eric R., 8

Schmidt, Leigh Eric, 8, 12
schools. *See* public schools
Schug, Phil, 197–98
scientific hope frame, 6; broadened from Paine's first use of, 46; deists echoing Paine on, 80, 127; Paine's *Age of Reason* and, 44–46, 99, 107, 129; Palmer's *Principles of Nature* and, 70; scientific study as act of worship, 44; second wave and, 127; third wave and, 137–38; Frances Wright's halls of science and, 45, 99, 105–8, 117–18, 129
scientific progress, 137–38, 176, 216
Scopes, John, and Scopes trial, 189, 191–94, 205
Second Great Awakening, 16–17, 89–91
second wave, 8, 12, 88–129; antiscripturalism and, 93, 99, 127–29, 216; Civil War onset ending, 8, 126; dormant years before start of, 89–91; free enquirers as term for, 88, 128; immigrants' role in, 127; Kneeland as blasphemy law martyr in, 99–110; nationally coordinated organizations' growth in, 129; Offen and, 8, 88, 91–93, 127; Owens father and son and, 93–99, 127; Paine birthday celebrations and, 88, 91–93, 105, 110, 120, 122–25; Paineite and Owenite strains merged in, 127; Ernestine Rose and women's rights in, 120–29; social reform agenda and, 128–29; Vale and, 117–19, 121, 127; Frances Wright as abolitionist and apostle of science in, 99–110, 127
Secular Coalition for America, 4, 42, 214, 216–18
secularism: disestablishment and, 2; fragility of, 9–10, 217; growth of, 1; present Supreme Court and Hamburger's misleading interpretation of history as threats to, 11; pressure to stop advance of, 218; public schools and, 139–40, 160; Revolutionary founders and, 56–57; spiritualism and, 149; third wave and, 138, 182–83; Unitarian embrace of secular humanists, 149; use of term, 2, 138
Secular Student Alliance, 214
Secular Woman, 214
Seneca Falls convention on women's rights (1848), 122, 155
separationism, 1, 6; American Humanist Association and, 190; Black and, 201–2; Blaine Amendment and, 140–42; Christian nationalist organizations seeking to weaken, 218–19; consequences of ending, 211–12; deists and, 80; early debates on (1784 & 1789), 83; *Everson* (1947) and, 81, 83, 201–2; *The Free Enquirer* and, 98; freethought thriving when focused on, 187, 204, 216; Grant on, 140; Hamburger on, 81–86, 184–86; Jefferson on, 10, 55–56, 83; Ku Klux Klan and, 205; Madison on, 56, 81, 83; original proponents as theistic, 56; Paine's *Age of Reason* and, 41–42, 129–30, 210; Palmer's writings and, 70, 209; political priority of freethought agenda, 42; present US Supreme Court and, 11; second wave and, 8, 129, 185; spiritualists and, 152; third wave and, 8, 12, 130, 133–34, 148, 182; Frances Wright on, 108. *See also* Nine Demands of Liberalism
Sermon on Natural Religion by a Natural Man (anonymous), 45
Shakers, 161–62
Le Siècle de la Raison, ou Le Sens Commun Des Droits De L'Homme. See *Age of Reason* (Paine)
Silver, Queen, 13, 190
Skidmore, Thomas, 109–10
slavery. *See* abolition
Slenker, Elmina, 171
Smith, Charles, 180, 182, 190, 213
social movements: clandestine activities distinguished from, 5–6; defined, 4; freethought movement omitted in literature on, 9; theory of, 6; visibility as trait of, 5
Society of Free Enquirers, 4, 17, 108, 112, 125, 128–29, 137
Society of Freethinkers, 4, 195–96, 204
Society of Moral Philanthropists, 4, 17, 44, 92, 105, 118, 121–22, 128
Spencer, John H., 61, 63
Spinoza, Baruch, 38, 49, 120, 176
spiritualists, 150–55, 182; antiscriptural stance of, 152; Davis and, 153; denouncing orthodox Christianity, 151; Fox sisters and, 150–51, 160; freethought movement and, 2; Garrison and, 153; Hammond and, 119; Houdini's debunking, 155; versus materialists, 154; as rational religion, 11–12, 151;

spiritualists (*cont.*)
  "Rochester rappings" and, 150; Ernestine Rose and, 153–54; third wave and, 11–12, 130, 138, 148, 150–52, 183, 217; Unitarians and, 131; Woodhull and sister Tennessee and, 159–61
Stanton, Elizabeth Cady, 123, 135, 155
state constitutions and laws: "baby Blaine" amendments, 183; major legislative reforms of third wave and, 187; religious freedom in, 47, 53, 113; separation of church and state in, 82. *See also specific states*
Stein, Lawrence B., 195
Stewart, Charles J., Craig Allen Smith, & Robert E. Denton: *Persuasion and Social Movements*, 4–5
Stewart, John "Walking," 76
Story, Joseph, 1–2, 83, 201
Sunday laws (blue laws), 59, 126, 185
Sunday morning meetings as alternative to Christian religious services, 11, 67–69, 81, 127, 129
Swedenborgians, 76, 215, 217

taxes: on church property, 140; to support state religion, 55, 201
Temple of Reason (newspaper), 45, 71–72, 76
Tennessee's Butler Act (1925), 191
Theophilanthropists and Theophilanthropic Society, 3, 16, 38, 74–75, 80
third wave (golden age), 130–87; Black freethinkers, 177–82; Blaine Amendment and, 140–42; Comstock and, 163–71; Establishment Clause, implications for current interpretation of, 184–86; eugenics, 158, 178–82; factions and alliances, 130, 148–59, 217; growth of freethinkers and freethought organizations, 130, 136–37, 148, 183; historians of freethought and, 175–77; Ingersoll and, 142–48; origins of, 130–34; periodicals published during, 159–63; post–Civil War revival, 8, 11, 134–39; Reynolds's blasphemy trial, 171–75; separationism and, 8, 12, 130, 133–34, 148, 182; social reform agenda and, 161
Thomas, Clarence, 219

Thomas Paine Memorial Committee, 196
Thomas Paine National Historical Association (TPNHA), 148, 177
Tilly, Benjamin, 117–18
Tilly, Charles, 7, 222n13; *Social Movements, 1768–2004*, 9
Tilton, Elizabeth, 164
Tilton, Josephine, 166–67
Tilton, Theodore, 159–60, 164
Toland, John, 38, 40, 49, 51, 65
Torcaso v. Watkins (1961), 204, 207, 212
Train, George Francis, 171
transcendentalists, 149
Treaty of Tripoli (1796), 55, 233n38
Trinity doctrine, 29, 49–50, 65, 71–72
Trollope, Frances Milton, 105, 245n70
The Truth Seeker, 69, 80, 115, 161–63, 169–73; advertising *Age of Reason*, 177; Bennett as founder, 159, 162; circulation of, 162, 182, 262n134; Comstock laws and, 168; eugenics and racism in, 178–80, 182; *Fifty Years of Freethought*, 135; on Ingersoll's defense of Reynolds, 174; MacDonald brothers as editors, 135, 152, 162; on obscenity prosecution of Bennett, 165–68; present day publication, 182
Turner, John, 16–17

Underwood, Sara, 176
Unitarians, 2, 29, 130–31; American Humanist Association and, 189; Blasphemy Act (Britain 1697) and, 49; compared to deists, 50–51; free religionists and, 149–50; fusion with Universalism, 149; Jefferson and, 1; National Conference (Saratoga 1894), 149; Palmer and, 65–66; Radical Enlightenment and, 51; as religious dissenters, 50–52; state support and, 59
Unitarian Universalist Association, 214
Unitarian Universalists (UUs), 12, 111, 149–50, 214–15
United States Moral and Philosophical Society for the General Diffusion of Useful Knowledge, 4, 111, 118, 125, 128
Universalists, 65–66, 111–13, 131, 149
utopian communities. *See* Nashoba community; New Harmony; Owenites

Vale, Gilbert: *Life of Thomas Paine*, 115, 117–19, 121, 127, 129, 162, 177, 240n154
Vanderbilt, Cornelius, 160, 165
Vaughan, William, 63, 87
Virginia Statute for Religious Freedom, 55–56, 201
Voltaire, 38, 67, 196
Vovelle, Michel, 37, 228n70

Wakeman, Thaddeus, 154, 167
War of 1812, 57, 91, 94
Warren, Sidney, 8
Washington, George, 20–21, 24, 56–57, 62, 74
Watson, James, 117
Watson, Richard, 61
Wesley, John, 32
Whitehead, Fred & Verle Muhrer: *Freethought on the American Frontier*, 8
Williams, Thomas, 16
Wollstonecraft, Mary, 22
The Woman's Bible, 156, 176
women's rights, 13, 98, 156; Know-Nothings' opposition to, 186; nativists' opposition to, 210; Putnam on history of, 176; reproductive rights, 219; Ernestine Rose and, 120, 122–23, 250n140; spiritualism and, 152; Frances Wright and, 99, 124
Woodhull, Victoria, 12, 157–65; eugenics and, 179–80; obscenity charges against, 163–65; speeches, 158, 161

Woodhull & Claflin's Weekly, 159–61, 163
Woolston, Thomas, 40, 51
Workingmen's Party, 109–10
Wright, Camilla, 99–101, 103–4
Wright, Frances, 14, 45, 88, 99–110, 127–28, 244n48; abolition and, 97, 99, 102–6, 110; antiscripturalism and, 99; background of, 99–101; *Explanatory Notes, Respecting the Nature and Objects of the Institution of Nashoba, and of the Principles Upon Which It Is Founded*, 104; feminism/women's rights and, 99, 124; first secular public address in US by woman (1828), 97, 99, 104–5; halls of science and, 45, 99, 105–8, 117–18, 129; Jefferson and, 102–3; Kneeland and, 112; Lafayette and, 102; as materialist, 149; neo-Epicurean, 128; *The New Harmony Gazette* and, 97, 106; Offen and, 105; Robert Dale Owen and, 103, 106, 108–9, 124, 246n82; at Paine birthday celebration, 110; Ernestine Rose and, 123–24; travel of, 101–2, 104; *Views on Society and Manners in America*, 101; Workingmen's Party and, 109–10. See also *Free Enquirer*; Society of Free Enquirers

Young, Thomas, 45, 62

Zen Buddhism, 215, 275n11